Enterprise Planning and Development:

Small Business Start-up, Survival and Development

David Butler

ELSEVIER

AMSTERDAM • BOSTON • HEIDELBERG • LONDON • NEW YORK • OXFORD
PARIS • SAN DIEGO • SAN FRANCISCO • SINGAPORE • SYDNEY • TOKYO
Butterworth-Heinemann is an imprint of Elsevier

Elsevier Butterworth-Heinemann
Linacre House, Jordan Hill, Oxford OX2 8DP
30 Corporate Drive, Burlington, MA 01803, USA

First published 2006

British Library Cataloguing in Publication Data
A catalogue record for this book is available from the British Library

Library of Congress Cataloguing in Publication Data
A catalogue record for this book is available from the Library of Congress

ISBN-13: 978 0 7506 8064 6
ISBN-10: 0 7506 8064 4

For information on all Butterworth-Heinemann publications
please visit our website at http://books.elsevier.com

Typeset by Charon Tec Ltd, Chennai, India
www.charontec.com
Printed and bound

Enterprise Planning and Development

David Butler is a Lecturer in Entrepreneurship at the University of Kent. He has over 25 years of experience in both large and small organisations including 15 years as a small business owner. He has been involved in small business training and research since 1997, and also works with the Small Firms Enterprise Development Initiative (SFEDI) and the Chartered Management Institute, but still finds time for some occasional fly-fishing to keep life in balance.

Contents

Acknowledgements

To my wife Wendy, with thanks for your patience during the many silent evenings of preparation, and the missed shopping opportunities at weekends. To Andy, thanks for keeping the computer in working order and the drinks flowing; and to Katie, thanks for the relentless ribbing and wind-ups that kept us all smiling.

Also, to Tony Robinson, Chairman of SFEDI, a source of encouragement and enthusiasm, and a passionate campaigner to rise the standards of support and training for small firms and business advisers.

Preface

This book is intended to update and to integrate two previous texts *Business Planning – A guide to business start-up* (2000) and *Business Development – A guide to small business strategy* (2001), and to discuss a number of other contemporary topics relevant to small- and medium-sized enterprises (SMEs). The aim is to provide a source of practical information for potential entrepreneurs, business practitioners, and students to encourage and support good practice in business planning, and to enhance the practical and strategic skills needed to survive and grow in business. It draws on a range of entrepreneurial theory and best practice, in addition to the author's personal experiences of running small businesses over a 15-year period – both good and not so good. It has been deliberately formulated to rise a continuous stream of questions, which are intended to prompt the reader to relate them to their own particular business situation at each stage, to help avoid some of the problems and pitfalls that may befall many new and growing businesses.

The text is aimed at a broad audience, including both students and practitioners and potential entrepreneurs each of whom may have very different but overlapping interests. For academic purposes, it will be relevant to a range of enterprise and business planning modules in undergraduate degrees, for aspects of post-graduate entrepreneurship studies, and aspects of professional management courses, as well as being useful to vocational students who might be considering self-employment. On a more practical level, Part I of the book is designed to assist private individuals who are considering the prospect of starting or becoming involved in a new business, by providing a readable and structured guide to producing realistic business plans that will both meet the requirements of potential lenders, and give the budding entrepreneurs the skills and knowledge needed to establish their enterprises and survive the difficult early days until they reach a break-even situation. It outlines the options for operating the business and the many risks involved. It also examines a wide range of aspects that must be considered and assessed as part of the process of setting up a business. But whether the reader's objective is to produce a Business Plan to simply achieve a qualification, or to produce such a document to convince a dubious bank manager of the viability of a business proposition, many of the aspects to be considered are the same. Most important of all, a careful and detailed analysis of those aspects can provide a yardstick by which potential entrepreneurs can objectively evaluate the true risks, pitfalls, and potential profits of their dreams.

The biggest problem faced by new firms is that of surviving the first year or 2, so a basic knowledge of the process of planning and organising a business can substantially increase the chances of survival. However, having faced the traumas of start-up and reaching break-even level, once that level of stability has been reached it is easy to become complacent and to focus on the day-to-day operation of the business rather than its longer-term development. Small business owners are often accused of being unable to think strategically, or of failing to plan for the long-term future. For owners and managers of established small firms who want or need to develop and grow them, Part II is intended to provide the knowledge, advice and planning skills that will enable them to move from operational to strategic thinking, in order to facilitate the long-term growth and development of the business. It encourages entrepreneurs to analyse and review current business practices, to define their own personal and business objectives, to identify and evaluate options that might achieve both the business and personal objectives, and to plan how the best fit options can be implemented. The structure of this section is aimed at following a logical sequence of questions to facilitate that process. It starts by asking the questions: "Where are we now?" – the strategic analysis of the business and its operating environment; and "Where do we want to go?" – the process of defining strategic objectives. It follows on with more tactical issues: "What resources will be needed to get there?" and "What sales and marketing policies will we need to develop?" It asks whether overseas exports are appropriate to the business and how these could be developed. It examines the personnel and staffing implications of the foregoing activities, and the efficiency and effectiveness of current financial management processes. It then looks at the overall financial implications of the strategy and how they will be met. Finally it looks at the way the whole strategy will be implemented to achieve the planned objectives.

This book will also be of interest to business advisers and other practitioners from enterprise agencies, chambers of commerce, and business links, etc., as a source of relevant information to assist the delivery of their business advice and support activities. The text has also been designed to broadly reflect the SFEDI National Standards for Business

Planning and Business Development as models of best practice for operation and management of SMEs. There are some excellent local business support services and business advisers across the UK, and some excellent textbooks, materials, and training programmes around to assist new and growing businesses – there are also some around that are not so good. Over the past 25 years the author has also seen and experienced a number of less than satisfactory examples, but the use and application of the National Standards for Business Planning and Development, plus those for provision of Business Advice and Information has gone a long way towards the promotion of good practice and reduction or poorer practices in those areas.

CHAPTER 1

The entrepreneurial ethos and environment

With the sheer number of small- and medium-sized firms or enterprises (SMEs) in existence, and the very diversity of the goods and services that they offer, it is little wonder that no one has been able to create a meaningful taxonomy to classify them, although it seems to be part of human nature that we insist on keep trying. In the process of trying, successive governments, research and educational institutions, have developed a range of overlapping and contradictory definitions, which vary from country to country.

Back in 1971 the British government had shown a little interest in the structure of small businesses when the Bolton Committee Report (1971) attempted, rather haphazardly to define the sizes of small firms across a number of key industries. For example, a "small" manufacturing firm had less than 200 staff whereas "small" mines and quarries had only 25 or less. In the motor trade a "small" firm had a turnover of under £100k but in the wholesale trade the turnover was £200k. "Small" transport firms had less than five vehicles, and catering businesses were small so long as they were not multiple outlets or brewery managed. With such vague definitions it was not surprising that the government had no clear or positive policies towards small firms, although the New Enterprise Programme of the 1970s was the first, albeit unsatisfactory, attempt to support small firms by encouraging them to undertake training and development to improve their staff and management skills.

It was only in the mid-1980s that the true importance of the small firms sector began to attract real government attention, particularly when larger organisations began to shed staff, and the skilled workers looked to use their redundancy packages to create opportunities in self-employment. As a result, the small firms sector emerged as the potential alternative to the large employers, and an alternative which could help to reduce the politically sensitive high and rising levels of unemployment. It was a solution to a big threat which could lose the controlling political party the next election. Various initiatives and support mechanisms were developed to assist small firms to start up and to grow, including the Department of Trade and Industry (DTI) Enterprise Initiative, and the Business Growth Training Option of the early 1990s.

In 1998, the DTI estimated that there were 3.75 million small firms providing 7.7 million jobs, and that of all UK firms, 84% had less than 10 staff, and 89% had less than 5 staff. This broadly correlates with the Small Firms Lead Body (now the Small Firms Enterprise Development Initiative) figures from 1998 stating that 96% of all UK firms employ less than 20 staff. This implies that the big companies, whose needs dominate the content of accredited management training provision throughout the UK, constitute only 1–2% of the total number of private sector employer organisations in the UK.

In the following 6 years that number of small businesses had grown to an officially recognised figure of 4.3 million in 2004. Interestingly, much of that data is based on registrations and de-registrations for value-added tax (VAT) and taxation, and that invariably overlooks the large number of self-employed individuals who fall below the VAT registration threshold and those operating in the grey economy who simply do not want to be known to any government agency. Butler (2004) reported on a survey in which over 7500 businesses were contacted, many of which simply refused to discuss their operations as they did not wish to appear on any database, "official" or otherwise. Realistically, the true number of "entrepreneurial" businesses and self-employed individuals could be as much as 40% higher than the government figures suggest.

The political context

One problem that still persists is the insistence of the government in using the term "SME". The DTI definition of a small- or medium-sized enterprise was that of having less than 250 employees or an annual turnover below £5 million. Unfortunately there is a continuing and confusing implication within this definition that prompts the assumption that the needs of a new small firm with just 5 to 10 staff are similar, or just a scaled down version of a firm employing 200 staff that may have been established for 20 or 30 years. With the current high value of new technology, a very small firm with just a handful of staff can be involved in high-value contracts exceeding £5 million or more, whilst another much larger business employing substantial numbers of unskilled staff on low-paid labour-intensive work, can have a turnover below that figure. In this context, annual sales turnover has become largely irrelevant, and it would make much more sense to subdivide the sector, e.g. into micro-firms (with under 20 full-time equivalent staff), small firms (with 20 to 50 full-time equivalent staff), and medium-sized firms as having 50 to 100 staff. In effect most firms with 100 to 250 staff are relatively large and well established these days, and certainly tend to employ the necessary specialist management skills that are usually found in larger companies. The difference in size also becomes critical in more rural counties where there are significantly fewer businesses in the 100- to 250-employee bracket, but a great deal more micro-firms which form the bulk of potential local employment. On this basis the current government definitions certainly need to be reviewed to focus support funding into the parts of the small firms sector which is likely to produce the most long-term growth and potential employment – which the government continuously tells us are the newly established and nursery businesses. It is these to which Part II of this book will apply most.

In 2003 in what many critics would regard as a rare example of common sense, the European Union (EU) came up with a framework definition of SMEs that will hopefully achieve general acceptance and credibility. Broadly, from January 2005 a micro-firm will be defined as having 10 or less staff, a turnover of no more than €2m, and an annual balance sheet total of no more than €2m. A small firm will have a maximum of 20 staff, €10m turnover, and €10m on its balance sheet. A medium-sized firm will have no more than 250 staff, a €50m turnover, and a balance sheet not exceeding €43m. Whilst these definitions will be accepted across Europe, two issues arise. First, with quite widely varying inflation rates amongst the EU member states it will be interesting to see how the thresholds are adjusted as time goes on. Second and more important, the new definitions still do not overcome the fact that a "medium-sized firm" with 51 staff and €10m turnover will be substantially different in terms of management skills and structure, access to resources, market influence, etc., than a firm with 249 staff and a turnover of €50m. Those differences are exacerbated with the insistence of bankers, government agencies, politicians, academics, and policy-makers of lumping the three very different groups together and treating them as a homogenous group called SMEs.

The training and education context

The provision of management and business training really started to expand in the 1970s, primarily through the polytechnics and some of the more technically focused UK universities (it was then still not quite a respectable academic subject at that time – except of course in the USA). This provision has expanded over the years both upwards to post-graduate level at most universities, and downwards through colleges of further education. One of the key problems however, is that the majority of the demand for such training is on a part-time basis, e.g. where employees are given day-release from work to attend college, or by distance learning through the Open University, Open College Network, or similar institutions. The major drawback is that historically this type of education or training does not attract the same levels of funding as full-time education, and as a consequence students are normally charged quite substantial course fees which in the vast majority of cases are paid for by their employers. In 2005 the funding structure for further education in the UK was revised to focus on the 14 to 19 age group, with reductions in funding for "demand-led" training and education, e.g. management training. This will have the further effect of increasing costs of essential training for the business sector that the government favours as the employment growth sector of the future.

In a survey of part-time business and management students carried out at South Kent College between 1997 and 1999 (Butler, 2000) less than 5% came from small firms, and the majority (75%) of that group were paying their own fees as their employers would not or could not afford to sponsor them. If, as is suggested above, the remaining 95% of students on these courses are derived from the 1–2% of large private sector employer organisations plus the public sector, whose training needs dominate the management education provision in the UK, then clearly there is a major imbalance and lack of proper direction in management training provision. In simple terms, there is a substantial and almost critical need for business and management training in the small-business sector, but central funding for this within the further and higher educational system is not readily available. Those who need it most can least afford to pay for it, and the educational funding systems are not designed to facilitate the provision of the sort of short, flexible, convenient training programmes that small firms need because they are invariably not qualification related! Added to this is the issue that college and university marketing budgets can achieve higher rates of return by focussing on larger institutions, whereas targeting the multitude of small firms can be a time-consuming and relatively unproductive process.

The predominance of students from large companies on management programmes has inevitably resulted in those programmes being directed towards the needs and interests of large organisations, with little or usually no reference to the needs or interests of their smaller counterparts. Corporate planning, public sector finance and international marketing are great subject options for employees of large organisations, but the big-company model of management training is woefully inadequate for the owner-manager, and it is only in very recent years that this problem has started to be redressed. In the mid-1990s there were only a handful of UK universities offering small-business programmes or options (Durham and Warwick being two examples also notable for their SME-related research) but the number is now steadily growing.

The owner-manager culture

Not only is the large organisation model inappropriate for business and management training, it fails to acknowledge the fundamental cultural differences between large and small organisations:

- Large organisations can afford to employ specialists to provide particular management or administrative functions, e.g. personnel, payroll, sales, marketing, purchasing, distribution, and accounts, etc. The owner-manager generally has, at least in the formative years of the business, to fulfil the majority of these roles without specialist support. In the small firm the emphasis is on breadth of knowledge and skills, in contrast to the specialist expertise and knowledge available in large organisations.
- Medium-sized and large organisations tend to produce corporate plans specifying their aims and objectives over a 3 to 5-year period. These "strategic" plans are produced at senior or Board level, and are implemented by middle managers at the "tactical" level. Below them, the middle managers have junior managers or supervisors to whom the day-to-day "operational" decisions are made. As the company has grown, its culture will have evolved to the point where it is less dominated by the entrepreneur who initially created it. In contrast, in the small firm strategic thinking or planning rarely takes place in the early stages of its development (see Figure 13.2), and the firm's culture may be heavily influenced by the motivations, attitudes and management style of its owner-manager.
- Until a small firm has reached a level of stability, the whole of its existence is a matter of and concern for survival, and

consequently its focus is on the short-term measures that will enable it to achieve survival. Long-term or strategic planning is non-existent, and in truth is often irrelevant – after all, what is the point in planning for next year if the business may have to close next month? Whereas large firms can afford to invest in staff development and training, this will only happen in small firms, and particularly the newer ones, where that training will offer a short-term payback for the time and effort invested, e.g. a very rapid increase in sales, or substantial cost savings. Similarly if the owner of a small firm takes time off, or sends a member of staff for training, it is highly unlikely that anyone will be available to cover for the absence. Lost time is lost revenue for the owner-manager, so compared with the big-company counterpart, the actual cost to the business of sending staff away for training is much more critical as it results in the loss of a higher percentage proportion of revenue income. Conversely however, it can be argued that as a matter of survival, the small firm owner cannot afford not to invest in training if that training provides the skills to survive. This is the Philistine view that if they don't take the trouble to arm themselves with the basic skills and knowledge to survive in business, then they don't deserve to survive anyway – an attitude totally contrasting with basic principles of quality management and customer care.

- Owner-managers, in particular those who have previously been employed as managers, tend to be fiercely independent and often reluctant to take advice, which may be fine if they actually have the necessary skills and expertise to establish a business. However, unlike the situation in large firms, when they hit problems there is often no one to consult or to provide expert advice. Again the tendency in such circumstances is to opt for the most immediate practical solution, or the cheapest short-term solution, perhaps to the detriment of the longer-term needs of the business.

- The finances available from lending banks and financial institutions tend to be much more restricted than for big companies. Interest rates tend to be higher, and the sums offered are frequently lower in proportion to the equity required to secure them. True, this is not a problem for well-established and profitable small businesses, but the financial system as it stands, makes the achievement of that condition much harder to achieve anyway. New small firms simply do not have any negotiating power when it comes to interest rates and terms of borrowing, and are often faced with a take it or leave it choice.

■ The political, legal and fiscal environment in which small firms operate is constantly changing, and in recent years has resulted in an ever-growing burden of bureaucracy. Whilst big companies may have the resources (if not the inclination) to handle these burdens, the pressure put on small firms is disproportionate to their size, turnover, and profitability. Unpaid tax collection responsibilities (VAT, PAYE (pay as you earn), etc.) in particular impose a disproportionate burden on smaller firms. In spite of frequent government pledges to reduce red-tape the burden continues to grow, largely due to our association with the European Community and its central-control culture. Compliance with the continuous influx of new legislation has become a primary issue for lobbying bodies representing small firms. Once again we see government policies having a negative effect on the sector most valued to create future growth and employment.

Enterprise, entrepreneurs and entrepreneurship

Not surprisingly with the sheer number of SMEs in existence and the disparity of their offerings mentioned earlier, coupled with the range of individuals both in and out of the public eye that we would describe as being enterprising, it is hard to find a consensus of agreement for the definition of these terms, and the different ways in which the words are used causes further confusion. The primary differences are between the economic school of thought where enterprise is what entrepreneurs do by creating new businesses, jobs and wealth, all of which contribute to the economy; and the educational school of thought. The latter takes the view that not all firms are enterprising, and those that are involve use of imagination and creativity, generating new ideas, dealing flexibly with changing situations, taking responsibility and making decisions. As such it is closely linked with the principles of life-long leaning and continuous professional and personal development. In some ways it can almost be viewed as a reversal of the 20th century approach to education in which personal creativity, initiative and imagination were educated out of people to make them employable in large conventional and conservative-minded organisations.

Enterprise is a word generally applied to businesses set up and operated by individuals, more often within the size range of SMEs. It can be, but rarely is used in the context of major companies or international organisations, as it tends to reflect a level of venturous, opportunistic and risk-taking attitude less typical of large organisations. However, with the government's aim to promote enterprise cultures at all levels of education, the word is being increasingly used in schools in a much broader context as an aspect of the curriculum to promote changes in attitude towards venture creation.

The term *entrepreneur* typifies an individual attitude of opportunity-spotting, and the creation and exploitation of business opportunities to create wealth – often with the implicit use of innovation, imagination, and risk-taking. The entrepreneur creates and operates the enterprise, and in doing so displays the characteristic of *Entrepreneurship*. However, too often the latter has been used in the restricted context of new business start-up, particularly by academics and educationalists – but the people who tend to care least about academic definitions are the entrepreneurs themselves who are just interested in getting on with the job. Entrepreneurship is also referred to as the process of growing and sustaining the business after the start-up stage, implying a broader definition. Furthermore, the definition attributed to Harvard University is that: "Entrepreneurship is the pursuit of opportunity beyond the resources you currently control", which opens up scope for the word to be applied equally to non-profit social enterprises, and to intrapreneurship within large commercial and public sector organisations to reflect entrepreneurial behaviour amongst staff. It is in this context that we start to consider the entrepreneur in terms of the characteristic which he or she exhibits or demonstrates, and which will be considered in more detail later in this chapter.

Much is also spoken about the importance of generating and promoting enterprise cultures within organisations, in which staff are positively encouraged to use initiative and imagination for the benefit of the organisation, and ultimately also for themselves if the enterprising behaviour is acknowledged and rewarded. An enterprise culture in society is one where business is seen as a positive contributor to society and creation of social capital, and where society positively supports entrepreneurial activity. Within organisations it is a climate that recognises and reinforces both business success and individual initiative, and accepts that there is a risk of failure in new ventures that is both acceptable to the organisation, and which does not attract blame. It is a climate in which innovation and creativity can thrive.

Just to confound the issues further we must not forget to mention several other related definitions. We have the *Social Enterprises* which are essentially those set up for charitable or philanthropic purposes, or for the benefit or welfare of their members; and these usually operate on a not for profit basis, or plough back any profits into the organisation. Then there are the *Serial Entrepreneurs* who find a challenge in the process of creating and growing a new business and then selling it for a profit, only to move on to create another business, often in a totally different and unrelated market. In this situation the personal objective is not just one of financial profit or capital growth so much as the repeated and ever-greater challenge to create something perhaps bigger and better – a bit like the mountaineer who starts with Snowdon and Ben Nevis, moves on to the Eiger and progresses via Anapurna, to Everest as the ultimate challenge. Then there is the idea of *Intrapreneurship* – the practice of entrepreneurial behaviour within a large organisation or in the public sector. The Intrapreneurs are usually easily recognised within an organisation as the energetic ones who will spot the new ideas and the find resources to match them – almost like Belbin's Resource Investigators, a member of the team but working at the edge of it, and often the one who others turn to for ideas when problems arise.

Entrepreneurial attitudes and characteristics

Invariably any discussion of entrepreneurial characteristics sooner or later involves reference to archetypal high-profile entrepreneurs – Bill Gates as the technocrat entrepreneur who created Microsoft, Richard Branson as the risk-taking builder of the multi-faceted Virgin empire, and Anita Roddick of Body Shop fame who is seen to reflect the social conscience of entrepreneurship. Their high-profile achievements as global entrepreneurs are held up as charismatic examples, almost role models, of what is best in entrepreneurship. However, in some ways such examples deflect the focus away from the characteristics and attitudes that make up the nature of the millions of smaller-scale entrepreneurial operators who may be comparably enterprising in their own smaller way, but who do not share either the ambition or the ability to create large-scale wealth on a multinational basis, and yet still create employment opportunities, and generate wealth from their profits.

Entrepreneurship students are frequently encouraged to ponder the question: are entrepreneurs made or born? Is entrepreneurship an inherent characteristic, perhaps inherited or present at birth, which gives them a unique capacity for spotting opportunities, taking calculated risks, and using imagination and innovation, to create profit and wealth from business activities? Alternatively, do we all start life from a level playing field, and whilst most people head are educated and aim for employability, there are those who acquire or develop the entrepreneurial characteristics perhaps from experiences in early life that force them to become resourceful, or by exposure to other entrepreneurs or entrepreneurial activities? Certainly, children growing up in traditionally enterprising Asian cultures seem the acquire the attitude and perception that to go into business is a highly positive and respectable ambition, whereas modern western cultures have tended to educate out entrepreneurial attitudes in favour of preparing people for the more socially acceptable ambition of employability and having what is perceived as a "good" pensionable career. If entrepreneurial characteristics can be acquired by exposure to enterprising environments, then it follows that those entrepreneurial characteristics and attitudes could be treated as transferable skills to be taught or learned, and that with the right form of guidance and tuition, we should be able to raise the entrepreneurial capacity of the working population. Individuals, such as Gates and Branson are often held up as prime examples of people with inherent entrepreneurial characteristics and skills, but with design and content, educational and training programmes can certainly equip people with the knowledge and skills to create and develop new enterprises and to thrive in highly competitive environments. Whilst the existence of inherent entrepreneurial skills and characteristic cannot be completely ruled out, the capacity to develop such skills by appropriate training and/or exposure to enterprise cultures has got to be a stronger argument. This is further reinforced by (often negative) factors of personal experience and environment particularly in younger developing years that are often quoted by successful entrepreneurs. For example experience of poverty or hardship may act as a strong motivator in later life to create and accrue wealth. In the case of Richard Branson, he has often recounted his mother's actions to make him self-reliant from an early age, as a strong influence on his subsequent entrepreneurial development.

One of the biggest issues in attempting to describe or categorise entrepreneurial characteristics is that they vary so widely from one individual to another both in terms of the range of skills and characteristics possessed, and those that predominate in any one individual. The characteristics, or the way in which they are exhibited, may also be influenced by the personal motivation and ambitions of each individual. For example, a not uncommon situation occurs where a person is motivated by the need for a life-balance, so in spite of possessing highly developed entrepreneurial skills in terms of ability to spot and act on opportunities and to develop profitable enterprises, the individual makes a personal decision to restrict the scale of their enterprise once they have achieved a level of income or return to match their desired lifestyle. This is one of a number of reasons why potentially large businesses cease to expand once they reach a certain level. This will be discussed further in Chapter 13.

Various attempts have been made to define the entrepreneurial personality. Timmons (2003) described 19 behavioural traits or characteristics, whilst Lessem (1986) used examples of seven specific high-profile entrepreneurs which he described as respectively reflecting imagination, intuition, authority, will, sociability, energy, and flexibility, these being based on specific combinations of attributes and personality traits.

Bolton and Thompson (2005) explain entrepreneurship as a balance between three characteristics:

- *Talent*: abilities, such as creativity, opportunity-spotting, and networking.
- *Temperament*: personal needs, such as desire to take responsibility, focus on performance, opportunity taking, feelings of urgency to act.
- *Techniques*: personal skills sets and techniques to develop talents and to manage temperament.

Bolton and Thompson have adopted a more pragmatic analysis than some previous theorists, by looking at what entrepreneurs do in practice rather than by attempting to analyse personality or behaviours, although that practice will of course reflect personal attitudes and characteristics. They defined entrepreneurs in terms of action factors, i.e. the key action roles that can be associated with entrepreneurs or entrepreneurship in any context:

1. *Entrepreneurs make a difference*. They challenge accepted norms and often exhibit the ability to convert vague or ill-defined ideas into practical and profitable reality.
2. *Entrepreneurs are creative and innovative*. They combine opportunities with imagination to address new challenges in innovative ways.
3. *Entrepreneurs spot and exploit opportunities*. They are able to identify new opportunities in situations that other people would miss or ignore, perhaps again because of their ability to use imagination. They may not be the originator of an idea but they can

see how to developer exploit its potential. This is closely linked to the previous example.

4. *Entrepreneurs find the resources required to exploit opportunities*: This reflects the Harvard definition of entrepreneurship mentioned previously, of pursuing resources beyond those currently controlled.

5. *Entrepreneurs are good networkers*: This is a key attribute that more conventional academic analysts frequently ignore, i.e. the practical skills of making, maintaining and exploiting contacts, in both short and long term, for mutual benefit. This is a key characteristic in finding resources.

6. *Entrepreneurs are determined in the face of adversity*: They do not give up easily as they are motivated to succeed, and possess determination and self-belief. They can also face up to and address unexpected problems and occurrences that may occur.

7. *Entrepreneurs manage risk*: They are prepared to accept and take responsibility for calculated risks that perhaps less enterprising people might avoid, but they will not take on unnecessary or excessive risks. One outcome of this is that they also quickly learn from their mistakes.

8. *Entrepreneurs have control of the business*: They make themselves aware of the on-going performance of the business, they control the business by attention to detail and by identifying what is important, but do not allow it to dictate their response or activity – a situation of strategic rather than operational control.

9. *Entrepreneurs put customers first*: Another issue sometimes overlooked by other theorists. Entrepreneurs have a strong customer focus and maintain constant awareness of changing customer needs and demands. This also contributes to the identification of new and evolving opportunities.

10. *Entrepreneurs create capital*: Whether financial in the business context, or social or aesthetic for non-profit making organisations, entrepreneurs create wealth, capital, or added value for the community. This concept is compatible with business enterprise, social enterprise and intrapreneurship.

As can be seen, there is some considerable inter-relationships and overlap between these various characteristics. Bolton and Thompson take the idea further by describing how the entrepreneur as opportunity spotter, identifies the idea (action factors 2–5 above) and then moves into the role of what they describe as a project champion to be able to engage and implement the opportunities that have been identified (action factors 1, 6–10) to make it happen.

The entrepreneur is then a complex combination of interacting factors:

- *Personality*: in terms of possessing resilience, tenacity, opportunity spotting and taking, and risk-taking.
- *Attitude*: having awareness of the importance of customer focus, the application of creativity and imagination, defined personal standards and values, the perception of enterprise as a positive activity.
- *Skills*: such as ability to network, to think strategically, business knowledge and acumen, interpersonal skills and people management, to gain access to resources.
- *Motivation*: personal drive and ambition, the desire to make an impact, need for achievement or self-satisfaction, desire for status, to create and accumulate wealth, social responsibility.

The presence, combination and interaction of these factors will determine both the way in which an entrepreneur engages in enterprising activities, and ultimately the degree of success that will be achieved. Unfortunately, there is no single model that can be applied to ensure success in every case. The object of the ensuing chapters is to identify some of the key aspects of knowledge and skills that can be developed to improve the chances of success and to minimise risk of failure for the budding entrepreneur.

The Made or Born argument

Without going into great depth or detail into what is a well documented and sometimes laboured argument for which there will never be a clear-cut conclusion, we will just briefly mention the "Are Entrepreneurs Made or Born?" question, our entrepreneurial equivalent of nature versus nurture from educational psychology. In short, the Born side of the argument quotes instinctive creative, innovative and opportunity spotting behaviour, with a range of personality and character traits that go alongside it, such as self-reliance, the need for esteem and self-actualisation (as per Maslow's hierarchy of needs), the hunter-gatherer instinct to provide for the family by creating wealth, etc. The Made side of the argument quotes development of entrepreneurial attitudes by exposure to business and enterprising environments during developmental years or subsequent working life, to the transferability of entrepreneurial skills, such as networking and creative thinking both by learning and by practice; and by the provision of additional business skills by training and empirical experience.

From a cynical and pragmatic view point, whilst the Made or Born argument may be of some academic interest, but it is surely the very last thing on the mind of the practical entrepreneur who just wants to get on with running and developing the business, as it is the process of being entrepreneurial that makes things happen, not just talking about it.

References

Bolton Committee (1971). *Report of the Committee of Inquiry on Small Firms*, HMSO, London.

Bolton, B. and Thomson, J. (2004). *Entrepreneurs: Talent, Temperament, Technique*, 2nd edition. Elsevier, Oxford.

Butler, D. (2004). Breaking down barriers to training uptake in small firms. *ISBE Conference Paper*, Newcastle.

Butler, D. (2000). "Business Planning – a Guide to Business Start-up". Butterworth-Heinnemann, Oxford.

Lessem, R. (1986). *Intrapreneurship: How to Be a Successful Individual in a Successful Business*. Wildwood House, London.

Timmons, J. A. *et al.* (2003). *New Venture Creation*. McGraw Hill, New York.

Further reading

Carter, S. and Jones-Evans, D. (2000). *Enterprise and Small Business*. FT Prentice Hall, London.

Chell, E., Haworth, J. and Brealey, S. (1991). *The Entrepreneurial Personality: Concepts Cases and Strategies*. Routledge, London.

European Commission Recommendation 2003/361/EC. The New SME Definition, Brussels.

Kirby, D. (2003). *Entrepreneurship*. McGraw Hill, Maidenhead.

PART I

Start-up and survival

The first part of this book, Chapters 2–12, are concerned with the initial planning of the business, and the stage from actual start-up through to when the business starts to break even and to make profit for its owners and investors.

From the owners' perspectives, the key objective here is for the business to survive and grow until it reaches that key point of break-even level before the working capital becomes so depleted that the business can no longer continue trading. Sadly, that is an all too common situation. The actual timescale may vary from several months to 1 or 2 years depending on the nature of the proposed business and the market in which it operates, so the business must be adequately capitalised to last out that period.

In an ideal world the initial business planning stage should incorporate some personal development for the would-be entrepreneurs to ensure that they have the necessary skills and knowledge to enable them to reach break even. Part I therefore, focuses on exploring the range of skills and knowledge that is required to plan and start a new business and to survive that first critical period.

CHAPTER 2

The importance of planning for start-ups

There are a whole host of reasons to justify the preparation of business plans, not just simply for business start-up enterprises, but as a model of good practice for established organisations; and any one of these reasons in its own right, should make the planning process a worthwhile exercise, if it is done properly. However, the important thing to remember is that just producing a good business plan alone will not result in a sound, profitable, or prosperous business. The business plan is just that – a plan – and like any other plan, the only way to see if it really works is to monitor its progress at regular intervals, so that you can respond to any potential problems which may arise, and change or modify your business strategy as necessary. So, let us take a look at some of the reasons why people take the trouble to produce business plans:

First, the process of producing a business plan, acts as a very efficient method of focussing the ideas of potential entrepreneurs, in terms of defining their objectives, assessing their own abilities to organise and run the business. It also acts as a means of testing the viability of the business proposal before actually committing its proposers to any substantial expenditure or investment. Typically, this type of plan would be prepared before the start-up or acquisition of the business, and certainly before any substantial financial commitments or investments are made.

Second, the planning process establishes parameters and specific targets which provide a yardstick against which the progress and profitability of the business can be measured, i.e. this is the process of converting the proposers' objectives into quantifiable financial forecasts and targets against which progress and achievement can be measured.

Again, this planning activity is a prerequisite to starting or acquiring a business, but beyond that, it is also an essential part of the on-going process of running a business, and should be continued on an on-going basis long after the initial start-up period.

Third, as there are relatively few aspiring entrepreneurs who have the resources to be totally self-financing. Most are faced at some time with the need to raise external finance, if not at the start-up stage, then later when they wish to expand and grow the established business (see Chapter 17). For these persons, possession of a good business plan is crucial to their future – their first appointment with the potential investor, financier or bank manager to discuss the proposal, is a bit like an audition for a part in a Hollywood film – if you blow your lines you blow your chances – or at least, you reduce your prospects of getting the part you really want! So it is most important to prepare the plan thoroughly, and to present it in a professional and competent manner. In this respect it is also important to remember that the business plan is essentially a sales document that will be used to convince the potential lenders or investors to engage with the business. As such it must be presented in a positive and honest manner to project the viability of the proposal and the competence of the proposer(s) to convert the idea into a profitable business, in order to persuade the lenders or investors to engage with the idea.

The business plan as a means of focusing ideas

The production of a comprehensive business plan is really centred on a process of questions and answers; and the deeper you move into the plan, the more questions arise which must be answered. Most people who are considering buying or setting up a business, or becoming self-employed, have a fairly general idea of what they would like to achieve. Typically this may take the form of a range of activities or options, perhaps linked in some way, or built around a central idea. It is only when someone asks them the question "What are your specific objectives?" that they actually start to define the precise parameters within which their proposed business will operate. Often, this question is only asked for the first time when they start to fill in the bank's business plan form. The primary objectives (often called the Mission Statement) of the business need to state clearly and specifically, the purpose for which the business exists, and the market in which it will operate. For example, "I intend to operate a high quality and profitable mobile catering service specialising in wedding receptions and private parties in the Kent and Sussex area", or, "We will be providing a service which designs, constructs and maintains heated swimming pools for large private homes in London and the South East". Invariably, statements such as these will invoke the immediate question – How will this be achieved? – which leads the budding entrepreneur into the examination and explanation of the financial, operational, marketing and control aspects of the proposition, which forms the core of the business plan.

The next aspect on which our new-businessperson must consider is the viability of the proposition, and yet another question – "Yes, it sound like a good idea, but what makes you think it will work?" Unfortunately, hunches, gut-feelings, innate beliefs, and even feminine intuition, cannot guarantee the viability of a business venture, so in answering the question, we must offer some more tangible ideas, e.g. "I am offering a service for which there is a growing awareness and demand, and at the current time, the nearest alternative supplier is located one hundred miles away". Viability may involve a range of considerations including market research and segmentation, feasibility studies, assessment of potential sales turnover and profit margins, break-even analysis, availability of regular supplies, availability of competent staff, adequate working capital etc. Again, our budding entrepreneur is required to focus in much more detail on the practicalities of the proposition, not the least of which is his or her own personal skills. The subject of business viability will be examined in more detail in Chapter 4.

The business idea itself may be perfectly viable for any competent or experienced businessperson, but the other area which must be considered is whether or not our budding entrepreneur actually has the necessary skills and competencies to pull it off. Does the person have the necessary technical knowledge of the product or service? Do they have knowledge of the market? Have they had any sales experience? Can they manage people and delegate work? Do they have the necessary financial skills for book-keeping and credit control?

If any of these skills are lacking, can they be acquired in time, or will it be necessary to buy them in, and if so, can we afford the cost? The biggest single difference between managers of large and small firms, is that the big-company manager can afford to be a specialist, and can usually tap-in to someone else in the organisation if there is a skills shortage in a specific area, e.g. finance or marketing. In contrast, in the small firm, the manager needs a breadth of general business skills, as well as a depth of knowledge of the product or service. Barclays Bank (1998) highlighted the fact that business owners only seem to fully appreciate the skills required to run a small business once they had experienced the process for themselves. Less than one-third of business owners undertake any basic business skills training prior to starting up, with 80% of the others believing that they already have adequate business skills to adequately manage their business ventures.

However, personal aptitude is not just a question of possessing a broad range of basic business skills. The clearing banks have recognised this in the past few years, and as a result, have started to incorporate questions into their standard business plan forms which relate to personal skills i.e. the management of yourself and your time. For example: Are you self-motivated? Are you persistent, or do you give up easily? Can you take responsibility? Do you find it easy to make decisions? Are you a good organiser? Can you lead and motivate others? These again are aspects which can be developed and explained within your business plan as part of your personal profile and action plan. The business plan gives you the opportunity to emphasise your personal strengths in these areas, and to propose how you intend to improve on those skills which are not so strong. Those who ignore these questions, do so at their peril; as the lending banks are unlikely to have little sympathy with anyone who cannot answer these questions openly and honestly, and admit to their own weaknesses.

It is interesting that in a survey carried out by Cranfield Management School on behalf of the Small Firms Enterprise Development Initiative (SFEDI 1998), contact was made with 1000 firms which had recently closed down. Of those, some 70% claimed to have lacked the basic business skills which they needed to survive. The business planning process provides an ideal opportunity to assess the range of skills which are needed in order for the business to succeed, and at the same time to identify any potential gaps within that range. The subject of self-assessment and self-appraisal is covered in more depth in Chapter 5.

The business plan as a yardstick to measure progress and achievement

As explained above, it is imperative that every new business has clearly defined objectives and parameters within which it will operate, however it is not sufficient for these to be expressed simply as bland statements. In order for us to be able to determine whether or not the objectives are being achieved, it is necessary to define them in much more detail. This is achieved through the process of financial planning (Chapter 10) and by the preparation of marketing plans (Chapter 6).

These plans provide us with specific measurable targets against which we can compare and monitor progress and achievement on an on-going basis, for example:

- Annual budgetary plans, forecasting income and expenditure on a month by month basis, against which actual income and expenditure can be monitored.
- Forecasts of gross profit margins and net profit margins, derived from the budgetary plans, which can be monitored to pick up any problems due to rising costs, falling sales, or seasonal fluctuations in sales, etc.
- The effects of specific sales or promotional activities on sales revenues or profit margins.
- Cash flow forecasts, and the effects of giving or taking credit.
- The need for additional working capital to sustain business, e.g. by means of short-term overdrafts; or longer-term loans to facilitate expansion of the business.
- Affordability of capital investment – Do we replace or repair? Do we produce components ourselves, or buy-in? Do we use loans or hire purchase to buy equipment, or do we lease?

The planning and monitoring of progress and achievement is an integral part of the formulation of business policy. The initial business idea formulates the initial policies which determine the financial and marketing plans and targets. Achievement of those targets, or modifications to the plans in response to external influences and change, will influence the resources available for the future, which will in turn have a bearing on future business policy. This is the constant cycle of Plan, Implement, Monitor, and Revise, although ideally, the revisions should take the form of proactive plans made in anticipation of future events, rather than a series of reactions in response to past events or circumstances.

Raising finance for start-up or expansion

As we have already considered, very few start-up businesses (apart, i.e. from some self-employed trades, or ex-lottery winners!) have the luxury of not needing some form of finance, if not at the outset of trading, then later as the business starts to expand and grow. Even those not requiring funding are now often asked to provide a basic business plan in order to qualify for the initial period (usually the first year of trading) of free bank charges on their business bank accounts that are offered to new firms by most of the main high street banks in the UK.

The various potential sources of business finance are discussed in Chapter 11, but for the great majority of small firms, the first port of call is their local bank manager. Inevitably, the first question asked of our budding entrepreneur is "Can I see your Business Plan?" (a question which is usually closely followed by "What forms of security or collateral can you offer?"). The simple fact of the matter is that these days banks just will not readily lend to anyone who cannot present them with a viable business plan. Fortunately, this requirement also constitutes a much more responsible attitude to lending on the part of the banks; who at one time in the eighties, were frequently accused of being willing to lend to anyone with adequate security, irrespective of the viability of their business proposition. At that time, when the going became tough, some bank managers simply closed down the struggling small businesses and called in their security against their loans.

Today, the clearing banks take a much more responsible attitude to potential business customers seeing themselves as stakeholders in the businesses, and this is reflected in the questions which are asked within their standard business plan packs. The business plan has become an essential prerequisite of any dialogue with the bank manager, and forms the core means of assessing the prospects of survival and growth of any business. This attitude is best illustrated by three extracts from recent customer information packs for business start-up from three of these banks:

HSBC Bank plc: "The more you plan, the better placed you will be to seize opportunities and anticipate threats. Not only will it help you but it enables anyone else involved to take an objective look at your business."

Lloyd's TSB Bank plc: "A business plan can provide you with a clear sense of direction. It can give your business something to measure its progress against – helping you identify any problematic issues early on and take appropriate action."

Royal Bank of Scotland plc: "A Business Plan is a written summary of how you see your business idea developing. Whether you're thinking of starting a new business or planning to grow an existing one, creating (or amending) a business plan is the best way to ensure you are clear about what you want – and need – to achieve."

The ability to prepare a comprehensive and coherent business plan is an absolute imperative for anyone starting in business, and particularly if finance is required from outside of the business. Value added tax registration statistics suggest that only half of new businesses survive more than 5 years, so the better your planning is, the more likely you are to succeed. Preparing a plan is not too difficult, given the many standard formats which are available these days; but preparing a *good* business plan requires a great deal of careful thought and effort. Take a look from the point of view of the bank manager – he or she is charged with the responsibility of controlling money which other people (possibly including yourself) have invested in the bank, and using that money to generate a profit. How would you feel if the bank manager went down to the local bookmakers and "invested" your money on an outsider in the 2.30 p.m. horse race at Haydock Park – you would most definitely not be very impressed? From the bank manager's view, it is your business plan than reduces your chances of winning from those of a rank outsider, to those of an odds-on favourite, or at least an even chance. Your business proposal provides the bank manager with a risk analysis of your prospects, so it is in the interests of both of you to take all practical precautions to minimise those risks. You do so by preparing a detailed and comprehensive business plan, and the bank manager does his part by checking it objectively for potential hazards and risks, before lending you any money.

How often should I update my business plan?

Most business plans are updated on an annual basis. For most small firms it is unrealistic to prepare budgets and cash flow forecasts for more than a year ahead, but preparing them for less than a full year would be too short a time to generate useful information. Some firms revise their plans quarterly or at the half-year stage if there look like being any major changes afoot.

The important thing to remember is that business planning is an on-going process – it is not just something you prepare for the bank manager at the start of the year, and then chuck in the filing cabinet and forget it until next time around. Plans need to be monitored on a regular and frequent basis if they are to be of any productive use. Budget outcomes (actual figures) should be compared with forecast figures at least once each month, and then within 2 weeks of the end of the month. This will enable prompt identification of any major discrepancies or problems which lie on the horizon. When discrepancies occur they must be questioned: Why has this happened? Is it a one-off occurrence, or the start of a longer-term trend and potential problem? What has to be done to resolve the situation? Unfortunately too many people faced with apparent problems are more concerned with asking: "Who is to blame?" rather than identifying the cause of the problems and working to find a solution. The subject or financial monitoring and control will be examined in more detail in Chapter 11.

One other aspect which must be considered here is the fundamentally different approach to planning by small firms compared with their big-company counterparts. Welch (1995) states that "the big-company model of managing and career development does not apply to small businesses". Larger organisations have the resources, stability, and security to facilitate the luxury of long-term strategic planning, perhaps 3–5 years ahead, or possibly more; and the immediate year ahead is seen as the short term. For the owner-managers of small firms, the immediate problem is often simply one of survival – where is the next order coming from? – particularly in the early stages of development of the business, when planning even 1 year ahead counts as long term. In the early stages, most small firms are essentially focussed on short-term plans and goals with survival as the first priority. Consequently they look to the equally short-term policies that will enable them to meet the short-term goals. Only when they have achieved some measure of stability and security can they start to look at longer-term planning and investment, staff development, and training, etc.

How much detail should the business plan contain?

The answer to this question will very much depend on the type of business for which the plan is being prepared. For example, the self-employed window cleaner with no overheads or equipment apart from just a car, ladders, bucket, chamois and scraper will have quite simple requirements – in fact the biggest problem will probably be in planning where to get the clean water from, on each part of his daily round. In comparison, someone setting up a wholesale or manufacturing business, as a hotelier, as an import/export agent, or as a specialist holiday tour operator; where longer-term capital funding is required or where specific and possibly complex legislation applies, may have quite a detailed business plan.

Some self-employed people who have no need of external funding simply do not bother to prepare business plans. Others working on a part-time basis may have a very simple plan, as their income may be regarded simply as a bonus to pay for holidays or luxuries, as they may not depend on that particular activity as their main source of income or survival; e.g. part-time hairdressers, beauticians, or therapists who have a working partners, or a regular day job. In reality no prescriptions can be made about the size and content of any particular business plan, as it will depend on the personal circumstances and resources of the owner-manager, the borrowing requirements needed for the business, and the size, complexity, and operating activity of the proposed business itself. The content and layout of the business plan will be considered in more detail in Chapter 3, which contains a generic template that meets the requirements of most lending banks, corresponds with best practice for business planning as defined in the SFEDI National Occupational Standards, but which can be adapted for most types and sizes of new enterprise.

References

Barclays Bank (1998). Training: the key to success. *Barclays Bank Small Business Review*, May.

Lloyds TSB Bank plc website (2005): www.lloydstsbbusiness.com/support/businessguides/startingup.asp

HSBC Bank plc website (2005): www.hsbc.co.uk/1/2/business/needs/starting-a-business/business-plan

Royal Bank of Scotland plc website (2005): www.rbs.co.uk/Small_Business/Opening_an_Account/Starting_your_Business/default.htm

Small Firms Enterprise Development Initiative Newsletter (1998). Northampton, London.

Welch, B. (1995). Developing Managers for the smaller business: a report on training and development needs. Institute of Management, University of Cambridge, UK/IM, London.

Further reading

Barrow, C., Brown, R., Burke, G. and Molian, D. (2005). *Enterprise Development*. Thompson, Harlow.

Bragg, A. and Bragg, M. (2005). *Developing New Business Ideas*. FT Prentice Hall, London.

Stokes, D. R. (2002). *Small Business Management*, 4th edition. Thompson, London.

CHAPTER 3

Structuring the business plan

In Chapter 2 we examined the reasons and justification for preparing and using business plans, both for new and established enterprises. This chapter examines the ways in which business plans are presented, and suggests a basic structure which meets both the best-practice features of the Small Firms Enterprise Development Initiative (SFEDI) National Occupational Standards for business planning, and the range of content and information required by the main high street lending banks in the UK. The structure is deliberately quite generic to allow flexibility in its content and presentation, so that it can be used as the basis for quite simple or highly complex business proposals. It also meets the learning outcomes or NVQ evidence of both the Chartered Management Institute and Institute of Leadership and Management Certificates and NVQ qualifications in business start-up.

What format should the business plan take?

There are a multitude of "ideal" business plans around, any or all of which will do the job for which they were designed, some better than others, and sadly some are quite inadequate. Each of the major clearing banks has its own version available to potential business customers in disk or paper format, along with explanatory notes to assist completion, and often with templates that supposedly simplify the process, but often just restrict the entrepreneurs opportunity to project their proposals in the best light. Other formats are available from local Business Links or Enterprise Agencies, or from the plethora of "Start your own business" books which abound on the shelves of most town centre bookshops. Most of these business plans ask a range of specific questions, providing a specific amount of space for the specific answers which are required, as well as specific pro-forma spreadsheets with specific headings – and this is where the problems start!

Probably the most common single feature that most new start-up businesses all share with each other, is the very fact that they are all different from each other; and the one feature which standardised business plans with their specific questions cannot accommodate, is that same disparity and uniqueness that pervades those new firms.

One of the biggest problems of standardised business plans is that they tend to restrict individual expression, because they focus on factors of commonality between firms, rather than encouraging them to focus on the factors which make them different or unique from their rivals. No one should doubt or underestimate the value and use of a good budgetary plan and cash-flow forecast to monitor the progress of a business, but even the finest of these will not help to sell the firm's products or services.

Not only do standardised business plan formats tend to restrict the expression of individual flair and ingenuity, by virtue of the fact that they must also accommodate a range of differing business structures, they inevitably prove onerous for some business prospects, and inadequate for others. For the individual who simply wants to operate for example, as a self-employed window cleaner with a regular round, and whose customers tend to pay cash on the spot; the contents of the average standardised business plan are largely superfluous, as the range of business skills, and the start-up capital needed to operate the business are quite modest. In comparison, in order to set up a limited company operating chain of several Cyber-cafes, most standardised business plan formats would probably be too inflexible and therefore inadequate from the user's perspective, as such an enterprise would need to consider preparing budgets on a multiple-location basis, and consolidating these into an overall working budget and cash-flow forecast. Also, the range of technological, management and staff-supervision skills needed by the proprietors would be more extensive than in the one-man-band situation; and the finance and resources required to establish the business would equally, be much more substantial.

Another issue that arises is the longer-term value of the business plan to the business proposer. Whilst a very basic version might provide the local bank with enough information to open a business bank account and offer a small overdraft facility; it will often fall short in terms of meeting the broader objectives of the business planning process, i.e. to provide the proposer with enough knowledge, awareness and information to survive long enough for the business to start making a profit. The planning process should be as much for the benefit of the success of the business as for the standard information needs of the bank manager. One of the most common reasons for business failure cited by insolvency practitioners is lack of business planning, and in particular the need for awareness of profit margins, break-even levels, and the possession of realistic budget and cash-flow forecasts to monitor business progress.

The layout of the business plan

As stated above, the following proposed layout for the business plan has been designed to cover the needs of the business proposers to help them to survive the early stages, and to meet the information requirements of lenders and investors, whilst allowing flexibility in its use as a framework around which the potential owner-managers can construct their own individual business plans, by adding further material, or by omitting certain sections as may be appropriate to the size and type of business which they are planning to operate. It is also suitable as a model of good practice for business planning students in further and higher education. Each section has been deliberately numbered to allow for ease of cross-referencing in order to avoid repetition.

Section 1: The business idea

This is the preliminary section to provide the reader with some basic background information about the proposal, and to hopefully stimulate enough interest to persuade the reader to look further. It must be remembered here that the business plan must act as a sales document to convince the lender of the viability of the proposal, so this section is key to that process and must therefore be concise, positive and upbeat!

1.1   The type of business proposed and services to be offered

This consists of a simple statement which acts as an introduction to the business plan. For example: "I am proposing to work as a self-employed complimentary therapist providing a range of treatments to my clients including aromatherapy, reflexology, reiki, and holistic massage. I am qualified as a practitioner, and experienced in each of these areas, and having worked in a health clinic for the past 2 years, I am ready now to branch out on my own." This statement shows in clear and simple terms, the type of work envisaged, the employment status of the owner, and the range of services that will be offered, and why the owner has chosen to do it.

1.2 Method of operation

This section describes briefly the way in which the business will be operated, to provide the reader (or potential financier) with an overview of the trading status and how the business will operate. Taking up the previous example: "I shall be operating as a sole-trader, working primarily from a dedicated treatment room in my home, which has been converted from a spare downstairs study. In the case of a few of my clients who are less mobile than others, I shall be visiting them in their homes to carry out their treatments. As the business grows I may later consider a move to dedicated premises as and when that becomes affordable".

At this stage it is not necessary to go into a great amount of detail, as the method of operation, and the reasons for its selection, will be considered later in the business plan. Again, the idea is to provide the potential financier with a preliminary insight into how the business will operate, and to describe the framework or structure of the proposed business in order to create an overall picture in the reader's mind. Once the reader has a basic understanding of your proposal, you can progress to add the details at a later stage, by which time the reader will have formed questions in his mind which you will need to answer with those details.

1.3 Personal parameters

This is where you can explain how the business will fit in with your personal circumstances or vice versa. For example, in the case of a website compiler perhaps: "I plan to start the business on a part-time basis alongside my full-time job until I have established enough regular clients to enable me to transfer to full-time activity". Or in the case of a part-time book-keeper "I plan to work from home on a part-time basis initially to enable me to work around my children's school hours. When the children are older I will have the basis to develop a full-time business activity and eventually to start employing others".

1.4 Outline of market and customers

This is where you provide a brief summary and outline of the type of the anticipated customers, or the target market that will be interested in your goods or services. Remember, at this stage an outline is all that is needed, as a more detailed analysis of your marketplace will be given in the marketing section (Section 5) of the business plan. For our mail order supplier: "The customers will comprise mainly male teenagers and single adults who either belong to model aircraft clubs, or who build model aircraft as a hobby". For our therapist friend they might consist of: "Affluent middle-aged housewives, prosperous businesswomen, or wealthy widows who feel they need relaxation to relieve stress and tension", or perhaps "A cross-section of people with physical or muscular problems for which the more conventional methods of treatments have proved inadequate".

1.5   Location and operating area

You will need to explain the geographical base and catchment area from which you expect your customers to come. For some businesses, such as a mail order outlet, this is a simple matter: "I shall be based in Rotherham, but my mail order customers will be spread throughout the UK". Or, in the case of our complimentary therapist: "I shall be based in my hometown of Maidstone, and most of my customers will come from the surrounding towns and villages within a 10-mile radius of the town. The clients which I visit will mostly live within 5 miles of my home".

1.6   Statement of viability

This is the initial assertion of the proposer's belief in the viability of the business, giving a summary explanation of why he or she thinks that the business will succeed. For our mail order supplier this might be the fact that "There is currently no other supplier in the UK who is importing and distributing this particular brand of model aircraft from Japan". For our therapist it might be that: "I already have a regular customer base on which to build, which keeps me occupied for 3 days per week, and I have a waiting list of twenty other clients as a result of word-of-mouth recommendation". Again, please remember that the business plan is a sales document so it is important to be positive and upbeat about the prospects in this part.

Section 2: The proprietors of the business

In this section we name and describe the proprietors or the key people who will be involved in setting up and running the business, along with their respective skills and abilities which will contribute towards its success. These people may not be one and the same, as the owners may have identified others who have key skills or abilities necessary to the business, but who will be employees of those owners; however, they will still be important, if not essential, to the potential success of the business.

2.1 Details of key personnel

In the case of a one-person business, this could comprise a quite simple *curriculum vitae* and personal profile of the business operator. However, in the case of a partnership or limited company, there may be a number of key personnel involved, the role and background of each of which will need to be described in some detail. If there are a number of people involved, and particularly if they have extensive *curriculum vitaes*, it may pay to just include a summary of each in this section, and to put their full details as an appendix to the business plan.

At the same time, in the case of business proposals involving a number of partners, directors or key personnel; this is the stage at which the management structure of the organisation can be outlined in the form of an organisation chart that specifies the respective positions and responsibilities of the key staff.

Having presented an organisation chart, then for each of the proprietors or key personnel shown on chart, you should provide a *curriculum vitaes* (ideally one page only) detailing your personal information i.e. nationality, date and place of birth, marital status, family details, etc. It should also list your current and any on-going qualifications or professional memberships which you expect to complete in the near future. It should summarise your career history, starting with the latest employment and working backwards, and identifying any training or experience relevant to the current business proposal. Finally, it should mention any hobbies or non-working activities or interests which may enhance your personal profile, e.g. school governor, club secretary or treasurer, charitable activities, publications, etc.

2.2 Personal profile(s) of the proprietor(s)

A personal profile for each of the business owners (as opposed to all key staff or employees) in which you describe yourself, your motivations, any past experiences which have had a major influence on your lifestyle or your career, and your personal ambitions and plans or long-term objectives for the future. It may also contain reference to any personal circumstances or family or social commitments which may influence or be of relevance to your business proposal. For example, you may have a family to support, or perhaps children with special educational needs. Alternatively, you may be in the fortunate position where you already have some alternative form of income, such as a working partner, or a pension, so that you do not have to rely on the income from your proposed business alone.

2.3   Your reasons for the choice of business

In this section you should explain in more detail the various occurrences or motivating factors which have caused you to develop your plans to run your own business, and why you want to go into business. In some cases this may be the result of redundancy forcing a change of direction – some people yearn for years to be their own boss, but it is only the shock and the insecurity of unemployment which forces them to take the risk. In other cases, it may be as a result of an opportunity which has presented itself, giving the chance to fulfil a long-standing personal ideal or ambition; e.g. a lucrative hobby gradually expands to the extent that it finally becomes viable as a full-time activity. Here the primary motivation is often one of personal satisfaction rather than financial security.

If there is only one proprietor involved then this section can be combined with the personal profile (Section 2.2).

2.4   Personal skills and experience relevant to the proposed business

This is where you can describe the various skills which you already possess or which you are currently working towards, and which you would typically evidence by certificates of qualification or references from previous employers. The important thing to remember is that it is not just certificated skills that are important. To a bank manager or prospective financier, it is not only the academic (or vocational) qualifications that are taken into consideration; it is relevant previous experience that also counts. Very often, previous experience, e.g. in book-keeping, cash-management, credit-control, budgetary planning, etc., is as important to a potential financier, as the technical knowledge of the potential entrepreneur. This is why it is important to dredge your memory to think back across your past working life to identify all possible experience which might be relevant to the business proposal. It is quite amazing how many people assume no prior knowledge or experience of business; and yet when asked, can describe previous jobs which involved the development and use of business skills (such as cash handling or stock control), without actually realising that this knowledge, acquired by experience, is now relevant to their prospective business.

Where several people are involved in the business you might want to summarise this section in the form of a skills matrix or table, with the names on one axis and range of skills on the other. This can be used in conjunction with the next section to identify potential gaps and development needs for each person. You may also wish to include a SWOT (strengths, weaknesses, opportunities and threats) analysis for each person, although if there are a number of individuals involved, these should be put in the appendices alongside each person's *curriculum vitae.*

2.5 Appraisal of available skills, and identified development needs

This section of the business plan constitutes the skills audit and skills gap analysis, and asks four key questions:

1. What skills are needed in order to achieve efficient and profitable operation of the new business? These may be technical skills or expertise such as trade or professional qualifications, business skills such as book-keeping or credit-control expertise, or management experience, such as staff supervision or production planning. The important thing is to list the full range of potential skills which will certainly, or might possibly be needed. Ideally this should be carried out in conjunction with someone who has experience either of the type of business activity which you are proposing, and who preferably has past experience of running such a business. An objective opinion can be a most valuable asset, particularly if that opinion can help you to ensure that you take a realistic view of your own capabilities.

2. What skills or experience have I (or my staff) accrued to date, or are in the process of developing? The key to answering this question is total honesty and objectivity. Since the mid-1990s the lending banks have increasingly acknowledged the importance of self-assessment within their own standardised business plans, by questioning the potential borrower's capacity for the demands of self-employment. There are various methods and techniques of self-assessment, some of which will be considered in more detail in Chapter 5.

3. What gaps or differences currently exist between the skills needed and the skills available? Having assessed the skills requirements of the business, and those available from existing or potential staff, it is necessary to define the gaps. This is the process of skills gap analysis which is designed to identify potential development areas for existing staff, or other areas where new staff skills may need to be brought in or recruited. Again it is important to be totally honest and objective in identifying any gaps in skills and experience. In the face of financial or operational pressures of running a small business it is all too easy to overestimate your own capabilities, or those of your staff; or to underestimate the full range of skills which might be required in order for the business to succeed and grow. Reference to a SWOT analysis can be useful in compiling this section.

4. How will we bridge the gap? There are two main options here: either to train and develop the skills of yourself or existing staff, or to import (i.e. recruit) new staff who possess those essential skills, assuming of courses, that such staff are available locally. When working capital is tight, the reaction of most small businesses is to make do and mend, i.e. to do nothing. If the business cannot afford new staff, then ideally it should provide training for current staff, but with a vast majority of small firms the tendency is to skimp on investment in training. Training is often regarded as a luxury which cannot be afforded. Small firms have a fundamentally different attitude to training compared with their larger counterparts which treat training as a long-term investment. In contrast, small firms look for short-term benefits which will offer immediate measurable returns on their investment. Such training needs to be provided at low cost, and convenient times so as not to lose productive working time. For most small firms, unless staff training can meet these short-term needs, it is unlikely to take place at all.

It may be useful to cross-reference this section with Section 3.5 to avoid duplication.

Section 3: The resources required

Before any attempts can be made at financial planning, it is essential to identify the capital investment requirements of the business (premises, transport, plant and equipment) and other resources required (personnel, raw materials, consumables, etc.), and the reasons why they are needed. The process of identifying and listing them will also assist the potential owner-manager to distinguish between those resources which are desirable to have, and those which are essential to have. It is surprising how many resources which were initially perceived as being "essential" suddenly become regarded as luxury items when the full cost is identified, especially if the money needed to buy them has to be borrowed at high interest rates!

3.1 Inventory of required plant, equipment, and materials

This is a list of all of the necessary machinery, equipment and materials which might be needed to start up the business, including not just essential production equipment, but the administrative systems (computers, office furniture), and ancillary furniture and fittings (burglar alarms, safes, chairs, tables, toilets, fire extinguishers), raw materials and consumables, etc. It is only when the list is complete, and costs have started to be allocated to the various items on the list, that questions start to be asked about the real necessity for individual items. Do I really need a Rembrandt on the wall of the executive toilet? Or on a more practical level – does the business really need three computers, or can I make do with two for the first few months?

Once the list has been compiled costs can be allocated to each item, and a differentiation made between those resources that are essential to actually start the business, and those which that can be acquired in the next few months or bought from trading profits when they can be afforded. These costings need to be carefully researched with potential suppliers, as they must be realistic and accurate in order to feed into the budgetary planning process. Without an accurate basis for calculating the expenditure, the whole budgeting process becomes a waste of time, as there is no credible or realistic basis against which subsequent expenditure and performance can be measured.

3.2 Schedule of available resources

Many people who are starting a new business have already had some partial involvement in their trade or activity, and may perhaps possess some of the resources needed to start the business. For example, if equipment has been progressively acquired whilst working on a part-time basis, the additional resources needed to turn the business into a full-time activity may not be too great. It is important therefore, to be able to list any resources which are already available, and to put a value on these, as they will constitute part of the business owner's capital. Bank managers are always reluctant to lend money unless they can see a corresponding investment on the part of the borrower. Whilst the person setting up the business may not have a lot of spare cash to invest, the possession of equipment, materials, a car or van, or the goodwill of an existing customer base, can form part of their equity in the business, and often a very significant part. Again, it is important for the purpose of the budgetary plan, to identify just how much of the cost of necessary equipment is already available, as this will reduce the net outflow of cash in the early stages. Potential lenders such as bank managers are also always interested to know the size of both cash and non-cash equity involvement of the business proposers.

3.3   Premises requirements, availability, necessary modifications, etc.

Identifying the required premises, and finding and preparing suitable premises, is a major and time-consuming part of setting up a new business. Chapter 8 examines the various alternative forms of acquiring a suitable site, and the various contractual and legal implications involved therein. If anything, this is the aspect of establishing a new business which can have the single biggest impact (usually in terms of delay) on the commencement of a new venture, as so many of the factors are beyond the control of the owner, particularly when solicitors and town planners become involved, and more so when they decide to go on holiday, invariably one after the other! Obtaining approval for change of use, or for modifications to premises can often add months to the start-up timetable.

3.4   Transport requirements

For any new business, transport is a major item of medium to long-term investment, and so it is of paramount importance to ensure that any transport which is used or acquired, will be both suitable and adequate during the lifetime for which it has been purchased. It is no good taking out a 4-year hire purchase agreement on a small van, if that van is likely to be too small for the needs of the business within 12 to 18 months. So, not only we must ask the question "What do I need right now?" but "Will the same thing still be suitable in a few months time?"

Finding the right vehicle will involve a number of considerations. For example:

- Is it to be used for sales and/or deliveries?
- What physical dimensions are needed or what payload is required?
- Who will drive it? Does the driver need a Heavy Goods or Public Service Licence?
- Will it incur high mileage usage, and if so, what is most economical, petrol or diesel?
- Should I buy a new or second-hand vehicle, and can I really afford a new vehicle?
- How easy is it to load and unload?
- What are the expected maintenance and running costs?
- Does it create the right image for my business?

The answers to these questions will largely determine the choice of suitable transport and the appropriate method of purchase or acquisition, and again this information will feed into the budgetary plans and cash-flow forecasts for the business.

3.5 Personnel requirements

This section will be determined to a great extent by the information gathered in the skills gap analysis in Section 2.5 of the business plan; but the skills gap analysis will only identify the range of skills in deficit, and not the numbers of individuals needed to perform each role. Assessment of the personnel and staffing needs of the business reflects not just the range of skills needed to operate the business, but the numbers of individuals required to work within the business. There may be a need for one person with supervisory management skills, but several with identical basic production skills to do the same job as each other, under the watchful eye of that supervisor. The numbers of each type of worker, and the associated costs of employing these must be identified in order to be fed into the budgetary plan.

3.6 Insurance requirements

The precise insurance policy requirements of the business will depend on the type of business which is proposed. As a very minimum, the owners will need to consider Public Liability insurance; as well as cover for theft or damage to equipment, fixtures and fittings, and possibly stock or goods in transit. If any staff are employed, albeit just a part-time cleaner, it is a legal requirement to take out Employer's Liability cover against accident or injury to employees, and for many businesses Public Liability is a legal obligation, and in reality it is essential for all, even if not legally required. These and other insurance options are examined in more detail in Chapter 8.

Section 4: Financial plans

4.1 Budgetary plans and cash-flow forecasts

For the very small business which deals largely in cash, and neither gives credit to its customers, or receives credit from its suppliers, the budgetary plan and cash-flow forecast may be one and the same. For larger businesses, of where credit is given or received, it will be necessary to differentiate between the two. In the eyes of the bank manager or potential financier, these are the two key documents on which much of the assessment of the viability of a potential new business is based. As such, it is important to get them right.

The budgetary plan attempts to forecast all items of income and expenditure, and details them according to when the sale is invoiced, or when the stock, goods or services received and a financial commitment is incurred. As such it can be used to assist in the forecasting of potential sales turnover and profits, and the forecast figures can be used as a basis against which actual financial performance (income and expenditure, profit margins, etc.) can be compared.

The cash-flow forecast is basically similar in structure to the budgetary plan, but it is modified to take into account delays in receiving money from customers, and paying money to suppliers, due to the giving and receipt of credit. So, although the budgetary plan may show a piece of equipment as being purchased in January, payment of that invoice may not be made until a month later. Similarly, goods sold to a customer and invoiced in January, may not be paid for until February or March, and in the meantime, the money due for those goods is inaccessible. A company can be making a healthy profit in budgetary terms, but can have an appalling cash-flow problem due to late payment for its goods or services, which might interfere with its ability to continue trading.

4.2 Explanation of basis for planned budgets

This section acts as a narrative explanation to the figures which appear in the budgetary plan. For example, how sales volumes and revenue have been forecast, or why the business has used hire purchase rather than leasing to finance its vehicles. It may also outline the basis for loan interest or repayment terms, or reasons for fluctuations in levels of trading activity. It can describe the equity input from partners, the thinking behind planned stock levels, rates of pay for staff, etc.

Similarly, the narrative will explain the basis for credit terms given to customers, and received from its suppliers, and the impact this has on cash flow and working capital. The cash-flow forecast may also indicate when finances are tight, i.e. if any overdraft facilities are required, or longer-term borrowing needs and the size of those.

4.3   Personal survival budget

This is the summary of personal expenses that the proprietor(s) will need to live on whilst the business is being established – typically for the first year or two. The information needs to be both realistic and comprehensive in terms of outgoings and financial commitments, and as it represents net income after tax, so must be grossed up for proprietors who are running limited companies. For sole traders and partnerships that are taxed on business profits the total will define the minimum level of drawings that business profits must cover. Either way it is an essential component of the budget and cash-flow forecasts, and is nowadays a standard information requirement of lending banks.

4.4   Break-even analysis

It is a fundamental requirement of any business to be able to identify its break-even level, i.e. the point at which its sales are generating sufficient contribution (surplus income) to cover both the cost of the sales, and the cost of the overheads of the business. It is equally important that the business should be aware of its profit margins (and mark-up) so that it is able to forecast its expected profits from its anticipated sales turnover. Like the budgetary plans, this information will be an item of key interest to any bank manager or prospective financier, as without an identified profit from its trading activities, the business will be unable to repay any money which it has borrowed from them. This is a critical aspect of the assessment of the viability of any new small business as far as the banks are concerned. Chapter 10 describes how to calculate break-even levels and figures.

4.5   Profit forecasts

Ideally, summary profit forecasts should be provided for the first 2 years of operation, simply because the figures in the first year will include the initial build-up phase so will probably not reflect the profit from a full year of trading. Remember to include all expenses but to leave out loan repayments, and for sole-traders and partnerships, to leave out drawings for personal use as these should be taken from net profit after tax.

4.6   Value of available capital and resources

The capital which the owners of a business put into their enterprise does not just have to be in the form of hard cash. It can also consist of premises, vehicles, equipment, materials, saleable stock, or even good-will in the form of an established customer base. In some cases, the capital may comprise a second mortgage, a charge on property as security, or a personal guarantee offered against a loan. The important factor is that whatever form the capital takes, it should be measurable, and have a tangible value to demonstrate what the investor is putting into the business. Not surprisingly, bank managers are reluctant to lend money to anyone who is not apparently prepared to back the venture themselves.

4.7   Further finance required and potential
sources of funds

It is rare for a new small business to have all of the available finance required to start it up and survive the first few months, let alone to expand itself once established. It is usually necessary at some stage to look for some form of external finance, even if that is just a short-term overdraft. Lenders will normally expect any business borrower to be investing a similar sum to that which they are asking to borrow, in order to verify their own commitment to the venture; except of course when the loan is secured against an asset such as a house or other property. Even then, although larger sums may be available, in practice the bankers' rule of thumb is that the value of the security should be roughly double that of the sum borrowed.

The various options for raising finance are considered in Chapters 10 and 17, and the appropriate options and sources of finance should be identified and described within as part of the financial requirements section (Section 4) of the business plan.

4.8   Chosen sources of finance and reasons for choice

Having examined the various potential sources of finance, the business plan should identify the chosen sources, i.e. those which are most appropriate to both the owner-managers, and the type of business itself. Some firms may choose longer-term secured loans at lower rates of interest, to ease cash flow in the earlier years. Others may only need short-term initial financing, in which case the higher interest overdraft facility may be more suitable, where interest is only paid when the overdraft facility is in use.

Whatever the choice, it is necessary to describe the chosen option and the reasons for its selection over and above the alternatives.

4.9   Financial monitoring procedures

Describe the main processes that will be used to monitor and control your finances once the business starts trading – these can be bulleted and then briefly explained, e.g.:

- Book-keeping systems.
- Budgets: comparison of forecast and actual figures.
- Credit control and bad debt recovery processes.
- Profit margins: planned compared with actual.
- Monitoring of changing operating costs and overheads.

Section 5: Marketing

After the financial plans, it is the marketing aspects of the proposed new business which will be of greatest interest to any financier or potential investor. The marketing section (Section 5) of the business plan will analyse the market sector in which the business plans to operate, and the problems or barriers which might be encountered in trying to break into that market. It will then proceed to define a marketing policy which should facilitate entry and generate sales for the business. Chapter 6 covers in more detail the type of information needed for this section.

5.1   Target market and operational area

It is important that the budding entrepreneur should have a clear idea of the market for his or her goods or services, and the physical or geographical areas in which the business will operate. This was briefly mentioned earlier in the introduction to the business plan (Sections 1.3 and 1.4). Using the same example of the mail order business, the overall market is in which the business plans to operate is that of model makers or hobbyists, but within that market the owner is focussing on a particular sector, in this case model aircraft. This is in itself quite a broad sector with plenty of competition, and for that reason the owner has decided to focus on a specific sub-sector i.e. the supply of a particular brand of Japanese model aircraft which are currently hard to obtain in this country. The specialised nature of the product means that there is likely to be insufficient trade within the geographical vicinity to make the business viable, so the owner has decided to extend the range of potential customers across the whole country by offering the product for sale by mail order.

5.2 Explanation of unique features of proposed products or services

Although stated in the marketing plan, it is a good idea to emphasise to potential lenders or investors, those features of your products or services which distinguish them from the opposition and that will make your customers buy what you are selling. These can be expressed in terms of quality, competitive price, durability, value for money, fashion, practical usage, or even sheer sex appeal. The important thing is that you can show that you have identified those key aspects which will help to sell your product or service in the open market, and that you are making use of that information.

5.3 Market research: completed and planned

In this section we investigate and analyse the particular market sector in which the proposed business expects to be operating. We must ask questions about the nature and size of the market, how easy is it to enter the market, who are the other operators within the market, and how do their products and prices, etc. compare with our own. This is the process of market research, and any potential lender or investor will ask two key questions about this topic: "What market research has been carried out to date?" and "What other market research must be carried out before the business can be launched?" In order for any potential lender or investor to have confidence in the prospects of the business venture, it will be necessary to demonstrate that these questions have been addressed and answered in a competent and comprehensive manner; and to present the results of the research in a clear and comprehensible fashion. The process of market research is examined in more detail in Chapter 6.

5.4   Identification of any special market influences or seasonal factors

Some markets, by virtue of their nature are subject to specific trends, patterns or influences. The majority of postcards are sold during the summer holiday season, whilst Christmas cards tend to sell at the end of the year. The cash receipts for holiday companies follow a definite pattern, with deposits for bookings taken at the beginning of the year, followed by short peaks in trade at Easter and Whitsun, and with the bulk of sales income being received during June, July, and August, then tailing off in September. The pattern is well established and recognised, and cash flow can be planned accordingly. The biggest potential disruption that can occur (apart from a war) is prolonged bad weather, and that is one factor which we cannot forecast well in advance.

In a similar vein, the operators of any new business must also attempt to identify any seasonal influences or market characteristics which will influence levels of sales, income or performance. Very often this will only be achieved as a result of direct experience gained from within the particular market, and then often only in hindsight, or as a result of analysis of sales and performance figures over a period of time.

For example, when I was wholesaling beers and wines to the licensed trade in the 1980s, I identified over several years, a sudden substantial drop in sales around the first weeks of February and October each year, irrespective of weather etc. In spite of recent end of month salary payments, the public were not spending their money in the pubs, and so the publicans were not buying my stock. Why not? Well, quite simply, the first weeks in February and October were the deadline dates for payment or settlement of credit card balances accrued during the summer holidays in August, or in the run up to Christmas, so disposable income was at a minimum at those times. Once the pattern had been identified, then stock levels could be reduced for those particular weeks in future years, in order to avoid cash being tied up in unsold stock.

Whilst it is imperative to be aware of seasonal and other influences on trading levels, actually identifying these as an outsider to the market, can in fact be very difficult, so it is important to ask questions about these potential problems as part of the market research process. Better still, try to get some experience of working within the market, or talk to someone who has done so recently.

5.5   Analysis of competitors products and services

This analysis can be carried out by answering a series of simple questions:

- Who are my direct competitors in the marketplace? That is those providing the same or very similar products or services. In the case of our complimentary therapists, e.g. who else is offering Aromatherapy massage in the district?
- Who might be competing indirectly with me? That is those providing other services which are not in direct competition with me, but which might detract from my sales? For example, those offering other forms of therapy which might compete with Aromatherapy.
- What prices are they charging? Are they lower, higher, or comparable with my own? Why should they differ?
- How do their services differ from mine, and is this reflected in their prices?
- What geographical areas do they cover? Do these overlap with my operating area?
- Are they operating in the same market sector as myself, and what proportion of the market do they occupy? Is there space for me within that market sector?

Obtaining this information is again, part of the necessary process of market research, and the questions must be answered in order to produce a convincing and realistic marketing plan.

5.6   The marketing plan

The marketing plan constitutes the methodology statement of the business plan – "This is how I will sell and promote my goods or services", and the plan is typically presented using four key headings, usually described as the four "Ps":

1. The *Product* is about the goods or services being offered, their purpose, quality, unique features, usefulness, appeal to the customer, etc.
2. The *Price* of the goods or services forms the basis for comparison with competitors. Price can be a selling feature in itself, e.g. by being less than that of competitive products; or if equal, leads

the potential customer to compare quality and uniqueness with that of the competitors' products.

3. The *Place* is concerned with the outlets and distribution channels through which the product will be delivered; and again, the perceptive marketing plan will look for opportunities or gaps in the marketplace, where demand is not being met.

4. *Promotion* is concerned with the ways in which the products or services will be promoted or advertised to potential customers, and how the effective use of promotional activities will lead to growth in sales and expansion of the business.

Again, this topic is considered in more detail in Chapter 6.

5.7   Samples of advertising material

The inclusion of samples of marketing material may not be appropriate or practical for all potential businesses. If you do have them available, it is always a good idea to include some simple samples of advertising materials such as business cards, newspaper adverts, or leaflets, within the business plan; although of course these need to have been produced to a professional standard and quality, otherwise they could well do your case more harm than good. With the widespread availability of computers and desk-top publishing programs, most people should be able to produce a basic design of advertising material to illustrate their ideas for advertising and promotion. The actual material can be included in the appendices if it is substantial or bulky.

5.8   Schedule of fees and charges

As in the previous section, inclusion of price lists may not be appropriate to all types of businesses, but even if you do not have a full price list like a bar or restaurant, you may have standard rates at which you will charge out your time, or perhaps you have standard hourly rates for certain types of service, and this section is where you describe them. The simple list of the fees or prices which you will be charging for your goods or services serves as a reference point for comparison with the prices charged by your competitors, as a basis for calculating profit margins, and to assist in the calculation of the sales revenues which are included in your budgetary plans and cash-flow forecasts. It will no doubt be influenced by the prices which are being charged by your competitors, but it should also reflect the quality of your goods or services, and any distinctive or unique features which differentiate them from the competition, and for which a premium price might be justified. The use of low prices to attract business in the short term might be a justifiable strategy, but in the longer term, it is the maintenance of profit margins that ensures survival. The golden rule when fixing prices is that if you sell yourself short, you will almost certainly be the loser in the long term. Competitors will either reduce their prices (and profit margins) to compete with you, or look to sell their goods or services on the basis of differential features such as those described above. Finally, remember to keep a copy of your old price lists, as they are a good point of reference should the tax man start to query the profit margins you have been achieving.

5.9   Statement of quality standards and policy

This is a formal statement of the quality standards for the goods and services which are being provided, as well as for the behavioural standards of the staff which are supplying them. The statements constitute a simple description of the operating standards against which the business can be visibly measured. For example, an extract from the standards used by a wedding caterer:

- All staff will be smartly dressed at all times, and will present a friendly, smiling, and caring attitude to the customers.
- All staff involved with the preparation of food will possess a Basic Food hygiene Certificate, and will adhere to the standards of hygiene required to comply with Environmental Health legislation.
- All food will be prepared on site, no more than 1 hour before the time of serving, and covered to protect it from contamination. All food will be stored at the appropriate cold temperatures prior to preparation, and before it is served.

These are just a few simple examples, but they demonstrate not just the need to comply with relevant legislation, but the emphasis on providing quality products and services to the customer, as well as the standards which the customers can expect to experience from the supplier.

5.10   Monitoring sales and marketing activities

It is a good idea to conclude the marketing section (Section 5) with a summary or description of how you will monitor the effectiveness of sales and marketing activities. For example:

- Are sales volume and revenue matching forecasts and if not, why not?

- Are the patterns of sales indicating any possible long-term changes in the market?
- Is advertising producing results? Record and compare numbers of enquiries and actual sales for each type of activity.
- By monitoring competitor marketing activities and prices, as well as new product developments.

Some methods of monitoring quality will be determined by legislation or by industry standards, e.g. the safe temperatures at which food can be stored, and the types of thermometers, and the records which must be used to ensure safe storage. Others will need to designed for the specific goods or services which the business is offering, such as the use of customer feedback questionnaires, the monitoring of the frequency of complaints or the return of unsatisfactory goods. Customer turnover or retention rates can also act as a yardstick to monitor levels of satisfaction. This section requires you to answer the question "How will I ensure that my goods or services meet the necessary quality standards?" and to describe or give examples of suitable methods. You may wish to describe some of the quality monitoring activities relevant to your business that are outlined in Chapter 11 under Customer care.

Section 6: The implementation of the proposals

Having planned the financial and marketing aspects of the business, this section of the business plan focuses on the way in which the business will operate, the timetable for implementing the proposals, and the importance of giving due consideration to potential risks or hazards that could disrupt or delay the implementation of the proposals; and of course, what contingencies might be needed to prevent that from happening.

6.1 Chosen means of operation, and justification for choice

Here, we are identifying the legal status of the business, e.g. as a sole trader, a partnership, or as a limited company; and the explanation and justification of that particular choice. The chosen method of operation may also be linked to any personal parameters, influences or ambitions which may have been identified in Section 1.3 or 2.2 of the business plan.

6.2   Relevant legislation

It is important to identify any key areas of legislation which may have an impact on the business or with which you will need to maintain compliance. This section should comprise a brief list which identifies the relevant legislation, accompanied by an explanation of its relevance to the business. It may also create confidence in potential lenders if some explanation is given for certain items of legislation which are not relevant to the business or its operating procedures. For example: "I do not require planning to operate my business from my premises as there is no change of use involved, as the site already has planning consent for commercial use. However, I shall need Building Regulations approval to carry out modifications to the external drainage system."

6.3   Timetable and phasing of business start-up

The budgetary plans will have identified the expected start of trading, but for many new firms there may be a lead time before trading can actually commence, e.g. where planning permission is required, or where premises have to be modified. This is usually a time of net expenditure which can inevitably result in a drastic drain on available cash. It is important that realistic lead times are identified, and contingency plans made if there is any possibility of prolonged delays.

You may wish to present your planned sequence of events or dates at a flow chart or Gannt chart, identifying key dates or events that are critical to the successful launch of your business. You may also want to link or combine this section with 6.4 to identify key activities that must precede or run alongside each of these events. Again, if you wish, any substantial information can be included in an appendix to keep the main text concise and focused.

6.4   Key stages of implementation

These will vary from business to business, but they might include factors such as dates for acquiring premises, delivery of stocks or raw materials, the commencement of trading, approval of available loans or finance, key review dates, or the start of an advertising campaign. The question "What makes them key stages?" invariably invokes the answer that "if certain events are not completed by those key dates, then there could be subsequent delays in the overall implementation of the business proposal". For example: In order to open a shop on a certain date, the shop fitting must be completed at least 3 days before the opening; and stock must be ordered at least 3 weeks before that date. A delay in receiving financial approval could mean that there is no money available to pay for the new stock on the date by which it must be ordered, so the opening date would need to be postponed.

You may want to present a risk analysis in this section to identify the potential impact of possible problems on the start and development of your business. This can be expressed in terms of how likely or probable is the risk, and how significant would the impact be if I should occur.

6.5   Longer-term plans or prospects

You may wish to include this section to describe to potential lenders or investors how you see the long-term development and growth potential of the business, for example, where you would like it to be in 3, 5 or 10 years' time from now, or what options there might be for expanding or diversifying the markets in which the business operates.

6.6   How you will measure the success of the business

You can explain here how you will measure the success and achievement of the business from your perspective, perhaps in terms of:

- growth or maximisation of profitability,
- capital growth or value of the business,
- market share achieved, or expansion of the customer base
- growth in sales turnover,
- number of employees in the organisation,
- the personal income or wealth it will create for you.

There may also be other personal objectives that you have outlined in Section 1.3 or 2.2 that will act as measures of success. Monitoring the overall success of the business goes beyond the on-going processes of monitoring financial, marketing and quality performance within the business. It is important to identify which individual factors or combinations will represent suitable measures of achievement for you as the owner and entrepreneur in the light of your own objectives and expectations, and possibly those of your family.

Section 7: Summary

This is where you move back into sales mode to summarise and confirm your belief in the potential profitability and viability of your business proposal and its potential for success. This could take the form of a list of key points, each stating a reason and a corresponding justification for the anticipated success of the business. For example:

"I believe that the business will be profitable for the following reasons:

1. I already have a core of regular customers who are satisfied with the products and services that I offer, along with a waiting list of potential clients.
2. I currently have no direct competitors within a 20-mile radius of my operating area, and I am not aware of any others who are planning to work in my locality.
3. I have adequate finance and working capital to buy all necessary plant and equipment, and sufficient working capital to finance the first 12 months of trading, even without expanding my current turnover.
4. I have sufficient collateral in my own home to raise any necessary finance for expansion, even though I fully expect longer-term growth of my business to be financed from its own profits.
5. I have all of the necessary skills and experience to successfully operate the business, along with two experienced and reliable staff who can back me up during holidays, or in the event of illness. My domestic partner is an experienced and qualified book-keeper, and my brother is a solicitor, so I can access sound financial and legal advice when needed.
6. I have a low-rent, long-term lease on premises which are adequate both for current output and foreseeable growth."

It sounds just like heaven, doesn't it? If only all business start-ups were that straightforward!

Section 8: Appendices

List and number each of the appendices and check that they have been correctly referenced in the text of your business plan. Appendices can be useful as a means of including bulky information such as market research date, that might otherwise detract from the readability of the main text. Similarly, it is the place for additional supporting information that might be of interest to lenders or investors, such as letters expressing interest from customers or suppliers, or letters of support from other potential investors.

Further reading

Bragg, A. and Bragg, M. (2005). *Developing New Business Ideas*. FT Prentice Hall, London.

Stokes, D. (2002). *Small Business Management*, 4th Edition. Thompson, Harlow.

Williams, S. (2003). *Lloyds TSB Small Business Guide*, 16th Edition, Vitesse media, London.

Writing a Business Plan: Chartered Management Institute Checklist No. 021, Corby.

CHAPTER 4

Developing the business idea

The objective of this chapter is to help the new or prospective owner-manager to make a realistic, and hopefully, objective assessment of the viability of the proposed or new business venture. As mentioned in Chapter 2, the business plan document serves a number of functions from defining the business objectives and resources needed to deliver them, quantifying the objectives and resources in financial terms to generate forecasts and targets, identifying further financial needs, and also acting as a sales document for potential lenders or investors. It is in the latter role that the business idea section of the business plan comes to the forefront as the initial taster that whet stimulate interest and whet the appetite of potential financiers. As such it is essential that this section is geared towards just that:

- by providing a concise and easy-to-read outline or summary of the proposed enterprise and its main activities;
- by positively promoting the strengths of the proposal and its commercial viability;
- by projecting a confident and positive attitude to the idea by the proposer(s) and their awareness of, and capability to handle any risks involved.

The business idea section of the business plan, the structure of which was outlined in the previous chapter, plays a key role in introducing the proposed venture to any banker or potential investor. It is intended primarily as an overview of the business plan, and as such, it does not have to be crammed full of detail – that can follow later on – but it must be regarded as a principle opportunity for promoting and selling your business. The fact is, that unless the introduction can provide a concise, positive and optimistic (but still realistic) summary of the business opportunity that will whet the appetite of the reader, then the chances are that any potential banker, financier or investor, will simply not bother to read any further. It must therefore, project and reflect the proposer's confidence and belief in the proposed business; and emphasise and justify that same belief. It is simply no good stating "Well, I think that it might work", as the bank manager would be quite justified in saying "Then come back and see me when it has!" It is important therefore, to sell the idea, to think positively, and to use positive language throughout the business plan: i.e. you do not *hope* to succeed, you expect to succeed; or you will do something, rather than *might* do it.

In my experience, most new or aspiring entrepreneurs tend to overlook two fundamental points. First, that bank managers do not have unlimited funds to lend, so that your proposition needs to stand out from the crowd and justify the bank manager's decision to lend to you. Second, that the business plan is not just a factual document. One of the primary skills that any owner-manager needs in order to succeed in business is the ability to sell their goods or services to the customers. Naturally, when a bank manager is appraising any business plan, then he or she will be looking for evidence of those selling skills. So for that very reason, it is important that the initial part of the business plan not only grasps their attention, but also starts to demonstrate the presence of those selling skills. Put yourself in the bank manager's shoes – if you are unable to project to the bank manager your own belief in the viability of the business, then why on earth should he or she believe in it?

The purpose of the business

The very first point that must be explained is the nature of the business activities. It may well be that the business will focus on providing just one type of goods or services – a chiropodist, e.g. carries out medical treatment to peoples' feet. However, in some cases, the central goods or services may be accompanied by a secondary line; e.g. some chiropodists also carry out reflexology (foot massage) treatments alongside their mainstream work.

It is important from the outset that the primary and secondary activities are clearly defined in an initial statement, so that the reader is immediately informed of the nature of the business. For example: "I intend to set up in business as a mobile caterer specialising in private functions such as weddings and parties. Alongside the provision of food and drink for weddings, I can also offer secondary associated services. These will include the supply of wedding cakes, licensed bars, chauffeur driven cars, discos, flowers, and wedding photography; which I will arrange as part of a complete package for my clients, and for which I will receive a percentage commission from the specialist suppliers". In this case, the primary service of food and drink for functions is clearly stated, and the secondary income from supplementary services is also explained.

Is this a new or existing business?

This is an obvious, but still important question to answer for the benefit of any potential financier, as the answer to it will invariably raise a series of further questions:

- Is this a new business which you are setting up from scratch? If so, assuming that you have done your market research and justified the viability of the prospect, then you must identify the lead time between start-up and reaching an on-going operating profit. This leads to the questions: "Are your financial resources adequate to cover that period?" or "What could possibly go wrong that might delay your trading at a profit?", and "How would you cope with that problem?". You need therefore to be in a position to answer these questions if asked, and ideally your business plan should demonstrate that you have considered them.

- Are you setting up a franchised business? If so, you should be able to demonstrate the type and level of support available in the early stages from the operators of the franchise, and confirm their reputation as franchisers. How well-known are the franchised products or services? Have you spoken to other franchisees to investigate their experience in the early stages? Do you have any exclusive operating area rights to protect you from neighbouring or new franchisees? Are you tied in to a long-term contract? Do you face any penalties if your franchise fails? Would it be possible to sell the franchise on if you chose to do so?

- If you are buying an established business, are you sure of its long-term viability? Is it threatened in any way by new developments in the area, or by incoming competition? Will it be affected by any economic or legislative factors? Are you paying a fair price? Has your contract to buy been checked by a solicitor and the financial books examined by an accountant? Are there any planned local developments or planning conditions or restrictions that could adversely affect the business in the future? Why does the vendor want to sell in the first place, and is the reason given genuine? Will you be able to make a reasonable return on the capital invested?

The legal format of the business

In the process of describing the proposed business, the reader will need to have made some basic but rational decisions about the format and trading status of the business, e.g. whether it will be operated on a sole trader basis, as a partnership, or a limited company, and possibly the tax implications of these options. In doing so, the reader may also need to consider some of the legal aspects described in Chapter 7. First, however, it is worth examining the various options of trading status in more detail.

Sole trader

Being a sole trader is not simply a case of being a one-man-band, as many sole traders actually employ quite a few staff – just think about some of the local builders or tradesmen in your vicinity. Sole trader status means that the person who owns and runs the business is solely responsible for its profits, losses, legal and statutory obligations, liabilities, etc.

On the positive side, this means that the sole trader does not have to answer to anyone else (unless married or with other domestic commitments that might influence the proposal), and is solely responsible for decision-making. It is easy to start trading as a sole trader, as all that is necessary is to inform the local office of the Inland Revenue (now combined with HM Customs & Excise from 1st April 2005 as HM Revenue & Customs) by completing a standard form, which is available from the tax office, Department of Social Security, or the local value-added tax (VAT) office. All profits are retained by the proprietor, and he or she can determine the hours worked, duration of their holidays, etc. With the aid of a good accountant, they can also minimise tax liabilities, as they are taxed on the profits of the business rather than the wages or drawings taken from the business. In fact, the overall operation of the business can be quite simple.

This all sounds very attractive, but naturally there is also a downside. As well as retaining all profits, the sole trader is directly liable for all losses, without any limit to the liability. If the business folds, then creditors can pursue the sole trader's own personal assets: home, car, jewellery, savings, and most but the very basic possessions. Attachment orders can also be made against future earnings. Unless the business is sufficiently large to employ staff, working hours can be long, holidays are often few and far between, and there is often no backup in the case of illness or accident. It can also be lonely having to make decisions without anyone with whom you can discuss issues or problems, or ask for an objective and honest opinion. Capital is also hard to raise without security, although that same problem can be true of most new businesses.

Legally, unless they are subject to special registration or reporting requirements for a particular trade or industry (e.g. environmental health registration for caterers), the statutory reporting requirements are quite simple. If sales turnover is less than £15k per annum, then a simple three-line tax return is sufficient (sales, less expenses, gives profit), and above that level the sole trader need only to complete the appropriate parts of the annual self-assessment form for tax purposes, profit and loss account details, etc. Once sales turnover reaches £50k per annum, then like any other business it is necessary to register for VAT with HM Revenue & Customs, and to make the necessary quarterly returns and payments, as described in Chapter 7. Also, if employing staff, then income tax and national insurance must be deducted from their wages or salaries under the PAYE (pay as you earn) system. Sole trader accounts do not have to be audited by a chartered accountant, but all records do have to be retained for a period of 6 years. Profits, less legitimate business expenses and personal allowances, are taxable; and every sole trader must pay Class 2 National Insurance Contributions (NIC), unless income is low. Class 4 NIC is also levied by HM Customs & Revenue according to the level of profits, the rate of which tends to change yearly in line with government fiscal policy.

Partnerships

A partnership is a business involving two or more partners who are trading together as a single business. Typically the business relationship will be formalised under a legally constituted and legally binding partnership agreement (see Chapter 7, Partnership Act 1890), and again the Inland Revenue have to be informed when the partnership starts or is closed down. It is also possible to set up a limited partnership by registering the partnership with the Registrar of Companies, and this is often used for partnerships of professional people such as solicitors, surveyors or accountants.

Many people find the added security offered by a partnership to be attractive. For example, with two or more people working together, there is usually a better interaction of ideas when it comes to decision-making – two heads are better than one. There is also the mutual support available in the event of illness or accident, and to facilitate more flexible working hours, and holidays. Profits are retained by the partners, and whilst shared, will often be greater than the same individuals could achieve by working separately, because of the savings gained by sharing administration and overhead costs, and by using specialist skills and expertise. For example, one partner may have strong sales skills, whilst the other may have better financial and administrative abilities than the first. A partnership may also provide an easier means of raising finance or of providing a greater sum of available finance; where, e.g. available monies ore pooled, or security for loans is shared.

Again, however, there is a negative side to partnerships which should not be underestimated. It is often said that there is nothing like a business partnership to test a friendship, or to divide a family in two! Differences of opinion can arise over what direction the business should take, or over who is working the hardest or longest hours, or drawing the biggest income from the business. The cracks become more noticeable when the business is under financial pressure, or when individual partners come under pressure from their own spouses or families. It is hard to convince your wife that you can't afford a holiday this year, because the business needs a new van, and then to see your business partner clear off to the Costa del Sol a week later!

The biggest drawback of partnerships is the personal liability of the partners for the debts of the business, i.e. the "joint and several liability" wherein each partner is liable for their own proportion of any debts plus the liability for the debt as a whole. Consider the following cases: Example 1, a two-woman partnership is assessed for a tax liability of £20,000. Partner A pays HM Revenue & Customs her half of the liability on time, i.e. £10,000. Partner B then defaults on her share, and disappears to South America with her new toy boy. Partner A now becomes liable for B's share of £1000 as well as the money she has already paid. Example 2 is based on true circumstances wherein two partners running a private club got into debt with HM Revenue & Customs for late payment of VAT. The bailiffs entered the premises, removed all assets and closed it down. Partner X had a heart attack and died, so partner Y declared himself voluntarily bankrupt, leaving the widow of partner X having to pay all business debts from her late husband's estate and insurance. It is true that legal redress can be obtained, but the cost, aggravation, and lengthy time scales involved often do not justify the initial financial outlay or the commitment in terms of time and effort.

The moral is to be very sure of the person or persons with whom you are going into partnership. Can you fully trust them? Are they honest? Are they reliable? Are their objectives for the business the same as yours? Do they also regard it as a long-term prospect, or is it just a get-rich-quick idea in which they will lose interest when the going gets tough? How does their level of investment compare with your own, i.e. who is taking the most risk? Do they have any business skills or experience? What can they offer you that you cannot get by employing someone? These are just a few of the questions you may need to ask yourself before making a full commitment.

From the point of view of legal reporting, the requirements for a partnership are very similar to those of the sole trader. The same accounting returns have to be made on turnover, expenses and profits for tax purposes. The PAYE and National Insurance requirements are the same, as is the VAT threshold, and that figure is more likely to be reached when two or more people are generating income for the business.

Limited company

Limited companies are generally regarded as being of a higher status than sole traders or partnerships. They can be purchased quite readily off the peg, via weekly UK national advertising publications such as Dalton's Weekly or Exchange & Mart. The new companies are often set en bloc up by specialist firms or solicitors, offered for sale for a couple of hundred pounds, and then renamed as required by the new order, ready to start trading. Assuming there are no anticipated problems with the proposed trading name, once the company has been purchased and company officers nominated, then the company can start trading almost at once. Alternatively, they can be set up very cheaply from scratch under the proposed operating name, in about 4–5 weeks without much legal advice. In reality, for the time delay and administration involved, it is much simpler to pay a little more for a company from a specialist supplier and then simply change the name.

The main documents required in order for the company to operate, are the Memorandum and Articles of Association which define the company's legitimate trading activities, and powers to raise finance. The company must also maintain a Minute Book which records the share capital, issue of shares, details of company officers, minutes of annual general meetings, etc. Every limited company also has a company seal which is affixed to official documents and contracts. Responsibilities and duties of company officers are established in law, and necessary statutory returns (and penalties for non-compliance) are specified by the Companies Acts.

The key difference between sole traders, partnerships, and the directors who own or manage limited companies, is that whereas the former are self-employed, the directors cannot legally be so, as they are employees of the company. This is because the limited company is a "body corporate", i.e. it has a legal existence in its own right, irrespective of the persons who own it, invest in it, or manage it. Similarly, whereas self-employed sole traders and partners are taxed as individuals and pay income tax, a limited company having a corporate identity, is liable for corporation tax. It is the same corporate status that makes the liability of its owners limited. This means that unlike the case of sole traders and partners where their liability for business debts is total, the owners, investors, shareholders, etc. of a limited company are only liable for the sums which they have already invested in the company, or which they have guaranteed on its behalf. (That liability also includes the value of any shares which are issued but not fully paid up.) If therefore, the company becomes insolvent, then the creditors can only pursue the assets of the company itself, and cannot take action against the shareholders or directors, except in the case of fraud or negligence by those same persons.

On the face of things, this seems a very attractive and low risk way of setting up a business, as the limited company approach ostensibly takes the owner one step back from the potential creditors. However, things are not that simple. I once heard of a retired middle manager from a water authority who had no direct experience of small firms, but who as a local business adviser was telling a business start-up group, that if they wanted to be taken seriously they must set up a limited company. This was because "sole traders and partnerships have no real credence in the business world". In reality this is total nonsense where new businesses are concerned, because a newly established limited company with no financial track record, and with only £100 of issued share capital, is no more attractive in the eyes of a potential creditor, as any partnership or sole trader, and with the added risk of limited liability, it may take the limited company a good deal longer to obtain credit facilities.

For any start-up business the two foremost problems consist of finding the finance to get started and then obtaining credit from suppliers to trade and expand the sales of the business. It matters not whether you are a sole trader of a limited company, if you have no proven track record, and no tangible assets, or security to offer, then borrowing money or obtaining credit will be hard. This is because you will be unable to provide any necessary trade references; and in the case of limited companies, a search via Companies House will show no accounts as having been returned. Quite often, suppliers of goods to limited companies will take a harder line than that taken with sole traders, simply because they know that it is easier to recover debt from a sole trader than from the owners of a limited company. It is quite common for initial terms of supply to be based on cash-with-order, or cash-on-delivery, with credit facilities being withheld until the buyers have proven their reliability. Even then, credit may be limited to a fixed monthly maximum figure, or to payment within a fixed period of time, until a good working relationship has been established.

In terms of legal and statutory reporting requirements, owners of limited companies have more onerous obligations than their self-employed counterparts. For those companies with a relatively low turnover and balance sheet (under £5.6m and £2.8m respectively), the submission of abbreviated accounts is permissible, but for the majority, it is necessary to submit full audited accounts annually to the Registrar of Companies. The annual returns, etc. are examined in more detail in Chapter 7. In addition, as all directors are employees of the company, all staff fall the under PAYE and National Insurance Regulations; plus the additional requirement to provide HM Revenue & Customs with separate details of all expenses for directors and higher paid staff. VAT thresholds are the same as for any other business.

As sole traders and partners, tax liabilities are assessed against the profit of the business against which personal tax allowances can be offset. Tax is paid at the standard and higher rates (currently 22% and 40% respectively), whereas corporation tax for limited companies is currently 19% on profits up to £300k and 30% on profit between £300k and £1.5m. Interestingly, the government's 1999 budget contained an incentive of zero corporation tax on the first £10k of profits to effectively encourage sole traders and small partnerships to convert to trading as limited companies, as those are easier to monitor and control via the Registrar of Companies. This incentive was reversed in 2005 leaving many small traders who had been advised to convert (such as taxi drivers) feeling aggrieved. In summary then, the limited company option is probably more suited to the type of business which employs staff, foresees steady and continuous growth, and eventual long-term profits exceeding £300k; whereas the smaller business which is not looking for substantial expansion would probably benefit from remaining as partnership or sole trader status.

Co-operative

The fourth trading status option for smaller businesses is to become established as a co-operative or joint ownership venture, wherein the business is owned and controlled by a minimum of seven members, normally but not necessarily its own employees, as there can be non-working members. This is usually described as a workers' co-operative to distinguish it from the various Co-operative Retail Societies (Co-op shops) across the UK which are in effect customer-owned co-operatives. Although co-operatives are normally limited companies, they can be societies or even partnerships (the John Lewis Partnership of department stores is a good example of this), as they are regulated and registered under the Provident Societies Acts (1965–1975). This means that all of the business policy, the assets, and the profits of a co-operative are controlled by its own members (or staff) who all have equal voting rights in how the business is organised and managed. Wages are paid to staff, and surplus profits (dividends) shared between them, according to their level of participation in the business. Like limited companies, registered co-operatives are classed as a "body corporate" and are subject to corporation tax, although if unregistered, they are treated as partnerships with unlimited liability for the losses or debts of the business. When registered in the form of a limited company, their reporting requirements will be the same as those of normal limited companies, as will be the operation of PAYE, tax liabilities, VAT registration, etc.

Involvement in a co-operative does usually generate a high level of commitment from its members, as they are effectively working for both the good of themselves as well as the co-operative, and participate in the management and decision-making processes. At times, however, this democratic process can be counter-productive, when business decisions are based on personal feelings or interest rather than sound business practice. Where co-operatives have been created as worker-buyouts of failing businesses when faced by possible redundancy, the result is often the continuation of inefficient labour-intensive working methods to maintain employment for members, which can threaten its own success or survival.

The government's Co-operative Development Agency exists to advise any potential co-operatives as to how to set themselves up. These days, apart from special areas of mutual interest (e.g. organic farming, social or environmental interests), co-operatives are relatively uncommon, and certainly there is little or no commercial advantage to be gained from setting up as one.

External influences

It is relatively easy to identify the factors which will impact on the viability of a business from within the business itself (staff, management skills, available finance, etc.) and from the market environment (size of market, demand for goods and services, competition, etc.). However, most aspiring owner-managers find it much harder to focus on the broader influences, particularly if they are not familiar with economics, or do not have a great deal of interest in politics or current affairs.

One of the most widely used methods of analysing these factors is the political, economic, social, technological, legislative, and environmental (PESTLE) analysis, which categorises them under the six main headings of PESTLE influences. The precise relevance of these will of courses, depend on the individual organisation, its particular geographical location, and the market in which it operates. The Pestle analysis is described and explained in more detail in Chapter 14, as it is an ideal tool for strategic analysis of the wider environment in which firms operate, and is therefore useful when planning long-term growth and development. However, it can also be used in the pre-start-up situation to identify potential constraints or opportunities that might affect the business, e.g. political initiatives to encourage new businesses, or fiscal policies that may have a negative impact on the potential business by pushing up operational costs (road fuel tax, minimum wages, etc.).

As explained earlier in this chapter, the business idea section is meant to be a sales pitch that promotes the concept of the new enterprise, and as such it should be concise and focussed. It would be easy to slip into a great deal of descriptive detail about the choice of trading status or the political and legal changes that might affect the business. They key to a good, well-presented business plan is to make brief reference to show awareness of relevant issues, but not necessarily to explain them in huge detail that would distract the focus of a potential investor or lender (or possibly bore them senseless!). However, at the same time you should be prepared to answer more detailed questions during a subsequent interview with the lender or investor, so make sure that you can explain or justify your material.

Further reading

Bragg, A. and Brabb, M. (2005). *Developing New Business Ideas.* Prentice Hall, London.

Clayton, P. (2004). *Law for the Small Business.* The Sunday Times, London.

Registrar of Companies Booklet (2003). *The Limited Partnerships Act.* http://www.companieshouse.gov.uk/about/gbhtml/gb02.shtml

Stokes, D. R. (2002). *Small Business Management,* 4th edition. Thompson, Harlow.

Williams, S. *Lloyds TSB Small Business Guide,* 16th edition. Vitesse Media, London.

CHAPTER 5

Developing entrepreneurial skills

There have been many people in the past who have nursed a secret aspiration to running their own business. For most the prospect remains just a wishful thought. For others, something happens in their lives which presents an opportunity, perhaps an unexpected inheritance; or an event which forces a change in direction, such as redundancy. But simply having the capital available to start a business is not enough. Even in the case of the tradesman who is made redundant and possesses both the technical skills needed to work and the redundancy pay to out start on his own, surviving in business requires a much wider portfolio of skills. The problems lie firstly in identifying which specific skills are most relevant to the business proposal, and secondly in determining objectively whether or not they are available. In the event that the required skills are not currently available, then those deficient skills must either be developed or imported. The process of identifying the necessary skills and assessing their presence is called the skills audit.

The objectives of this chapter are to assist the reader in understanding how to carry out a skills audit, and to provide some practical methods of self-assessment which will assist him or her, as a potential owner-manager, to define the skills gaps which need to be filled. Following on from that, the reader will be able to define his or her own personal development plan to acquire the further skills needed to succeed in business.

This chapter also links to Chapter 16 in the second part of this book, as the processes of identifying staffing levels and skills requirements is similar both in the case of business start-up and as the business starts to expand and grow.

The process is concerned with four main stages:

1. To objectively analyse and identify the current and foreseeable skills' needs of the business, in terms of management, administrative and technical skills, and the relative importance of these.
2. To identify the entrepreneur's own personal goals and objectives, and accurately analyse and evaluate his or her own skills and resources in relation to these.
3. To produce a realistic personal development plan for the potential entrepreneur.
4. To monitor the on-going performance of the entrepreneur once the business has started and the progress made towards developing the new skills that had been previously identified as necessary for the success of the business. This applies both to the entrepreneur's personal needs and to the process of assisting employees to develop new skills that will also benefit the business.

What skills does my business need to make it successful?

First, when answering this question, it is important for anyone preparing a business plan for a new or potential enterprise to remember that they should not just be looking at those skills which are needed right at this moment, but also those which will be required as the business starts to expand. As a rule of thumb, the smaller the business, the wider the range of skills that the owner-manager will need to operate the business, particularly in the early stages of its development. It is important therefore, to draw up a skills profile for the business identifying the diverse range of expertise required:

- *Technical knowledge or expertise*: Knowledge and expertise of the goods or services which you plan to provide, and how the customers will make use of them. From the customer's perspective, the supplier is the specialist who is expected to answer all of the awkward questions.
- *Marketing skills*: To enable you to research your market, to design a marketing plan to promote and distribute your goods or services. Many owner-managers set up in business in an area with which they are already familiar, and so have some basic knowledge of their market, but there is still a need to maintain

objectivity, particularly when estimating market share and sales volumes.

- *Sales skills*: These are often assumed to be the same as marketing skills, but there is a distinct difference. You may have an excellent product, and a market ripe to take it, but you still need the skills to persuade your customers or your distributors that it is your product they should be using or retailing, rather than one supplied by a competitor. In the early stages of developing your business, you may not be able to afford to pay a full-time sales person and may have to do the job yourself.

- *Organisational skills*: The ability to plan and organise yourself and your business, to ensure that your staff, resources, materials, finished goods, etc., are in the right place at the right time. Careful planning and attention to detail enables you to make the most productive use of time and resources, and to avoid costly waste.

- *Decision-making*: The facility to analyse problems, identify and evaluate options, and to make objective and rational decisions, including how they will be made to work effectively.

- *Financial skills*: Keeping day-to-day accounts is not necessarily the best use of the owner-manager's time, as a part-time bookkeeper or accountant would probably be much more cost-effective. However, it is still important for the owner to be able to understand the accounting procedures. In particular, it is essential to have a basic understanding of budgetary planning and control, in order to keep the business on-track, and to spot any potential problems. There may also be a need for the owner to be involved in credit control and debt collection.

- *Customer service skills*: This is not just the case of keeping the customers satisfied by providing a consistently high standard of service. For small firms one of the biggest headaches in dealing with customers is debt collection, and persuading your customers to pay their bills on time without the risk of offending them or losing their business.

- *Staff management*: The ability to supervise, delegate work, train and motivate staff to get the best out of them. The importance of this is often underestimated, and for new owner-managers who have never previously been involved with managing staff. One of the hardest aspects is that of delegation – trusting the staff to get on with their own jobs without constant close scrutiny, so that the owner can get on with the job of running the business.

▨   *Management of information and computer literacy*: The use of word processing, databases, desktop publishing, accounting software, e-commerce and internet sales and marketing, electronic communication, etc. Alongside this goes the growing significance of compliance with data protection regulations.

The skills audit: What skills do you (or your staff/associates) already have?

Once you have identified the range of skills which the business will need, the next stage is to identify which of those you, as the owner-manager, already possess, or those which can be provided by staff or associates. Where there is an obvious gap in the skills, you have to decide whether or not it can be filled by developing them within yourself or another person within the business. If so, then you must consider how this is going to be achieved, e.g. by attending a training course. In some cases it may just be easier and more convenient to buy in the skills, as in the earlier example of accounts, where a part-time book-keeper employed for a few hours per week may be sufficient for the first year or two of the business. Sales skills are another good example, as full-time sales staff are expensive to finance until the business becomes established, and yet without them the business will never be able to grow. Very few owner-managers can devote sufficient time to do as much selling as they really need, so the short-term answer is often a compromise, involving a part-time or commission only sales agent to supplement the owner's sales activities. Then once the firm is established, it can look to employing permanent sales staff. But before we can think about employing staff, we need to examine some methods of self-assessment which will assist in identifying both the skills which are present and those that are needed. There are a whole host of different methods of self-assessment, including psychometric tests, learning style questionnaires, etc., but the examples described below have been chosen because they are easy to use, are relevant to the needs of owner-managers, and provide good examples for inclusion as appendices in the business plan for presentation to the bank manager, as this has become a standard expectation by lending banks in recent years.

SWOT analysis

It is becoming increasingly hard these days to find anyone who has never completed a SWOT (strengths, weaknesses, opportunities and threats) analysis in one form or another, but its popularity is a reflection of its simplicity and usefulness in a range of contexts. The idea is that the person making the analysis lists their own personal **S**trengths and **W**eaknesses (i.e. those factors which are a part of themselves) affecting the proposed business. They also examine and list the **O**pportunities and **T**hreats (i.e. the external factors) which might affect both them and the business. For example:

- *Strengths*: Sales skills, good technical product knowledge, enthusiasm.
- *Weaknesses*: No knowledge of accounts, poor computing skills.
- *Opportunities*: Offer of cheap premises, existing customer base.
- *Threats*: Lack of working capital, strong local competition.

In view of the subjective nature of the SWOT analysis, it is quite possible for people to under- or overestimate their personal skills and capabilities. Ideally the person carrying out the analysis should ask another person (preferably one with an objective insight into the business) to carry out an independent analysis so that the results of the two can be compared, evaluated and if necessary mediated. This is particularly important when the SWOT analysis is being carried out to assess the skills of the owner-managers and key staff. It is all too easy to overestimate management capabilities, and to underestimate weaknesses. The SWOT analysis is a useful element to include in a business plan, and is becoming a key requirement to meet the criteria of a number of lending banks.

Exercise: What makes a successful entrepreneur?

This exercise is designed to get the participants thinking about a whole host of different management skills, their relative importance or usefulness, and which of them the participants need to develop for themselves. On the following page (Figure 5.1) is a list of 72 entrepreneurial and management skills, which illustrate a broad range of technical, organisational, business, and inter-personal characteristics and skills typically found in varying proportions in successful entrepreneurs, and certainly of major use and value to the budding owner-manager.

- *Stage 1*: The participants examine the 72 skills, and categorise them under three alternative headings: Managing Yourself, Managing Others, and Managing Tasks.

Figure 5.1
What makes a good Entrepreneur?

1. Showing enthusiasm
2. Making an impact
3. Being assertive
4. Taking responsibility
5. Adapting and being flexible
6. Being objective
7. Managing under pressure
8. Showing resilience
9. Dealing with uncertainty
10. Being self-aware
11. Valuing oneself
12. Being an active learner
13. Developing oneself
14. Exercising self-discipline
15. Setting high personal standards
16. Showing sensitivity to others
17. Learning from mistakes
18. Measuring performance
19. Listening and questioning
20. Influencing
21. Handling conflict well
22. Understanding customers
23. Developing other people
24. Challenging and confronting
25. Being supportive
26. Being at ease with people
27. Encouraging ethical behaviour
28. Motivating people
29. Working effectively in teams
30. Networking
31. Envisioning
32. Admitting own short-comings
33. Seeking opinions of others
34. Encouraging quality and excellence
35. Being "one of the boys"
36. Grasping new opportunities
37. Being honest with staff and customers
38. Valuing continuous improvement
39. Managing change
40. Monitoring
41. Sales and marketing skills
42. Being proactive
43. Implementing
44. Handling complexity
45. Collating and organising information
46. Thinking conceptually
47. Logical and analytical thought
48. Focusing on problems
49. Thinking strategically
50. Being creative
51. Making judgements
52. Possessing common sense
53. Using time efficiently
54. Being decisive
55. Being consistent
56. Treating people fairly
57. Respecting others
58. Avoiding waste
59. Being respected by others
60. Setting clear targets and objectives
61. Belief in equal opportunities
62. Book-keeping skills
63. Putting people at ease
64. Optimising use of resources
65. Delegating responsibility
66. Allocating work efficiently
67. Managing budgets
68. Communicating information
69. Prioritising work
70. Remaining slightly detached
71. Willing to consider innovation
72. Encouraging initiative

Figure 5.1
What makes a good Entrepreneur?

Skills/competencies to be improved	Activities/methods of improvement	Means of measuring achievement	Degree of success/reasons for failure
Example: Effective delegation: work needs to be delegated to release time for other management duties.	Review daily/weekly job activities to see which of these could be delegated. Select potential staff and assess their suitability to take responsibility, and any training needs, etc. Define staff objectives and how their progress and achievement will be monitored and assessed against their targets. Review own workload once more.	Is delegated work progressing suitably well? If not, why not? Are there more jobs that I can delegate? What else am I doing with my time? Review progress after 30 days, and 60 days.	Are there still jobs to be delegated? What problems have occurred?

Figure 5.2
Action plan for self-development.

■ *Stage 2*: The participants identify what they regard as the 10 most important skills in each of the three areas, and list them in order of priority.

■ *Stage 3*: The participants grade themselves against each of the 30 selected skills, on a scale of 1 to 5, with 5 being the highest. As a double check, they can also ask a friend, colleague or manager to grade them against the same 30 skills.

■ *Stage 4*: The participants select the two weakest skills from each category, as being potential areas for self-development, and complete an action plan for developing these. A sample action plan is shown in Figure 5.2.

Planning and prioritising your work

1. Make a list of all of the daily activities that waste your valuable time, e.g. talking to the secretary, making coffee, smoking breaks, failing to delegate routine tasks, cluttered desk, allowing interruptions, lack of self-discipline, unfinished work brought forward, attending unnecessary meetings, responding to crises, long lunch breaks, playing golf during working hours, etc. Make a second list of ways in which you could save time: e.g. better use of diary to plan work, delegate more work, keep meetings to tighter agendas, and time scales. How do these compare? Highlight key areas for improvement, and work out how the improvements can be achieved, and how you will measure their achievement.

2. List all of the items of work that you have to do over the next 2 weeks, under two headings: First, the proactive work that will lead to profit or development of the business (sales meetings with customers, planning new products or services, etc.). Second, list the reactive and routine work which has to be completed, but which does not really contribute to the profitability or growth of the business (value-added tax (VAT) returns, reports for bank managers, filing and administration, etc.). Then prioritise your tasks in terms of four headings:

   (i) *Important and Urgent*: typically the proactive tasks that need a prompt response, such as customer enquiries, ensuring the completion of customer orders and the delivery of goods on time.

   (ii) *Important and Less Urgent*: typically the proactive work that will lead to growth of the business in the longer term. This may involve negotiations for future contracts, development of new products and markets, negotiations with suppliers, etc.

(iii) *Less Important but Urgent*: The day-to-day work that needs prompt action, but which does not necessarily involve substantial time commitment, e.g. writing cheques and letters, paying bills, renewing insurance policies, advertising for staff.

(iv) *Less Important and Less Urgent*: The routine work which is not due for completion in the next week or 2, e.g. the quarterly VAT returns, monthly PAYE (pay as you earn) records, non-urgent replies to letters, etc. But beware of this category, as less important and less urgent work, if repeatedly deferred, has a habit of suddenly becoming both urgent and important, particularly if it involves late VAT returns!

How did you perform in these two activities? Are you already using your time effectively? Are you already planning and prioritising your work, or was this a new experience for you? Have you identified any scope for further improvement? If so, then what changes will you make, and how will you start to implement these?

Identifying personal goals and objectives

The previous exercises have been concerned with identifying the skills needed to ensure the efficient operation of the business, but it is equally important not to neglect the personal aspirations and objectives of the owner-manager and his or her family:

- Where am I now, and where do I want to be in 5 or 10 years time?
- What material benefits do I expect from running my own business, in terms of my salary, my home, my car, holidays, etc.?
- What benefits do my family expect from the business?
- Are my family aware of the potentially substantial commitments of time and effort involved in establishing and running a business? Are they prepared to accept possible disruption to family routines, and possible financial pressures during the early stages of setting up the business?
- What price am I prepared to pay in terms of stress and risk to personal health, in order to ensure that the business succeeds?
- How will I measure the success of the business in material terms?
- How will I measure the success of the business in terms of my job satisfaction and self-fulfilment?

■ What will I do when I have achieved my targets?

■ Will I be able to handle failure if the business does not work out?

■ Are my family fully aware of the risks involved?

■ Do I have the will to succeed?

These are just a selection of the questions which potential owner-managers should be considering, not just on their own, but in consultation with their spouses, domestic partners, or families. There may be times when owner-manager needs the support of friends and families, and that support is likely to be more forthcoming, if their own objectives and aspirations have been considered. Once again, where targets are identified, action plans can be prepared to monitor progress and achievement, and the review of those plans should be carried out not in isolation, but in conjunction with partners and family.

Action plans for self-development

Apart from a common component of the business plan formats required by a number of major lending banks there is a very sound reason for the preparation of action plans, because with the best will in the world, personal objectives can easily slip or be pushed into the background. Just think back to last year, how many New Year's resolutions did you actually manage to keep, or have you simply given up trying? Owner-managers are very busy people, and in their case it is even more important to make some public or tangible declaration of intent, in the form of a self-development action plan, to make it stick, otherwise it will be forgotten or relegated into oblivion by the sheer pressures of work. A simple action plan, in the form of the example shown in Figure 5.2, pinned in a prominent (although not necessarily public) location, will act as a regular reminder.

Another reason for the use of an action plan is to provide a means of monitoring progress on a regular basis, and to set specific review dates. To take an analogy, how many times have you heard someone say: "I'm going on a diet and I intend to lose 10 pounds". Okay, when will you start, right now or after the barbecue next week? When will you lose the 10 pounds, by next month, next year, or by Christmas 2012? How often will you check your progress, daily, weekly, monthly, never? And if you do manage to hit your target weight, how will you ensure that it does not go up again? The answer is easy: "I will use my action plan to set specific targets and review dates to monitor my progress, and to highlight any problems or reasons for failure, along with the necessary corrective action" – but is not that just exactly how the Weight Watchers organisation helps its members to succeed, albeit in a slightly different format, and with a bit of added guilt for motivation? Most budding entrepreneurs simply do not need the guilt factor to achieve their development aims as they already have the motivation, but they do need to appreciate that the self-development process will make a valuable contribution to their enterprise.

So, to review the process of action planning:

1. What skills' gaps do I wish to fill? What competencies do I wish to improve? List them.
2. What methods or activities will I undertake in order to facilitate the development of those skills and competencies? Again, list them, and review them to ensure that they are appropriate.
3. How will I measure my progress or success? Set specific targets, set review dates, and set target dates for achievement. Define the criteria for success.
4. How well has the process worked? What problems were encountered? What were the reasons for success or failure? Where do I go from here?

Effective management requires regular self-evaluation

The self-assessment process is not a one-off activity that you go through when you set up a new business. It is a measure of an effective manager that personal skills and capabilities are reviewed on a regular basis. If you were employed by a large organisation, you would almost certainly be involved in some form of annual or twice-yearly appraisal system. You may well have plans for setting up such a system in your own business. So why should you not bother to carry out regular assessment on yourself? Self-evaluation is not just a process of assessing skills' gaps and development needs, it is also about your overall performance as a business manager:

- *In the achievement of standards*: meeting objectives and deadlines, ensuring consistent quality of work, achieving targets, achieving and maintaining customer satisfaction.
- *In the efficient use of time*: prioritising work, effective delegation and allocation of work, monitoring progress of work, and avoiding time wasting activities.
- *As part of self-development*: improving and upgrading skills and abilities, improving personal knowledge. This is the process described as continuous professional development (CPD).

■ *In the style of management*: employing and varying management styles according to the needs of the situation (autocratic/ democratic, etc.); being proactive and in control, thinking ahead and anticipating problems, rather than being reactive and constantly fire-fighting in response to problems.

Further reading

Palmer, S. (1998). *People and Self Management*. Butterworth-Heinemenn, Oxford.

Palmer, G. (1999). *Personal Effectiveness* (You & Your Business booklets). SFEDI/MCI, London.

Market research and planning

Whilst the vast majority of people who are setting out to start a new business can usually tell you about how their goods or services will be made or provided, what basic resources are needed, and roughly what each item will cost, their most common deficiency is a lack of marketing knowledge and sales skills. Unless they have worked in a marketing environment, they will often lack the knowledge of how to research their market and how to prepare a marketing plan. Similarly, without having worked in a sales capacity, they are likely to be unaware of the skills needed to identify potential customers, to investigate and match their needs, and to close the sale. In fact there are many who do not even realise that sales and marketing are two fundamentally different disciplines. Marketing is concerned with identifying the level of demand for the goods or services, where potential customers might be found, the competition which exists, and creating a mixture of product features and means of delivery that will ensure the goods or services will be desirable. Sales is about actually persuading the customer to buy the goods, to pay the right price for them, and then to come back to you for more at a later date. It is quite possible to make excellent goods for which there is a potentially high demand in a ready-made market, but without the sales skills to actually make the customer buy them they will just sit on the shelves.

The objective of this chapter is first to describe the processes of market research, identifying suitable market segments, and then designing a marketing plan. Second, we will examine some basic sales skills and techniques that should assist the reader, and how these will be implemented to meet the objectives of the marketing plan.

Stokes (1998) describes small business marketing as something of a paradox. On the one hand small firms regard marketing as being an activity for larger organisations, and yet their very flexibility and responsiveness to customer needs is the epitome of good marketing practice. Certainly by the very nature of their limited size, turnover, and profit, small firms are much less able to commit such large chunks or percentages of their gross profit to marketing activities, compared with their larger counterparts. Many owner–managers lack marketing skills apart from those they may have picked up empirically and then often through making mistakes along the way, or as a result of following gut instinct. Others do not go beyond basic essential sales activities, having to focus on day to day survival, with little time or inclination for long-term strategic market planning. So then, what are they missing?

Market research

Market research is an on-going process which seeks the answers to a range of questions in the ever-changing market environment:

- How large is the market for my goods or services?
- Is the market growing, static, or shrinking?
- What proportion of the market do I command?
- What potential proportion could I achieve?
- What would I need to do to achieve that?
- Are there any barriers to entering the market or to expanding within it?
- What resources will I need, and over what time-scale?
- What problems can I anticipate?
- Is the effort worthwhile, or should I consider an alternative?
- Who are my competitors and what are they offering?
- Are their goods or services as good as mine?
- What are the key features my customers are looking for, and can I meet these?
- What are the prevailing prices, and can I meet or beat these and make a profit?

It seems hardly surprising when faced with this package of questions that many owner–managers do decide to take the simplest option of reacting to demand rather than forecasting and planning ahead to meet it. Unfortunately little research has been carried out into the relative survival and growth rates of those owner–managers who do employ market research techniques as part of their business planning, compared with the numbers of those who do not. Nevertheless, simple common sense tells us that the more we know about our customers and our markets, then the more chance there is of maximising opportunities and minimising risks, which has got to improve the chances of survival and growth of any business.

If we summarise the main aspects which are covered by the range of questions above, we are looking at four main areas: the size and nature of the market itself, the proportion which we hope to gain, our competitors and their offerings, and the prospects for our own goods or services within the market. We need to examine these in more detail:

The size and nature of the market

The first question we must consider here is about the scale of the market. Is it an international market or part of one, such as the oil or motor vehicle industries? There may be little hope of competing directly with Ford or Toyota, but there still may be an opportunity to supply them with specialist components. Is it a national industry like the market for cheddar cheese or English sausages? Here there may be a good chance of overcoming any barriers to entry such as high levels of competition, by targeting a special niche in the market. Is it a local market, such as a therapeutic service provided within a small geographical area? Here you would need to be even more aware of the importance of identifying and targeting the needs of the customer, rather than by simply promoting the quality of the product or the service. There is usually plenty of research data and findings about specific markets, available at international level and national level, through trade journals and associations, economic reports and analyses, national and regional statistics, etc. Not only can the overall size and growth potential of the market be established, but the respective share of key players can usually be realistically estimated by someone who knows the market well. It is possible to buy reliable market research information about national and international markets from published sources, albeit sometimes quite expensive. However, at local level and in smaller, more specialised markets it is much harder to find the necessary direct information, and even at regional level the information may be aggregated with that of other markets within economic development reports, rendering it too general to be of much use to a new small firm. The problem is compounded if the proposed business is aiming at a new or niche market for which there may be no existing established data. If therefore, the published sources are inadequate or irrelevant, then this should be pointed out within the business plan, along with details of alternative sources used, and the reasons why these are suitable. It is then down to the business proposer to investigate the potential market to establish the extent of any potential demand.

The target market share

If the level of supply within the particular market has not reached full capacity, then the target market share may well be determined by the capacity to produce and supply for that market. But if there is already a good deal of competition within it, then the target may need to be more modest, as without heavy investment, it may prove hard to break into a new market, let alone to subsequently sustain and expand market share. Almost certainly the competitors will have something to say about a new entrant to the market and may vigorously compete to keep the newcomer out. Actually determining the target market share usually requires some specialist knowledge of the market sector to ensure that the targets are reasonable and realistic. It also implies some knowledge of the sort of sales and promotional activities that would be required in order to penetrate the market to the required extent.

The nature of the competition

At international and national level the key players within an industry or service sector are usually well known to each other, and in many areas, have regular contact with each other on matters of mutual interest (e.g. credit control, lobbying against new legislation etc). Where formal links do not exist at company level between rival organisations, there are still nearly always informal links existing at a personal level. These may be between former work colleagues who have changed companies, or who may have trained together in the past, or who may even have met at trade exhibitions or conferences. Having worked in the licensed trade, computing, and horticultural industries, I can vouch for the fact that even the most serious business rivalry usually breaks down in a social situation or after a few drinks! It has been said in jest that men network and women gossip – whether or not this is true or false is immaterial, but what is important, is the amount of business which is transacted by networking, through formal and informal contacts, and the marketing knowledge which can be gleaned and shared simply by talking to other business people. Networking is probably the most valuable sales and marketing tool available to the small business owner and is a skill that should not be neglected. It is not just a case of meeting and talking to people, but listening to their ideas and problems, sharing opinions, passing on contacts and information to help solve those problems; and eventually when the wheel turns full circle you find other contacts are talking about you and passing on your details to others. It is a long-term investment in time and effort, but can produce a good payback in generating new unsolicited business, if your reputation is sound.

Where goods and services are concerned, anyone who is not a total newcomer to the market will normally have a good idea of who the competitors are and what they have to offer. More detailed technical information or price lists can usually be obtained by telephone request or by posing as a potential customer. Don't feel guilty or apprehensive about this approach, it happens all of the time, and sooner or later someone will do it to you. Other information can be obtained from a simple Google or Yell search on the internet, or from local trade directories, Yellow Pages, Thompson's Local etc., and very often your own bank manager or local enterprise agency may be able to help. Remember though, you are not just interested in finding out who your competitors are, but what goods or services they offer, at what price, and with what unique or special selling features.

Your own goods or services in comparison

Having examined the competition and their offerings, you now need to turn to your own goods and services to determine how the stand up against both the competitors, and the nature if the demand within the market as a whole. What unique benefits can I offer my customers? Is the price right or is it too high or too low? If I pitch my prices lower than those of my competitors, will I sell more? Is the quality right? Should I sell my products on the basis of quality rather than price? Does the market want a solid but cheap belt-and-braces product, or would a more refined and expensive alternative sell better? Just how more refined and expensive does that have to be? Perhaps there is even a place for both of those, amongst different types of customers.

Another aspect of market research into the goods or services is that of product testing, wherein the products are test marketed to establish consumer reactions and response. Depending on the product this may also have to involve some advertising or promotion such as might normally be expected to accompany a product launch. A good example of this is the consumer testing of specific goods in discrete television franchise areas before they are launched on a national basis. Other products or services may be tested by market research surveys in supermarkets, town centres or door to door, where quality can be evaluated against price bands, using questions about how much people would be prepared to pay for the product, and their reactions to the presentation and packaging, etc.

At this point we also need to examine the relative costs and profitability. Which products will provide you with the best contribution to your overheads and profit? What proportion of less-profitable goods or services can you afford to sell without adversely affecting your chances of survival? In Chapter 10 under break-even analysis, we looked at an example where a higher sales volume at a slightly lower level of contribution, caused a drop in overall sales revenue and subsequent profit. This is where it is important to link the marketing aspects of the business to the financial planning process, as they are essentially inter-dependent. The expectancy from this part of your market research is that it will help you to decide the position of your goods or services in the market place, and your pricing policy for them. Invariably you may find that you have a combination of products or prices appropriate to different sectors of the market place. This leads us conveniently into the next section which is concerned with the different segments which occur within an overall market.

Market segmentation

Market segmentation is best described as the process of analysing the demand for specific goods or services, breaking them down into distinctive segments, and then identifying the characteristics of each segment to produce a marketing plan for that particular segment. In more simple terms, we are trying to identify the various groups or types of customers which share similar patterns of demand, to which we will be attempting to sell our goods or services, and then to target our sales effort towards those groups. This process is most easily illustrated in case study 6.1 by using an example.

The process of identifying market segments allows you to select those which are worthy of the most effort and investment, based on the potential returns which they offer. Each segment will require a different approach in terms of the marketing mix, as described in the case study. Segmentation can be based on a number of differing factors including customer needs, location, potential contribution or profit, age, sex or social status, buying habits, or simple points of common interest. These can be prioritised in various ways, in terms of the number of customers in each segment, the relative profitability of each segment, their location or accessibility, or the amount of time and investment required to generate business. Once the factors have been prioritised, we can then start to formulate our marketing mixes to target the individual segments, to address those priorities.

Case study 6.1

Ivor Mop is in the process of setting up a contract cleaning business. He has identified four basic types of client who will provide the bulk of his business (Figure 6.1) and the specific characteristics of these clients in terms of their types of service, quality, and price motivation, relative profit margins, and percentages of the total expected business. As a result of this process he has established a combination of client-types which give him a balanced combination of regular high-value but low profit contracts as his bread and butter business, tempered with less regular but very profitable special work. His marketing plan can be set up to target the needs of each of these four segments. He knows that for large local authorities and school contracts he must be competitive on price whilst meeting prescribed standards of cleanliness. For office based private companies, price is still relevant, but reliability and quality of service are most important. Private individuals are willing to pay more for quality service coupled with flexibility, but still expect value for money. Special deep-clean contracts are the most profitable, often resulting from pressure by local environmental health inspectors, needing rapid response at inconvenient times. It would be hard to concentrate on this type of work as core business as it is not sufficiently regular, but when it does arise it makes a very healthy contribution to profit margins, and it complements the less profitable but more regular core business which forms the bulk of his sales turnover.

The marketing plan

The marketing plan for any product or service is concerned with formulating the right mixture of characteristics of the product and the way in which it is supplied and presented, so as to maximise its value and interest to the target groups of customers which have been identified within the market research process. To explain this more simply, if we take the Ivor Mop case study example from the previous section, he has identified catering kitchens as a potential market segment for his services. His marketing mix for that service will involve specifying the type of service (deep-cleaning of kitchens preparing for, or in response to environmental health inspections), the way in which it is delivered (response at short-notice, working overnight and weekends), the key selling points (minimum disruption to working activities) which justify the premium price and high profit margin. His promotional activities will involve the direct targeting of customers by trade journal adverts, mail shots, and by sales appointments with local potential clients, and the environmental health officers which inspect them.

Traditional marketing theory expounds the four key elements of the marketing mix as being product, price, promotion, and place, although it has been argued (Booms and Bitner, 1981) that for service industries

Type of organisation	Examples	Contract value per annum	Profit margin (%)	Service criteria	Financial or quality motivation	Service requirements	Percentage of total business
Public sector, large	Government departments schools, local authorities	£200k–£500k	10–20	On-going reliability	Cost motivated within specified standards	Regular full-time and part-time staff	30
Private companies	Office based service, and high-tech companies	£100k	15–25	On-going reliability, and often security sensitive	Quality service at reasonable price	Regular morning or evening	50
Private individuals	Owners of large private homes	£10k–£15k	30	Regular service with flexibility when needed. Honest staff	Quality service but value for money	Daily cleaning with periodical special work, e.g. pool cleaning	15
Hotel and catering trade	Hotels and restaurants	£3k–£5k	75	Available at short notice, and anti-social hours	Rapid efficient high quality service, with minimal disruption	Annual and special "deep cleans" to kitchens for EHO visits	5

Figure 6.1
Market segmentation example.

people, process, and physical aspects should also be considered. The idea is that for each product or service being offered, there is an appropriate combination of these factors which will optimise the sales potential to the respective market segments. Where a product or service is relevant to more than one segment, then the components of the marketing mix will be modified accordingly to match the needs of the respective segments. In reality, it is a common-sense problem-solving process applied to the needs of marketing, the value of which is acknowledged by the fact that it has been in use without challenge or major modification, for many years.

Product

The product element of the marketing mix is essentially concerned with the customers' perceptions and expectations of the goods or services, and covers a broad variety of aspects. There is the basic quality of the product, its durability and whether or not it will be fit for the purpose for which it was acquired. Linked to this are the aspects of warranty, and after sales service in the event of there being faults or problems with the quality of product or service. The product may be of a very satisfactory or high quality, but there is also the question of its perception by the customer as giving value for money, i.e. does the quality correspond to the cost. If the quality is seen as being low, compared with the cost, it will constitute poor value for money; but if it is perceived as being high in relation to cost, it will be good value for money. This aspect becomes particularly significant at times when money is tight, at the lower or utility end of the market, and when there is an abundance of competitors' products around. Also related to value for money are the range of applications or uses of the product, i.e. the uniqueness or relative usefulness of the goods or services. A good illustration of this is the range of gadgets or extras that are offered with goods such as food processors and electric drills to make them appear more versatile than the competitors' tools.

The Product part of the marketing mix is not just concerned with the quality and utility of the goods or services; it must also consider aspects of style and appearance as perceived by the potential customer. In particular the packaging and presentation, the brand name and the image it creates, and again the uniqueness of the product. This is especially true in premium markets where the image and uniqueness, often coupled with restricted outlets or supply, can attract status value to the product, with commensurately higher prices and profit margins. This is precisely why you cannot by Versace clothes in the local Co-op or Gucci handbags in Woolworths; for that matter, why you won't find jellied eels in a Fortnum and Mason food hamper!

Price

In practical terms, price is concerned with finding out how much we can charge for the goods or services to maximise profit margins without reducing the level of sales volume. Again this is a matter of customer perception, as we need to consider the price level in terms of value for money, and the price level in terms of competitors' products and prices. We may be able to charge a higher price than our competitors if the customers perceive the quality and value for money of our products as being substantially better than the competition. But the lower the differential between the products, then the lower the price difference must be. We may in fact choose to, undercut the competition to buy market share through increased sales. However, such a move can also adversely affect sales, in that a substantially lower price may encourage the customers to infer that the products are in some way inferior to those supplied by the competitors.

When formulating the pricing policy of the product we must also consider aspects of discounts, credit terms and payment terms, particularly if we are distributing via a wholesales and/or retailer network. If favourable, the terms and discounts can act as substantial incentives to stock or promote our products. Conversely, if poor, the terms and discounts may be a disincentive to sell the product, or result in the vendor selling it at an unfavourable price compared with competitors goods. After all, the wholesalers and retailers are as much concerned with their profit margins as we are with our own.

Place

The place aspect of the marketing mix is not just concerned with establishing where the customers can obtain the goods or services. Certainly it is important to define the geographical areas in which the business will operate, and within those areas, outlets and their locations can be specified. Place is also about establishing and defining distribution channels, e.g. via wholesaler of retailer networks, by direct supply and delivery, by mail order etc. The choice of distribution channels will also have implications for the availability of the products, in terms of transport and supply lines, stock levels, and inventories etc, which raises a number of further questions. Will you be supplying retailers through regular weekly deliveries, enabling them to hold relatively low stocks; or perhaps monthly where stock-holding will need to be higher, with consequential implications for the payment terms of your distributors? Will you choose to operate on a reduced profit margin to enable you to use wholesalers who will hold regional stocks for the retailers, thus reducing your own distribution costs? Will you be allocating exclusive sales areas to your distributors, or will they be competing against each other?

Promotion

Promotion encompasses the whole range of sales and advertising activities which could be employed. You may decide to employ a sales force to carry out direct personal selling to your potential customers. Alternatively, this work could be carried out by sales agents, or by sales staff employed by your distributors. The latter may be cheaper for you, but will it be as effective, as those same sales people may also be selling competitive products.

The promotion part of the marketing mix also involves identifying the appropriate forms of advertising your goods or services, whether it be through the internet, national TV, local radio, newspapers, and magazines, specialist trade journals, mail shots, advertising hoardings, tethered balloons, Yellow Pages, exhibitions, trade fairs, County shows, telesales calls, sealed tenders for contracts, or a stall in the local market. Not only must you identify the most suitable forms of advertising, you must select those which are the most affordable, and which are likely to give you the best return on your investment. Word of mouth recommendation is a very cheap and superb form of promotion, but it is both slow and outside of your control, and so cannot be relied upon to produce results. In contrast, trade fairs and exhibitions are expensive and time-consuming, but if chosen carefully, they can offer a captive audience with a potentially high level of interest in your products, and a good chance of achieving immediate orders.

Another aspect linked to advertising is the use of special offers or sales promotions to generate interest in your products and to persuade potential customers to try them. We see this used frequently in supermarkets where new products are launched on the basis of "buy one and get one free" bargains, or tasting sessions for food items accompanied by money-off vouchers. Obviously, these methods are not appropriate to every form of goods or services, so the promotional activity must be designed to match the product. Beauty and therapy treatments are often offered on a five for the cost of four treatments basis. Gyms and fitness clubs offer discounts for annual membership to encourage regular patronage, magazines offer discounts for prepaid subscriptions etc. Breweries offer publicans large discounts for bulk purchases in advance of the busy Christmas period, to ease delivery problems. Effective promotion is all about finding out what appeals to your particular customers and then using a little imagination to trigger their interest in your product.

People

Where services as opposed to physical goods are being supplied, then People become a more important element, particularly in terms of the image which they project to the prospective customers. This is not just a question of the impressions created by dress or physical appearance; it applies to knowledge and behavioural aspects of the interaction with customers. We are talking about technical knowledge of products and services, which can create (or if absent, can destroy) customer confidence. It is also about the attitude shown to customers in terms of behaviour e.g. friendliness of reception staff, helpfulness of sales staff, a positive interest shown in solving customer problems etc, and in building long-term customer–client relationships, which together reflect the overall culture of the business.

Physical

The physical aspects include the sales environment, and in particular the impression created by the parts of the premises seen by the customers. Is the reception area clean and tidy, tastefully decorated, or are the furnishings tatty and the space cluttered? Does the organisation project an image of being well organised and professional? If you are in doubt about your premises, ask yourself the question, "How would I feel about walking into this environment if it belonged to one of my suppliers? Would I feel comfortable, embarrassed or downright disgusted?"

Process

The process part of the marketing mix is really related to the general provision of quality products and customer service. It involves ensuring that company policies and procedures are conducive to meeting the customers' needs and to providing smooth provision of service to consistent standards. It can relate, e.g. to the discretion given to employees to apply flexibility or to modify procedures in order to assist customers, or it can relate to involving customers in product development, or in seeking ways to improve the standards of service. In a perfect situation the processes operating within the business should be invisible to the customer in so far as they should be designed to work for the benefit of the customer rather than the convenience of the firm's staff, or becoming a barrier to customer transactions.

The sales plan

Sales activities

The promotion section of the marketing mix should provide the basic structure for determining the methods of sales activity which will be employed according to which are the most appropriate for reaching the customer target groups. Typically this would include a combination of several of the following:

- Internet advertising – in its simplest form this can comprise a simple website with key words or phrases that will ensure a prominent position for any potential customers using the most popular search engines. On a more sophisticated basis it may involve a secure interactive website through which customers can place orders and pay for them securely. This could be promoted via a pay-per-click facility with primary search engines to ensure prominence on the first page of any keyword search. A company website is really an imperative for any small business now that the convenience of internet searches have largely replaced conventional directories such as yellow pages as the first choice method of researching sources for products or services.
- Cold-calling by telephone. This is basically a numbers game, with large numbers of contacts, at relatively low unit cost, but usually resulting in quite a low rate of positive interest or response, even when the targeted calls have been carefully selected. The normal approach is to try to identify categories of businesses who might possibly be interested in the product (often from Yellow Pages or Thompson Local listings), and then

to make telephone contact to find the appropriate person or decision maker within those organisations. In recent years the double glazing industry has given this type of sales activity a bad name, and of course, the results largely depend on the skills of the individuals who are making the calls being both competent at doing the job, and being able to talk convincingly about the product if they get through to the right person. To achieve positive indications of interest from 5% to 10% of those called would generally be regarded as very good, and typically to convert 10% of those into an actual sale would also be very good.

■ Mail shots, like cold telephone calls, have seriously declined in value in recent years, simply due to the sheer proliferation of junk mail which falls through our letter boxes just about every day of the year. Personally speaking I just throw circulars and all junk mail straight in the bin with no more than a cursory glance, and any obvious circular remains unopened in the envelope. Circulars containing personalised letters are read to the bottom of the first paragraph at least (unless they bear insurance company logos) to determine any relevance or usefulness, before being discarded. Sadly though, the amount of money uselessly wasted every day on postage and printing is vast, and all too often because business owners are too lazy to take a more proactive attitude towards other methods of sales or promotion.

■ Cold-call visits are much more time-consuming and costly, and therefore need to be carefully planned to avoid wasted effort by calling on the wrong type of customer. They also need to be well organised to minimise the cost of travelling between calls and to optimise the use of the sales-person's time. For this reason a good sales person will often use calls for information gathering for future reference. For example, Mr Dai Appy is a salesman employed to sell farming products in rural Wales, where distances between customers are quite long. If he has two positive sales appointments in a particular area, then he will use the rest of the day to make a number of cold calls on other local farmers. This serves three purposes: in maintaining the profile of his company by regular contact, seeking information about future possible needs which will lead to subsequent sales, and making new contacts which can be followed up at a later date. Cold-calling then is more of a longer-term sales activity best used to complement other sales effort. It is not the easiest thing to do, and takes time and practice and quite a bit of nerve to do well, which is why many people dislike doing it. However, as a long-term process it can produce positive results.

- Planned sales activity involves a combination of the previous methods, and constitutes a much more professional approach, resulting in better use of time and a higher proportion of positive results. For example, a cold-telephone call might be used to do no more than to find the name of the key person or decision-maker in an organisation. This is followed by a short and concise personal letter of no more than one page which outlines the products or services offered, and tells the key person that they will be contacted within a few days to request an appointment for the sales person to meet them. After that it is down to the skill of the sales person and the quality of goods or services on offer.

- National or regional television or local radio advertising is relatively expensive but does guarantee coverage of a wider audience. National TV is excellent for consumer products but highly expensive. Local radio stations are cheaper, but with lesser coverage, although they always seem to do quite well in promoting regional events.

- The national press is again expensive and often too broad to be of value to many businesses, although the travel industry always seems to find it productive. Local papers are good for local products and particularly local services, and are more reasonably priced. Most specialist products or services are advertised in trade journals or magazines where the cost is justified by the readership, which will have been identified as a potential customer group.

Sales skills

For a new or aspiring owner–manager with no previous sales experience the most daunting prospect is that of having to sell their goods or services. Salesmanship is a profession, which has to be learnt and practised if it is to achieve good results on a regular basis. The biggest mistake that most new sales people make is to try to push and sell the range of products in their portfolio, whereas someone with more experience will listen carefully to the clients, and probe to identify their specific problems and needs. Only then are the products revealed, and in such a way that they offer potential solutions to the customer's needs. A Dexion salesman once told me: "I sell solutions to problems and benefits to the customer, not storage and materials handling systems". It is important to sell on quality and benefits rather than on lowest price. If nothing else, there is then still scope to negotiate on price at a later stage, but if a competitor beats you on both price and quality, you are out of the running.

It is also important to be open and honest with the client, to retain both credibility and the opportunity of returning at a later date. Don't promise what you can't deliver, and don't be afraid to say if you cannot meet the client's requirements on this occasion. Buyers are as much professionals as sales people, and they not only appreciate an honest answer which saves their valuable time, but they will usually be receptive to a later approach when your product might be the real answer to their problem.

Many people who are new to sales find it hard or embarrassing to close the deal, or to actually ask the client for an order. In fact some buyers will make a point of waiting to be asked before committing themselves, particularly with young or new sales people. If you are uncomfortable about asking outright for an order "Can I take your order today?" then try "When can I expect to receive our order?" or "When would you like us to deliver?" Another approach is to ask the question "Can you see any reason why our products will not meet your needs?" If a reason is given then you have an open opportunity to answer and overcome it. If the client has no objections then you have a direct lead in to ask for the order.

Finally remember that not all business is good business, so don't be afraid to walk away from a contract or a sale if you are not happy about the terms of trade or your potential profit margins. You deserve to make a reasonable profit just as much as the people to whom you are selling, and most professional buyers appreciate this fact. The sale should be treated as a potential starting point for a longer-term customer–supplier relationship, and as such needs to be established on equitable terms, so don't sell yourself or your business short!

Setting targets and measuring achievement

The sales plan is then about defining the range and combination of promotional activities which will be employed to persuade the customers to buy the products. The hardest part however, is actually setting the targets for sales volumes and revenues. If the market research has been done properly then there should be some positive indications as to the overall size of the market and the potential volume, which can be achieved within that market. The next problem then is to try to realistically identify how much of that potential volume could realistically be achieved. This may be influenced not just by sales capacity, but by restrictions imposed by the capacity of production and/or distribution facilities, or the time available for the provision of a service. For example, a consultancy firm employing three staff may be able to offer up to 120 hours of service per month per member of staff, an overall total of 4320 hours per annum, but it could not meet a contract requiring 2500 hours of work in just a 3-month period.

Monitoring the sales and marketing performance can be carried out as part of the on-going financial monitoring of the business described in Chapter 10, and by some fairly simple methods of evaluating the effectiveness of sales activities:

- In preparing the budgetary plan for the business, certain sales volumes will have to have been identified and formulated. These in effect constitute targets against which actual performance can be monitored on a month by month basis.
- The budgetary plan itself constitutes a summary of sales revenue targets which again can be monitored on a monthly basis.
- The budget will also include forecasts of expenditure for advertising and promotion. How does the actual expenditure compare with those forecasts? When expenditure has occurred, has it resulted in the expected increases in sales that it was designed to generate?
- What sort of response rates are you receiving from sales activities. For example in terms of the numbers of enquiries generated by each advertisement, and the numbers of those that were converted in actual sales. Similarly, you can measure the response rates and achievement rates for cold telephone calls, cold sales calls, planned sales visits, mail shots etc. If you had actually set targets for these beforehand you may well want to compare the targets and the outcomes, probably using the results to set more realistic targets for the coming year. If not, then you will now have the data to enable you to set targets for the future.
- From your expenditure figures, you can calculate the relative costs of different sales activities, cold calls, telesales, mail shots, and various forms of advertising. The figures showing response rates and rates of conversion into sales can then be applied to these various activities to identify e.g. the cost per enquiry for each advertisement, or the cost of each sale resulting from cold calling.

■ Finally the relative costs of the various sales activities can be compared to the revenues generated, to determine the most cost-effective methods which will then feed into your marketing and sales plans for the forthcoming year.

References

Booms, B. H. and Bitner, M. J. (1981). *Marketing Strategies and Organisational Structures for Service Firms.* American Marketing Association.

Stokes, D. (1998). *Small Business Management: A Case Study Approach.* pp. 239–244. Letts., London.

Further reading

Chaffey, D. (2003). *E-business and E-commerce Management.* FT Prentice Hall, London.

Kotler, P., Armstrong, G., Saunders, J. and Wong, V. (2004). *Principles of Marketing.* FT Prentice Hall, London.

Macdonald, M. and Dunbar, I. (2004). *Market Segmentation. How to Do it, How to Profit From it.* Elsevier, Oxford.

Fell, C. (2005). *Marketing Communications: Engagement, Strategies and Practice.* FT Prentice Hall, London.

Robinson, T. (1999). *You and Your Business: Marketing.* SFEDI/CMI, London.

CHAPTER 7

Identifying relevant legislation

In recent years the sheer volume of legislation, rules, statutes, and directives facing small firms seems to have increased at an exponential rate; and even more so as the UK is drawn ever closer into the tangled web of the European Union (EU), where bureaucracy rules supreme, and the harmonisation of the laws of its member states appears to be the sole acknowledged route to Nirvana. Why, I ask, should anyone want to go to heaven if they can get a job as a bureaucrat, or better still, a solicitor in Brussels? However, coming back to the real world, actually identifying the legislation which is relevant to any particular new small business can be a nightmare, even without the fact that the laws are constantly changing, and thereby placing additional demands on owner-managers who have to keep informed of changes, understand and comply with them.

The objective of this chapter is to list and briefly describe a range of the most important pieces of legislation which might affect small businesses and their owners. The intention is not so much to produce a legal compendium or reference text, as to assist the readers to identify those areas of the law which are relevant their own particular businesses, and where they will need to examine the implications of that legislation in more detail. Remember, ignorance is no excuse in the eyes of the Law, so if a piece of legislation sounds remotely relevant to your business circumstances then make sure you check it out!

Many organisations will be subject to very specific legislation which is only really relevant to their own particular field of operation (e.g. abattoirs, breweries, fishing, road transport, or zoos), and it is simply not practical to try to address all of these. Instead, this Chapter looks at the main items of legislation, which have applications to broad sections of business operations, and groups these under six headings:

- Health and Safety and related legislation
- Environmental Legislation
- Trading Legislation
- Employment Law
- Financial and Company Law
- Anti-discrimination Law

Health and safety legislation

Health and safety legislation has existed under a number of guises for many years, but it was only in the 1970s that its real importance was acknowledged and made properly enforceable. Prior to that the emphasis was made, e.g. on provision of safety guards on machinery, but without enforcing their use; or for ensuring adequate toilet facilities where more than five staff were employed. Post-1974 the emphasis switched to that of care for employees, visitors, customers, and passers-by; and to risk assessment and prevention of accidents in the workplace.

Factories Act (1961)/Offices, Shops & Railway Premises Act (1963)

These were effectively the first examples of legislation relating to the health and safety of employees. Under the Factories Act the employer ("occupier" of the factory) has the responsibility of protecting the employees against any risks of the industrial environment to which they might be regularly exposed. This involves ensuring safe systems of work, safe access, and clear gangways, fenced and guarded machinery. Occupation of premises and the name and nature of the business must be notified to the Health and Safety Executive, including notification if any mechanical machinery is used. Written details of any death of serious injury resulting from industrial accidents must also be notified within 3 days of the incident. Under the Offices, Shops and Railway Premises Act, prospective occupants must notify the appropriate local authority at least 1 month before the start of occupation of the premises; and must subsequently notify of any accidents or industrial diseases. Safety requirements required by the Act are similar to those specified under the Factories Act, but employers must also avoid overcrowding premises, must provide adequate water and sanitation facilities, heating, lighting, ventilation, and first aid facilities.

Health & Safety at Work Act (1974)

Whereas the previous two Acts were fundamentally concerned with the provision of basic minimum standards of safety and hygiene in the workplace, the Health and Safety at Work Act was designed to extend this provision (and the employers' liability to ensure it) much further. It is the duty of the employer to provide safe working systems and a safe and secure working environment for all staff, customers, and visitors to premises, as well as the general public, passers-by, and in some cases, even to potential trespassers. The Act applies not only to business premises, but to all public places, local authority premises, hospitals, entertainment sites, community halls, shopping centres, etc. Responsibility also extends to any staff working away from the main place of work, such as lorry drivers, or contractors' staff working on site. It also requires sites to be securely fenced against intruders who might inadvertently injure themselves on a hazard within the site, again including trespassers. Long gone are the days when building site workers would lean over the side of scaffolding to wolf-whistle at passing girls. Today, apart from probably being accused of sexual harassment, the chances are that most scaffolding will be covered by a mesh screen to prevent any loose objects falling on passers-by, and leaning over the scaffolding would be regarded as an unsafe practice, and likely to be disciplined. If recent TV adverts for a certain popular fizzy drink are anything to go by, it will probably be the girls doing the whistling anyway!

Another major requirement of the Act was the need for every employer with more than five staff to produce and regularly update a written Health and Safety Policy Document for the organisation or premises, and to ensure that all new and existing staff are all made aware of its contents. Employers are also required to carry out a regular risk assessment and hazard analysis throughout their premises, and across working practices, to identify and minimise any likely potential harm to employees, or potential users or visitors to the premises. Appropriate Health and Safety posters must also be clearly displayed within the premises, and these can be obtained from the local Health and Safety Executive offices (HSE). Employers must record all accidents or injuries in an Accident Book kept for that purpose. The HSE must be notified of any deaths or major injuries resulting from accidents at work, and can prosecute employers or owners or operators of premises for negligence if appropriate; the penalties for which are potentially high, and in extreme cases might include imprisonment.

Control of substances hazardous to health

All employers and operators of premises where potentially hazardous chemicals are stored, manufactured, or used in a commercial or industrial process, must carry out specific risk analyses under the control of substances hazardous to health (COSHH) regulations. As part of this process, they must identify suitable preventative actions or remedies in the event of accident, leakage or spillage of any such substances. They must also display appropriate warning notices detailing the nature and potential hazards of the substances, and have the means available to deal with any such events. Staff must be instructed in the safe handling and storage of hazardous substances, and informed of what to do if leakage or spillage should occur.

For example, most agrochemical distributors are required to have impervious flooring and some form of concrete bund around the site so that and leakage can be contained within to avoid the contamin ation reaching local drains or watercourses. Within the site they would have to have sand or other inert substances to soak up spillage, and masks for staff to avoid breathing noxious fumes. Whilst this might sound like an extreme example, most industrial cleaning agents contain bleach or chemicals which might come under COSHH regulations, and even the peroxides and perm lotions used by hairdressers can have some quite damaging effects on human skin if mishandled!

Reporting of Injuries, Diseases, & Dangerous Occurrences Regulations (1982)

These regulations, often referred to as Reporting of Injuries, Diseases, & Dangerous Occurrences Regulations (RIDDOR), and require the owners or operators of businesses or premises to notify the responsible authorities of certain specific events or illnesses. For example, the local Environmental Health Authority would need to be notified of an outbreak of food poisoning, particularly if it involved the staff of a food manufacturer or distributor, or the customers of a specific catering outlet. The Health and Safety Executive must be notified of any major accidents of substantial injuries to employees, and the Local Medical Officer must be notified of outbreaks and individuals who contract specified illnesses such as meningitis, polio, and presumably bubonic plague.

Fire regulations

The local fire brigade is responsible for advising operators of premises, and inspecting the premises to ensure that they comply with fire regulations. These will vary according to the size, type, and use of premises. For example, a small workshop may just require a specified number of water and powder fire extinguishers, whereas a restaurant kitchen will also usually need to have fire blankets available to cover any burning cooking oil. At a more complex level, a residential home or hotel will have to provide fire exits and escape routes, emergency lighting, regularly tested alarm systems, staff training, and fire-doors at regular intervals along corridors, which are designed to withstand fire for certain minimum periods. Unless the premises comply with the regulations, the fire brigade may refuse to issue or renew the necessary licence, and the hotel will be unable to operate. Fire regulations may also be relevant to materials used for partitioning within offices, to storage of inflammable materials, and to the external access routes to premises. The requirements for fire safety also link in with health and safety policies and hazard analyses within premises where fire may be one of the inherent potential hazards in the business activity.

Environmental legislation

These pieces of legislation are quite diverse but have been linked together as being in the interests of members of the public at large as protecting their interests in the protection of the living and working environment as a whole.

Environmental Health Act

The Environmental Health Departments of local authorities are particularly concerned with aspects of public hygiene and food safety. In the case of public health and hygiene, the Environmental Health Acts empower local authorities to carry out or enforce the safe removal and disposal of refuse, and the extermination of vermin, or other risks to public health. They are also responsible for monitoring and licensing the operation of funeral parlours.

In recent years the food safety role has become much more prominent, with all manufactures, suppliers, distributors, and retailers of food or drink having to register with their local authority. Specific standards are prescribed for the safe preparation, handling, and storage of food, and premises are regularly inspected to ensure that these standards are met on an on-going basis. There is the risk of enforced closure of premises in cases of default, and heavy fines where food poisoning is found to result from poor food handling or contamination; and this is quite realistic when we remember that the clostridium and streptococcal bacteria found in kitchens are potentially lethal.

The food handling regulations prescribe minimum levels of training for staff i.e. the Basic Food Hygiene Certificate, with higher levels for super. visors. They also prescribe the types of washable materials suitable for covering walls, ceilings and floors; fly screens for protecting windows and vents, the quality of stainless steel for work surfaces, and the colour coding of knives, etc., used for different purposes to avoid cross-contamination. Operators of food premises are expected to produce adhere to, and record, regular planned cleaning programmes for all food production areas; to provide staff with all necessary protective clothing, and provide instruction and supervision in safe food handling practice.

Town & Country Planning Acts 1971

The principle of Development Control was introduced in 1947 under the first Town and Country Planning Act which was updated in 1971. Local Planning Authorities such as the district councils are responsible for producing local development plans, controlling and approving new developments, approving the change of use of premises, and monitoring the use of specific "listed" buildings and conservation areas. County Councils have a role in producing strategic plans, and for development control of more major items such as mining, gravel extraction, waste disposal etc.

For any new or expanding business which is planning to occupy premises, it is necessary to ensure that planning approval exists to cover the type of activity for which the premises will be used. For example, if I wish to convert the front room of my home into a shop, I will need to obtain permission for change of use from domestic to retail use. If I wish to rent a farmer's barn to manufacture and sell rustic furniture, I will need to apply for change of use from agricultural to commercial use. Remember, simply applying for change of use for premises does not mean the new use can start straight away. The change of use still has to be approved, and very often there will be specific planning conditions attached to the approval. For example, it may be granted for a fixed period such as 3, 5, or 10 years;

it may prohibit any structural change to the premises without further specific approval, or it may limit hours of opening or public access.

Applications for planning consents are usually made via the local Council Offices for the district in which the premises subject to the application are located. The application is considered by the professional planning staff and recommendations are made to the next Council Planning Committee meeting. There meetings usually take place at 6 to 8 weekly intervals where the Committees discuss, approve or reject the recommendations of the Council's planning officers. In some cases where further information is requested, applications can be deferred to the next meeting so it can therefore sometimes take several months from the time of application. In view of this, it pays to ensure that adequate time is allowed between the date of the application, and the date when the approval is needed for use of the premises.

Building Regulations

Whereas the planning regulations affect the use which can be made of premises, the Building Regulations relate to any changes or modifications to the structure of the premises, including drainage. If I wish to build a conservatory on the back of my house, so long as it falls within a certain size limit, I will not need planning permission; but I will still need Building Regulations approval for the new structure. When an application is made, the plans are submitted to the local council, and a Building Inspector or Surveyor will check and approve the structural details, e.g. whether or not the foundations are adequate to support the proposed building. Once building commences, the Inspector will visit the premises at specific intervals, to ensure that the builder is actually complying with the details of the plans, and the Inspector has the power to stop work, or order work to be replaced or improved if inadequate. Naturally, the local council charges a fee for the Building Regulations approvals and each of the inspections, but at least the approval of the works is delegated to Council Officers and is not subject to the prolonged Committee approval process – except of course where planning consent is needed before the works can commence.

Local Government Miscellaneous Provisions Act (1982)

This is an interesting piece of legislation which gives local authorities discretionary powers to licence and/or inspect various business activities.

For example, in some districts, all beauticians and massage parlours need to register with the local council. In other districts, only those performing functions which penetrate the skin (such as tattooing, ear-piercing, or electrolysis) need to register and be inspected for hygiene purposes. The Act also covers licensing of pet shops, and less common businesses such as zoos. So, in view of the discretionary nature of this Act, if in doubt, then call your local council offices to check first. Interestingly it does not cover houses of ill repute, but with the current government's approach to taxation by stealth that must be just a matter of time!

Control of Pollution Act (1974) and related legislation

The first stage of the Control of Pollution Act was introduced both to update and reinforce some previous legislation, such as the Clean Air Act; and to cover emerging problems and gaps in environmental controls. These included the emission of gases and toxic fumes, pollution of watercourses, and the licensing and control of the tipping and disposal of waste materials. For example, every tip site or waste storage or waste transfer station, has to be licensed, usually by the County Council, or local authority with responsibility for waste disposal (as opposed to waste collection). The licence will specify the materials which can be processed or tipped at the site. If any toxic or problematic materials are to be handled, then the conditions of the licence will usually specify the measures which need to be taken for safety purposes. Certain toxic materials can only be disposed above impervious clay soils, as a sandy or chalky sub-stratum might allow them to permeate into an underground aquifer and pollute a water supply. The author was once involved in a site in Sheffield, where a limestone barrier was proposed to stop an underground fire in a very old coke-breeze tip, from reaching a coal seam on adjacent land which ran through to Rotherham a few miles away. These are problems inherited from an industrial past, which the Control of Pollution Act is intended to prevent from recurring in the future. It does have very significant implications for any manufacturers whose processes result in the need to store or dispose of toxic materials.

More recent legislation relating to reduction of environmental pollution has been instigated to reduce emission levels of gases, and in particular vehicle exhaust fumes, and gases used in refrigerators. In line with European Commission policies to increase recycling and to reduce landfill, there are now also strict regulation relating to recycling of packaging materials, and specified minimum levels of component materials of vehicles that must be capable of being recycled, and this is something that will grow considerably in the future. Another environmental regulation relating to exposure to asbestos in the workplace is to be introduced in 2006 as part of Health and Safety legislation as a result of the European Asbestos Worker Protection Directive.

Trading legislation

Fair Trading regulations relate to a wide range of aspects of trading including misrepresentation and trades descriptions, business names, civil law concerning the sale of goods, labelling of packaging and safety of products, pricing and competition. Aspects of fair trading have also been updated as part of the Enterprise Act (2002) including the establishment of an independent Office of Fair Trading.

Sale of Goods Act (1979 & 1995)/Consumer Protection Act (1987)

These two pieces of legislation are designed to protect the interests of the consumer, and are primarily administered by the Trading Standards Officers employed by local authorities. They define the rules under which warranties can enforced, goods exchanged, refunds obtained etc. At one time the key definition was that when goods are sold, they must be "fit for the purpose" for which they were designed, or of "merchantable" quality. The latter phrase has now been replaced by the term "reasonable quality", which in many ways swings the balance more in favour of the consumer. Basically, goods must correspond to their description whether verbal written or illustrated, they must be of satisfactory quality, and fit for the purpose for which they were supplied. Services must be carried out with reasonable care and skill, in a reasonable period of time, and for a reasonable charge unless previously agreed with the customer.

In the first instance it is the vendor of the goods who is legally responsible to the consumer for any faults or problems including those inherent in the product itself, but ultimately the cost of repair or replacement goes back to the manufacturer (or importer). In the case of death or substantial personal injury, the liability may extend to all parties with involvement in the product, from manufacturer, importer, carrier, wholesaler, to retailer. The law requires that terms of trade are expressed in plain and intelligible language. They must not contain any terms which bias the transaction unfairly or unreasonably against the consumer, and inclusion of such terms would render the contract null and void. In particular, they cannot seek to restrict liability or enforce broad indemnities indemnity for personal death or injury; and any clauses seeking to restrict liability for loss or damage must be reasonable in the circumstances. For example, the manufacturer's warranty or guarantee cannot limit or restrict the consumer's rights as defined in law; neither can it attempt to limit the manufacturer's legal liability for negligence.

Where vendors and manufacturers fail to meet their responsibilities to the consumer, or where goods are considered to be dangerously faulty, then the Trading Standards Officers have powers of prosecution. These days it is quite common for most of the larger high street chain stores to offer refund and replacement facilities which go far beyond the minimum legal requirements; which can reflect badly on the smaller independent traders who do not have the resources to provide the same terms.

In the case of on-line selling there are further conditions relating to disclosure of facts to potential customers including requirements that the vendor must display a business name and postal address, must give a description and full price of the goods or services offered including how long that price is valid, must define payment and delivery arrangements, and must state any cancellation rights and the duration of any contracts for services.

Advertising Standards/Trades Descriptions Act

Advertising Standards are not so much statutory regulations, but a code of standards which are designed to encourage good practice within the advertising industry, and to discourage adverts which are considered in bad taste, offensive, inaccurate misleading, or libellous. The code of practice is administered by the Advertising Standards Authority, which itself was set up by the Government for the purpose. The Trades Descriptions Act requires that the description of good or services must be accurate – to provide false or misleading information or information that is misleading by implication is an offence with unlimited fines or up to 2 years' imprisonment. There is also separate and more specific legislation relating to particular industries or trade sectors, e.g. food and drink, precious metals, holiday operators, and hotel accommodation.

Data Protection Act (1984)

Under this Act, all computer users who store details or information about private individuals, or information of a personal nature; must register with the Data protection Registrar. This ruling applies whether the holders of the information are private individuals, sole traders, partnerships, limited companies, or public limited companies. It does not apply, however, to information about individuals which is stored on manual systems such as a card index file. The onus is on the holder of computer data to register under the Act, and not to wait until registration is queried or challenged. Anyone who thinks that their personal data might be stored within a computer system has a right to be informed if that is the case, and a right to see the stored information on payment of a reasonable fee. For example, the two biggest credit reference agencies which operate in the UK will provide a copy of any information held against a named individual or private address on payment of a fee, which is currently two pounds. This enables people who are refused credit, to check on whether or not the reason for refusal might be based on erroneous or inaccurate information.

A recent update of the Data Protection Act (DPA) was introduced in response to the growth in e-commerce and on-line trading to provide more specific guidance about the retention of private data. Businesses may now only hold information which is actually needed and is directly relevant to trading (as opposed to general market research data about individuals that could be sold to other organisations). It must ensure that information is current and up to date and must review and delete superfluous information at regular intervals. Above all, date must be stored securely. The latest amendments also require that data holders must observe subjects' rights to privacy, and must not mail them without pre-agreement – an attempt to eradicate unsolicited mail and spam e-mails.

Employment Law

Employment law is a very complicated and constantly changing subject. For that very reason, all businesses are well advised to seek professional guidance where disputes or areas of doubt might arise, as the consequential expenses and risks of facing industrial tribunals can be crippling to a small business which is struggling to establish itself. Even for professional personnel managers who subscribe to receive regular updates to changes in the law, still have to think carefully when giving advice; so it is even more important for the owner-manager who must double as the firm's personnel specialist, to tread carefully.

Employment Acts

Many of the provisions of the various Employment Acts overlap with other legislation, described below. Fundamentally, in law the employer is obliged to:

- Provide a safe and secure working environment.
- Pay staff at agreed rates and at agreed intervals, including the observance of minimum pay requirements.
- Provide staff with contract of employment.
- Inform staff of health and safety policies, and discipline and grievance procedures.
- Ensure that staff do not exceed permitted working hours.
- Provide staff with paid leave for holidays, statutory sickness pay, paid maternity leave (and now for paternity leave).
- Observe the statutory rights that staff have for time-off for jury service, parental responsibilities, trade union duties for which time-off cannot be refused.
- Pay staff for redundancy as appropriate, and give suitable notice to terminate employment.
- Treat staff fairly and reasonably, particularly where dismissal is concerned.
- Not discriminate against staff in any way.

In return, the employer has the right to expect staff to:

- Put on a fair day's work for a fair day's pay.
- Observe workplace rules, and health and safety policy.
- Act in a safe, competent and reasonable way alongside other employees.
- Act honestly, and not against the employers' interests.
- Take care of the employer's property.
- Honour the employer's ownership of any patents or inventions developed within work time or in the workplace.
- Not disclose any confidential information about the business to outsiders.
- Obey lawful and reasonable instructions from the employer.

Employment Protection Act (1975)

This gives employees who have been with an organisation for at least 2 years, automatic rights to, and guarantees of the minimum levels of statutory redundancy pay, if faced with that prospect. They are also allowed paid time-off work to look for alternative work if facing redundancy. After 6 months of employment, female staff are entitled to receive statutory maternity pay, and after 2 years in employment, their jobs must be kept open for them if they wish to return to work after their period of maternity leave. Also after 2 years, employees have the right (with legal redress via industrial tribunal) not to be unfairly dismissed from employment. Since 1995, all of these rights apply to part-time as well as full-time workers. Male parents are also now allowed to take optional paternity leave to which the employer must pay them a fixed proportion of their wage for up to 2 weeks.

Reservists (Territorial Army and Royal Naval Reserve members) must be allowed 15 days unpaid leave per year to attend training, and if they are called up for service they must be re-employed on return – from April 2005 there is a limited financial contribution towards the costs of temporary replacement staff.

European Working Hours Directive (1998)

The UK, by opting out of the EU Social Chapter, had previously avoided having to implement the Working Hours Directive, however as many EU countries felt that the opt-out gave the UK an unfair trading advantage; it was resurrected under the auspices of EU health and safety legislation. It came into force in the UK in October 1998, and basically requires that no employee shall work in excess of an average of 48 hours per week over any 17-week rolling period. Employers must take "all reasonable steps" to ensure compliance with the Directive. As is immediately obvious, for any substantially sized organisation running a shift system, the calculations and administration involved are horrendous; but whereas larger organisations should be more able to accommodate the cost incurred therein, for smaller firms that cost constitutes another substantial overhead burden.

Certain professions (such as doctors) are exempted from the Directive, and there is a clause which permits employees to opt voluntarily for exemption from the 48-hour limit. However for that voluntary option to be valid, it there must be no pressure from the employer, and the employees approval must be given in writing. For it to continue, employees must regularly (e.g. at 6-month intervals) be given the option to change their minds, or to renew their decision to opt out of the Directive.

The Directive also specifies minimum breaks (11 hours) between periods of work, plus a minimum break of 24 hours in each 7-day week; and a compulsory rest break if working more than 6 hours in a day. The minimum paid annual leave entitlement of at least 3 weeks, was raised to a minimum of 4 weeks per year in 1999. Again the resulting financial burden of funding extra paid holidays will have a substantial impact on the operating costs of many smaller businesses.

Contracts of Employment Act (1972)

Within 2 months of starting employment, every employee must be provided with a written contract of employment which specifies the nature and location of their work, rates, and methods of payment, hours of work, holiday entitlement, period of notice, etc. If the employee has not already been informed of the organisation's health and safety policy, this should normally be provided at the same time, along with a copy of any discipline and grievance procedures. Whilst these do not actually form part of the contract of employment, their provision both constitutes good practice, and in the case of the health and safety policy, forms part of the employers' duty under that legislation. Under the Employment Acts every employee is entitled to a minimum of 4 week's paid leave per year (pro-rata for part-time staff) although statutory holidays can be included in that 4 weeks.

Employer's Liability (Compulsory Insurance) Regulations (1972 & 1998)

All organisations, whether they are sole traders, large commercial businesses, public sector bodies, educational institutions, or charities; if they employ any staff whatsoever in any capacity, part-time or full-time, must take out Employer's Liability Insurance to cover their staff for the risk of accident or injury in the workplace. A copy of the current certificate of insurance must be displayed in a prominent position in their premises, where it can be seen by employees. From January 1999 the minimum sum to be insured increased from £2m to £5m for any one

claim, and employers are now required to keep all past insurance certificates for a period of 40 years.

Minimum wage regulations

In October 1998, under a EU Directive, the government introduced a
basic minimum wage for all employees aged over 21, with a slightly
lower level for very young employees, with the actual rates increasing
each year under annual reviews. Whilst seen by many people as a positive social move, the wisdom of this is still arguable, as some employers
have simply removed other staff benefits (such as paid tea breaks) to offset the cost. In some cases, others who may have previously paid higher
rates, now regard this as the industrially-accepted standard, and have
reduced wages accordingly. Certainly for some poorly paid staff such as
carers, domestic and security staff, the minimum wage is a positive
move; but for many newly established or struggling small firms, it simply increases overhead costs. Either way, it is a legal requirement with
which businesses must now comply.

Stakeholder pensions

It is a legal requirement that if you employ five or more staff, unless you
already offer a personal pension scheme or an occupational pension
scheme to those staff that they can join within a year of starting to work
for you, then you must make provision for them to have access to a
Stakeholder Pension Scheme, although currently you do not have to
make employer contributions towards that scheme – at least not at the
present time, but don't relax as that will happen sooner or later as the
pension age rises and as state pensions come under financial pressure.
The current requirement is a case of providing access to a scheme and
does not apply for new employees in the first 3 months of employment,
to those who are below the lower earnings limit for National Insurance
purposes, or to those who belong to, have declined to join or are ineligible to join an occupational pension scheme.

Financial & Company Law

These are grouped together primarily because the laws which relate to the
legal format and structure of businesses invariably, within the definition of

those, become involved with the financial aspects of capitalisation and distribution of profits, which in turn have implications for taxation etc.

Finance Acts

The Finance Acts are the means by which the government is able to raise money by taxation, and to operate its fiscal policy. As such, they are effectively revised or modified every time there is a new government budget, which is usually at least once a year. However, they also define some of the processes and procedures within which businesses must operate, and act as a convenient mechanism to modify other more significant pieces of legislation. As example of the latter is shown below under the Partnership Act section.

H. M. Revenue & Customs VAT Regulations

Value-Added Tax (VAT) is another legacy of membership of the European community, the rates of which have climbed slowly but steadily since its introduction, to the current standard rate of 17.5%, with lower rates for insurance and fuel supplies. Some products, such as food, childrens' clothing, animal feeds, books, etc are zero-rated and attract no VAT. The tax is based on the concept that at each stage of the supply or production of goods or services, value is added to those goods or services, and that added value is taxed. Currently in 2005–2006, any business which has a sales turnover of £58,000 per annum or more, (which is reviewed annually in the Chancellor's budget) must register with H. M. Revenue & Customs, and must charge VAT on the value of its invoices to customers. It must pay to H. M. Revenue & Customs every quarter, the sum of all VAT collected in that quarter, less any VAT which it has paid to its suppliers during the same period. Dates for payment are fixed, and penalties for transgression can be heavy. Be warned, unlike other creditors, H. M. Revenue & Customs do not need to obtain a Court order before sending the bailiffs into your premises to confiscate your stock or equipment, and they will not hesitate to do so if necessary!

Laws of taxation

These are essentially derived from the Finance Acts as principles in law, but the specific operation of the tax system (in terms of rates of taxation, tax-free allowances etc.) are modified by the government each year as part of the annual Budget. Amendments to taxes and the introduction of new taxes are usually made under changes to tax Regulations, rather than by introducing specific new Acts of Parliament. The influence of the EU on tax law is expected to become more and more significant over the next few years, because of the pressure from several continental companies for the UK to "harmonise" its tax laws with those of other parts of Europe. This is largely because some of our European neighbours regard the UK's less onerous company tax system as giving UK businesses an unfair advantage! Whatever happened to the old adage "If you can't stand the heat, get out of the kitchen"? The laws on taxation are quite complicated, and this is one particular area where the advice of an accountant or taxation specialist can often more than pay for what it costs. Remember, tax avoidance is legal, tax evasion is not. The two are often finely divided, with the difference between them being only accurately determinable by an experienced taxation expert.

Companies Act (1985 & 1989)

The Companies Act formulates the rules under which all limited companies, and public limited companies operate. It specifies the registration requirements, and the annual returns which have to be made, reporting the accounts and financial situation of the company etc., including:

- The annual accounts: profit & loss account, balance sheet, cash flow statement, debtors, and creditors figures, details of any material changes in methods of accounting.
- The capital value of the company, numbers and types of shares issued, paid-up share value, details of loans and debentures, and any investments made by the company.
- Proposed dividend payable to shareholders.
- Names of directors, details of directors' expenses, remuneration of lowest and highest paid directors, schedule of directors' interests, directors' annual report.
- Names of auditors, details of auditor's remuneration, auditor's annual report.

For small companies with a turnover of under £350,000 and balance sheet of under £1.4 m, un-audited accounts with an abbreviated balance sheet can be submitted if supported by an accountant's statement confirming that the accounts agree with company records. A copy of the directors' report and the profit and loss account must be provided to shareholders.

In either case, the company must hold an annual general meeting to which all shareholders are invited to attend. Day to day management is carried out by the Board of Directors.

Partnership Act (1890)

As can be seen by the date, this is a very long-standing statute. When a partnership is established it is usual for the partners (or their legal representatives) to produce a legally binding partnership agreement, which specifies a number of details:

- The names and addresses of the partners.
- The name and the nature of the business, and its trading activities.
- The effective date of commencement of the partnership.
- Decision making procedures, and any arbitration or dissolution arrangements.
- The relative capital inputs of the partners.
- Banking arrangements, accounting periods, production of annual accounts etc.
- The way in which profits and losses will be divided, and if necessary, arrangements made with creditors.

The partnership agreement, once signed and witnessed, is a legally binding document. In the absence of a formal partnership agreement, the Partnership Act specifies that profits and losses will be allocated equally between partners in the business. It also prescribes that if a partner wishes to resign, the whole partnership must be wound up, and a new partnership formed by any remaining partners. This is obviously an onerous process, particularly in professional partnerships (accountants, solicitors etc.) where changes are relatively frequent. To overcome that problem Section 113 of the Finance Act 1988 allowed for the production of a "Notice of Election to Continue Partnership" wherein a partner could leave, or another join, without having to dissolve of rewrite the partnership agreement, thereby simplifying the whole system for Income Tax purposes.

Another key aspect of the Partnership Act is that it specifies the "joint and several liability" of all partners for partnership debts, wherein each partner is liable, not only for their own share of the debt, but for the debt as a whole, in the event of default by other partners.

Business Names Act (1985)

Names of limited companies are registered with the Registrar of Companies at Companies House, and obviously before a name is registered there is a search process to ensure that the name has not already been used by an allocated company, or allocated to a newly formed but inactive company. The Registrar can provide advice on names, which must not be offensive or constitute a criminal offence.

In the case of partnerships or sole traders, there is no registration requirement by law, and proprietors can use their own names, or can trade under other names, e.g. "John Smith trading as Wonder Web Internet Services". It is a legal requirement however, for company letterheads and documents to show the registered company name and number, and the names of company directors, and the registered office. In the case of partners and sole traders, where they are not trading under their own names, they must be identified as proprietors on all business documents.

Copyrights, Designs & Patents Act (1988)

This legislation is covered in more detail in Chapter 19 as part of the management of intellectual property.

Consumer Credit Act (1974)

There are two aspects of this legislation of relevance to small firms, the first of which is that any business advising, giving or arranging extended credit for customers, such as hire purchase or leasing agreements, must first be licensed to operate under this Act. The other aspect is that of unincorporated businesses (sole traders and partnerships) where any loans raised by individual proprietors for business purposes, and which are less than £15,000 are regulated under the terms of this Act. These terms include appropriate "cooling off" periods after signing, during which the borrower can change their mind; and the requirement that once a fixed proportion of repayments have been made, recovery of goods or enforcement of payment requires a Court Order.

Insolvency Act (1986)/Company Directors Disqualification Act (1986)/Enterprise Act (2002)

One of the main objectives of the Insolvency Act was to curtail the legal but improper practice of operating what were known as "Phoenix" companies, particularly in the building and double glazing industries. That is, the practice trading for a while, accruing debts, bleeding the business of cash by paying high directors' salaries, and then liquidating businesses overnight. A new limited company then surfaces a few days later under another name, with the same directors, operating from the same premises, producing the same goods or services, but having dumped previous creditors without much hope of payment. The Insolvency Act made it a criminal offence for any individual or company director, to knowingly continue to trade whilst insolvent. The penalty for failing to take corrective action, or for failing to inform creditors of an insolvent situation, involved the company directors being made personally liable for all company debts, from being barred from future directorships, and in some cases for facing charges of fraud.

It was also no longer possible for company directors to put businesses into voluntarily liquidation and appoint themselves as liquidators. One spin-off of this was the upsurge in private Insolvency Practitioners (often described as vultures with accounting qualifications) and their agents, for whom this was almost a licence to print money, particularly during the early nineties when the rate of bankruptcy amongst small firms hit an all-time high. The Insolvency Practitioners operated almost in a monopoly market, charging fees well above those of their fellow accountants, so that by the time the assets of the insolvent business were liquidated, and the fees paid, there was rarely anything left for the remaining creditors. But on a positive note, it did mean that all bankruptcies and insolvencies were investigated and the reasons subsequently reported to the Department of Trade and Industry. It also facilitated a monitoring system so that company directors who were repeatedly involved in liquidated companies could be identified, and if necessary, barred from holding directorships or positions of authority in future, for up to 15 years.

Businesses which were profitable, but insolvent due to cash flow problems, could continue to trade by virtue of voluntary agreements with creditors, wherein if at least sixty per cent of creditors agreed to forestall action to recover debts, the insolvent business could negotiate a planned schedule of repayments to creditors. If the required proportion of creditors agreed, then the voluntary agreement was legally binding on all creditors, and on the schedule of repayments. The Act also introduced the Statutory Demand for Payment, whereby creditors could demand payment within 21 days, and if this was not made, they could apply for an immediate Winding-up Order against the business.

The Enterprise Act (2002)

This Act covered a range of business areas including competition and mergers, but it also updated the 1986 insolvency regulations in several key areas (source: The Insolvency Service.):

- To streamline the procedure of administration to make it more efficient and accessible in order to aid the rescue of viable companies.
- To restrict the ability to appoint an administrative receiver only to lenders holding pre-existing floating charges, or to financiers involved in certain capital and other transactions where the appointment of an administrative receiver is essential to efficient market operation.
- To introduce powers to extend certain insolvency proceedings to foreign companies, Industrial and Provident Societies, and Friendly Societies.
- To reduce the number of restrictions that are imposed on undischarged bankrupts and to allow for the automatic discharge of nearly all bankrupts after a maximum of just 12 months.
- To introduce Bankruptcy Restrictions Orders (BROs) to protect the general public and the business community from bankrupts whose conduct before and during bankruptcy has been found to be culpable.
- To introduce voluntary income payments agreements (IPA) as an alternative to court-based income payments orders (IPO). IPAs will carry the same conditions as IPOs and both will be able to run for a period of up to 3 years.
- To enable the official receiver (OR) to act as nominee and supervisor of new fast-track voluntary agreements begun after bankruptcy order has been made.
- To require the OR to investigate why a bankrupt failed only where he thinks that this is necessary.
- To limit to 3 years the period in which a trustee may deal with a bankrupt's interest in the sole or principal home of the bankrupt, the bankrupt's spouse or a former spouse before that interest revert to the bankrupt.

■ To remove the Crown's preferential rights in all insolvencies and make provision to ensure unsecured creditors are major beneficiaries – a major change effectively removing preferential creditor status and downgrading government" and local government organisations to the status of ordinary creditors.

■ To reform the financial regime of The Insolvency Service, making it simpler, fairer to creditors and more transparent.

Contract Law (debt recovery etc.)

This is essentially different from any Statutory Law in that the laws of Tort or contract have not been established and precisely defined by Act of Parliament, but have evolved over a period of time as a result of numerous cases in Civil Law which have formed established precedents. However, as a result of this process, there are established procedures within the Civil Courts which facilitate the recovery of debts which are proven under Civil Law, e.g. where failure to pay within a specific time has resulted in a breach of contract. These recovery processes are discussed in more detail in Chapter 8.

Property Law

Like the civil law relating to tort or contracts, the laws which affect purchase, ownership, and leasing of property, are a mixture of statutes and case law. If anything, this is an area where proper legal advice is more important than just about any other, particularly where legal liabilities are concerned. One example which has always been contentious is that of long-term leases, where a leaseholder who sell on the remaining lease to another party, will still remain liable for any subsequent debts on that lease (such as non-payment of ground rent by the new leaseholder). Similarly, if the new leaseholder becomes insolvent, the responsibility for the lease will revert to the original leaseholder.

Anti-discrimination Law

Broadly speaking, you are not allowed to discriminate against any employees or applicants for vacant jobs, on the grounds of race, colour, religion, ethnic origin, gender or marital status.

Race Relations Act (1976)/Equal Opportunities Commission

This was one of the earlier moves to prevent discrimination in the workplace, wherein it became illegal to discriminate against individuals on the basis of skin colour, race or ethnic origin, or nationality. When recruiting, you must not discriminate when advertising the job, or in determining the terms of the job offered. An employer must not knowingly allow discrimination to continue in the workplace, or to discriminate against staff when considering training or promotion opportunities, or when involved in selecting staff for redundancy or dismissal. A Code of Conduct has been produced by the Commission for Racial Equality to guide and assist employers.

The Equal Opportunities Commission (EOC) takes a more positive approach to the problem of discrimination, by expounding the fact that not only should we be discouraging discrimination on the basis of race, religion, colour, ethnic origin, gender, age, size, and disability; but that employers and communities should take a more positive role in giving people the opportunity for employment, promotion, and training. The key to this is to judge people on their abilities and potential, rather than their disability or ethnic origin. The EOC also produces and updates Codes of Practice for the guidance of employers to provide recommendations and guidance on how to avoid unlawful racial discrimination and harassment in the workplace. The Code recommends that employers should have an equal opportunities policy from recruitment to dismissal and a corresponding action plan to put the policy into practice – great in theory but in reality for most new and very small businesses a case of pie in the sky, as most owner-managers are much too preoccupied with the day to day running of the business to start preparing paper-policies that they might (or might not) just need in the future. This comment is not meant in any way to detract from acknowledgement of the important principles of equal opportunity, but it simply reflects the pragmatism of running a modern business in the face of increasing pressure for compliance with political correctness before the event actually arises. In many ways it presupposes that entrepreneurs will fail to meet their equal opportunities obligations unless forced to do so, which many small business owners would regard as a totally offensive and inappropriate attitude.

Disabled Persons Employment Act (1944)

As a result of the many injured and disabled servicemen returning from military service, this Act was introduced to facilitate and improve employment opportunities for them. Any organisation which employs more than 20 staff has a legal duty to ensure that at least three per cent of its employees are drawn from those registered as disabled; and that facilities are available in the workplace to accommodate them. This may sound quite onerous for employers, but it must be considered within the context of the Department for Work and Pensions definition of disabled persons as those who are registered as disabled for employment purposes. This does not mean that all such people are wheelchair bound or physically incapacitated, as many people registered as disabled for employment purposes are simply restricted in the range of work which they can do. For example, someone with a back or leg injury may not be able to move heavy loads in a factory, but could be fully competent in a sedentary or clerical position in an office, where their disability would probably not even be noticed by their colleagues, but they still contribute towards the three per cent quota of disabled staff.

Disability Discrimination Act (1995)

Following on from the previous legislation, the Disability Discrimination Act (DDA) is really an attempt to promote the inclusion of disabled persons in the workplace; and again, we are not just talking about severe disabilities, but anyone who qualifies for a DfWP Green Card. There has always been a tendency in the past, and not necessarily a conscious one, for anyone who admits on a application form to being registered as disabled, to be overlooked during the recruitment process – even if the disability is only relatively minor. As per the example quoted above, a person with arthritis may be "disabled" in terms of having limited leg movement or lifting capability, but could have excellent analytical, financial, or computing skills which can be exercised whilst sitting down.

Under this Act, disabled individuals have the right not to be discriminated against, either during the process of recruitment, or within their employment. This also means that they must be given equal opportunity to receive training, or to be considered for promotion. Employers must also provide reasonable means of physical access and working systems to allow them to exercise their rights. This includes access ramps for wheelchair-bound customers, wide doors, provision of disabled toilets for staff and customers as appropriate in large retail outlets and commercial employers etc.

When the DDA was first implemented in 1995 small firms were exempted from many of the requirements, having been allowed several years to achieve compliance. The full effect of the Act came into effect from October 2004 at which time the regulations requiring provision of access were extended to include all small businesses. For most non-retail small firms this was not a major problem but for small retail outlets it was necessary to widen doors and to provide wheelchair ramps etc. Also, if toilet facilities were provided, these had to be accessible for disabled people.

Sex Discrimination Acts (1975 & 1989)

When advertising job vacancies, or when interviewing staff, it is unlawful to discriminate on the basis of gender. Certain exemptions do exist, where e.g. gender is specifically relevant as a genuine qualification for the job, such as mineworkers where the working conditions are deemed unsuitable for women; or rape counsellors where a male counsellor would be entirely inappropriate or unacceptable for the needs of the clients. No longer can a pub landlord advertise for a barmaid, the advert must be for a bar-person. There are of course, still those inventive characters who try to find a way around the system: "Bar-person wanted – must be capable of filling a size 12 red rubber gym-slip". The mind boggles! This still constitutes sexual discrimination, as it gives preference to one gender over the other – in theory at least!

Equal Pay Act (1970)

The Equal Pay Act stipulates that an employer must pay men and women equal pay and other employee benefits and pensions, terms of contract etc, where they are carrying out the same or similar jobs as each other. However, in some circumstances differences in pay and conditions are acceptable, e.g. for jobs where specialist skills or knowledge are required differential rates can be paid to reflect differing levels of qualifications and/or experience; or perhaps extra annual leave may be allocated as a reward for long service. In the event that an organisation pays disparate rates of pay between men and women for equal work it is now imperative that there is a robust case or justification for doing so – an "objective justification" that shows that the reason for difference is unrelated to sex, is a real need of the employer, is appropriate and necessary to business objectives, and conforms with the principle of proportionality.

Trade Union Reform & Employment Rights Act (1993)

It is illegal to discriminate against members of staff on the grounds of trade union membership or participating in trade union activities (unless this interferes with normal working duties and has been carried out without the approval of management). You do not currently have to recognise trade unions, although this situation may change if the EU has its way; but you cannot prohibit staff from belonging to a trade union. Even if there is no trade union involved, staff consultation is still required where redundancy is a possibility, or where the potential sale of the business would affect the livelihoods of more than 20 staff. You are entitled to receive at least 7 days' notice of any official industrial action by trade union members, during which time members must be balloted. Failure to do so could render the trade union liable for any losses resulting from a breach of contracts with your commercial customers. Unofficial activity is not the responsibility of trade unions, but would not doubt constitute a breach of the contracts of employment by the participants, possibly justifying termination of employment.

Sources of information

The important thing to remember when considering any aspects of legislation is that the tenets of business and employment law are constantly changing, so any attempt to reference legal sources or information must be carefully managed to ensure that the information accessed is current, accurate and relevant to the situation. The main purpose of this chapter has been to summarise the purpose and significance of the various items of legislation which are relevant to a small businesses but these will continue to change. So, basic good practice for investigating legal issues requires that:

- When consulting or using any published sources of information you must check to make sure that they are not out of date, of that the usefulness of information has been superseded by changes in circumstances, or more recent events. For example, government population census information may be well prepared and quite reliable, but if it is only updated once in every 10 years, then the 2001 census data will not be of much use in the year 2007. In contrast, internet data is often relatively new and regularly updated, but coming from a wide range of sources must be checked and validated for its accuracy.

- The source of the data needs to be checked for its reliability. Again, although very dated, the population census data is generally accepted as coming from a reliable source, whilst the provenance of internet data, although it is more current, may be less reliable. Data and statistics can easily be manipulated or modified to prove or disprove a particular argument, so the source and objectivity should be checked carefully evaluated, particularly if it is to be used as the basis for market research. Is the source reliable? Has the data been verified or evaluated by any external agency or academic institution?

- If you are unable to find the necessary information, or you need help in utilising it, then you should turn to an appropriate person to get the right advice. For example, in the case of financial information, you might turn to an accountant, bank manager, or a business counsellor from the local enterprise agency. For advice on insurance, an independent insurance broker might be appropriate. In each case, it is important to ensure that the chosen adviser is suitably qualified and experienced for the job. There are many people who advertise themselves as offering accounting services, but a properly qualified accountant will display their qualifications, such as FCA, ACCA, CIMA. A few years ago financial advisers shared some dubious reputations for the lack of truly objective advice provided to clients, but with the imposition of Financial Services Agency standards that has largely been eradicated.

- As a rule of thumb, if you are in doubt about who to turn to for proper advice, try your local Citizens Advice Bureau, or Enterprise Agency, who will generally be able to provide a list of names of suitable local people. Failing that, the local library will be able to give you the address of the relevant professional organisation who can put you in touch with a local member. Finally, bear in mind before committing yourself to using a professional adviser that these people have to make their living from the provision of advice and professional services, so be prepared to pay the going rate for their professional fees. If the thought of this bothers you, do not be afraid to ask them what the advice will cost before you commit yourself.

References

www.insolvency.gov.uk/faq/eactfaq.htm
www.businesslink.gov.uk

Further reading

Clayton, P. (2004). *Law for the Small Business: An Essential Guide to All the Legal and Financial Requirements.* Kogan Page, London.

Croner's Guide to Employment Law 2005, Croner, Kingston upon Thames.

Equal Opportunities Commission: Codes of Practice. www.eoc.org.uk

CHAPTER 8

Resource requirements

The objective of this chapter is to assist the potential owner-manager to review his or her options when considering potential premises, and to understand some of the legal implications of buying, leasing, or renting commercial premises. It will also enable the reader to assess which types of insurance cover he or she should be considering for both premises, and for the business as a whole, including the physical resources other than premises, as the two tend to be interdependent. The size, volume, and extent of physical resources may well predetermine the premises requirements, or conversely, the availability of premises may place limitations on the physical resources which can be utilised. The first part of this chapter is concerned with the processes of identifying the space required for various activities, the most suitable types of premises, their locations, their relative costs, and the legal aspects of acquiring premises. The second part is concerned with associated issues of insurance related to premises, but broadening out into a general overview of different types of insurances and their relevance to the owner-manager.

What sort of premises will I need?

Well first, just what type of business are you running? A mobile hairdresser or complimentary therapist, who visits the clients in their homes, may be able to simply work from their own home, with just the need for some small space for storage. A self-employed professional consultant may also be able to do likewise by converting a spare room at home into an office; however, a small office in a commercial location might create a better image in the eyes of their clients and customers should they need to visit. An engineering or manufacturing process would almost certainly be looking for premises with planning consent for light industrial use, particularly if the work involved noisy machinery, dusty of dirty processes, etc. For a retail business, the location of the premises will be a primary factor as the business will need either to be in a place where the customers already go, such as a shopping mall; or in a place where it is easy and convenient for the customers to get to them, such as a retail park. A wholesaler would need to be in a central position from which the customers could be supplied, and ideally close to a good road network.

There is no specific formula for finding the ideal location for business premises although clearly, the nature of the market will have fundamental implications for the location and vice versa. With the exception of e-commerce and mail order firms whose clients are distance-based, the business needs to reflect the community it serves, and therefore its location within that community must be selected to match the needs of that community. A business selling commercial hydraulic hoses and their fittings is ideally situated in an industrial estate where its commercial clients can call and can park easily, but it would be as much out of place in the high street as a fine China shop would be in an industrial estate. Equally, the location of competitors must be considered. Where the market community is large, it is not unusual to see competing businesses located nearby each other, but in a smaller community, two rivals competing for the same small market would probably put each other out of business as neither would make enough profit to survive. It is also important that the location should match the image of the product or service on offer, and more so that the premises themselves should reflect that image. It is not sufficient that the fine China shop is situated in the high street, it must be at the right side or end of the high street where more affluent customers are likely to be found, and it must project an image of up-market quality.

The cost of retail premises is largely determined by their location. Town centre shops are always expensive to rent, lease, or to buy, although because of those same high costs, many town centre shopping malls or arcades frequently have a proportion of empty property due to the high turnover rate when businesses either fail, or move because of the high rents. Shops located in retail parks are also relatively expensive to rent because of the cost of the provision of the infrastructure of access roads and parking. In comparison, retail outlets just outside of town centres and on main access routes tend to be cheaper, and those in residential areas or on the outskirts of towns can be cheaper still. The relative cost of premises on industrial or commercial estates will depend on a number of factors including their proximity to road networks and motorways, the age and condition of the premises themselves, and the extent and quality of customer parking, security and services. The same basic principle applies to storage and warehousing. To rent space in a farmer's barn may be very cheap, but remote locations and muddy access roads may not be so good in winter. On the other hand, a modern warehouse will be much more secure and accessible, but correspondingly more expensive to rent.

So, in answer to the question: "What sort of premises will I need?" we have to be considering a number of factors:

- The type of business which is proposed and the type of premises most appropriate to that business. The physical environment may be important to the product or process, e.g. hygienic and easy to clean for food preparation, secure for storage of valuable products, or perhaps needing a specialist environment for sterile services.
- Whether or not customers will need access to the premises on a regular basis, where those customers will be coming from in terms of distance, and how they might be travelling, e.g. for car parking or public transport links.
- The visual appearance of the premises particularly if they will be visited by customers on a regular basis. This is discussed as an aspect of customer expectations in Chapter 11.
- The need for easy access to motorways, road networks, rail links, airports, etc.
- The likelihood of obtaining planning consent for the proposed use.
- The need for services and facilities such as customer parking.
- The need for security to prevent intrusion, or to protect valuable stock.
- What the business is likely to be able to afford in the early stages.
- The space requirements, both present and future.
- Convenience of access for the owner-manager and staff.

What size of premises will I need?

A good starting point for estimating this is to look at the inventory of physical resources which you will need for the business, and which is discussed later in this chapter. Until you actually identify what fixtures and fittings, machinery, furniture, etc., that you will need to run the business, and how these will need to be laid out, then it is impossible to make a realistic judgement about the working area required. Probably the easiest way to start is with several large sheets of graph paper on which you can sketch out various layouts of the "ideal" premises. First, work out the different work areas that will be required and which need to be separated or partitioned off from each other. Let us take several examples:

Example 1: In a reasonably sized high street shop the main area will obviously be the retail sections where the customers come to inspect the goods. There will also need to be a stockroom for the storage of back-up stock, toilets for staff, a small office space for a desk and telephone for the manager, somewhere secure for staff to leave their bags and coats, and somewhere to make tea or coffee and to wash up. If the shop anticipates a large turnover, there may also need to be a safe within the office.

Example 2: For small wholesaling business the main premises requirement is for storage space for the products, with a small office for dealing with customer enquiries and producing invoices, etc., a toilet and wash room, and small room for the delivery drivers or warehouse staff to use during breaks and store their clothes. More important however, are the dimensions of the storage area, as vertical storage of stock on pallets is far more economical and efficient than having the stock spread around the floor. The space also needs to be planned to allow access for handling equipment such as fork-lifts when goods are received or despatched, and this too has implications for floor surfaces which must not be too rough, and adequate door widths.

Example 3: A self-employed complementary therapist setting up a in practice would only need a main room in which to treat the clients, a small reception area, and a washbasin and toilet. The treatment room would house a desk and filing cabinet, the treatment couch, some cupboards with a work top and sink, and some screened space for clients to change behind. The space requirements here are simple and modest, but the room itself would need good heating for the comfort of clients, a washable floor, and there would need to be parking space outside for the use of the clients. In fact the parking area would probably need to be greater than the treatment area.

Having worked out how the space would need to be sub-divided, the second stage is to ask yourself how big these areas need to be? To do this it is first necessary to work out what is going to go into each of them, and then to look at the way they will be laid out. You should allow plenty of space to move around as well, especially if there is a need for any equipment to move stock or heavy items using barrows, pallet trucks, or fork-lifts. This exercise should generate a rough idea of the area needed, although of course, real premises are invariably always the wrong shape, and with power points and water supplies in the most inconvenient of places, so it pays to allow for a margin of error. There is bound to be something you have forgotten anyway!

Another aspect which must be considered is that of growth or expansion. All too often owner-managers of new businesses fail to plan ahead and take on the smallest premises that they can manage with, just to save on short-term rental costs. As soon as the business starts to grow, those premises are outgrown, and the proprietor has to go through the expensive and time-consuming process of looking for bigger premises. Apart from the cost of moving and the disruption of trade, this can be particularly expensive if the premises are subject to a minimum rental period, where an early move might invoke a penalty clause in the rental agreement. So, you must ask yourself what size of premises might be needed to meet your planned rate of growth over the next 2 or 3 years, as the answer to this may well influence your final choice of location.

What are the options for acquiring premises?

The most appropriate way of acquiring premises is usually pre-determined by the financial resources which are available within the start-up business. A lot of potential owner-managers like to start very cautiously by utilising existing space at home, so as not to commit themselves to heavy regular expenditure on premises until they are sure that the business will take off. This is fine for some activities such as those involving the provision of services by sole-traders, but for manufacturing, wholesale or retail activities; commitment to expenditure for premises is usually unavoidable. This is particularly true if the new business involves buying out another established business such as a shop or garage, or setting up a franchised business associated with a corporate image (e.g. a MacDonalds or Wimpy outlet) where the design, décor and facilities within the premises are specified under the terms of the franchise.

The most common methods of acquiring premises are for freehold or leasehold purchase or some form of rental agreement:

■ Freehold ownership of premises can take two forms. In some cases the business (or its owners) will buy land and develop custom built premises. This is typically associated with well-established cash-rich companies for whom the land is often a long-term capital investment. More often in small businesses, freehold premises are purchased along with the business within them (e.g. shops, pubs, off-licences), or a warehouse may be bought to house a specific business. Typically the process of freehold purchase requires the purchaser to provide 20–25% of the purchase price from their own resources, with the balance being funded through a commercial mortgage with a bank or financial institution, repayable over 10 or 15 years. As a longer-term capital investment it is good, the premises are an asset on the balance sheet, and of course there is no rent to pay. Full tax-relief can be claimed on interest payments, and capital allowance can be claimed against the purchase cost. Very few small firms however, have the spare cash or resources to find the 25% deposit for the mortgage without selling or mortgaging their own private homes. Solicitors are essential for the conveyancing of freehold premises, both to ensure the legality of the process, and to check that no undeclared mortgages or charges exist against the premises, or planning consents which might adversely affect the site. In some old cathedral cities it is not unusual for former church property to carry legal covenants from one or two centuries back that restrict the potential use of the site.

- Leasehold purchase provides a method of acquiring a capital asset for balance sheet purposes, without the same level of expenditure as freehold purchase. In the case, the business buys the leasehold rights to premises for a period of years (typically 25, 50 or 99 years on a new lease) and then pays the owner of the freehold rights an annual ground rent. The ground rent was traditionally paid on the four quarter days, i.e. 23rd of March, June, September, and December each year, although that tradition is now fading in favour of monthly direct debits. Once again, the deposit sums are usually around 25% but as the sum borrowed is lower than needed for freehold purchase, the repayments are more affordable. The repayment period is normally about 15 years, as per most commercial mortgages, but could be longer for a long residual period or less if there are only a few years remaining on the lease. Leases can also be resold if the firm outgrows the premises. The big draw back with selling leasehold property is that if a subsequent leaseholder goes bust, the liability for outstanding and future ground rent payments can fall back on the original or previous leaseholder. Again, solicitors are necessary for the conveyancing of leasehold purchases, and are essential for the checking of potential liabilities in the event of a future leaseholder defaulting on the lease, and the liabilities reverting to an earlier lessee. It is also worth checking for any restrictive covenants which may occur in leases for older buildings, as these could restrict the way in which the premises could be used.

- Medium or long-term rental agreements are quite popular on modern industrial estates, and sometimes new businesses are enticed with an initial rent-free period of 3 to 6 months. Typically the agreement period will be for at least 3 years during which the monthly rent payment is fixed at a pre-agreed level. In longer-term rent agreements, the rent may be reviewed at specified intervals.

- Short-term rental agreements are quite popular for very new businesses as they do not incur such long-term commitments as other arrangements. Typically rental agreements might be renewed year by year, with an annual rent review. The actual monthly or quarterly payments may be slightly higher than those of a medium term agreement, but it is normally possible to terminate the agreements with between 1 and 3 months' notice. Another bonus is that the agreements do not require the involvement of solicitors and the associated fees. It is of course still advisable to get a legal or informed opinion (such as an estate agent or surveyor) before signing contracts for any rental agreement, in case of any adverse clauses hidden in the small print. It is worth paying particular attention to any clauses relating to the liability of occupants to pay for, or contribute towards the upkeep and maintenance of premises. If these are included then it is reasonable to expect the rents to be adjusted downwards to reflect the liability.

Other aspects of obtaining premises

The reader is reminded of the requirements for planning consent for change of use of premises under the Planning Acts, and the need for Building Regulations approval for any structural changes to premises, or drainage, etc. These are discussed in more detail in Chapter 7. Similarly, according to the nature of the use of premises, it may be necessary to obtain licences for specific activities from the local authority, under the Local Government Miscellaneous Provisions Act, and to register with the local authority for any food-related businesses under the Environmental Health Regulations.

Information about available premises can usually be obtained from commercial estate agents, most of which are usually listed in yellow pages or advertise in the local press, although agents are increasingly using the Internet to advertise property. Alternatively, the local enterprise agency or bank business adviser may be able to suggest suitable options, and may well know of special incentives or assistance available to potential tenants.

What insurance cover will I need for the premises?

There are basically three types of insurance related to premises – the insurance for the building itself, insurance for fixtures and fittings, and insurance for stock of other contents:

- Buildings insurance is taken out to cover the structure and fabric of the premises. It is usually the responsibility of the owner, i.e. the freeholder or leaseholder of the premises, and any person renting business premises should check to make sure that this is the case. The insurance covers the cost of repair or rebuilding work for any damage to the structure or fabric of the building by fire, storm, flood, Acts of God (or presumably, Allah) and all-perils, e.g. from a runaway lorry crashing through the walls. It does not cover damage to anything inside the building or to loss of trade during the rebuilding process. Cover for damage resulting from acts of war or terrorism is normally excluded.
- Buildings Contents Insurance excludes the structure of the building, but covers all fixtures, fittings, furniture and equipment, etc. within the building, for a similar range of perils. For business premises it is normally prudent to keep an up-to-date inventory of all fixtures and fittings, office equipment, machinery, etc., with original costs or values, to ensure that the buildings contents insurance is adequate to cover the cost of all contents. This form of insurance only usually covers permanent items of business property, excluding resale stock.
- Cover for the value of goods held in stock within premises is essential in case of fire, flood, theft, etc. Most insurance companies are interested in the value of a realistic average level of stock, and policies will typically allow for seasonal increases in stock levels without extra charge. Again, check to make sure that the level of cover is adequate, as some insurance companies reduce the levels of pay out if they believe the value of stock to have been underinsured.

What other types of insurance should I be considering?

- Following on from the previous item, any business involved in the sale and distribution of goods should consider Goods in

Transit Insurance. Premiums are normally based on the maximum value of each consignment (e.g. van or lorry load). Don't let the insurance agent try to set the premium against the total value of stock sold over the year, as this will result in a horrendous premium, and does not reflect the risk of the value of goods which could be lost in one incident.

- Employer's Liability Insurance is a legal requirement for anyone employing staff, to cover those staff against accident or injury in the workplace. This cover is also required for directors of limited companies as they are also employees of the business. Even private householders employing au pairs or part-time cleaners need to comply with this insurance requirement.
- Public Liability is another essential insurance. It covers accident or injury to any member of the public or their property, including people visiting or passing by premises.
- Product Liability Insurance provides you with cover against injury or illness affecting your customers or members of the public as a result of the use of your products. For example, food poisoning from food products, or skin damage caused by beauty treatments.
- Professional Indemnity covers professional individuals against claims for negligence or misconduct, such as a hairdresser who uses the wrong concentration of bleach and causes the customer's hair to turn orange and fall out. Another example would be a design engineer who gets the structural calculations wrong, and the bridge he has designed subsequently collapses. This is also an essential if the proposed business is employing any staff who might provide financial, technical or other professional advice.
- Loss of Profits Insurance is designed to provide an on-going source of revenue when normal trading is interrupted due to some external factor. For example, if a fire damages a building and its contents stopping trade for 2 months, the Loss of Profits Insurance would cover the expenses of paying on-going overhead costs (rent, rates, insurance, staff, etc.) until the business starts trading again. Payments are based on the calculated profits (not turnover) which have been lost. Good in principle, but can take time to be paid out, and for new businesses without a trading record or previous year's accounts, it can be hard to prove the real level of profits which have been lost. In the short term, having this insurance should at least facilitate a temporary bank overdraft, to help until the insurance pays out.

- Motor Vehicle Insurance – essential for vans and trucks carrying goods, but also for private cars used in association with the business, for odd deliveries, visits to suppliers or customers, or for carrying tools or work-related equipment.

- Health Insurance: private health insurance can provide a way to prompt treatment in private clinics, by-passing the National Health Service waiting lists. Good, but very expensive for better levels of treatment. The extent of cover is restricted in the lower bands. Health savings schemes are very cheap, and offer cash payments for periods of hospitalisation, and other medical expenses.

- Accident or long-term disability insurance is designed to provide a pension-type income for people who become permanently disabled or unable to work as a result of serious illness or injury. Quite expensive for a good level of cover, but pay-outs only begin 6 months after the illness starts, and premiums have to be maintained in the meantime. Existing health problems are usually ineligible for consideration.

- Key Person Insurance is often required by banks when loans are made to partnerships. Apart from picking up lots of commission on the insurance premiums, this insurance is often linked to the loans so that the bank loans are automatically repaid if one partner dies. The other purpose of this is that it enables the surviving partner in a partnership, to buy out the share of the deceased partner, if the deceased's estate should require it. It can also be taken out on people whose expertise or abilities are key to the profitability of a business, and upon whose death the business would suffer financial loss.

- Life Assurance – worth having to cover the value of any loans or liabilities of a business if the proprietor dies, to protect the inheritors of his or her estate. This can take the form of Term Assurance – flat rate payments for flat rate cover, with no payback at the end of the period. Term-with-Profits insurance gives the life cover but for an additional premium pays back a lump sum at the end of the period of cover. Endowment policies are a longer-term savings-related form of life cover. Premiums are higher, but so are end-of-term pay-outs if you survive the term.

- Private Pension Plans are not insurance at all, but must be mentioned in the context of life insurance and personal financial planning. They are increasingly essential for anyone who is self-employed, and whose state benefits are therefore likely to be reduced. Tax relief can also be claimed against the pension contributions by people who are self-employed. Small firms employing more than five staff are now legally obliged to make arrangements for employees to have access to a stakeholder pension if a company pension scheme is not operated. At present employers are not obliged to contribute towards stakeholder pensions, but with the likely raising of the compulsory retirement age and the poorer performance of share-based pension schemes combined with loss of certain tax reliefs since 1997, then as state pensions become less affordable it seems inevitable that employers will be forced to contribute in the future.

■ Combined policies – often called Shopkeeper's policies – are special insurance packages for various sectors of business. For example, a Hairdresser's policy might cover a core package of Employer's Liability, Public Liability, Professional Indemnity, and Theft and damage to equipment, linked together for a very competitive premium. There is also the option of extending the cover beyond the core parts for additional premiums.

Finally, Insurance Brokers deserve a mention, as a means of obtaining fairly objective advice, and normally very competitive quotes for business insurance. They earn their income (from the insurance companies, not from their clients) by matching the policies to their clients' needs and pockets. In recent years they have been hard-hit by the growth of direct insurance over the telephone, but for small firms with widely varying insurance needs they can provide an efficient and cost-effective means of searching the insurance market for the right policy. Most of them are also small businesses too!

Physical resources

As stated above, premises and physical resource requirements are often interdependent. This section examines the ranges of physical resources which may be required to operate a business, plant and equipment, furniture, office machines and computers, stock, delivery vehicles, etc., and the way these are purchased from suppliers and financed, the timing of their acquisition, and the control systems used to monitor them. It also relates to contracts of supply with public utilities which may be different from those encountered in a domestic situation. This will enable the reader to identify the range of physical resources which are likely to be relevant to his or her business in the early stages, to quantify these, and to estimate their costs, to identify potential suppliers, and the timing for acquisition. The resulting data will provide much of the information required to compile the budgetary forecast and cash flow forecasts for the first year of operation of the new business.

When people first start to think about the physical resources that they will be required to start their businesses there is usually a tendency to underestimate both the range of items required, and the full cost of these. It is only when the likely full cost is realised that the same people start to ask themselves which items are really necessary as opposed to nice to have. The process also raises further questions about which items are need right from the onset of trading and which could be acquired out of profits as the business grows. In some cases it will be far cheaper to use existing resources which may also be available in the home, e.g. do you really need a brand new computer for word processing, or will the old one at home do the job for the first few months?

Similarly, when looking at office furniture, e.g. the new stuff may look impressive to customers, but if cash is short, then it may be worth looking at second-hand alternatives which can still be of good quality and appearance, but which are often much cheaper. If the furniture is not in public view, it does not really matter anyway, so long as the furniture or equipment is functional and comfortable to use. The same principle applies to vehicles, as often it is cheaper to buy a two-year old van which still has a good potential life span, but for which someone else has already born the cost of the substantial depreciation in value during the first year or so.

The important lesson to remember here is that without adequate working capital the business will struggle to get off the ground. If too much of your capital is tied up in resources which are not all in immediate or full use, then working capital may be tight, cash flow problems will arise, and the business will be fighting to survive before it has even had the chance to become fully established. Equally however, we should not be sacrificing quality for the lowest price. As will be explained in Chapter 11, in the longer term a better quality but higher-priced component may work out cheaper if it reduces the cost of rejects and customer complaints.

How do we identify what physical resources are needed?

First, we need to identify the broad categories of the resources, e.g. transport, fixtures and fittings, plant and machinery, furniture and office equipment, resale stock, raw materials and components, and materials and consumables. Obviously the combination of the various groups will depend on the nature and complexity of the business. A manufacturing business will probably need most of these, except for resale stock, whilst a retailer or wholesaler will need to buy stock, but will have no use for raw materials or components, whereas a mobile hairdresser will probably only need some basic transport and equipment.

The second stage is to brainstorm and list all of the physical resources which could conceivably be required, and to sift through them eliminating those which might be nice to have at some point in the future, but which would not be essential for the first year of trading. Sorry, but the bright red Ferrari really must wait if what you really need is a delivery van! The remainder can be sorted under three headings: Already available, essential to purchase for start-up, and buy during first year.

The third stage is to go through the list and to allocate realistic prices or costs to each item. These will be used to feed into the budgetary plan and cash flow forecasts described in Chapter 10. The planned acquisitions can be phased over the first year according either to how soon they are needed, or when sufficient profit is generated to pay for them. Minor items will probably be paid for at the time of purchase, but for major items of capital expenditure like machinery or vehicles, decisions must be made about how these will be financed. The need to obtain and repay loans to buy equipment, or the payment of hire-purchase deposits and the subsequent phasing of payments for plant or vehicles, must also be accurately reflected in the budgetary plan and cash flow forecast. Some of the sources of funds and various options for financing the purchase of resources are also discussed in Chapter 10.

Transport

The selection of vehicles required will depend not just on the type of goods or services which are being produced, but on the distribution channels and the relative locations of the customers. If your goods are being sold on to wholesalers who trade them on to a retail network, then large articulated delivery trucks might be the most appropriate form of transport. For the wholesalers themselves, a medium sized truck, e.g. 7-tonnes, which can access narrower roads to reach the retailers. This size of vehicle is popular because it is not regarded as being a full Heavy Goods Vehicle, and can be driven on an ordinary driving licence in the UK. If the customers are concentrated in a fairly tight area, or if access is a problem, or if the goods are not too heavy, then vans with a payload of 1000–1800 kg are a better option, and unlike the 7-tonne options these do not even need to have a tachograph fitted. The choice of the type of vehicle and its payload or size is basically an operational one, but the decision to buy new or second hand, or to lease or buy, will be determined by available working capital, interest rates on finance, and the availability of the vehicles.

The same really applies to cars, as the type of car (estate or saloon) will be determined by what it has to carry functionally, the engine size by the fuel consumption and type of driving involved (local or long-distance) and they are by what the owner-manager can afford. For example, a mobile hairdresser working locally might need an estate car or hatchback for ease of transporting equipment, and being local, a small economical engine would be fine, and it would not matter too much if the car were to be a few years old, so long as it was reliable. In contrast, if you were buying a car for a sales person to drive long-distances around the country, you would almost certainly pick something new or nearly new for purposes of reliability. This may possibly be a saloon car so that samples could be kept out of sight locked securely in the boot, and with a 1.6, 1.8 or 2.0 litre engine giving sufficient power for comfortable distance driving, but without excessive fuel consumption.

Remember, when budgeting for vehicles, do not just think in terms of the costs of acquiring them, but allow for running costs such as road tax, insurance, MOT tests, repairs and maintenance, etc., and build them into the budgetary plan accordingly.

Fixtures and fittings

These are essentially the items within the premises which are attached to the structure, or which are necessary to the production of the goods or services, but not directly involved in their creation or provision. In terms of fittings we are talking about things like lighting and heating systems, electricity or water supply, telephones, sinks, toilets, etc. which have been fitted to the premises to make them habitable. It may be when moving into new premises that these are inadequate or need to be replaced or repaired. Perhaps extra power points are needed in the office, or the water supply has to be extended, or new toilets built for additional staff. When considering these, you should think also of the installation costs as well as the purchase cost of the materials.

When we talk of fixtures, we are normally referring to items such as safety rails, storage or racking systems, lifting equipment, mezzanine floors, etc. which have been fitted or installed within the building, to facilitate the operation of the business. What fixtures do you need for immediate use, and what additions will be required as the business grows? Is it cheaper to install the whole lot from the out set or is this beyond the capital currently available? If you take out a loan for the additional requirements, will the savings on installation costs and later disruption to your business, outweigh the arrangement fee and interest payments on the loan? With storage facilities, we should also be checking that not only are they of adequate size or capacity to meet current and forthcoming needs, but they are capable of being used in such a way to ensure proper stock rotation to avoid waste and additional expense. This includes ensuring that the environmental conditions, such as temperature and humidity, are suitable for the goods in storage.

Plant and machinery

There are many issues to be considered here, all of which will have a financial implication for budgets and cash flow. What essential plant or machinery is required to manufacture your products or processes? Do you have any of this, or can it be bought second hand? If it is very specialised, will there be a long lead-time for delivery? Will it take time to install and commission before becoming fully operational? Will the premises need to be modified to take it? Will you also need to maintain a supply of tools and spare parts for the machinery, and employ staff to maintain it? Will you need to make a substantial down payment when ordering it? How will you finance the period between ordering and becoming fully operational?

This heading not only includes things like production machinery, but items used in materials handling such as pallet trucks or fork-lifts, weighing, packaging and labelling equipment, pumps, cranes, lifts and pulleys, conveyor belts and rollers, power tools, and hand-held equipment. There are also implications for insurance and the safe and secure storage of some of these items, particularly if they are valuable and easily moved (or removed).

Furniture and office equipment

This category will include not just the items within any management or administrative offices, but also the carpets, easy chairs, display material that may be located in a reception area for visiting customers; and of course the tea and coffee cups, kettle, toaster, or microwave oven for staff use.

Within an office we are talking about items such as desks, chairs, filing cabinets, storage cupboards, computers or word processors, a safe or petty cash tin, telephones, fax machines and answering machines, franking machines, cleaning equipment, and the multitude of minor items such as staplers, hole punches, rosaries, and stress-busting toys. These are the things that are most often taken for granted or under-estimated when planning a new business, and when compounded, their total costs can be quite high. They do however, include items which the aspiring owner-manager may already possess.

Resale stock

Anyone involved in wholesaling or retailing will need to identify what stock has to be held at any one time. There will of course need to be a purchase of opening stock, and an on-going holding of a reasonable level of core stock – those items that will be in constant demand. The costs of buying this opening and core stock have to be built in to the budgetary plan. As stock is sold, more is bought in to replace it and to replenish stock levels, and as the business grows, so the average level of stock held may need to be increased. This can have implications for both storage space and equipment and for the availability of adequate working capital to fund the additional stock holding.

The frequency with which stock can be replenished, and the minimum order or delivery size from suppliers may also impact both on the need for storage space, and on the required levels of working capital. For example, a supplier based at some distance may only make periodic deliveries so either larger volumes of the stock items have to be held, or the retailer may have to pay additional carriage costs for intermediate deliveries. Some suppliers only offer free delivery where the order is above a certain minimum value, and others relate discount levels to the size of the order. Here the free savings from free delivery and better discount rates have to be weighed against having extra working capital tied up in stock, and the space which that stock is occupying.

Raw materials and components

This is a similar situation to the purchase and holding of stock for resale, only the initial purchase costs may be relatively larger, particularly if credit is given to distributors or customers. There is a need to buy an initial opening stock of raw materials and components, and whilst these are being turned into the finished product, further raw materials and components will need to be ordered to replace them. The wider the range of products offered, the greater the range of stock items will be, as will be the cost of buying them; and once again as the business expands, so usually does the need to increase the average levels of stock holding. Depending on the source of raw materials and components, there could be implications for delivery lead times, especially if components have to be shipped from the far Eastern countries that usually constitute one of the cheapest potential sources of supply.

Once again, the initial costs of buying the raw materials and components have to be realistically estimated, and the costs built into the budgetary plan and cash flow forecast for the business. The process would normally include identifying the various alternative suppliers, the range and quality of their respective products, and their costs, discount structures and terms and conditions of trade. For example, given that product quality and basic cost of a component are the same from each of the two suppliers, it may be that the extra 2% discount offered by one is more than offset by the extra 30-days' credit offered by the other, if working capital is freed for use elsewhere. If however, the discount were much larger, then it might pay the business to borrow money from the bank to pay for the components, as the costs of borrowing would be outweighed by the extra profit generated by the better profit margins. This is the sort of cost-benefit analysis that a bank manager will appreciate, and will normally be willing to accommodate. If adequate working capital is available, and interest rates are not excessive, then cash discounts beat credit terms any day!

Materials and consumables

These are the items which are purchased, used and replaced on a fairly regular basis as part of the administration or running of the business. In the office they would include stationery, envelopes, postage, computer disks, and printer ribbons, etc., and probably the tea, coffee, milk, and sugar. In the working areas it might include the provision of protective clothing, safety wear, or uniforms. In the business as a whole it would cover things like first aid materials, cleaning materials, disinfectants, paper towels, toilet paper, light bulbs, the costs of a window cleaner, etc. In a large organisation they would probably be accounted for under different headings, but in a small firm's accounts they might well be grouped together as "miscellaneous and admin expenses". The accounting classification is less important than the fact that they should be identified and included in the budgetary plan and cash flow forecast, because although they are all quite minor items of expenditure, when aggregated and taken over a year, they can amount to a noticeable sum.

Public utilities

By these we mean the suppliers of electricity, gas, telephones, water supply, sewage disposal, and waste disposal services. Most of us are familiar with these organisations through our own domestic contact with them, but it is worth mentioning them in a commercial context as they are able to offer business customers more flexibility and competitive prices in some cases. Now that the supply of gas and electricity has been privatised and is now controlled by overseas-owned monopolies as opposed to the former local state owned monopolies (i.e. the former regional gas and electricity boards) business users can often negotiate much more favourable terms of supply than were previously available. This is particularly relevant to those businesses with a large and regular or predictable demand. As the supply of North Sea gas and oil starts to run out over the next 10 years, gas and electricity prices will inevitably rise, so it will pay to give careful thought to levels of energy consumption when acquiring premises, or when purchasing vehicles or plant and machinery.

Telephone and broadband services are now available from a range of providers at competitive rates, using conventional systems and cable networks. The systems providers can be highly competitive on price, and efficient in installation, although problems of inter-organisational co-operation can often occur at the point where the various systems interface with each other, causing delays. These delays can be more critical for high-tech companies, or those relying on the Internet and e-mail marketing and communications. There are still some rural locations where broadband cover is not yet available, so do check on this if broadband internet connection is essential for your business.

In most parts of the UK the same water companies provide both water supply and sewage disposal services, for a single charge. In commercial premises this may be linked to the size according to rateable value, or more frequently to water metres installed on the premises. In some parts of the UK the water and sewage functions are provided by separate organisations, typically the small local water supply companies, and the former regional water and drainage authorities. In these cases the charges are divided, although where water metres are installed, the supply company will usually pass on details of volumes used to the drainage authority.

What business users do need to be aware of, is the fact that businesses which use high volumes of water as part of their production process, or where wastewater may be polluted, e.g. breweries and the paper industry, have a loading applied to their sewage disposal charges to cover the cost of re-processing the wastewater. For a new business these loadings may be imposed on an arbitrary basis, without actually testing the degree of pollution of the wastewater. For example, when running a small brewery some years ago, I found that the metered water supply figures were passed on to the drainage authority. The latter allowed a 5% reduction for evaporation, but levied a 20% loading for contaminated waste. After challenging the loading and submitting several samples of wastewater, the loading was reduced to 10%, and the allowance was increased to 30% on the basis that a fair proportion, having been consumed as beer, was recycled through someone else's sewer. It may sound a small thing to make a fuss about, but in fact it cut the annual sewage bill by almost 40%, and when your product is 95% water that can amount to a large budget item over the course of a year.

Uniform business rates levied by local authorities have spiralled in recent years, and now constitute a significant overhead cost for most businesses. On the face of it, they don't actually buy you much apart from the access roads and site drainage, and even these may be subject to private maintenance for some business locations, although many local authorities do employ economic development staff to promote and support local enterprises. The council rates also no longer cover waste disposal unless you pay for it separately, and most firms now make private contractual arrangements with private operators who supply and empty bins on a regular basis. With the recent addition of taxes on landfill tipping, waste disposal is now becoming an expensive business, so allowance for this should be made in the budgetary plan, particularly if any of the waste products of your business are classed as dangerous or hazardous, e.g. poisons, oils, or toxic chemicals. Above all you should be attempting to minimise waste to reduce these additional costs to your business. The recycling of waste materials will gradually become a statutory requirement at some time in the next few years, and the collection and recycling of specified proportions of packaging materials by companies that manufacture or distribute packaged products is already compulsory in the UK.

It is important to remember that the public utilities are now mostly privatised, and you are one of their potential customers. They no longer have a monopoly control over the market, and they themselves now have to answer to watchdogs such as Ofwat and Oftel. Don't be afraid to challenge them or to ask for better terms.

Supplier relationships

As a final note to this chapter, it is worth remembering several key points in dealing and negotiating with your suppliers:

- Your suppliers are just as much entitled to make a reasonable profit as you are. Don't be afraid to push them for a bit more when the time is right, but respect their position if they turn you down. They almost certainly still want your trade, but not at any price. Sometimes when a customer pushes too hard, you just have to walk away from the business if it is not worthwhile.
- The objective in dealing with suppliers should be to develop a long-term, honest and reliable relationship that will ensure continued supply of quality goods or services at a mutually acceptable price. Suppliers should be treated as stakeholders in your business just as you would treat your customers, the bank manager, or your accountant. They have an interest in the profitability and survival of your firm, just as you have in theirs, in that both businesses need each other as part of the supply chain to the end user. The cheapest price from a supplier is not always accompanied by best quality and reliable products, and long-term continuity of supply can be just as important to your business. It also pays to keep in regular contact with them, not only to find out about new products or opportunities, but also to talk about any trends or changes in the market place which might affect you both.
- If you have cash flow problems, don't lie to your suppliers or ignore their calls. They are not stupid and they can read the signs as well as you can. Be honest, contact them promptly and tell them about the problem, ask for their co-operation, and give them a firm and realistic date for payment, then honour it. If you can, then make a payment on account in the interim period, to show your goodwill. Sometime later it may be your supplier with a similar problem asking for a prompt or early payment, in which case if you can afford it, then help him out. This is what building long-term business relationships is all about, and it will do you no harm at all when a bank or another supplier asks you for a trade reference!
- Although price is important, it is not the only area for negotiation with suppliers. If the supplier is unwilling or unable to improve discounts or prices as the volume of your purchases increase, then look for alternatives, and be imaginative. Can you

get better payment terms, e.g. a longer period of credit, or a higher credit limit? Is there some advantage to you in varying delivery arrangements, such as weekly instead of fortnightly to reduce the levels of stock that you need to hold? Will the supplier contribute to some of your marketing costs, e.g. by paying towards the cost of a trade exhibition, sharing advertising costs, or by giving you some point of sale material or free samples for your customers? These are the sorts of possibilities that will benefit both you and the supplier.

■ You should ensure that you have suitable monitoring systems in place to check on the quality of goods received, and that quantities, prices, discounts, etc. are correct. Any discrepancies should be recorded and notified to the suppliers immediately. You can't realistically expect your suppliers to take responsibility for problems with goods which have been out of their hands for any length of time, so by reporting problems promptly you can avoid potential disputes. Again, be honest with them and don't try to rip them off by claiming more than is properly due. If your suppliers regard you as being fair to them, then they will tend to treat you fairly in future, and they will be more likely to respond to a request for help when you have a problem, or need an urgent delivery.

Further reading

Barrow, C., Brown, R., Burke, G. and Molian, D. (2005). *Enterprise Development*. Thompson, Harlow.

Bragg, A. and Bragg, M. (2005). *Developing New Business Ideas*. FT Prentice Hall, London.

CHAPTER 9

Recruiting and employing staff

Many people whom are setting up a new business already have the technical and product knowledge which will enable them to produce or provide their goods or services. A smaller proportion of them will also have acquired some basic sales or marketing skills along the way. Some may also have been involved with staff management and supervision, including the recruitment and selection process. Normally, however, unless they have worked for a relatively small organisation, they will have relied on the advice and support of a personnel specialist to guide them through the legal nightmare of the recruitment, selection, and employment legalities and processes. Even before the advent of the European Union, this was not a matter for the faint-hearted, but nowadays, the legal requirements and obligations demand an extensive and detailed knowledge of the subject to avoid the risk of being caught out and falling foul of the law just by overlooking the smallest of details. This may sound like bad news, but quite simply, employing people is now becoming a hazardous and difficult procedure that many small firms try to avoid. In spite of repeated government boasts about how small firms will be the employment growth area of the future, if the costs of employing staff and the red tape involved are allowed to become disproportionate to the benefits, then small firms will either avoid employing staff or just employ the bare minimum, which defeats the government policy; or they will employ people in the grey economy by paying them cash. The latter situation is the most problematic because not only does it deprive the government of revenue, it is almost certain that people employed illegally will not receive normal employment benefits (holidays, sick pay, etc.) but are also likely to be working under unsafe or unsuitable conditions.

The imposition of the European Social Chapter and various directives relating to working hours, minimum wages, leave entitlement, etc. actually mean that employing staff is becoming an increasing nightmare in the UK, and yet in comparison with mainland Europe, the UK is still perceived as relatively employer-friendly in that the government taxes on employees (National Insurance Contributions, etc.) are still much lower in the UK than in France or Germany. This is clearly evidenced by the sheer number of enquiries in recent years to Kent-based Chambers of Commerce and Enterprise Agencies, from continental companies who still see the UK as a cheaper and more attractive option in employment terms, compared with employing staff in France or Germany where national insurance rates are over 40%, and where sacking even the most unsuitable of staff can be a costly and difficult process, unless compensation is paid to terminate contracts of employment.

This chapter links to Chapter 7 where aspects of employment law are considered, and also to Chapter 16 where the subject is revisited in the context of planning staff requirements to facilitate growth.

Politics and Europhobia aside, the objective of Chapter 9 is to examine how to assess the personnel requirements of a business in its early stages, and how to go about the process of selecting, and recruiting suitable staff. We have already examined the processes of identifying the key skills needs of the business in Chapter 5, along with the personal skills and capabilities of the business proprietors. Where the skills of the owner-managers are either inadequate to meet the full range required, or where to utilise them would not be cost-effective (e.g. the owner-manager should not be typing letters or filing instead of selling the products or planning production), then it is appropriate to consider employing alternative staff. If we consider the primary objectives of the business, then the owner-managers' efforts should be focussed on these, and should not be spent on more mundane administrative matters, which can be delegated to less-expensive staff, who will probably do the job better anyway! Once we have carried out a skills audit to determine questions of what skills or staff the business really needs, then if those needs cannot be filled internally by delegation of staff development, then it will be necessary to employ someone for that purpose.

Aside from the various legal and health and safety implications of employing staff, especially once the firm employs more than five, there is the issue of cost, not just of the basic salary, but additional costs of recruitment, training, holidays and sickness, maternity (and now paternity) cover, pensions, National Insurance Contributions, etc.; and of course the risk of employment tribunals if you don't get it right! It is not surprising therefore that many owner-managers, particularly at the start-up stage, will try to avoid employing anyone. The other issue is that as soon as you start paying staff, the working capital requirements of the business increases, and at the start-up stage this is not always affordable until the firm starts to make a profit.

The first of a number of questions which we must be asking is whether of not we really need to be employing staff. Do we have to employ them directly, or could we make use of casual, temporary or agency staff, who may or may not be as reliable and productive as a permanent member of staff? Can we afford to pay the wages on a regular basis? Will the extra staff generate enough income to cover their costs, or will they release the owner-manager to spend more time working to produce extra profit? Will employing staff push up other overhead costs, such as insurance, protective clothing? Will there be a need for extra expenditure on furniture, machinery or equipment for them to use? Will there be enough work to keep them fully occupied? Can they be trusted in the owner-manager's absence? What will be the costs to the business or the effects on profit if they are not employed, e.g. will contracts be lost? How difficult or costly will it be to get rid of them if things go wrong? How soon will they be needed? What induction, training or supervision will be needed, and will this interrupt other work? So, assuming therefore that we have already identified the nature of the skills deficit, and then asked and answered these important questions then we can start to look at the process of recruiting staff, and the further implications for the business.

The first implication of employing staff is the extra time and cost involved in meeting statutory requirements. In addition to the legal requirement to take out employer's liability insurance, once staff are employed there is the need to set up and maintain a PAYE (pay as you earn) system, to deduct income tax and National Insurance Contributions from the employees' pay, and to remit these to the inland revenue on a monthly basis. In addition to the deductions from pay, the employer must also pay an employers' National Insurance Contribution, currently 12.8% of employees' pay, but subject to change in the Chancellor's annual budget. Staff are also entitled to be paid for holidays, sickness, and maternity leave; and whilst away from work, other temporary staff still have to be paid to cover the absence. In addition to the financial implications, there are, as we have seen in Chapter 7, legal implications in terms of health and safety which have to be met, particularly once more than five staff are employed in the business. In the early stages of a new business there may only be a need for one or two employees, but as the business expands and extra staff are taken on, the legal implications can easily be overlooked, particularly if the owner-manager is not familiar with employment law or procedures. The significance of this may not be immediately obvious, but a year or two down the line, when the employees are protected from unfair dismissal, etc. an over-looked issue may turn into an expensive industrial tribunal. It is important, therefore, that when staff are employed, their job descriptions and terms and conditions of employment should be clearly defined.

Of all of the resources utilised within a business, staff tend to be the least reliable in terms of the return they offer on the time and money invested in them, especially from the owner-manager's perspective. When a manager buys a piece of production machinery, the capital cost and expected annual running and maintenance costs are known, as well as the expected productive lifetime of the machinery. Unfortunately people are less predictable. The cost of recruiting staff can be high, and there is always an initial period of inefficiency when they are training or learning the job. Staff also have the annoying and inconvenient tendencies to fall sick, to want holidays, to become pregnant, or to leave for better pay elsewhere, and usually at the most inconvenient times for the owner! Is it any wonder then, that manufacturing industries prefer to use robotic systems on their production lines? Whoever heard of a robot suffering from PMT or taking an afternoon off for a football match or to go fishing? Seriously though, it is often hard to find staff who are willing to work hard and be committed to the business, and sometimes even harder to keep them, unless reward structures are sufficiently attractive. Levels of commitment and motivation in staff are invariably linked to remuneration and reward – if you pay peanuts, you get monkeys, and the monkeys will soon move off to join someone else who is offering more peanuts. A business which has a continuous turnover of disaffected staff will never reach its full potential level of efficiency or profitability, and will certainly suffer problems in achieving consistent standards of product quality and customer care. What owner-managers often forget is that their staff also have lives of their own, and should not be automatically expected to offer the same level of effort and dedication to the business as the owner-manager does, particularly if they are not well rewarded, or if their efforts are not appreciated.

To reiterate, recruiting, and training staff is an expensive and time-consuming process and in order for the investment in time and money to be recouped, it is essential to define most carefully the nature of the job and the type of person required. The recruitment and selection process should be a two-way situation. On the one hand it must be carried out objectively to match the candidates with the job requirements. On the other hand the remuneration package of the job itself, and the terms and conditions of employment, must be sufficiently attractive to the candidates to stimulate their initial interest in the job and to retain their services in the longer term. In this respect we are talking about job satisfaction and organisational culture as well as pay and conditions, as contributing to staff retention. For some people, high wages will adequately compensate for unpleasant conditions, over-bearing management and boring work, whereas others will tolerate low pay for interesting work in a friendly environment.

The process itself typically falls into three stages:

1. Defining the requirements – the job description, person specification, and the terms and conditions of employment.
2. Attracting the candidates – considering the use of internal promotion, training and development of existing staff, or advertising for external candidates; and then choosing and implementing the most suitable means of finding candidates.
3. The selection process – sifting the applications, short-listing, carrying out interviews, choosing the candidates, checking references, and making an offer of appointment.

In the case of new small businesses, this process tends to be somewhat simplified, firstly because there are rarely any internal candidates to consider for training or promotion, and secondly because new owner-managers seldom have the suitable skills or the time to spare for a full-blown recruitment and selection process. Unfortunately this can often result in the selection of candidates who may be less than ideal, especially if the job description of person specifications have not been produced carefully.

The job description

Once the decision has been made to employ a new member of staff, the first step must be to prepare a job description for the vacant position, which involves defining the scope, role, and responsibilities of the job. Obviously, the precise content of the job description will vary according to the complexity of the job, and the levels of responsibility involved, but it might typically include:

- The job title and location.
- The grade or salary range.
- The position in the organisation structure, and to whom the person is responsible.
- The main duties, i.e. the primary tasks, key activities, and the purpose of the job or the objectives the post-holder is expected to achieve.

- The main responsibilities, e.g. staff supervision, budget-holding, functional areas or processes.
- Supplementary duties, such as attending sales exhibitions, dealing with customer queries, health and safety, first-aid, or in a very small firm, making the tea or even taking a turn at cleaning the toilets!
- Special job features, e.g. the need for regular foreign travel or to deal with foreign customers, anti-social hours or shift-work.

The person specification

Whereas the job description was about the job itself, the person specification is about defining the characteristics, skills, and qualifications, etc. of the type of person who would be ideally suited to fill the job. Bearing in mind the person specification would have to be non-discriminatory and compliant with equal opportunities regulations, this might include:

- Age range, gender, or marital status (if relevant or appropriate, but beware of anti-discrimination laws).
- Essential qualifications and experience.
- Essential skills, e.g. experience of managing staff or budgets, or specific technical knowledge or expertise.
- Desirable skills, e.g. the use of specific computer applications, possession of further qualifications, fluency in foreign languages.
- Physical health, if, e.g. the work involves heavy lifting or manual work.
- Essential behavioural competencies such as the ability to work closely with a team of other people, or to negotiate with customers.
- Desirable behavioural competencies such as a friendly disposition, sense of humour (especially if the pay is low!) or willingness to travel abroad at short notice, if needed.

Terms and conditions of employment

These must comply with legislation relating to contracts of employment, and would normally include:

- The job title.
- The duties, main and secondary, locations of work, flexibility, and requirements to travel.

- Commencement date of continuous employment. This is important for the calculation of annual leave, statutory sick pay, maternity pay, and statutory redundancy pay entitlements, and to the dates after which the laws relating to unfair dismissal apply.
- Rates of pay (hourly, weekly, monthly, annual salary, etc.) and methods of payment, e.g. cash paid weekly on each Friday, by monthly bank transfer on 28th of month.
- Holiday or leave entitlements.
- Sickness arrangements, e.g. where the employer offers sick pay above and beyond the statutory requirements.
- The period of notice to terminate employment by either party, and any specific variations of this arrangement, e.g. suspension or summary dismissal for theft, violence, or gross negligence.
- Arrangements for termination of employment, such as the return of vehicles or equipment, confidential information, or special arrangements such as "garden leave" for sales staff moving to competitor organisations to avoid possible poaching of customers or theft of customer information during period of notice.
- Health and safety/discipline and grievance procedures – usually reference is made to standard organisational procedures, copies of which are supplied to the new employee on starting. In the case of new small firms, with less than five staff, these may not yet have been prepared.
- Workplace rules are not so much statutory regulations, as standards and procedures which are used within the workplace, e.g. standards of hygiene, no smoking rules, flexitime operation, logging of telephone messages and incoming mail, standards of dress when interfacing with the public, etc.
- Trade union status or recognition – whether or not the organisation recognises trade union or has negotiating arrangements with them.
- Special terms relating to inventions, patents, copyrights, etc. for products or materials developed in the firm's time, these will normally belong to the employer firm and not the employee, unless special arrangements to the contrary have been made.
- Variations to contract – at the end of just about everyone's contract or employment there is a section which prescribes for variations to be made to the contract of employment, subject to a reasonable period of notice to the employee, etc.

Advertising the position

Internal promotion is always an option worth considering, and not just from the viewpoint of "better the devil you know". Existing staff are more familiar with the firm and its products and customers, internal recruitment is good for staff motivation (apart perhaps from the one who didn't get the job!), and the process is cheaper and less time-consuming. However, as mentioned above, in most new small businesses there will simply be no existing internal candidates to be considered for promotion or for training and development, so looking elsewhere is the only available option.

So, how do we go about finding suitable applicants? The first choice to be made is whether to pay someone else to do it, or to do it ourselves. Advertising agencies have great expertise in designing and preparing adverts, and selecting the right places to advertise, but they also tend to have great fees, and the potential success is still largely dependant on the detail and quality of the requirements specified by the client. Similarly, recruitment agencies have a great deal of expertise in finding and sifting potential applicants for short-listing, but they tend to charge between 20% and 25% of the first year's salary as their fee, which is not so good if the new recruit leaves soon after. Once again the usefulness of their results is also largely dependant on the depth and quality of the briefing by their client. In short, if you give them a poor job description and person specification, you cannot blame them if they do not come up with the right candidates for the job.

The other alternative then, is to do the advertising ourselves. For the newcomer to this type of advertising, unless he or she has skills in desktop publishing or computer graphics, it may pay to get some assistance, particularly to ensure compliance with anti-discrimination laws. Some basic knowledge of designing adverts, the use of logos, bold wording, margins and white-space, etc., can make a big difference to the impact of the advert on the readers. A recruitment advert should be treated the same as an advert for the firm's products or services, as it needs to catch the reader's attention and to prompt a response or action. Very often, the advertising staff at local newspapers can provide this as a service to clients. If given the basic job information along with a company logo and details, etc. they will design the advert for an additional fee. Subsequent advertising then becomes less-costly as the basic artwork is already available. Assuming then, that we have some basic idea of what we want to include in the advert, where should we place it, or where else can we find our suitable candidates?

For a fairly straightforward vacancy involving no specialist skills or expertise, a vacancy notice outside of the firm's premises, a card in the local newsagent's window, of the local job centre all offer very low-cost options for finding staff at fairly short notice. As the level of necessary skills increases, then so does the importance of finding the right place to advertise. Local newspapers, particularly if they are part of a regional group, can reach a large readership in a concise geographical area, at a reasonable cost. Just how wide you advertise will depend on how far you think your staff will realistically be prepared to travel. For staff with high levels of skills or specialised qualifications and experience, it may well be necessary to consider advertising on a national basis, or in specialist trade magazines or journals, e.g. the Times Educational Supplement, the Engineer, the Architects Journal, or the Caterer magazine. Of course, advertising on a national basis has implications for the cost of interviews, the possible need for new staff to relocate, and the time-scale in which the vacancy can be filled. Specialist staff are also likely to cost more, and to attract special remuneration packages to retain them, which takes us back to the earlier option of whether or not it is worth promoting or training internal staff, and recruiting local replacements to fill their vacant posts.

Summarising then:

- The method of advertising will be largely determined by the nature of the vacancy, and the local availability.
- The advert must be designed to attract attention, create interest, and to stimulate action and response from potential candidates. Applicants expect to be supplied with basic information about the job, the salary, the location, and the employer organisation. If the information is insufficient, then you may loose some good potential applicants. If you are unsure of how to design the advert, then it is worth getting experienced help or advice, even if you have to pay for it.
- The advert should tell the potential candidates precisely what action is needed and by when. For example, you should state clearly whether application forms will be provided for completion and return, or if applicants should send a *curriculum vitae* and letter of application. You should also state the closing date for applications, and if you do not intend to write to all applicants after that date, you should state in the advert, the date by which applications will have been unsuccessful unless otherwise notified. This is both fair to the applicants and sensible from your perspective, otherwise, not only will your credibility as a potential employer fall in the eyes of some applicants, but there will be a proportion who will keep ringing up to find out about the progress of their applications.

- Once the advert is written, check for compliance with anti-discrimination legislation, etc. and again, if in doubt, seek advice.
- When the advert has been printed, measure the responses in terms of number of enquiries and applications, and the resulting cost per enquiry and per application. This will give you a yardstick against which you can measure the efficacy of future advertising, particularly if you have advertised in more than one publication.

Sifting and selecting the applicants

It is not uncommon these days to receive several hundred applications for one job, particularly if there is an attractive salary, and it is when we start to sift through all of these applications, that the usefulness of the job description and person specifications really comes through. The process of sifting is quite straightforward, although it can be time-consuming if there are many applications to read and process:

- If there are a lot of applications, then list them on a control sheet or database using a basic name and reference number, with space for a grading and comments.
- Discard immediate non-starters, e.g. those who have ignored basic instructions, e.g. by sending a *curriculum vitae* in place of your application form, or without the required covering letter, or with beer stains all over the application (and yes, it does happen!).
- Provisionally grade the applicants by one or two key criteria defined in the job description/person specification, e.g. essential qualifications and experience. Sort them into Possibles – the long-list, Marginals – the reserve list, and Unsuitables – which are rejected.
- Compare the Possibles with further selection criteria to produce a short-list of likely candidates. If the list is sufficient then reject the reserves and if it is insufficient then re-examine the reserves. If the reserves are still inadequate then either something has gone wrong with the advertising process (the advert itself, or where it was placed), or you are simply not offering the right package to attract the calibre of applicants you require, or even both of these.
- Start the interview process using the short-list, which will hopefully produce a suitable applicant. If not, go back over

your long-list. If this is also inadequate, you've made a pig's ear of it all, and its back to square one! So, where did you go wrong? Try to identify any mistakes that have been made, and review the alternatives.

Methods of selection

There are a whole host of various methods employed by larger organisations to select staff, including psychometric testing, personality questionnaires, 3-day assessment centres, interview panels, aptitude or intelligence tests, handwriting analysis, "informal" buffet lunches, selection boards, bio-data questionnaires, team-skills activities, etc. All of these may be great fun to design or organise, but for the owner-manager every one of them is either time-consuming or costly if carried out by someone else, and therefore detracts from the owner-manager's primary objective of keeping the business profitable to ensure survival and growth. So, for the majority of small firms, the obvious answer is to use the more conventional tried and tested options of one-to-one interviews supported by references. Even when very specific technical skills are involved, with a little preliminary guidance and advice, the owner-manager can normally find out ways of checking if the candidates have the necessary skills during the interview process. But one of the biggest advantages of face-to-face interviews is that it gives both parties the opportunity to ask themselves the question "Can I really work with this person?" and for the owner-manager who is now in the role of the customer or buyer: "Will this person fit in with my business, and will they create the right image with my customers?".

However, although interviews are probably the most practical form of selection for a small business, for an owner-manager who has never carried out an interview before, the process can be as harrowing for them, as for the person being interviewed. How then can we make the process more easy to manage and less frightening?

Interviewing staff

The whole process of interviewing becomes less fraught if it is well planned and organised, and if we follow some simple basic guidelines, e.g. before the interviews take place, the interviewer should:

- Give the candidates adequate notice of the time and date, with clear directions of where to go, and with details of overnight accommodation if needed.

- Tell them where to park and if possible, make sure that there is space for them. On arrival, ensure that someone greets them, tells them where to wait, and where to find the toilets. Ideally, offer them a cup of tea or coffee, and sit them somewhere in private where they will not be subject to the scrutiny of any other staff.
- Look at the room layout, avoid barriers between you and the candidates, and try to create an informal and relaxed layout. If you put the candidates at ease, they are more likely to open up in discussion.

During the interview process:

- Ensure that there are no interruptions from telephone calls or visitors. If necessary put the telephone on answer-service and leave a "do not disturb" notice on the door.
- Allow adequate time for each interview, and space between them to stretch your legs or to deal with any urgent calls. If you are using any tests or questionnaires, allow time for these to be completed, and time for them to be assessed before the candidates are interviewed.
- Plan the interview schedule to allow time for those travelling longer distances.
- Allow sufficient time for yourself, or any other interviewers, to read through the applications between each interview, to remind you about each candidate, and to highlight any specific questions you may wish to ask.
- When the candidate enters the room, introduce yourself and tell them briefly about your business, and about the job. Keep it fairly short, then ask any standard questions you may have prepared, and any specific questions relating to them individually.
- Invite the candidates to ask questions, encourage them to do the talking, and listen to their answers. Use open or probing questions to encourage them to express ideas and opinions. If you are unsure of the answer, revisit it later in another way. Use hypothetical questions to assess the candidate's responses to possible problems, and closed questions to clarify a point or fact. Above all, don't talk too much!
- Make notes of their answers and responses for later review.
- Finally, at the end of the interview, check that they are still interested in the job. Thank them for their time, and tell them when you will be making a decision and when you will notify them of the result.

After the interview:

- Review your notes, and consider some basic questions about them. Think about the impression they have created on you, and whether or not you would want the same impression created on your customers! Will they fit in with you, any other staff, and the way your business operates? Can they do the job you want them to do?
- Compare the candidates against the job description and person specification. Which applicant met the requirements more closely? Would they fit in with your business? Do they still want the job?
- Check on references, make your decision, notify the successful candidate and make them an offer. If he or she accepts the offer, then notify the unsuccessful candidates. Always keep your notes of the interviews for several weeks, in case any of the applicants want feedback on why they were unsuccessful, and if this is requested, keep it factual and objective. If your chosen applicant falls through, you may even wish to go back to one of the others.

Discipline and grievance procedures

Whereas most medium-sized and large organisations which can afford to employ specialist personnel staff, have written procedures for discipline and grievance, it is quite rare to find them in small firms, even though the risks and legal implications in terms of industrial tribunals and appeals, are the same. In fact the financial implications of a lost industrial tribunal, whilst they are an expensive nuisance to a big company, can be totally devastating to a small firm. Even winning a tribunal can still leave a business with hefty legal bills. It pays therefore, to think about having some simple form of discipline and grievance procedures if you are thinking of employing even just a few staff.

The Code of Disciplinary Practice and Procedures in Employment describes the three basic principles of natural justice on which the disciplinary process is based:

1. Individuals should know the standards of performance which they are expected to achieve, and the rules to which they must conform.
2. They should be told promptly and clearly of how and why they are breaking any rules, or failing to achieve the required standards.

3. They should be given adequate opportunity to improve before disciplinary action is taken, or dismissal is implemented.

When disciplinary action is taken, if the offence is serious, e.g. it relates to theft, violence or dangerous behaviour which constitutes a major risk to health or safety, then an employee can be suspended and sent home immediately pending dismissal. Otherwise it is normal to take a three-stage approach involving an initial verbal warning (although with details recorded on file), after which if there is no improvement, a formal verbal warning is given, usually with a letter which confirms the nature of the verbal warning. Finally, if the problem still persists, a formal written warning is given, with notification that further recurrence within a specified period of time will result in dismissal. The second and third stages are also recorded on file.

Grievance procedures tend to follow a similar pattern, depending on the size of the organisation. In the case of a complaint, every employee is entitled to a fair hearing within a reasonable period of time. In a very small firm this may just involve a straightforward discussion with the boss to resolve the problem, but in larger firms, it may involve successive appeals to higher levels of management through a standard procedure, e.g. supervisor, line manager, senior manager, or director. It may also involve colleagues, personnel staff, or trade union stewards, over a period of several days. In either case there has to be a cut-off point at which the process stops. It is always worth keeping a record of the process at each stage, on file, for later reference.

A large proportion of tribunals are based on dismissal, or more to the point, unfair dismissal. Dismissal by means of the formal period of notice, or upon expiry of contract is quite fair; but if, e.g. the employee is refused work after pregnancy, or is unjustifiably demoted, this may constitute constructive dismissal, which is illegal. Two key questions are asked by tribunals in these circumstances:

1. Was there sufficient reason for dismissal, i.e. was it fair or unfair?
2. Did the employer act reasonably or unreasonably in the circumstances?

When dealing with discipline or grievance issues, unless it is any area in which you have had previous experience, it is always worthwhile to invest in professional advice, e.g. from a human resources (HR) practitioner. The advice is not usually free but can save the risk of much larger bills resulting from industrial tribunals. There are some HR specialists who offer advice to small firms in return for a fixed annual or monthly payment.

Staff appraisal

There are still some hardened and cynical managers who regard it as regrettable that the P45 has been superseded as the primary form of staff appraisal, and there are still some staff around for whom it remains the most appropriate method. In the past two decades, staff appraisal systems have become almost universal within large- and medium-sized organisations, although formal systems are still relatively rare in very small businesses, apart from those which have implemented more formal quality systems such as Investors in People or International Standards Organisation (ISO) 9002; or where the owner-managers have come from larger businesses where appraisal was an accepted part of the organisational culture.

Appraisal is essentially a process of performance management. The basic principle is that every member of staff has a private and uninterrupted interview with their immediate superior or manager on a regular basis, e.g. annually or half-yearly. Prior to the interview, both parties will typically complete a form in which the manager reviews the performance of the staff member over the preceding period, and the staff member reviews their own performance over that same period. The two assessments are then compared and discussed. The appraisal process is meant to provide a constructive analysis of performance that can be used to set targets or objectives for the forthcoming period, for discussion and agreement by both parties. It is also used to identify any areas for staff development or training, either to redress weaknesses, or to prepare the person for a future extension of their job role. It is an opportunity for praise, as much as for criticism, and should certainly not be regarded as a mechanism for punishing staff. In many organisations, it is also used to form the basis for pay reviews or promotion.

In order for it to work properly, the appraisers are normally provided with training in listening skills, and in how to handle the interviews in an objective and non-threatening manner to put the appraisee at ease and facilitate a useful and productive dialogue. An autocratic style of management is not exactly conducive to achieving quality discussion in appraisals, where open and honest discussion is essential. A good appraisal system will encourage feedback from both parties on the relationship and interactions between each other. It should also be welcomed by employees, not feared or dreaded.

Further reading

Armstrong, M. (2003). *A Handbook of Personnel Management Practice.* Kogan Page, London.

Clayton, P. (2004). *Law for the Small Business: An Essential Guide to All the Legal and Financial Requirements.* Kogan Page, London.

Stokes, D. (2002). *Small Business Management.* Thomson, Harlow.

Thomson, A. and Thomson, R. (2002). *Managing People,* 3rd edition. CMI/Elsevier, Oxford.

CHAPTER 10

Planning and managing the business finances

Financial planning

Financial planning is a fairly generic term which covers a range of different activities, from the initial estimating of resource requirements and associated costs, forecasting sales revenue, identifying on-going operating costs, and preparing the budgetary plans which combine the former information. It also involves cash-flow forecasting to ensure that there are no gaps between income and expenditure, analysing break-even levels, and forecasting profits.

It is because the process draws together all of the other aspects of planning the business, and then expressing those plans in monetary form, that it is so important to prepare correctly, as it is the primary point of interest for bankers and any other potential lenders or investors, and is usually the first thing they will focus on when reading a business plan. If the financial forecasts do not look to be sufficiently detailed or realistic then it is highly likely that the business plan will be rejected or at least referred back for more information.

The objective of this chapter is to describe the various processes involved, and the reasoning behind them, so that the reader is in a position to prepare the necessary information for his or her own business plan, in particular the budgetary plan, cash-flow forecasts, and break-even analysis. As part of the process we shall also be defining and explaining some of the financial terminology which it is essential for the owner-manager to understand.

There are five key documents with which we are concerned, and all of which are inter-linked, as they are developed from the same, or over-lapping information, and certainly, the first two feed in to the others:

1. The owner-manager's own survival budget.
2. The break-even analysis.
3. The budgetary plan.
4. The cash-flow forecast.
5. The profit or loss forecast.

The personal survival budget

It may seem strange to start with this item, particularly as it is not really part of the information central to the business plan, but it does form an essential part of the budgetary plan and the cash-flow forecast, and is usually a specified requirement of the high street lending banks when considering a request for loans. The key question here is: "If I am going into business for myself, how much money do I realistically need to draw from the business to maintain a reasonable and comfortable lifestyle?" Note carefully the wording here, in that we are not talking about a luxurious lifestyle (that hopefully comes later) and neither are we looking to find the minimum figure that we can survive on. If you are working hard, with long hours, substantial stress, and risking your own personal resources, it is not unrealistic to expect to be able to draw sufficient income to enable you to live in some basic comfort, especially if you have a family to support. You may find it quite acceptable to live on a very minimal budget during the early stages of the business, but there has got to be a cut-off point beyond which you must expect some comfort. If you fail to realise that fact yourself, then there will certainly come a point when your domestic partner or family will soon start to remind you of it, and probably in quite a firm manner, as financial pressures can strain any relationship, no matter how sound. It really boils down to the fact that if you cannot achieve a basic reasonable lifestyle from your business, then you must ask yourself if the business is viable, or right for you in the first place.

The personal survival budget is effectively a summary of all of your domestic outgoings over a period, typically a year, although for the purposes of your business budget, you will no doubt break it down on a monthly basis. For example, for a family of two adults and two teenagers:

	£
Annual mortgages payments	4,800
Rates, water, sewage	900
Gas, electricity, telephone	900
Repairs & maintenance to home	300
Food & clothing for family	4,800
Loans, hire purchase, credit cards	600
Insurance policies, pension, savings	1,200
Car loan & running costs	3,600
Leisure, birthdays, Xmas, holidays	1,560
School travel, childrens' expenses	900
Total	15,960

Remember here, that the sum of £15,960 per annum (p.a.) (£1340 per month) does not constitute gross earnings, as it is the *minimum* sum which needs to be drawn from the business to pay for what is a far from exorbitant range of family expenses. As such it does not include any income tax or national insurance which must be paid on the gross figure. If the business is a limited company, then depending on tax allowances, the owner-manager would probably need to be paid a salary of at least £21,000 p.a. to achieve the required net figure. In the case of a sole trader or partnership, then the expected profit generated by the business would have to be sufficient to provide an after-tax profit of around £16,500 to allow for drawings and Class 2 National Insurance Contributions; otherwise the owners would be eating into their own capital and almost certainly creating future problems with cash-flow and a shortage of working capital. Please note that sole traders and partnerships are not just liable for taxation of profits, but those profits are also subject to Class 4 National Insurance Contributions.

The break-even analysis

First we must define what we mean by "break-even", and in order to do this, we must distinguish between fixed costs, and variable costs. Fixed costs are generally regarded as overhead costs, but the definition is that they remain "fixed" in relation to changes in the level of sales or output. Typically they would include things like rent, rates, management and administration costs (including the owner-manager's own drawings), insurance, etc. In contrast, variable costs are defined as those costs which vary directly in relation to changes in sales or output. This would include the costs of raw materials, components, labour production costs (particularly bonus pay or overtime), invoicing, packaging, and distribution, etc. The break-even point then is the point at which the revenue from sales equates to the variable costs incurred in achieving that level of sales, plus the full overhead cost. Put it in another way:

$$\text{sales revenue} = \text{fixed costs} + \text{variable costs} + \text{profit}$$

When we are breaking even, by definition we are making no profit, so our sales revenue must be matching our fixed or overhead costs, plus what it cost us to make the goods we have already sold.

Another useful concept here is that of contribution, which can be found by turning around the above equation:

$$\text{contribution (to profit and overheads)} = \text{selling price} - \text{variable cost}$$

Here we mean that the difference between the selling price and the variable cost of that item makes a contribution towards the profit and overheads of the business. For example, if it costs a second-hand car dealer buys a car for £1000 (variable cost) and sells it for £1500 (selling price) then the difference of £500 makes a contribution to the dealer's overhead costs and profits.

There are several ways of calculating the break-even point, including a graphical break-even chart, but the two most accurate methods involve fairly simple calculations based on the two above equations. To illustrate this we will use the following example where: selling price = £10 per unit, variable cost = £4 per unit, fixed costs = £150,000 p.a., and the break-even sales level = Y units.

(a) The Equation Method uses the simple formula mentioned above:

$$\text{sales} = \text{variable costs} + \text{fixed costs} + \text{profit}$$

$$10Y = 4Y + 150,000 + 0$$
$$10Y - 4Y = 150,000$$
$$6Y = 150,000$$
$$Y = \frac{150,000}{6}$$
$$Y = 25,000 \text{ units}$$

So we see that when sales levels reach 25,000 units, the income is sufficient to cover the variable costs incurred, plus the total overhead costs. However, it is only when sales start to exceed this level that the revenue will make a contribution towards the profit of the business.

(b) The contribution margin method uses a different equation:

$$\text{break-even level} = \frac{\text{fixed costs} + \text{net profit}}{\text{contribution}}$$

$$Y = \frac{150,000 + 0}{10 - 4}$$

$$Y = \frac{150,000}{6}$$

$$Y = 25,000$$

(c) In the case of businesses that work on a standards mark-up of goods and services to give a standard percentage profit figure, e.g. where the contribution equals 40% across all products or services, then the calculation is simply a case of dividing the annual overhead figure by the percentage profit. So with annual overheads of £100,000 and a profit margin of 40% we would divide £100,000 by 0.4 to give a break-even sales level of £250,000.

When calculating profit margins and setting prices it is important to remember the effect that small changes can have on break-even level. Using the above example, let's say that our marketing specialists had advised that a small change in the selling price (£9 instead of £10) would generate an increase of 10% in sales. It sounds good, but is it worthwhile? Using the equation method, $9Y = 4Y + 150,000$ we find that the break-even point Y calculates out at 30,000 units. Unfortunately for us, the increase of 10% in sales volume has only shifted a total of 27,500 units, so we are worse off than before, as we actually needed a 20% increase in sales to break even at £9 per unit.

The budgetary plan

A budget is a financial plan for an organisation, detailing income and expenditure over a fixed period of time, typically an accounting period. So, the primary purpose of setting a budget is to enable us to forecast levels of income and expenditure over the coming year to tell us where our money is coming from and where it is going to.

There are basically two ways of preparing a budget, the most popular of which is *Historically-based budgeting*, where we take the budget for the previous period and adjust it for known or anticipated changes. This is quite a simple and reliable process assuming of course that the figures from the previous year have been prepared carefully, and have turned out to be realistic. The other problem was that any contingencies or slack which had previously been built into the system is usually compounded by the effects of inflation, leading to ever-increasing inaccuracies. The alternative is *Zero-based budgeting* where the budget is formulated from scratch, ignoring the figures from previous years, and thereby forcing every single budget heading to be carefully analysed and individually justified. This process has tended to be unpopular, partly because it is time-consuming if done properly, and prone to error if shortcuts and guesswork are permitted to save time, and very often the justification of parts of the budget will be historically based anyway. Historical budgets can be too loose leading to inefficiency, whilst zero-based budgets can be too tight leading to inflexibility, but apart from the first year when all budgets are by definition zero based, the historical approach is by far the most popular and practical.

So, why do we bother with budgets? The answer is that they are a very useful and practical management tool, and act as a yardstick against which we can monitor:

- Levels and fluctuations in sales revenue.
- Sales trends and changes in demand.
- Profitability and cash flow.
- Changing costs of overheads, raw materials, labour, sales and marketing, transport and distribution, administration, etc.
- The impact of advertising programmes on sales.
- Working capital requirements, and the potential need for additional financing, loans, short-term overdrafts, etc.
- The effects of changes in interest rates and exchange rates operating costs.

So, if it can do all of this for us, how do we go about it? The budget calculations are produced on a spreadsheet which is basically a grid containing row and column calculations. If the rows and columns have been prepared correctly, then all the totals across, and all of the totals down, should correspond when carried to the bottom right-hand corner. However, even with computerised spreadsheets the budgetary plan rarely works out first time around, and will invariably require tweaking or adjustment to achieve a realistic and acceptable result. An example of a budget spreadsheet (Winston's budgetary plan) is shown in Figure 10.1. Please note that all budget figures always exclude value-added tax (VAT) charged and payable as that is money that belongs to HM Revenue & Customs, and not to the business.

Item	Jan.	Feb.	March	April	May	June	July	August	Sept.	Oct.	Nov.	Dec.	Totals
INCOME £													
Market Stall	9,000	12,000	7,000	9,000	8,000	10,000	9,000	8,000	10,000	11,000	15,000	17,000	125,000
Non-trading income	50	50	50	50	50	50	50	50	50	50	50	50	600
Total Income £	**9,050**	**12,050**	**7,050**	**9,050**	**8,050**	**10,050**	**9,050**	**8,050**	**10,050**	**11,050**	**15,050**	**17,050**	**125,600**
EXPENDITURE £													
Stall rent	750	600	600	750	600	600	750	600	600	750	600	600	7,800
Stall wages	500	500	400	500	400	400	500	400	400	500	400	600	5,500
Stall stock	5,400	7,200	4,200	5,400	4,800	6,000	5,400	4,800	6,000	6,600	9,000	10,200	75,000
Bags and wrappings	90	120	70	90	80	100	90	80	100	110	150	170	1,250
Stall fittings	–	–	50	–	–	–	–	–	50	–	–	–	100
Book-keeper	30	30	30	30	30	30	30	30	30	30	30	30	360
Administration and expenses	100	80	80	100	80	80	100	80	80	100	80	80	1,040
Advertising	30	60	30	30	30	30	30	30	30	30	30	60	420
Insurance	50	50	50	50	50	50	50	50	50	50	50	50	600
Transport – running costs	250	250	250	250	250	250	250	250	250	250	250	250	3,000
Transport – hire purchase	150	150	150	150	150	150	150	150	150	150	150	150	1,800
Bank loan repayments	100	100	100	100	100	100	100	100	100	100	100	100	1,200
Bank charges	–	–	300	–	–	250	–	–	250	–	–	250	1,050
Personal drawings	1,500	1,200	1,200	1,500	1,200	1,200	1,500	1,200	1,200	1,500	1,200	1,200	15,600
Total Expenditure £	**8,950**	**10,340**	**7,510**	**8,950**	**7,770**	**9,240**	**8,950**	**7,770**	**9,290**	**10,170**	**12,040**	**13,740**	**114,720**
NET INCOME £	**100**	**1,710**	**–460**	**100**	**280**	**810**	**100**	**280**	**760**	**880**	**3,010**	**3,310**	**10,880**

Figure 10.1

Winston Wight 12-month budgetary plan.

The first stage is to identify the key areas of income, distinguishing between income generated by sales of goods or services, and non-trading income, e.g. rent from subletting space. You may wish to subdivide the sales income to show revenue from different product groups, from different types of customer, or carrying different profit margins. For example, a beer and wine wholesaler would want to distinguish between those two major product areas, but the budget headings may also differentiate between sales to retail outlets where a 20% profit margin is expected, and sales to other wholesalers at 10% profit margin. The revenue figures throughout the year will also need to reflect seasonal trends. In the case of the wholesaler, this would involve peaks over the summer months and at Christmas, and much quieter periods in February–March and October–November. Any other sources of income are identified and included under a separate heading, e.g. capital receipts of loans, and then all items of income are totalled.

The second stage is to carry out a similar exercise for all known areas of expenditure, including overheads, operating costs, stock purchases (which should reflect sales levels) distributions costs, capital expenditure, and loan repayments, etc. As with income, these are totalled for each month and for the year as a whole.

The third stage is to calculate the net income or expenditure for each month and for the year as a whole. If done correctly, this can be quite a complicated and time-consuming exercise the first time around. It is particularly important then, that the time invested is not wasted once the bank manager has seen it, by simply showing the budget in the filing cabinet and forgetting it until next year. The budget is a working document, but it will only work for you if you use it properly. The monthly figures against each item of income and expenditure are your forecasts, and the benefit of budgeting is only gained by the regular monthly monitoring of actual income and expenditure against those forecasts. By comparing the two, you will be able to identify discrepancies, and in searching for

Case study 10.1

Winston Wight

If you have ever driven down Lewisham High Street in South East London, you may have noticed that the two predominant products on sale are greengrocery and ladies' underwear. Winston Wight is a bright lad who owns one of these ladies' underwear stalls. He has just completed his second year of trading, and has produced a budget for his bank manager, with whom he has a small bank loan. His income comes primarily from sales of stock, with peaks in the pre-Christmas period and just before Valentine's Day. On Mondays when he is not working, he sub-lets his market stall, for £50 per month (non-trading income). He works on an average gross profit margin of 40%, and apart from the rent on his stall, and the cost of running his van, his overheads are minimal. He pays no electricity, rates, water, or sewage, etc. He pays a book-keeper to maintain his accounts, and draws a regular sum of £300 per week from the business for his own living expenses. He also pays a wage to his girlfriend Sharon, who works with him part-time on the stall. His budget, shown in Figure 10.1, is a fairly simple and straight-forward example of a spreadsheet. All relevant areas of expenditure clearly identified, including adjustments for 5-week months, and of course, the figure in the bottom right-hand corner adds up correctly. We will come back again to our friend Winston in the next section.

explanations to these you will further identify potential problem areas. Ignore the process, and you may find that the problems continue to grow unnoticed, until it may be too late to rectify them.

One final point to remember on the subject of budgeting: budgets are not set in stone, they are essentially working documents to be used and revised during the financial year as circumstances dictate. If sales are higher than expected, revenue will be higher, but so will the costs of providing the goods or services, and the expenditure part of budget will need to be increased accordingly. Similarly, if sales revenue falls, income will fall, and expenditure will probably not be sustainable at the same level, so will need to be cut back.

The cash-flow forecast

In many respects the preparation of a cash-flow forecast resembles the process of preparing a budget spreadsheet, as the format and calculations are basically the same. However, the purpose of cash-flow forecasts is different, in that where the budget is concerned with identifying levels of income and expenditure for each part (e.g. month) of the budgetary period, the cash-flow forecast is concerned with when that income is received, and when payments are made for expenditure incurred. In order to do this, the cash-flow forecast will need to reflect:

- Cash balances brought forward from the previous period.
- Payments due to suppliers (creditors) incurred in the previous period.
- Payments due from customers (debtors) owing from the previous period, and adjustments for bad debts.
- On-going credit being given and received during the year.
- Receipts of loan income or capital.
- Capital purchases, lease payments, loan repayments, etc.

▓ In the case of sole traders and partnerships, the income tax liability for the business in the previous year, and with limited companies, the corporation tax liability for the previous period.

Again, as with budgets, cash-flow forecasts always exclude VAT charged on sales or paid on purchases. This is because VAT is essentially someone else's money, i.e. it belongs to HM Revenue & Customs. It is also seen as a positive influence on cash flow, in that all payments are offset against receipt and the balance paid to HMR&C quarterly in arrears, so that the balance payable is collected before it has to be paid out. In theory then, its short-term residence in the trader's bank account should improve cash flow temporarily.

So, why do we bother with cash-flow forecasting? The answer quite simply, is solvency, i.e. ensuring that the business can pay its bills and settle its liabilities, as and when they fall due. Unless that is the case, the business may be insolvent, and if so, it cannot legally continue to trade, unless steps are taken promptly to redress the insolvency situation. One of the biggest reasons for failure amongst small firms is lack of working capital (the money used to operate the business on a day to day basis), and irrespective of how profitable they might be, if they can't pay their bills, they often go bust.

What then, are the main influences on cash flow? I find that the best way to understand cash flow is to picture working capital as a bucket with holes in it. Cash receipts pour in through the top, and leak out as expenditure through the holes in the bottom. There are ways in which the rate of flow can be increased, to top up the level in the bucket, and there are factors which cause a faster outflow, thus reducing the level of working capital in the bucket:

▓ *Increased profits or net receipts from trading improve working capital.* As trading profits increase, the net profit from trading will increase the amount of working capital available (assuming of course that all debtors pay on time), but equally, any losses or net reductions in receipts from trading will diminish working capital.

▓ *The raising of loans, and repayment of loans.* The receipt of loans increases working capital. When a long-term loan is taken out (or any other long-term liability) the working capital pot is increased, however any regular repayments of loan capital and interest will progressively diminish the available balance. Similarly, repayment of loans, reduces available cash and working capital.

▓ *Injections or capital from investors.* This will increase the availability of working capital but the redemption of capital or the

Item	Jan.	Feb.	March	April	May	June	July	August	Sept.	Oct.	Nov.	Dec.	Totals
INCOME £													
Market Stall	9,000	12,000	7,000	9,000	8,000	10,000	9,000	8,000	10,000	11,000	15,000	17,000	125,000
Non-trading income	50	50	50	50	50	50	50	50	50	50	50	50	600
Cash balance b/fwd	9,800	–	–	–	–	–	–	–	–	–	–	–	9,800
Total Income £	**18,850**	**12,050**	**7,050**	**9,050**	**8,050**	**10,050**	**9,050**	**8,050**	**10,050**	**11,050**	**15,050**	**17,050**	**135,400**
EXPENDITURE £													
Stall rent	750	600	600	750	600	600	750	600	600	750	600	600	7,800
Stall wages	500	500	400	500	400	400	500	400	400	500	400	600	5,500
Stall stock	7,700	6,300	5,700	4,800	5,100	5,400	5,700	5,100	5,400	6,300	7,800	9,600	74,900
Bags and wrappings	90	120	70	90	80	100	90	80	100	110	150	170	1,250
Stall fittings	–	–	50	–	–	–	–	50	50	–	–	–	100
Book-keeper	30	30	30	30	30	30	30	30	30	30	30	30	360
Admin and expenses	100	80	80	100	80	80	100	80	80	100	80	80	1,040
Advertising	30	60	30	30	30	30	30	30	30	30	30	60	420
Insurance	50	50	50	50	50	50	50	50	50	50	50	50	600
Transport – running costs	250	250	250	250	250	250	250	250	250	250	250	250	3,000
Transport – hire purchase	150	150	150	150	150	150	150	150	150	150	150	150	1,800
Bank loan repayments	100	100	100	100	100	100	100	100	100	100	100	100	1,200
Bank charges	–	–	300	–	–	250	–	–	250	–	–	250	1,050
Tax liability previous year	3,200	–	–	–	–	–	3,200	–	–	–	–	–	6,400
Personal drawings	1,500	1,200	1,200	1,500	1,200	1,200	1,500	1,200	1,200	1,500	1,200	1,200	15,600
Transfer to pension fund	–	–	1,500	–	–	–	–	–	1,500	–	–	–	3,000
Total Expenditure £	**14,450**	**9,440**	**10,510**	**8,350**	**8,070**	**8,640**	**12,450**	**8,070**	**10,190**	**9,870**	**10,840**	**13,140**	**124,020**
NET INCOME £	**4,400**	**2,610**	**–3,460**	**700**	**–20**	**1,410**	**–3,400**	**–20**	**–140**	**1,180**	**4,210**	**3,910**	**11,380**
Cumulative cash flow £	**4,400**	**7,010**	**3,550**	**4,250**	**4,230**	**5,640**	**2,240**	**2,220**	**2,080**	**3,260**	**7,470**	**11,380**	

Figure 10.2
Winston Wight 12-month cash-flow forecast.

payment of dividends, profit shares and taxation, will reduce available cash.

- *Changes in the average balance of debtors and creditors:* These are major influences on the available working capital. Increased creditors (more credit from suppliers) and decreased debtors (faster payment by customers) will both improve the cash flow, whilst conversely, the reduction in creditors and any increase in debtors will worsen cash flow. The latter is one of the inevitable effects of any growth in trading.

- *Sale or purchase of fixed assets (e.g. land and buildings) or investments releases cash:* The sale of fixed assets will increase the cash available to run the business, but any corresponding or subsequent purchase of fixed assets will reduce that sum. When a vehicle is sold at the end of its practical working life, the residual value will be added to the working capital pot. However, any replacement vehicle (which will inevitably cost more on account of inflation over the intervening years) will probably result in a larger sum being taken out of the working capital pot, unless other financial provisions are made.

- *Changes in stock levels:* The reduction of stock levels can free cash previously tied up, but increasing stock levels ties up cash. Often the increased stock-holding is a response to expansion of sales, which if coupled with an increase in credit customers can reduce available working capital, quite quickly and severely, possibly leading to an over-trading situation.

The structure of the cash-flow forecast spreadsheet is broadly the same as that of the budget, with the exception of the bottom line. This is an additional line below the net income/expenditure line, which shows the cumulative effect of income and expenditure on cash flow. The basic rule of thumb is that the biggest cumulative deficit figure is the absolute minimum overdraft requirement for the period. If you bear in mind that the cumulative figures represent the roll-up for the month as a whole, there may be times within the month when due to late payment by customers, and creditor bills falling due, the actual, deficit is higher

Case study 10.2

Winston Wight

In Figure 10.1 we saw Winston's budget for the coming year. Figure 10.2 shows the same figures adjusted as a cash-flow forecast. Instead of showing when income and expenditure was incurred, this spreadsheet is concerned with the periods in which the money was actually received or paid. It shows the sales revenue, the tax liabilities and dates due, the payments to be made in each month (Winston gets 30 days' credit on 50% of his purchases), the net cash income or expenditure for the month, and finally at the bottom, the cumulative cash balance for the month. It also shows the money which he intends to draw from the business out of his after-tax profits, to make lump sum payments into his personal pension fund. These again, are not trading transactions, but do represent a substantial movement of cash out of the business. Note the variations in the monthly net income figures for the two spreadsheets, which illustrates just how different the budgeting and cash-flow forecasting processes are from each other.

than that shown by the cash-flow forecast. It is an irritating fact of business life that your customers will always seem to pay you late when you need it most. So it is sensible to build some contingencies into the overdraft requirement, as not only do bank managers tend to worry about requests for repeated increases in overdraft facilities, they charge you extra fees for arranging them!

The profit or loss forecast

The two primary accounting statements which are produced at the end of the financial year are the balance sheet and the profit & loss account. The balance sheet is like a snapshot taken at the final moment of the financial year. It shows the resources which have been put into the company by the owners or investors, and any long-term borrowing (capital and liabilities), and the way in which those resources have been deployed (assets) e.g. in the form of land, buildings, machinery, cash, stock, etc. In contrast, the profit & loss account for the financial year acts as a summary of the trading and profitability of the business over the year as a whole. The reason these two statements are read together is quite simple. Whilst the balance sheet tells us all about the assets,

Case study 10.3

Winston Wight

Figure 10.3 shows the profit forecast for Winston Wight's market stall. As can be seen, many of the financial sums have been taken straight from the totals column of Winston's budgetary plan (Figure 10.1); but it is the points of difference that we are interested in:

■   Winston's personal drawings are excluded from expenses section of the profit forecast as these are taken out of the net profit after tax. As a sole trader he pays income tax and Class 4 National Insurance Contributions on the profits of the business, and not on his personal drawings.

■ Loan repayments are also paid out of net profit after tax, only the interest payable on the loan counts as a business expense which can be set against profits. Winston has to obtain a certificate of interest paid, from his bank, to verify the figures.

■ Similarly, the capital part of hire purchase payments is claimed as a capital allowance for tax purposes, so capital payments are paid out of net profit after tax, but the interest does count as an operating expense. Winston's hire purchase agreement specifies the total interest payable over the period of the contract.

	£	£
Sales income	125,000	
Non-trading income	600	
Total income		125,600
Stock purchases	75,000	
Plus opening stock	3,000	
	78,000	
Less closing stock	3,000	
Cost of goods sold		75,000
Gross Profit		**50,600**
Less expenses		
Stall rent	7,800	
Bags and wrappings	1,250	
Stall fittings	100	
Wages	5,500	
Book-keeper	360	
Administration and expenses	1,040	
Advertising	420	
Insurance	600	
Transport running costs	3,000	
Bank charges	1,050	
Loan interest	300	
Hire purchase interest	600	
Total expenses		22,020
Net Profit Before Tax		**28,580**
Estimated Tax/NIC liability		5,800
Net Profit After Tax		**22,780**
Hire purchase capital repayments	1,200	
Loan capital repayments	900	
Personal drawings	15,600	
Lump sum pension payments	3,000	
Total payments from after-tax profit		20,700
Profit retained in business		**2,080**

Figure 10.3
Winston Wight
profit forecast.

capital and liabilities of the business, it tells us nothing at all about the profitability. Conversely, the profit & loss account tells us all about the profitability and efficiency of trading over the year, but it shows us nothing of the assets and liabilities.

As stated above, the profit & loss account is a historical prepared at the end of the year, but the profit forecast, which ideally follows the same format for ease of comparison, is prepared at the same time as the budgetary plan and cash-flow forecast. In fact, much of the information for the profit forecast will be drawn from the totals column of the budgetary plan.

In summary then, we have examined the five main forecasts which would be expected to be included in a business plan: the personal survival budget, the break-even analysis, the annual budgetary plan, the cash-flow forecast, and the profit forecast. It may be however, that depending on your circumstances you would not actually need all of these in your own business plan. For example, a non-profit making organisation by definition would not need a profit forecast, but it still needs to know if it is breaking even. Someone working part-time on a self-employed basis may only need a simple budget, and if working for cash, this could also form the cash-flow forecast. The important factor is that you need to know how these documents work and what they are used for, in order to decide whether or not they are relevant to your own particular business plan. Most important of all, you need to understand them in order to use them to monitor and control the growth and development of your business.

Financial controls

Following on from the previous section, having planned the finances for the business we now need to examine how to monitor and control the financial performance of the business. The objective of this section is to provide a practical understanding of some of the basic methods of maintaining financial controls, and of some of the simple techniques used for assessing financial performance; in order to make the reader aware of how these can be employed to the benefit of the business. These will include:

- Basic accounts and double-entry book-keeping.
- Monitoring budgets and cash flow.
- Profit margins and mark-up.
- Stock control.
- Aged debtors and creditors accounts.
- Credit-control procedures.
- Accounting ratios.

Basic accounting and double-entry book-keeping

It is a legal requirement for any business, charity, trust, voluntary organ-isation, public body, etc., to maintain a true and accurate record of its financial transactions. For tax purposes, these accounts have to be retained for a period of 6 years. Accounts are prepared on a yearly basis, and depending on the size and turnover of the business, can be completed in one of two ways. For businesses with a turnover of less than £350,000, accounting can be carried out on a cash basis, whereby the financial transactions are recorded only when money actually changes hands, i.e. when payments are made or received. Where the turnover exceeds that figure then the VAT regulations require that accounting is carried out on a commitment basis, whereby the transaction has to be recorded as soon as any goods or services are supplied or received, irre-spective of the subsequent date of payment.

Double-entry book-keeping works on the principle that when a sales or purchase transaction is entered in the appropriate ledger column of the accounts, a corresponding entry is made in the cash or bank columns to show where payments were made from, or into which accounts any receipts were paid. If this process is carefully maintained, then it provides an easy way of reconciling the accounts with bank statements and petty cash. Figure 10.4 shows an example of a simple double-entry accounts sheet suitable for a small business operating on a cash accounting basis. The number of sales and purchase column headings can be expanded to suit the needs of the business, and analysis books with varying numbers of such columns are readily available from high street stationers.

As the accounting process becomes more complex, i.e. where credit is given for goods and services sold, and received from the business' own suppliers, then the system will need to be more detailed. For example it will be necessary to differentiate between those entries which are paid, and those which are still outstanding, and the dates when the payments were made or received. For a newly established business the paper-based system may be adequate in the early stages, but there comes a point (typ-ically around 120 to 150 transactions per month), when hand-written ledgers are no longer cost-effective and where a computerised system is required. These are available quite cheaply and are relatively easy to install and to learn to operate – they and are often provided free of charge to new businesses by the high street banks. They also offer the added benefits of integrating the various component parts of the system. For example, the production of invoices is linked with entries in the sales ledger and the stock control systems. Similarly, payroll systems, stock con-trol and purchase orders can be linked to purchase ledgers. The various

Date	Item	Cash in	Cash out	Bank in	Bank out	Rent and rates	Resale stock	Transport	Administration and expense	Wages and drawings	Sales and adverts	VAT on inputs	Total purchase	Sales revenue	VAT on outputs	Total income
01/05/05	Balance b/fwd	852.17		1,972.83		430.00	5,120.00	152.25	33.48	2,220.00	15.00	929.47	8,900.20	7,741.50	1,354.76	9,096.26
03/05/05	Rent				300.00	300.00							300.00			
04/05/05	Petrol		23.50					20.00				3.50	23.50			
04/05/05	Stock purchases				1,527.50		1,300.00					227.50	1,527.50			
04/05/05	Expenses		28.00						25.20			2.80	28.00			
07/05/05	Wages		180.00							180.00			180.00			
07/05/05	Sales w/e	258.92		2,000.00										1,922.49	336.43	2,258.92
10/05/05	Telephone bill				262.35				223.28			39.07	262.35			
11/05/05	Van repair				235.00			200.00				35.00	235.00			
11/05/05	Stock purchases				1,386.50		1,180.00					206.50	1,386.50			
12/05/05	Petrol		35.25					30.00				5.25	35.25			
13/05/05	Newspaper Ad				17.63						15.00	2.63	17.63			
14/05/05	Wages		180.00							180.00			180.00			
14/05/05	Sales w/e	253.52		1,950.00										1,875.34	328.18	2,203.52
17/05/05	Stock purchases				1,433.50		1,220.00					213.50	1,433.50			
18/05/05	Expenses		19.57						17.47			2.10	19.57			
19/05/05	Rates				130.00	130.00							130.00			
21/05/05	Wages		180.00							180.00			180.00			
21/05/05	Sales w/e	200.80		1,900.00										1,787.92	312.88	2,100.80
23/05/05	Petrol		35.25					30.00				5.25	35.25			
24/05/05	Stock purchases				1,586.25		1,350.00					236.25	1,586.25			
24/05/05	Stationery		11.75						10.00			1.75	11.75			
28/05/05	Wages		180.00							180.00			180.00			
28/05/05	Sales w/e	154.98		2,250.00										2,046.79	358.19	2,404.98
30/05/05	Drawings		150.00		1,350.00					1,500.00			1,500.00			
31/05/05	Balance c/fwd	896.64		1,844.10		860.00	10,170.00	432.25	309.43	4,440.00	30.00	1,910.57	18,152.25	15,374.04	2,690.44	18,064.48

Figure 10.4
Double-entry book-keeping.

components of the system are usually integrated via a nominal ledger which is used to produce monthly budget out-turn reports, monthly debtors and creditors analysis, etc., and the annual balance sheet and profit and loss account at the end of the financial year. These provide accurate and up to date information which is invaluable in monitoring and controlling the finances of the business, and which is much harder and more time consuming to extract from a manual accounting system.

Monitoring budgets and cash flow

The first section of this chapter explained in detail the importance of producing detailed cash-flow forecasts and budgetary plans, but apart from keeping the bank manager quiet for a whilst, these are of little value to the business if they are not monitored on a regular basis. At least once a month, and preferably as soon as possible after the end of each month, the actual sales volumes and revenues, and the actual expenditure incurred in each area within the business, needs to be compared with the forecast figures to identify any significant discrepancies. Where such discrepancies occur, they need to be analysed to determine the cause, and to identify whether or not they constitute a one-off situation or part of a developing trend which might adversely affect the longer-term prospects of the business. Having identified them, it is then necessary to assess the impact that that they will make on business operations and profit. If the budgetary plan has been prepared on a computerised spreadsheet, this is a relatively simple process, as the actual data can be entered into a copy of the original budget to produce revised out-turn figures.

This process is even more important when forecasting cash flow, as relatively small changes in sales revenue or credit terms, can over a period of time, compound themselves to create a major cash-flow problem. However if the problems can be spotted in time, then it is often possible to address the problems before they become too great, e.g. by arranging a short-term overdraft, by tightening credit limits or the length of credit given to customers, or by extending the credit received from suppliers, although ideally of course, they should be consulted first!

Profit margins and mark-up

This is a topic which many people who are relatively new to business find hard to comprehend. When we talk of *profit margin* we mean the difference between the selling price and the cost price. If we buy an item for £60 and sell it for £100 the profit margin is £40 which constitutes 40% of the selling price. When we talk of *mark-up* we mean the amount of percentage by which the cost price is increased to produce the selling price. Using the same example, if we buy an item for £60 and mark it up by £40, it will sell for £100, but the mark-up as a percentage of the cost price is 66.7%. Similarly, a 100% mark-up gives 50% profit margin, a 50% mark-up gives 33% profit margin, a 33% mark-up gives a 25% profit margin, and a 25% mark-up gives a 20% profit margin.

Failing to distinguish between these two is probably the commonest and most significant mistake made by people who are new to business. The anticipated 50% gross profit was in reality only 33%, and with a few unexpected expenses, some increases costs during the year, and a small drop in sales revenue, the forecast 10% net profit on sales turnover has suddenly become a 15% net loss, and there is no spare cash to pay the bills that are due next week! There is little detailed published data on reasons for small business failure and bankruptcy, but I would seriously contend that this all too-familiar scenario is probably one of the primary reasons why many emerging small businesses fail to survive beyond their first or second year.

Stock control

For providers of services, where the only stock which is held is likely to consist of stationery or consumables, then stock control will probably not cause any major problems, but for manufacturers, wholesalers and retailers the situation can be totally different. Stock related problems can include:

- Having inadequate volumes of raw materials to produce goods.
- Having inadequate volumes of completed goods to meet sales orders.
- Having the wrong types of goods in stock.
- Having too much money tied up in slow moving stock, causing cash-flow problems.
- Being unable to obtain stock from suppliers (particularly imported goods) on a regular or reliable basis.
- Having to handle a high proportion of returns of faulty or unsatisfactory stock.
- Being left with unsaleable or outdated goods.
- Careless storage or handling resulting in damaged stock.
- Inaccurate invoicing of stock sold, or poor stock control resulting in inaccurate stock records.
- Theft of stock, or slippage (e.g. removal of stock by staff for own use).

Most of the above problems are fundamentally concerned with operational issues relating to the ordering processes, and the physical storage and stock management systems used by the business, however all of them will have an impact on the profit margins which the business makes. Stock levels need to be monitored carefully to ensure that they are adequate to meet foreseeable demand but without tying up cash unnecessarily for long periods of time. This will involve both regular liaison will sales and marketing staff to assess future levels of demand, and an efficient system of ordering replacement stock, e.g. by identifying both minimal acceptable levels of stock, and levels at which new stock must be ordered allowing for lead times for delivery, etc. It is no good waiting until the stock reaches the minimum level before re-ordering, if that stock is likely to run out before the delivery is received. If the delivery takes 2 weeks to arrive, then the re-order level must be set at the minimum stock level plus the amount of stock that would typically be utilised during that 2 week lead time. Many larger organisations, particularly in the automotive industry, now use "Just In Time" ordering and stock delivery systems where stock can be ordered and delivered at short notice. This works well for them as it saves them the expense of holding large quantities of stock, but it often results in their smaller suppliers having to bear the cost of holding that stock on their behalf.

Whilst the physical monitoring of stock is important to detect any theft, damage resulting from storage or handling, and deterioration due to poor stock rotation, it is also important to monitor the financial aspects of stock control. Wholesalers and retailers who handle a large number of stock lines have to deal with a constant stream of changing prices, discount structures, special promotions, etc., all of which affect the purchase price of each of the stock lines. Unless these ever-changing costs are checked on a regular basis (ideally on the receipt of each purchase invoice) then profit margins can unknowingly become eroded. The larger the range of stock lines, the more important it is to use some form of database or financial stock control system to record the cost prices, profit margins, and selling prices, and to flag up any changes in the purchase price of goods.

It is also useful to monitor the rate at which stock is being turned over. For example, if I hold an average of £10,000 of stock and make an average level of sales of £60,000 per month, then I am effectively turning that stock around six times per month, or every 5 days, which means that I am making excellent use of my working capital. If on the other hand, I am holding the same level of stock but only selling £20,000 per month, then I am only turning the stock over once every 15 days. I am probably holding more in stock than I really need, which means that I have too much money tied up in stock, and I am not making the best use of my working capital. Obviously the ideal turnover rate will vary from one industry to another, for example, fast moving consumer goods such as foods will turn over far quicker than perhaps furniture that is held in stock for some time, but the basic principle remains the same in each case.

At the end of each financial year (and frequently at the half-year stage) it is necessary to carry out a full and detailed inventory of all items of stock, and to determine the full value of the stock (at cost). The annual stock-take forms part of the process of preparing the annual balance sheet of the business, and there are a number of ways in which the stock values can be calculated. Under the Last In First Out (LIFO) method, stock is valued at the price pertaining to the oldest items held, which can be a complicated process if stock has been received at different prices over a period of time. Under the First in First Out (FIFO) method, stock is valued at the latest price, which presents an easier method of calculation but with the risk of over-valuing the stock, particularly if much of it is old. A more practical and realistic method is to divide the total value of all items of stock by the number of units, giving what is called as Weighted Average Cost which reflects the true value of each line of stock. It is important to remember that the choice of method of valuation will influence the cost of goods sold in the profit and loss account, which in turn will affect the gross profit calculations, and subsequently the taxable profit of the business.

Aged debtors and creditors accounts

These are simple monthly reports which are readily available from computerised accounting systems, but which unfortunately many small businesses overlook unless prompted to produce them by their bank manager. They certainly do require more effort to produce from a manual accounting system, but in either case, if credit facilities are given to customers, or received from suppliers on a regular basis, these are essential.

The aged debtors analysis, an example of which is shown in Figure 10.5, is used to assess the performance of customers in paying their bills (and the performance of the business in collecting the debts). The aged creditors analysis is virtually identical in structure but it is used to measure the performance of the business in paying its debts to its own suppliers, the creditors. In the aged debtors analysis, each unpaid invoice for each credit customer is allocated to the 30-day period in which it was issued. Let us take, e.g. the fairly standard business credit terms wherein payment is required within 30 days of the end of the month in which the invoice was issued. Any invoices issued this month are not yet due, and

Customer	Current (£)	1–30 days (£)	31–60 days (£)	61–90 days (£)	91 + days (£)	Total debt (£)
Winston Wight	462.00	1,150.00	981.70	–	–	2,594.20
Helen Highwater Associates	112.80	534.60	–	–	–	647.40
Grabbit & Runn, Solicitors	227.90	722.50	847.10	693.30	–	2,490.80
Rojjers & Ammerstein	350.20	211.00	–	–	–	561.20
W & H Clinton Ltd.	–	–	987.50	675.80	992.30	2,655.60
Evan Elpus & Partners	–	125.70	–	–	–	125.70
Ben Dover & Sons	1,349.20	1,878.10	–	–	–	3,227.30
Lemmon & McArthney Ltd.	484.00	525.50	293.90	–	–	1,303.40
Totals	2,986.10	5,147.90	3,110.20	1,369.10	992.30	13,605.60
Total debtors (%)	21.95	37.84	22.86	10.06	7.29	

Figure 10.5
Aged debtors analysis example.

are regarded as current. Those falling due at the end of next month are classed as 0 to 30-days old, and are within the terms of credit. Those which are 30 to 60-days old should have been paid by now, and so are in need of chasing. Those which are 60 to 90-days old are of major concern, and unless they are part of an on-going dispute, must be regarded as being at risk, or in accountancy terms they are a "doubtful debt". The 90 days plus category is a definite sign of a bad debt, and debt recovery action should have been taken long ago. One of the basic principles of accounting, the Prudence Concept, requires that profits are not classed as such until they are in cash or near-cash form. Similarly, any doubtful or bad debts must be acknowledged as such at the earliest opportunity. If nothing else, then at least by acknowledging the post 90-day debts as bad, if you have taken recovery action then you can claim bad debt relief for them when making the next VAT return. although if the debt is eventually settled, then that relief will have to be repaid.

Credit-control procedures

So, it is becoming obvious that some of your customers don't want to pay you, or can't pay you, then what can you do about it? There are a number of options available:

- The heavy mob, i.e. send in some big lads armed with baseball bats to break a few bones. Once popular perhaps in certain Mediterranean countries, but strictly illegal, and there is always the risk that their lads might just be a bit bigger than yours! Not exactly the best or first choice option for a respectable growing business. Unfortunately there are still some areas of the grey economy where this method still occurs, particularly in the field of unlicensed credit.

- Telephone or send a reminder letter. Why not try? After all, the non-payment may simply be the result of an oversight. However, if the customer is a serial bad-payer this is likely to have no effect at all, as reminders will simply be ignored.

- If no further response within 7 to 14 days then try again, preferably more firmly. Contact the decision maker or person responsible for payment. Check that the payment is not in dispute. Ask outright if there is a cash-flow problem and ask for a firm date by which payment (or at least part payment) can be expected. Again, the serial bad-payer will probably just make empty promises at this stage, and will stretch their credit to the limit until forced to pay. There are unfortunately, still a few people in business who regard this process as being one big game, and seem to enjoy testing the patience of their suppliers to the limit.

- Once the payment becomes 30 days overdue, then unless there are special circumstances which you are prepared to accept, or unless you have negotiated an agreement for repayment, then you must seriously consider stopping further supplies. Some small firms find this a hard step to take, as they run the risk of the customer going to another supplier. But what is there to lose? A sale is not a sale until it is paid for, and if the customer is slow in paying you, then the same will probably apply to his next supplier, and you will be better off without him in the long term. It may come as a surprise to you, but some customers even respect this firm approach.

- If the customer is in difficulty, then you may be able to negotiate a structured programme of repayment without a loss of trade. I have found this to work on several occasions where, e.g. the customer pays cash on delivery for the regular weekly supply of goods plus an agreed minimum figure to reduce the outstanding balance. This sometimes formed the basis for a future long-term trading relationships, as once the customers had overcome the current problems then they remained loyal to the suppliers who had worked with them during the difficult period. But if you do agree to take this route, you must not allow the outstanding balance to increase at any stage until the debt has been cleared and normal trading terms have been re-established.

- Once you get beyond the 90-day stage, there is little option but to take formal debt recovery action. Most owner-managers are very busy people, and have little time to spare chasing bad-payers. Solicitors are one alternative, although expensive to employ, and often laboriously slow to get a result. Professional debt collection agencies are often a better alternative as apart from an initial assignment fee, and the reimbursement of their legal expenses, they work on the basis of taking an agreed percentage of the money they recover. They also tend to tell you up-front when faced by a hopeless situation, whereas a solicitor might run up expensive bills before reaching the same conclusion.

- For sums under £5000 the Small Claims Court is supposed to offer a quick and inexpensive form of redress, without involving solicitors. However, the sheer volume of small claims which the courts have to deal with means that the process can still take some months, even if uncontested. The downside is that if your customer lives at a distance from yourself, the court action will often end up being transferred to the defendants local County Court, leaving you with the cost and burden of travelling to their locality. For larger debts it is possible to take action by means if issuing a High Court Writ against the debtor, although the cost of doing so is quite high. The High Court tends to move faster than the County Court, particularly when applications are made for Compulsory Winding up Orders; but once again, the cost of action must be measured against the likelihood of recovering the debt.

- As part of the Insolvency Act 1986, the facility was created to issue a Statutory Demand for Payment, whereby if payment for a debt was not made within 21 days of the issue of the Statutory Demand, then the Plaintiff could automatically apply for the business to be wound up or declared bankrupt. This is okay in principle if the business has any assets which could be liquidated in the event of bankruptcy, although if that were the case, then the company could probably rise the money to pay the bill anyway. Realistically, it is only worth issuing a Statutory Demand if you are willing to go to the next stage of enforcing it, i.e. applying to have the debtor declared bankrupt or insolvent which will incur further legal costs. Also, bear in mind that if there are no tangible assets against which to claim, the pursuants of the claim could simply be incurring more legal expenses only to find themselves alongside a whole host of other unsecured creditors.

■ Where goods are supplied to customers it is possible to write the terms of trade which appear on the reverse side of business invoices, to include retention of title to the goods supplied, until such times as full payment is made for them. The owner then has the right to reclaim the goods if payment is not made, although of course this does not confer rights of entry to premises to recover them, neither does it help if the goods have already been sold. It can sometimes be of use when goods are confiscated by bailiffs or receivers in bankruptcy, as those goods cannot be subsequently sold, and have to be returned to the supplier once proof of Title has been demonstrated.

Accounting ratios

These are not so much methods of monitoring and controlling business finances, as tools which can be used to assess the performance of the business, particularly in term of solvency and liquidity. There are a whole host of ratios which can be applied to test business performance, but not all of those are of significance to start up of small businesses. A description of the relevant ratios is provided in Chapter 17.

In summarising this section, it must be emphasised that the effective monitoring and control of finances involves the use of a whole range of tools and techniques on a regular on-going basis. Moreover, those tools and techniques complement each other and are best used alongside each other rather than in isolation.

Sources of finance

The chances are that unless you win the National Lottery, inherit a fortune, marry a rich widow or toy boy, or find a sugar daddy, that you will sooner or later have to raise some short-term or long-term finance for your business. The most obvious source of funding for most owner-managers is from the local high street bank, but this is not necessarily the cheapest or the best way of financing a particular borrowing requirement.

On a more serious note, it must also be acknowledged that amongst a number of ethnic minorities, there are religious objections to what is referred to as "usury" – the payment or receipt of interest for lending money, and therefore the conventional high street banks are not regarded as an acceptable source of finance or borrowing, and the communities themselves or their member families will use their own resources to finance new or growing businesses.

The purpose of this section is to examine some of the potential sources of finance which are available for new and expanding businesses; and to examine their relative uses, advantages, and disadvantages. In many cases this will involve considering not just the finance required for the initial start-up phase of the business, to cover the period until the firm achieve regular profitable trading. It is just as important to consider and identify the available options for the next stage, when the firm starts to expand, possibly at a rate which is faster than receipts from profits can support. The effective planning of finance at this stage is critical to avoid over-trading, where the business is growing beyond the level which can be supported by its own working capital. This is one of the most common causes of business failure, when growth outstrips working capital, resulting in a cash-flow crisis and inability to pay suppliers, wages, etc., on time. In this situation, profits might be excellent, but the firm is still technically insolvent and therefore trading illegally. Some firms manage to hang on and trade out of this situation, but for the majority, the only sensible remedy is to rise finance to increase working capital to a level which will support the expansion.

Factors which influence suitable sources of finance

The most appropriate form of borrowing will be determined by a number of factors:

- The purpose for which the funds are required, e.g. whether it is to increase working capital, or to acquire a vehicle or an item of capital equipment. For the former, a medium-term loan would be suitable, whereas for vehicles or plant and equipment, leasing or hire purchase might be better.
- The size of the borrowing requirement. Most bankers will only lend against security. A personal guarantee may be adequate for a few thousand pounds, but for a more substantial sum the loan will need to be secured by a legal charge on some property. Borrowing small sums can also be quite expensive in that interest rates tend to fall as the size of loan increases, and with small loans, the initial set up fees form a larger proportion of the total cost.
- The anticipated repayment period. Short-term borrowing tends to incur higher rates of interest, whilst the rate usually falls when spread over a longer period. Some form of finance also have maximum repayment periods, such as commercial

mortgages; or repayment periods which are linked to the size of the borrowing, as in the case of car loans.

■ The affordability of repayments. The crucial question when assessing funding options is "Can the business afford to make the required regular payments from its current or expected levels of profit?" If not, then we must firstly question the viability of the business: "Is it really worth carrying on?" If so, secondly we must question the necessity of the borrowing: "Do I really need a new car, or will the current one last another year?" Thirdly we need to examine the alternative funding options: "Can I find another lender who will consider lower repayments spread over a longer period?"

■ The availability of security or collateral. As bankers will rarely lend against the full equity value of property (50% is a more realistic figure for some high street banks) the availability of the loan may be limited by the equity or residual value of the property against which it will be secured. If the net value of your home is £50k, then you may only be able to borrow £25k to £30k against it.

Funding options for start-up situations and small businesses

The following options are some of the most common sources of finance options most regularly used by smaller organisations. They are by no means the only options and a range of others are described in Chapter 17, but those tend to be more appropriate for firms with an established track record, or for larger organisations.

Equity or capital

This is basically the value of the resources which are introduced into the business by its owners or investors. These resources do not have to be in cash form only, as they can include just about anything of value that will be of positive use to the business, including saleable stock, vehicles, computer equipment, land and buildings, office equipment, plant and machinery, etc. In the case of sole traders and partnerships, the value of those resources is assigned to a capital account for each of the proprietors. In a limited company, the resources become the property of the company against which shares are issued. The investors cannot withdraw their capital investment, but if the company wishes and if it can afford to do so, then the company can redeem or buy back the shares from the investors.

Unsecured loans

Unless you have a long-standing and proven track record, obtaining an unsecured business loan from a bank, for anything but a small sum, is a virtual impossibility.

Many small businesses are started with unsecured loans from friends or family, as this can be a very low cost and flexible way of getting started. However, it is very much in the interests of both lenders and borrowers to be in some way formalise the loan arrangements in writing, even if only by means of a covering letter signed by both parties. For example, This would give details of the lender and borrower, the sum involved and the purpose of the loan, the date borrowed and the date when repayment is due, and details of interest payable (or not payable). Even a simple signed document would protect the lender in the case of default by the borrower. Similarly, if say, the lender died, then the deceased's estate could not demand immediate repayment of the loan prior to the agreed date.

Overdrafts

Overdrafts are essentially a short-term form of borrowing, designed to cover temporary periods when cash flow may be poor, or during seasonal troughs such as those experienced in the coastal holiday trade. They are usually only granted for up to one year, and approval and re-approval incurs an arrangement fee charged by the lender. Interest rates are quite high, but then again, interest is only charged when the overdraft facility is in use. The important thing to remember, is that if you find that you need a permanent overdraft, then you do not need an overdraft at all, you really need a longer-term loan or capital injection.

Loan Guarantee Scheme

This was introduced by the government in the early 1980s to encourage banks to lend to new and small firms whose proprietors could not offer any conventional security but it has never been that successful due to the reluctance of banks to take any risk (albeit a small proportion of the total debt) by lending to small firms with no proven track record.

The loan guarantee scheme (LGS) is therefore more suited to established firms that want to finance growth, and is covered in more detail in Chapter 17.

Short and medium-term bank loans

These typically involve repayments over 2 to 5 years, but sometimes up to 7 years. For sums in excess of £5000 security would almost certainly be required, in the form of a charge against private or company property, of a fixed and floating charge over the book debts and assets of the business. For short-term loans for sums below £5000, a personal guarantee of payment in the event of default, would probably be acceptable, so long as it was given by one or more persons with tangible assets (e.g. home-owners). Interest would typically be fixed at between 2% and 5% over the base rate prevailing at the time the loan was taken out. The precise rate of interest may be influenced by the type of security offered, in that better security may attract a lower rate of interest. Arrangement fees are also charged on new loans.

Long-term loans from banks

High street banks will make long-term loans to businesses, typically on over 5 to 10 years, on a secured basis. Beyond that period, the loan is more likely to be treated as a mortgage, being secured by a specific fixed asset belonging to the business or one of its proprietors. Again, arrangement fees are charged and there may be some solicitor's costs incurred in setting up legal charges on property.

Share capital from private investors: ordinary shares

Private limited companies cannot offer their shares for sale to the general public, as only those companies listed and quoted on the Stock Exchange or the Alternative Investment Market can do that. However, private limited companies can still sell shares privately to individual investors or to other companies. These transactions normally involve the purchase of a fixed number of Ordinary shares for an agreed sum which then belongs to the company. Ordinary shares confer voting rights on the owner, and dividends are paid annually from company profits, usually in the form of so many pence per share.

Share capital from private investors: preference shares

These are sold in the same way as ordinary shares, but are fundamentally different in that ownership of them confers no voting rights, and that there is normally an option for the issuing company to buy them back (redeem them) after a fixed period of time. In lieu of those rights, preferential shareholders receive guaranteed dividends, which are fixed, or have a minimum payment level; and which are paid even when no dividends are paid to holders of ordinary shares. If no dividend is paid 1 year, then the next time that one is declared, the preferential shareholders will receive recompense for any past unpaid dividend. In the event of liquidation, holders of preference shares have priority over ordinary shareholders if any residual funds are available for distribution.

Grants

Grants to assist in the setting up of a new business are quite scarce, although for those who are under 25 years, it is worth applying to the Prince's Youth Trust which makes grants available to unemployed young people who wish to start up on their own. Some relocation grants are available for businesses starting up or moving to development areas, particularly in more remote rural areas. Local authorities in urban redevelopment areas often have access to European Social Fund (ESF) monies, which are sometimes issued in grant form to assist small firms, and local councils or chambers of commerce can often advise on the availability of these, as they will differ from area to area. However, from 2007 the availability of ESF funding is likely to decline as the European Union (EU) directs it towards new member countries in Eastern Europe. Grants to subsidies training for employees can be obtained from some local authorities, Regional Development Agencies, Business Links, and local Enterprise Agencies. Up to 50% of the cost of training can be currently be obtained by firms working towards Investors in People status.

Commercial mortgages

A person who is buying their own home will normally take out a mortgage with a bank or building society typically over 25 to 30 years. A commercial mortgage arranged through a bank, insurance company or financial institution, is basically the same, but would normally be repaid over 10 to 15 years. These are covered in more detail in Chapter 17.

Venture Capital

Venture Capital organisations are specialist companies which invest in new businesses and unquoted companies to help them expand and grow. It is relatively rare that a venture capitalist will invest in a start-up business unless perhaps there is a high-growth opportunity linked to based on well-protected intellectual property, or unless the business proposer has a sound track record in setting up, growing and selling on businesses. Venture Capital is discussed in more depth in Chapter 17.

Hire purchase

This is usually used to buy a fixed asset such as a vehicle or piece of plant or machinery. Under a hire purchase agreement, the business would typically pay 20% of the cost of the asset plus the full VAT sum up-front, with the hire purchase company financing the balance. The VAT is claimed back at the next quarter, and fixed monthly payments are then made over a specific period of time, perhaps 3 to 5 years, at the end of which the asset belongs to the business. In case of default on monthly payments, the hire purchase company, which still technically owns the asset until the final payment is made, can recover and sell the asset. If the business has already paid at least two thirds of the money due, then recovery will require a Court Order. Hire purchase is useful to a business which wants to show the fixed asset on its balance sheet, but being a capital purchase, capital allowance taxation rules apply.

Leasing/contract hire

In the case of hire purchase, the asset eventually becomes the property of the business, but in the case of lease hire or contract hire, this transfer of ownership does not occur. The business simply makes regular monthly payments to the leasing company over the duration of the contract, and has the use of the asset during that time. Leasing is cheaper to set up, usually requiring an up-front deposit of only 3 months' payments, with VAT being charged on each payment. Leasing is good for cash flow, and tax-effective as all payments count as a business expense, but as ownership of the asset never changes hands, the leased item cannot be shown included in the company balance sheet. At the end of the period of the lease, the item can usually be purchased via a third party if desired, but for tax and legal reasons the leasing company is not allowed to sell the asset direct to the lessor.

Factoring/invoice discounting

Factoring involves the management of the firm's sales ledger by an out-side organisation, typically a bank. First, all company customers are given a very tight and careful credit check, and once approved, the factoring company guarantees to pay the business a fixed percentage (e.g. up to 80%) of the value of every invoice within 14 days of the issue of the invoice. The balance, less a factoring charge, is paid once the debt has been settled. The system is excellent for cash flow, but factoring companies are very strict and can be heavy-handed in dealing with customers, which can result in the loss of trade. There is also usually a minimum turnover requirement of £250k, so the system is hardly suitable for new or start-up businesses. Invoice discounting works in a similar way, but the sales ledger is controlled by the company itself, with advances of up to 80%, being made against specific invoices. The company repays the advance when the debt is collected, and interest is paid at between 2% and 5% over normal commercial rates.

Further reading

Bragg, A. and Bragg, M. (2005). *Developing New Business Ideas*. FT Prentice Hall, London.

Broadbent, M. and Cullen, J. (2003). *Managing Financial Resources*. Elsevier, Oxford.

Owen, A. (2003). *Accounting for Business Studies*. Elsevier, Oxford.

CHAPTER 11

Integrating and maintaining quality

In Chapter 10 we examined some of the financial monitoring and control systems which are suitable for use by a small business. In this chapter we are concerned with the non-financial systems, which essentially fall under the heading of quality management. This involves defining quality standards, examining the ways in which we build quality systems into our products and services, and identifying the methods that are suitable to monitor and control the effectiveness of those quality systems.

The objective of this chapter is to assist the reader to:

- Identify the aspects of the business which are critical to the provision of quality goods and services.
- To establish realistic quality standards for the business which are relevant to the aims and objectives of the business.
- To set up monitoring and control procedures which will enable those standards to be achieved on a consistent basis.
- To examine examples of good practice in terms of customer service.

The three most frequently used quality procedures against which businesses can be assessed for accreditation are the International Standards Organisation standards, ISO 9002, for quality systems and procedures (formerly British Standard, BS 5750), the EN14001 standards which relate to environmental quality, and the Investors in People (IiP) award for organisations which meet specified standards in staff training and development, personnel systems, equal opportunities, and other people-related quality systems. The important common feature of these is that they are not just a one-off process. Once awarded, the standards of accreditation have to be maintained, and the organisation is subject to periodic inspections by independent assessors which it must satisfy in order to retain the accreditation. The assessment criteria are rigorous and comprehensive, and unless the standards are maintained on a consistent basis, the organisation can have its ISO 9002 or IiP approval suspended or withdrawn.

Developing quality systems

Why does a business need to bother with IiP or ISO 9002?

For many businesses the desire to achieve ISO 9002 or IiP accreditation is not always altruistic, as possession of one or other of these is becoming an increasing requirement for inclusion on lists of preferred suppliers, or for competitive tenders, particularly in the public sector and in the automotive industry. In the case of some major organisations which are themselves accredited, they simply refuse to buy from any suppliers who are not already accredited or working towards accreditation. At first glance, this approach may seem rather harsh, but it does in fact make a good deal of sense in that a supplier's possession of a quality accreditation should ensure that goods or services obtained from that supplier will be of the right quality. The ISO standards, which superseded the BS 5750, are accepted on a European-wide basis, so possession of one of these is particularly important for firms trading in international markets. The implementation of quality systems can also bring about a range of further direct benefits including:

- Reduced customer complaints, and returned or rejected goods. In addition to the obvious cost savings of not having to process complaints or to handle returned goods and replace them, in the longer term the enhanced reputation of quality goods or services will increase sales.
- Customer retention is improved leading to a reduction in selling costs, as less sales effort goes into replacing lost customers. This means that the sales effort can be directed to expanding the customer base to increase turnover and profits. This is discussed in more detail later in this chapter.
- Quality production systems work towards eliminating faults or problems by ensuring that they do not occur in the first place. This idea of "quality by design" is aimed at ensuring that all aspects of design and production are geared towards getting

the product right first time and every time. In the short term this may result in an initial increase in costs, but in the longer-term costs will fall, as there is no longer the need for extensive and detailed inspection. Similarly, as more goods are produced to the correct standard, the costs of rejection or reworking are also greatly reduced. For example, quality systems will discourage the purchase of components from the cheapest supplier on the basis of price alone. The cheapest supplier's components may have a failure rate of perhaps 10%, which if they remain undetected could result in a failure or rejection rate in the finished article of 10% or more. However, for a small increment in the cost of the components, the failure rate might be reduced to 1% or 2% resulting in huge savings on reworking, repairs or replacement; and of course savings resulting from the reduction of amounts of waste materials generated.

■ The use of quality circles and an ethos of continuous improvement amongst staff tends to result in problems being noticed before they develop. Staff also become more positive about their roles and duties, as the quality process encourages ownership or responsibility. Planned training and development programmes for staff also enable them to become more efficient at their work as they gain more detailed knowledge of the processes. Staff involvement in regular quality meetings in work time (quality circles) where supervisors have the same status as ordinary staff, promote a coherent approach in working towards the achievement of quality systems of work and quality standards.

■ Regular internal audits, and periodic external assessments or inspections ensure that quality standards are maintained on an on-going basis. Initially this may be viewed as a threat or a matter of fear of outside criticism, but as time goes on, the ability and confidence to face audits knowing that systems and procedures are good, usually develops into a matter of pride in the organisational systems.

■ Management and communication systems and procedures are improved which allows for better planning, easier decision-making, and problem solving. In particular, the improved communications between levels of staff tends to promote earlier warnings of possible problems. It is the difference between shooting the messenger who is the bearer of bad news, and praising the same person for being astute enough to spot a potential difficulty, which demonstrates a basic shift in organisational culture from punishment by blame, to motivation by praise.

So, how does the process work?

In the first half of the 20th century great emphasis was placed on quality control in the manufacturing and production environments. This was based on the idea of ensuring that customers received quality products by inspecting them at each stage of the production process and rejecting any faulty or substandard items. Perversely, high (and costly) rates of rejection were often regarded as a sign of good quality products, as only the best were allowed to pass. Naturally, the more thorough and rigorous the inspection, the more costly the process became. Following on from quality control came the idea of quality assurance, where operations management systems were employed to make production processes more efficient, and to eliminate faults in the production process. This was perhaps a move in the right direction but it still did not address the problem of tackling problems which were inherent within products and systems by virtue of the way in which they had been designed.

The total quality management (TQM) approach had in fact been around since the post-World War II period, and the American TQM guru W. Edwards Deming, started to employ its principles in the re-establishment of post-war Japan, the Americans having failed to take it on board at home in spite of Deming's efforts to persuade them. TQM started to grow in popularity in the USA and Europe in the 1970s. It focussed initially on the marketing principle of identifying the customer's needs, both the customers in the market place, and those internal customers in the production chain within the organisation. Once the customer need is identified, TQM works on the basis of designing standards of excellence within that product, and then designing quality systems in the organisation, which would ensure that the excellence of the product can be achieved and delivered to the customer on a regular and consistent basis – hence the phrase: "getting it right first time and every time".

How do we go about achieving it?

In larger organisations the usual route is to either employ a firm of quality management consultants to examine all of the various systems used by the organisation, or to appoint a trained quality services manager to carry out the same process, to design the standards to which the organisation will work, to produce the manuals and procedures, and to seek and subsequently maintain accreditation. Overall this can be a long and very expensive exercise which is likely to be well beyond the resources of most small businesses, especially those just starting up. If accreditation is essential, then some expenditure must be expected, although advice, and sometimes financial assistance, can be obtained from local councils, enterprise agencies, business links, etc. If however, you just wish to design and build quality systems into your business without gaining formal accreditation, then the process can be simplified, although not to the extent that you can start cutting corners, i.e. not what quality management is about.

For someone starting up in business, probably the easiest way to go about formulating a quality management policy is to start by looking at all of the systems and procedures which operate within the business, both now and in the foreseeable future; and having listed these, for every one of them, ask yourself "What can conceivably go wrong?" A good starting point might be to look at what happens when a customer enquires about your products or services, and then to follow the sequence through, from receipt of order, production, delivery, invoicing, after-sales service, etc.; and of course, don't forget the administrative processes which support each of these stages. We will take a hypothetical example of a plumber, Mr Mick Sturbs, who is a sole trader employing a young lad to assist him, and we will work through the various stages of handling a customer enquiry and carrying out the work:

1. Mick has a weekly advertisement in the local paper which generates most of his business. What can go wrong? Does he pay the paper promptly and regularly to ensure continuity of advertising? Is the advert clear about the types of services he provides, and how to contact him? Does it project a professional image? Does it produce results in the form of enquiries for work?

2. A customer sees the advert and enquires about his services. Does the customer find it easy to contact him? Does someone take messages for him whilst he is out? Are they positive, helpful and competent in answering, or do they appear rude, indifferent or disinterested? Are they knowledgeable about the business? Will they know how to contact him in an emergency? If Mick uses an answer phone, does he check it regularly during the day? Does he follow up enquiries by promptly returning

the call, or do customers get tired of waiting and go elsewhere? Does he use a mobile phone to make contact easier? Are the mobile phone batteries charged regularly so that it is ready for use when needed? Are the details of each enquiry recorded carefully, or does he tend to lose details of customers and their telephone numbers? Does he respond to enquiries within a specified period of time, or do the customers have to wait until he is ready?

3. A customer arranges an appointment for Mick to fix a new central heating boiler. Does he allow sufficient time in his diary to do the job properly or does he try to cram it in between other jobs? Does he build in contingency time in case he encounters a problem, or does he leave the job unfinished to return a few days later? Does he arrive on time at the customer's premises, or turn up half way through the day? Is he polite and friendly, or rude or indifferent? Does his appearance create the right impression with the customer, or is he scruffy or wearing greasy overalls and muddy boots? Does he project a professional attitude, or does he give the impression of being a bodger? Does he make sure that he has all of the necessary equipment with him, or does he keep having to go back to get them? Has he ordered the materials in advance to ensure that they are available when needed? Has he given the customer a written quotation for the work and explained what is, and what is not, included in the price? Has he explained his terms of trade and the arrangements for payment? Does he pay his own suppliers regularly and reliably to ensure that his supplies are always available? Is his assistant competent and knowledgeable, or just a gopher?

4. Mick fits the new central heating boiler for his customer. Has he used good quality materials that will ensure a lasting job, or has he cut corners to boost his profit? Has the work been completed to a professional standard, or has he bodged it because he is short of time? Has he checked any work carried out by his assistant? Has he advised the customer of any safety measures needed, and how to use the boiler properly? Has he checked that the customer understands these? Has he provided the customer with the manufacturer's warranty for the boiler? Does he offer a warranty for his own workmanship? Has he left the premises in a clean and tidy condition and removed any rubbish? Has he provided the customer with a detailed invoice, and explained any variances from the estimated cost? Did he

obtain the customer's approval for any extra expenditure before it was incurred? Did he check that the customer was satisfied with the work? Did he thank the customer for payment? Did he leave the customer a business card for future reference, or in case of emergencies?

5. After the job was finished. Did he call the customer a few days later to check that all was going well? On completion, did he record his sales income, and the various items of expenditure in his sales and purchase accounts books or petty cash book? Was any value-added tax (VAT) paid or collected, recorded correctly? Were his tools cleaned and stored, and any materials such as solder, replenished ready for the next job? Were any problems with the boiler reported to the manufacturer or supplier? Did he remember to top up the petrol in his van ready for the early start the following day, or will he be arriving late yet again?

The questions above are by no means exhaustive, but a wrong answer to just about any one of them could result either in a problem arising, or in the client receiving an inferior level of service. Quality systems do not have to be complex to be effective. In Mick's case, his quality systems and procedures could probably be organised using a simple job sheet which incorporates a checklist of the various items. His procedure for dealing with clients' enquiries could just involve organising an efficient answering service and mobile phone, and setting himself simple standards for response times. For example, he could check his answering service at regular set times during the day and then make a point of returning any call within no more than 3 hours of its receipt. He could diarise follow-up calls to clients within a week of the work being completed. He could have standard quotation forms printed, with his terms of trade on the rear. He could set his own administrative standards and systems to maintain his accounts on a weekly basis, to pay all bills promptly on the dates due, and to chase his own debtors for payment. He could also arrange vocational training for his assistant, and take a short course in customer care for himself. As a qualified plumber he could maintain his membership of the appropriate trade association, and of necessity he must maintain his Corgi gas fitting accreditation to operate legally.

The idea of TQM still remains very much within the domain of larger organisations, although it is gradually becoming more noticeable in smaller firms. The great thing about designing and building quality into systems and procedures for small firms is that when there are still relatively few firms employing these systems, the opportunity for developing and enhancing a reputation for quality is tremendous, and so are the potential benefits for putting the business ahead of its competitors. Many larger firms state within their Mission Statement, the objective of becoming a "first-choice supplier", but there is absolutely no reason why a small firm or a sole trader cannot employ quality systems to achieve the same objective within its own local market.

Monitoring quality

How can a small business monitor its quality systems?

Not only do small businesses lack the staff and resources which larger organisations can employ to develop and maintain quality systems, they face similar problems when it comes to monitoring their quality standards and measuring their performance. But pressure of work or lack of resources should not be used as an excuse for an owner-manager to neglect the monitoring process. As we have shown in the case of Mick the plumber above, it is perfectly possible to implement quality systems within very small and simple businesses. If the systems are capable of being established quite easily, then they are equally capable of being monitored without the need for complex computer systems, or substantial staff time. In Mick's case a simple checklist against which he could check each job would probably be sufficient so long as the list was sufficiently detailed to cover all relevant quality issues, and it would also for his staff to know clearly what standards are expected of them.

In retrospect, the most obvious indicator of potential problems or of the failure of quality systems is to look at the sales volume and revenue figures which were used in the preparation of the budgetary plan. Are the figures on target? If not, then do we know why this is so? Is it due to external factors beyond our control, or something we are doing wrong within the business? Have our competitors been affected in the same way? Is it due to poor forecasting, or inadequate sales effort, or to a problem with the quality of the products or services we are offering? If it is apparently a problem of quality, then there are a number of options we can employ to isolate and identify the problem or problems within our products or systems.

The obvious starting point for any business is to examine the nature of the complaints received, or goods returned in order to determine whether or not these affect the whole range of products, or a specific group of them. If the complaints have been received across a whole range of goods or services, then it is probable that the source of the problem will lie within the systems used by the business. In this case it will be necessary to examine the complaints more closely, perhaps by contacting former customers who have complained, in order to seek out any common points or issues which might pinpoint the problem. If the owner of the business has proper quality systems in place, these types of common issues should already be being picked up anyway as part of the on-going review of quality standards. If that is not the case, then there is clearly more than one flaw in the system which must be addressed.

If however, the complaints have been focussed on a single product or product group, then it is more likely that the problem will lie within the product itself rather than the systems which deliver them, and it should be a fairly straightforward process to isolate the problem. In the case of physical goods it may be a specific component or assembly process which is the continuing source of the problem, and which can be identified as a common element amongst returned goods. If we know that the problem started at a specific time, it may be traceable to change of supplier, or a variation in the assembly process. If on-going, but gradually increasing, it may be due to a problem of wear and tear, or deterioration of production machinery which once discovered, can be rectified.

Another indication of problems are the changes in levels of customer retention, although the monitoring of these is really only applicable to businesses which supply customers on a regular basis, as opposed to one-off sales. There is always a certain amount of "natural wastage" or turnover with customers, and over a period of time this can be established, but when these rates start to increase, it is usually indicative of either a decline in the quality problem within the products of services, or an indication that they are not up to the same standards being provided by competitors. Once again, the monitoring of these is more of a longer-term process as short-term fluctuations in customer activity tend to distort the picture in the short term.

Analysing changes in sales volumes and revenues, and customer retention levels, and monitoring volumes and patterns of complaints after the event it is very much a reactive process, which by definition is not what quality management is all about. A more proactive approach is to monitor sales and customer responses on an on-going basis, and this should be an inherent part of the quality systems of any business. One option is to establish a positive procedure for customer care which will provide a prompt and efficient means of responding to and rectifying customer problems. Another way is to use customer feedback, either verbal or obtained by questionnaire, to monitor the customers' perceptions of the quality of the goods and services which you are providing. Again, the quality approach relies on prompt response and positive action to any problems identified by the feedback.

Customer care

Customer care or customer service is really the outward facing aspect of quality, focused on formulating and implementing policies and standards of behaviour and practice, which will ensure that customers' needs are identified. Customer care is also about developing procedures which ensure that customers are treated politely, fairly, and positively if and when things go wrong. The term customer service often has negative connotations in so far as the phrase is often used a label for what is effectively the complaints department of many businesses, hence customer care is often used as an alternative to emphasise the more positive focus on quality. To further differentiate between the two: customer service is often described as the way in which we respond to customers and their problems. In contrast, customer care goes a stage further in that a customer care policy (like a TQM policy) tries to build a policy of awareness and responsiveness to the customer within the provision of the product or service as a whole, and with the intention of avoiding possible problems at a later stage. Customer care is about minimising the occurrences that are likely to give rise to complaint, and responding quickly and positively when complaints do occur.

Invariably the customer service policy will overlap and reflect the sales and marketing plans, and the quality policy of the business, as it does in effect define the way in which quality standards are implemented within the sales environment. We have already examined the marketing context of identifying customer needs in the market research section of Chapter 6. The service aspects of customer needs can most effectively be determined by asking the customers, directly face to face, by telephone, or by written questionnaire, whether the business is meeting the full range of their needs and expectations, where, if any, are the gaps or shortfalls, and how the customers would like to see those addressed.

Apart from the details and specifications of the products themselves, in most cases when we are talking about customer needs we are in reality talking about customer expectations. By this we mean what the customers expect from us as suppliers, and what the customers themselves perceive to be their needs, as opposed to what we believe them to be.

What type of things then, do the customers expect?

This topic is discussed in more depth in Chapter 18, but to summarise and put the subject into context:

- *From the business*: Pleasant and suitable surroundings which are clean, welcoming, well-lit, safe and hygienic, and living up to the general image of the business and its products or services.
- *From the staff*: Sufficient staff to be available. Staff to show a friendly, interested and welcoming attitude, and to be pleasant, and certainly non-threatening. Staff should also be smart in appearance, competent and knowledgeable. Customers also expect that dealing with the organisation's staff should be a pleasant experience, and free of problems, antagonism, or excuses.
- *From the products, goods, or services*: These should be available when wanted, fit for the purpose for which they were acquired, and at a reasonable price which constitutes value for money. User-friendly information should be provided as to where the product can be found, and its use and operation. The product should also be supported by a friendly, helpful and efficient after-sales service in the event of any problems arising.

So why should we bother with customer service or customer care?

The primary objectives of customer care policies are to:

- Retain customers for repeat business. The use of sales staff and advertising, etc. to find new customers is an expensive process. If we can retain, or at least reduce the rate of natural turnover of existing customers, then sales effort can be invested in finding extra new customers which overall will increase the sales revenues and profits of the business.
- Increase the level of trade with existing customers by improving their confidence in the business and its products or services. Dealing with the business should constitute a pleasant and problem-free experience. This again will generate extra sales revenue and profit in the longer term.
- Enhancing the reputation of the business and its quality standards. This is aimed at increasing customer loyalty and

recommendation, which again adds to turnover and profit. Even customers who complain, but who are treated well in response, tend to return, and to tell others about their positive experience. In contrast, poor service leads to loss of reputation and customers, and consequential reductions in turnover, or the need for extra sales effort to replace lost trade.

- In the longer term, the implementation of customer care policies tends to reduce the costs of operations. As in the case of quality management described in the previous chapter, by building in quality systems it is possible to reduce the need for checking and inspection, leading to a reduction in the cost of quality control. Similarly, a good customer care policy tends to reduce the occurrence of problems and to correct them before they get out of hand. Customers who don't complain often tend to go elsewhere anyway, so the idea is to avoid complaints arising in the first place, to prevent the loss of customers. Overall the process should result in a reduction of costs as the need for inspection and remedial action is reduced.

- Within the business itself, a positive customer care policy should also have the effect of increasing job satisfaction of staff, both by the positive interaction with their customers, and by avoiding the stress and aggravation which accompanies customer complaints. Once again, this should contribute to the overall efficiency of the business.

Customer expectations do not always relate to the object in question but to the potential benefits that object offers. People do not just go to restaurants for food, they go to spend a pleasant evening with friends in relaxed and convivial surroundings. Cars are not just sold on engine size, they are sold on the pleasure of driving in comfort, their reliability, economy, the exhilaration of speed and acceleration, and the image they convey. Think back to the Dexion salesman quoted in Chapter 6: "I sell solutions to problems and benefits to customers, not storage or materials handling systems". Similarly, within the sales transaction and subsequent interpersonal contact, customers do not just want efficiency, they need to be made to feel important and that their custom is valued, and to have esteem and respect from the sales staff, even if it is just a one-off transaction. Most important of all, the attitude projected by staff must be perceived as being genuine, no matter how obnoxious the customer may be in reality, and given time, the positive attitude may even rub off on them! Customers are a complex mixture of personality, emotions, motivations, attitudes and needs; and the more that you understand of their perspectives, the better you can meet those needs.

The implication of this is that the quality ethos and customer care attitude must be an inherent part of the internal culture of the business, which implies a high level of commitment on the part of the owners, to motivate their staff and to treat them in a similar equitable fashion. The bottom line is that you can hardly expect your staff to treat your customers with respect and to demonstrate commitment to customer care, if behind the scenes you are treating them like dirt! Remember, if you treat your staff badly, e.g. by being rude or arrogant when dealing with them, they will often wreak revenge through your clients by treating them in the same rude or arrogant fashion, and usually at a time and place where it is guaranteed to hurt you the most! Like charity, customer care starts at home, and you cannot expect your staff to be caring and considerate to customers if that care and consideration is not reflected in aspects of your management style.

How do we go about formulating a customer care policy?

As we have just said, the customer care attitude must become an inherent part of the culture of the business, and the policies which are developed must work towards that end. In larger organisations this normally takes place as part of an overall TQM strategy affecting all systems and operations, and relating to the internal customers as well as those in the external marketplace. In a new business the initial primary objective is usually that of survival and growth to a level of financial stability, and only once that stability has been achieved, can the proprietors move further towards enhancing growth and profit using quality systems. The fact is that irrespective of any desire to employ quality systems, most new businesses do not have the time or resources to implement these in the early stages of their existence. However, once a basic level of stability is achieved, they are then in a position to move from reactive to proactive methods of working, of which the introduction of customer care policies is an obvious choice and priority.

Probably the most important aspect of the customer care policy is that it should coincide with, and work towards meeting, the primary objectives or mission statement of the business. In fact most businesses which actively promote policies of customer service and customer care invariably end up including reference to those policies within those objectives, particularly in service industries where the process generates the profit. The mission statement might be something like: "The company will aim to provide a high quality, reliable service to its clients which will establish it as a first-choice supplier in the market place, leading to maximisation of profits and sustained and continuous growth". The corresponding customer care statement might be something like: "To provide a high standard of customer service and care which will enhance the reputation of the company's services leading to an expansion of its customer base and enhancing the profitability of the business".

The policy also needs to identify how the customers of the business will be made aware of the customer care policies. Some organisations do this by incorporating their customer service standards within their printed terms of trade, although there may be a tendency for the information to be lost in the small print and seldom read. Some clearly publicise their policies in their advertising material, or on printed sheets which accompany receipts or sales invoices. Where physical products are produced, the information may be contained within the printed warranty or product guarantee. Others have their policies displayed prominently in their reception areas where visitors and clients can readily view them.

Most of the conventional textbooks on customer care are geared towards larger organisations, and propose commendable ideas such as creating posts of customer service manager, increasing levels of teamwork and multi-skilling, integrated audio, video, and data communications. These may be great for a large company, but are somewhat grandiose and impractical for the average owner-manager of a new business, who struggles to afford a secretary. What is needed then is to take some of the ideas from the big-company model, and to apply them on a smaller scale. So in answer to the question: "How do we go about formulating a customer care policy?" we revisit the customer expectations which we examined earlier and apply them to the small business environment. For example, we know that our customers expect to receive a positive and prompt response to enquiries. So in place of the "integrated communications systems" of large organisations, we look at practical ways of ensuring that no call from a customer is overlooked, and that all enquiries receive a response within a specified period of time. In fact within small firms the formulation of the customer care policy becomes more a case of identifying where there is a potential problem, resulting from a customer expectation not being met, then finding the most practical and affordable solution for that problem, and setting basic standards for ensuring for operating the solution.

Quality standards for customer care

It is the prescribed standards of performance that form the backbone of any customer care policy, as unless the various processes of interaction with customers are measurable against defined standards, there is no way of telling whether or not the policies are working. The process then involves defining a comprehensive range of standards for each stage of the interaction with the customers, i.e. before, during and after the transactions, and then monitoring the achievement of those standards.

Pre-transactional standards are concerned with the stage prior to the transaction, when contact with the customer is first established. These define the processes and responses required to keep the customer satisfied in the preliminary or enquiry stages of the sale. For example, a catering business providing wedding reception services might have for its pre-transactional standards:

- All enquiries will receive a telephone response within 24 hours.
- The owner will arrange an appointment with the clients within 7 days to discuss their needs, and will provide sample menus, and photographs and references from previous functions.
- A written quotation will be posted to the client within 48 hours of the visit, giving a detailed schedule of the services to be provided, any options available, and a firm estimate of costs for those items, and a summary of payment terms, etc. This will form the contract with the clients.
- On receipt of confirmation of the booking, a letter of acknowledgement will be sent to the clients requesting the agreed deposit or booking fee.
- Four weeks before the event, the client will be contacted to confirm any variations to the requirements, and an invoice will be risen for the balance.
- A week before the event the client will be contacted again to finalise details of access arrangements, times, and any special requirements, e.g. vegetarians, young children or wheelchair users.
- All necessary food and sundries will be ordered 5 days before the event for delivery on the day before the event, or early the same morning.

The transactional standards relate to the quality and provision of the actual transaction itself, the production and quality of goods or materials, the processes by which it will be delivered, and the standards that can be expected from the people involved. This is best illustrated using the same example of the catering business:

- All food items will be fresh, of high quality, and will be stored in suitable containers at safe temperatures prior to preparation, and before they are served, in compliance with Environmental Health Regulations.
- Food will be prepared as close as possible to the time of the event to ensure freshness and safety. It will be prepared in hygienic conditions, under the supervision of staff trained and qualified in food hygiene.
- Tables will be laid with clean cloths, crockery and cutlery, with decorations in the colours and designs prescribed by the customers using.
- Waiting staff will be clean, tidy, polite, and friendly. They will be dressed in a standard formal style appropriate to the event. Food will be served promptly and tables cleared quickly once the diners have finished eating.

Post-transactional standards are used to define levels of after-sales service, warranty conditions for products, locations of service centres, response or turnaround times, etc. They would also include how the service is completed, and how feedback on service provision would be sought. Again using the above example:

- After the meal all items will be cleared promptly, washed, and removed from the site. Kitchen areas will be left in a clean and tidy condition, and all rubbish will be bagged for disposal.
- At the end of the event, the clients will be approached by the person in charge to check that there are no further requirements, and then thanked before departure.
- A week later the clients will be sent a letter enclosing a brief questionnaire and pre-paid envelope, requesting their feedback on the service provision.

The last of those post-transactional standards is particularly important as there is little point in establishing a comprehensive list of standards and associated targets without some form of monitoring to ensure that they are being achieved. The feedback should be evaluated and used to modify the standards or to develop new standards.

How do we implement the customer care policy in practical terms, and ensure that it is achieved?

To answer this question, let's take several examples of customer expectations which might be problematic, and potential solutions to these are given in the following examples.

Example 1

Problem: Customers expect someone to respond quickly to their enquiries.

Solution: If the owner-manager is not available to answer enquiries, then nominate another person to take that specific responsibility, ensuring that they have or are given basic training in telephone answering skills, and some knowledge of the products or services which you supply. Insist that all details of enquiries are logged. If no one is available, then ensure that an efficient remote-access answer phone or voicemail system is in place, preferably supported by e-mail and fax facilities.

Standards: Make regular contact with the designated staff, at least two or three times per day, to ensure that there are no outstanding queries, or to provide answers to any questions which may be beyond their scope. If using answering facilities, check them at 2 to 3 hour intervals, log all details of enquiries and dates and times received, then ensure that all messages are acknowledged immediately by telephone. Ensure that any actions arising are implemented within 24 hours.

Achievement: Monitor log entries to ensure that responses have been made within standard times. Check the frequency of incidents which fall outside of the standards and investigate the cause of these.

Example 2

Problem: Customers expect the business premises to be clean, tidy, well-lit, and pleasant to be in. This can be particularly difficult for a small firm with very confined working space.

Solution: Try to divide the working part of the premises from the part accessed by customers, e.g. the reception area. Ensure that it is warm, dry, reasonably decorated, well-lit, and that it is cleaned on a regular daily basis. Provide some basic seating to make clients comfortable, and information about the firm's products or services to keep them occupied if waiting. Ensure that they are greeted and acknowledged on arrival and not kept waiting. Ensure that your staff are aware that the area must be treated differently, and reserved for clients, and why this is so.

Standards: Daily cleaning and watering of any pot plants, regular replacement of reading materials and information, e.g. weekly/monthly, periodic painting or redecoration, and replacement of damaged furniture.

Example 3

Problem: Customers expect a prompt response to problems and complaints.

Solution: Establish a procedure for handling complaints, recording details of the complainant, the nature of the problem, the customer's desired solution, etc. Allocate responsibility for handling complaints to a specific member of staff and train that person in the procedures to be followed. Establish a tracking system to ensure that complaints are followed up and resolved within specified times, and that any exceptions are flagged for action.

Standards: All complaints to be acknowledged within 24 hours and action taken to rectify problems within 72 hours of the complaint. If further time is required beyond the target response time, the client is to be notified of reason why, and given an estimated time for the resolution of the problem. Within 1 week of the problem being rectified, designated person will telephone the client to check on satisfaction, and to obtain client's feedback on the complaints procedure, along with any outstanding problems or adverse comments. These will be formally recorded and risen for discussion at next weekly staff meeting.

The above examples have looked at just three customer expectations, the first being an example of what the customers expect from the staff of a business, the second of what is expected from the premises, and the third of what is expected of after-sales service for the products. If we look back at the rest of the customer expectations described at the start of this chapter, we can see that the process used in those three examples can be extended and applied to most of the others in some form or another, within just about any small business. The list of customer expectations are useful as a starting point for identifying ways of implementing customer care, but the owner-manager still needs to analyse the full range of other expectations which might arise from customers of his or her particular business. Each and every one of them can be treated as a potential problem area, in response to which a customer care policy will need to be formulated. Once this solution to the potential problem is proposed, and a method of implementation identified, standards can be established which will be used to define its success. The final part of the policy then, is to identify the process and frequency with which the achievement of those standards will be monitored. That in a nutshell, is how customer care policies can be implemented in even the smallest of businesses.

To summarise this chapter:

- Oakland (2003) states that "quality begins with marketing". In the first instance we must establish the customers' needs for the goods or services we aim to provide.
- Secondly we must establish the customers' expectations of the products and services, and of the businesses which aim to provide them.
- We must analyse every stage of the production or provision of the goods or services, and the systems which support that provision, to identify potential problem areas, and to design those products and systems to avoid the anticipated problems.
- We must set precise, accurate, and realistic standards for our products and systems which will act as targets against which we can monitor our success in providing quality products and services.
- We must ensure that all staff involved in the business are committed to the principles of providing quality products and services, and are knowledgeable about the standards required of them, and that they have received any training necessary to enable them to achieve those standards.
- We must monitor the compliance with standards on an on-going basis, by monitoring customer feedback, complaints, product returns, etc., to ensure that any problems are promptly addressed and rectified. In the longer term, we must monitor changes in sales volumes and revenues for our products and services, and overall customer retention, to assess the impact these are having on the overall performance of the business.
- We must review all products, systems and procedures on a regular basis to ensure that quality standards are maintained, or are modified as needed, and that these are redesigned to eliminate future potential problems when required.
- We must define and regularly monitor a customer service policy that will enable the business to maximise customer retention and loyalty so that sales effort can be focused on developing new business rather than on replacing lost customers.
- Finally, we must continue to ask ourselves the question: "If I were one of my own customers, would I really be happy with the quality of the service and products which I am receiving from this business?"

Reference

Oakland, J. (2003). *Total Quality Management.* Elsevier, Oxford.

Further reading

Bell, D., McBride, P. and Wilson, G. (1998). *Managing Quality.* IM/Butterworth-Heinemann, Oxford.

Canning, V. (1999). *Being Successful in Customer Care.* Blackhall, Dublin.

Sadgrove, K. (1995). *Making TQM Work.* Kogan Page, London.

Smith, I. (2003). *Meeting Customer Needs.* CMI/Elsevier, Oxford.

Tricker, R. (1997). *ISO 9000 for Small Businesses.* Butterworth-Heinemann, Oxford.

CHAPTER 12

Putting the business plan together

In Chapter 3 we examined in some detail, an example of business plan layout which would satisfy the requirements of most bank managers or financial institutions, and which complied with the best-practice model defined in the Small Firms Enterprise Development Initiative (SFEDI) National Occupational Standards for Business Planning.

The purpose of this chapter is twofold: first, to round-off the business plan by explaining how the proposals will be implemented and to consider what might possibly go wrong in that process. Second, to encourage the potential entrepreneur who is going through the motions of formulating his or her business plan, to pause, and to take a step back to re-examine the work they have carried out so far. This review of the overall business plan is intended to ensure that the content, structure, and presentation of the document are suitable for submission to a potential lender or investor.

Implementation and risk analysis

The implementation and risk analysis sections of the business plan are just as important to potential lender and investors as the finance or marketing sections, because they will want to see that the entrepreneur has planned the process carefully in terms of identifying each of the key stages in sequential order, has allowed sufficient time to carry them all out, and has given due consideration to risks and hazards that could potentially cause problems along the way.

Trading status

In Chapter 4 we looked at the options for the trading status of the business – sole trader, partnership, limited company, etc. Assuming that the choice of trading status has been made, the entrepreneur will need to make the necessary registrations in readiness to start trading. In the case of sole traders and partnerships this is relatively simple as "all are required" is for the business owner(s) in the UK is to notify that HM Revenue & Customs that the business has started or will be starting to trade, and the date thereof. This can be done quite simply through a specific HM Revenue & Customs contact telephone line, currently 0845 915 4515. The registration has to be made no later than 3 months after the date when the business started but can be made before trading starts. The trading name should not deliberately duplicate that of any other local businesses, although similarities do occur. In some cases where services are purely local and there is no geographical overlap this may not be a problem, but where it does occur then litigation may follow, with action typically being instigated by the firm that has been using the name for the longer period.

For limited companies there are two options, either to buy a dormant company from a specialist supplier and then change the trading name to whatever is planned for the business via the Registrar of Companies (see Chapter 4), or to apply to the Registrar at Companies House to set up a totally new business. The latter may be marginally cheaper but the former option is simpler and quicker to achieve. In either case the Registrar will check to ensure that the chosen trading name is not already in use elsewhere. It may be sensible when thinking of potential business names, to have a fallback idea in case the preferred name is already in use.

Legal compliance in order to trade

Legislation has been discussed in Chapter 7 in more detail, but when the business is about to start it is always worth double-checking compliance with regulations, particularly where registration with a statutory body may be required. Apart from registering the trading status of the business, other typical examples of this might be the need to register for value-added tax (VAT) where likely sales turnover will exceed the prescribed threshold, the need to set up a PAYE (pay as you earn) system where staff are to be employed, the need for a risk/hazard analysis and written Health and Safely policy if more than five staff are employed or where the work activity may be hazardous. There may also be a need for any industry-specific registrations, e.g. for food handlers or suppliers to register with the local Environmental Health Office, or for licensing of certain activities such as bookmakers or pet shops.

Planning the pre-start-up timetable

The pre-start preparation will vary widely from one business proposition to another simply because of the degree of complexity involved. A window cleaner, once he has equipped himself with a van, ladder buckets, etc. is ready to go and can start knocking on doors to find customers; but in contrast a manufacturing business may need to find premises and negotiate contracts for them, to order and commission plant or machinery, and to source raw materials and skilled staff before work can commence, and that could feasibly take 3 to 6 months.

The starting point then, is to try to identify a date by which trading would ideally start, and then to identify and examine all of the key stages and events that must take place before that date. Some operations' managers would say that logically we should start by working out the critical stages and time involved in implementing them before we even consider fixing a target start date, but this is not always possible as there may be good reasons for aiming for a specific start date, such as the need to be ready to take advantage of seasonal sales. For example, someone opening a seaside guest house or restaurant, would want to be ready for the Spring to take advantage of the Summer holiday season, and the last thing they would want to do is to delay the opening to October when the season has ended and there will be little sales revenue for the following 6 months. For some home-based new businesses the start date may not be critical at all as they may be initially working on a part-time basis with the intention of working up to full-time activity as the customer base is expanded. The first questions to be asked then are: Have you identified a specific start date and how critical is that start date, e.g. to meet a customer's deadline or to take advantage of seasonal trade?

Identifying key or critical stages

When you start to identify the work that needs to be done before the business can start trading some items will obviously be sequential in that one must be completed before another can start, whilst others can run alongside each other. The sequential items, such as finding and equipping premises, will typically be the ones that take the longest time to complete, especially if planning consent is required. Others such as negotiating contracts with suppliers or ordering marketing materials can be carried out at the same time. Figure 12.1 shows a simple Gannt chart example of some of the activities that might be involved in opening a new shop and they might be phased and implemented prior to the start date.

Many of the items or activities will have been identified in the Resources section of the business plan but at this stage it is necessary to identify:

- Those items or activities that will require lead times, i.e. must be planned and ordered well ahead of when they are required. For example, complex machinery may have to be ordered from the manufacturer perhaps 6 months before it is required, and may take further time to install and commission before it is ready to be used. Where contractors are to be employed, e.g. for shop fitting, they may need to be booked weeks or months in advance, and often the better their reputation is, the more notice they will require to be available. Pre-launch advertising and staff recruitment are other items that may require lead times, particularly in the latter case where staff may have to work out periods of notice to terminate other employment.

- Those items or activities that are critical in terms of having to be implemented or completed before others can commence, and where any delays in their implementation could have a knock-on effect causing delays with other parts of the project. For example, in the case of premises , the negotiation of leases or purchase contracts can take weeks or months, and likewise obtaining planning consent for change of use of premises can take months if there are any objections from members of the public, or in the case of Listed Buildings where changes of use may have to be advertised. Delays can be costly if you have to pay rent on unoccupied and unusable premises, and they can be compounded if, e.g. contractors are postponed and then cannot return precisely when you need them, due to their other work commitments.

Risk analysis and contingency planning

It is widely accepted as one of the general laws of nature that what can go wrong in a project will go wrong, so when planning the implementation

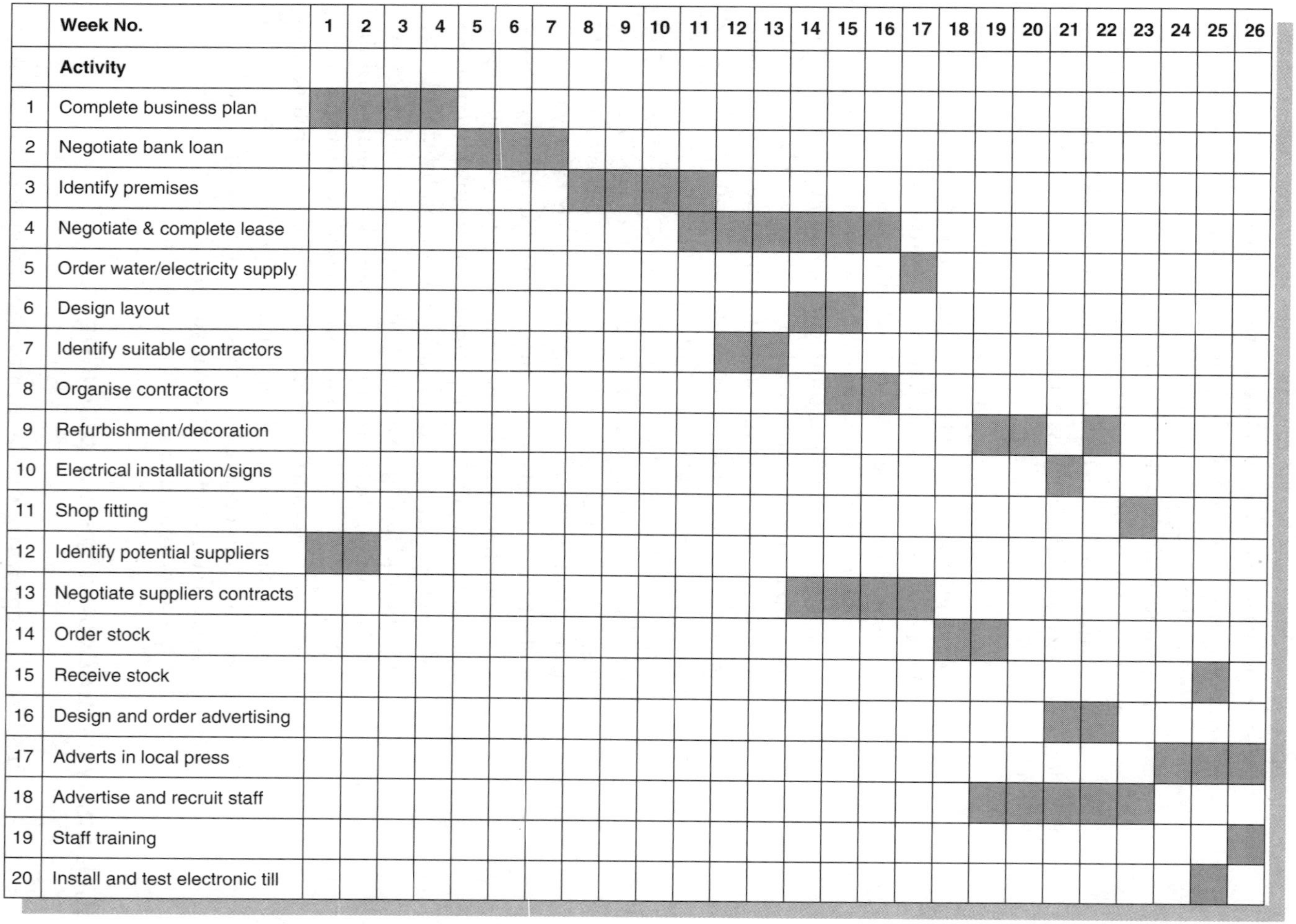

Figure 12.1
Gannt chart for preparation activities prior to new shop opening in week 27.

of a new business it is worth bearing this in mind, evaluating the extent of potential risks or delays, and making contingency plans for them. For example, in Figure 12.1, you will notice that in week 18 there is little going on apart from the ordering of stock, so in effect a spare week has been left as a contingency in case of any contractual delays, and similarly there is space in week 24 in case of an over-run in the refurbishment and shop fitting.

The process of risk analysis when applied to projects planning and implementation looks at three important questions:

1. What are the main risks that could occur, or what could possibly go wrong?
2. What is the likelihood or probability of each one of those risks occurring?
3. What impact would each of them have on the successful implementation of the project in terms of delays, monetary cost, or the risk of survival of the business?

Some project planners like to plot the comparative probability of occurrence against the impact on a table. Figure 12.2 illustrates how some of the implementation activities described in Figure 12.1 might be evaluated in terms of risk. Other practitioners prefer to use a score of 1 for low, 2 for medium, or 3 for high, and to multiply the probability score by the impact score, so that each risk can be evaluated on a scale of 1 to 9. In either case the purpose of the risk analysis is to identify which activities are most likely to disrupt the successful implementation of the

		Probability of occurrence		
		Low	Medium	High
Risk impact	Low	Suppliers contracts late	Not all staff available for training before opening	Contractors one week late starting work
	Medium	Over-run on shop fitting	Electronic till fails to work	Premises delayed
	High	Bank loan refused	Delays in planning consent	Delays in delivery of some stock items

Figure 12.2
Evaluation of risks.

business so that appropriate contingency plans can be made, like starting certain activities earlier to build in extra time in case of delay, or by allowing funds to cover the extra costs of any delays.

Reviewing the business plan

Within the SFEDI National Occupational Standards for Business Start-up there is a useful checklist that enables the person writing the business plan to work through their material to ensure that all relevant items have been covered in sufficient detail. The process recommends that the potential entrepreneur should:

- Review all of the data gathered during the research process about the business, its requirements and its markets, to ensure that the resulting information is both accurate and correct. This is an eminently sensible and obvious suggestion as it is easy to leave gaps with the intention of covering them later, only to fail to do so. It is also important to ensure that there are no inconsistencies between what has been described in the various sections of the business plan.
- Review all of the financial research and figures, checking them for accuracy, and ensuring that they are still relevant and not in need of revision. It is so easy to make minor changes within the business plan as it is developed, and then to fail to adjust the final calculations to reflect those changes. For example perhaps, you have decided to employ an extra member of staff within the business, or to revise the sales revenue without adjusting your cash-flow forecast and/or profit forecasts. You can be certain that the very item you have failed to adjust will always be the first one that the observant bank manager spots and chooses to ask you about!
- Ensure that the reviewed data enables the reader of the business plan to clearly identify the objectives of the plan, and that those objectives are realistic within the context of the plan. This is partly a matter or the style of presentation, in ensuring that the objectives stand out within the business plan. But it is also a matter of producing reasoned argument backed up by factual data, to justify to any potential financial backer, that the objectives are both realistic and achievable.
- You review the sources of the information which you have used, to ensure that the information is still up to date. This is

particularly important where, e.g. calculations have been based on current interest rates or exchange rates. It would also apply to any overheads and materials costs which have been included in your budgets. Are they still current, or have they increased for any reason?

- You should confirm with any potential lenders, investors, or backers that their requirements will remain the same, i.e. that they have not changed the terms or conditions of their funding or support, or their expectations of returns from the business. It can sometimes take quite a long time from first devising an idea for a new business to the stage when the final details of the business plan are produced, and many things can happen during the intervening period. It is also important therefore, to double-check that that none of your backers or financiers have had second thoughts, or have invested or tied up their money elsewhere in the meantime. If there is likely to be any substantial delay, it is often worth asking them for a Letter of Intent, which confirms their interest and support for your proposals, subject to negotiation of final terms and conditions, and the signing of formal agreements, etc. Such documents can be placed in the appendices to the business plan and used to support your case for the viability of the proposal.

- Some plans can take a period of time to put together so when you are checking and reviewing the accuracy of your data and information, make sure that you update or correct your business plan to reflect any other changes that have occurred since you started. If those changes have been substantial, such as additions to the proposed range of goods or services to be offered, you should identify any significant impact which might have on your proposed operations, and refer to this in the business plan. Will the changes affect the marketing of your goods or services, or your turnover or profitability? Will they impede or interfere with the way in which you plan to operate, and if so, how will you deal with this problem? Will you need to change or improve your control systems to manage the changes? Will you need to employ any additional staff or resources, and what are the cost implications? If you have already completed your business plan, you may wish to show this information as an addendum or an appendix to the plan, along with any published data or information which might support your modifications to the business plan. Do not be put off by thinking that by adding extra bits on to the end, it will detract from the overall appearance or impression of your business plan. If anything, it will add to your credibility by showing that you are perceptive to changing influences and that you can respond to them and revise your plans accordingly. In the world of small business, flexibility and adaptability are the keys to survival!

- The various component parts of the business plan should be integrated to form a coherent document which is consistent throughout, and which contains no self-contradictions or discrepancies in facts or figures. It should be comprehensive but concise, factual, honest, and accurate. It is often a good idea to provide an abstract or overview of the document (300 to 400 words is sufficient) which summarises the business idea, its potential profitability and the key points of its implementation. If your financiers have requested a particular format for the plan, then so be it. It may well be the case that they employ some form of scoring system which assists in evaluating the relative merit of the plans which they receive, or that the specific format helps them to utilise the criteria which they apply to approve applications for funding.
- The business plan should clearly state the nature of the business, its feasibility within the market place, the necessary resources required for start-up, its revenue, cash-flow and profit forecasts. It will also need to identify the key personnel and their respective roles, and to show the way in which it will be managed and organised. This information is not just for the benefit of potential backers, but as an on-going management tool for the owner-manager of the business.
- The plan should also show how and when the plan will be implemented, including the identification of any key or critical stages of implementation. It must also analyse any potential risks, and propose the contingency plans that would be used to handle them if they can during the implementation of the plan.
- Finally, the plan should contain sufficient information to allow any potential financier or backer to make a reasoned decision about its viability. Remember, key information should be included within the business plan itself, whilst supplementary or secondary information is best referred to and included in an appendix to the plan.

When assembling your business plan ready for submission to the bank manager or financier, it pays to give careful attention to the quality of presentation. You should be aiming to create an impression of professionalism in the way you present your proposals. The document itself should be prepared carefully, and should comply to certain basic minimum standards:

- The document should be bound in some form of flexible binding. Most high street stationers can offer a wide range of inexpensive transparent or coloured plastic bindings used for reports, dissertations, and business plans.

- At the front you should provide a header page which states clearly the name of the business, and the proprietors. For example: "Business Plan for Acme Wedding Services. Miss Helen Highwater. November 2006". The main title of the business should be centred; about one-third down the page, in large bold letters (20 to 24 point). The name of the proprietor(s) should be lower down, to the left-hand side, and in smaller letters, e.g. 14 point size, with the date of preparation opposite on the lower-right-hand side of the page. The font used for the text is optional, with Times New Roman or Arial as common favourites, although educationalists will tell you that Tahoma or Gill Sans MT are more reader-friendly, particularly if your bank manager should happen to be dyslexic. Whilst the choice remains yours, it is good practice to avoid large blocks of italic text, and Comic or Script fonts do not create the sort of professional image that you should be projecting in a professional business plan.

- Immediately inside you should provide a brief contents page, listing the key sections of the plan. It is also useful, if the business plan is quite a lengthy document, to provide a short summary or abstract which describes briefly the nature of the proposal, as suggested above.

- The bulk of the document should be word processed or typed (hand-written documents do not create a professional image) on single side A4 size, paper, with margins of at least 1 in./2 cm all round. It is usually best to use either white, or another light coloured paper for ease of reading, and always use a good quality paper of at least 80 or 90 g. Single spaced lines are quite acceptable, although it is a good idea not to make paragraphs too long. If you have word processed the document, don't forget to use the spell-check, otherwise, proof read it carefully, as again, silly typing or spelling mistakes do not create a good impression. Spreadsheets and tables should also be checked for silly errors. The use of bold text is quite acceptable to emphasise key points, especially if they contain favourable or impressive profit forecasts.

■ It is always a good idea to use a numbering system for each section and subsection (e.g. 1. The Business Idea, 1.1 Type of business proposed and trading status, 1.2 Range of services to be offered, etc.) There are two main advantages of this: first that it provides a clear and sequential structure that the reader can follow, and second and most important, it allows for easy cross-referencing between sections which can help you to avoid having to duplicate material in different sections.

■ Any bulky supporting information of research material which is not directly relevant to the main content of the business plan should be confined to the appendices. Whilst it is useful to have such data available for reference, too much indirect information within the central text can be distracting, and may well deter the reader from moving on to the important parts of the text. The use of coloured diagrams has become standard practice in recent years, but they should be included to show relevant data only, and not simply to impress the bank manager with your computing skills (unless of courses, that is the nature of your business).

■ Finally, it always pays to have one or two spare copies available, in case the bank manager has mislaid the one you sent; or perhaps in case of accident. It does not create a good impression to proffer the bank manager your one and only copy covered in beer stains, and a second copy is always useful for reference when you are asked questions. If you really do only have one spare copy, then either wrap it securely in waterproof material; or avoid tea, coffee, wine, and any other coloured food or drink which will invariably be drawn to it like a magnet, and just stick to clear gin and vodka, or preferably water if you are just about to go for the appointment with the bank manager!

Further reading

Bragg, A. and Bragg, M. (2005). *Developing New Business Ideas*. FT Prentice Hall, London.

Burke, R. (2004). *Project Management: Planning & Control Techniques*, 4th edition. Wiley, Chichester.

Williams, S. (2003). *Lloyds TSB Small Business Guide*, 16th edition. Vitesse Media, London.

PART II

Developing strategies for growth

In the second part of this book, Chapters 13 to 21 are concerned with the post start-up stage. Once break-even level trading has been achieved, most enter a phase of consolidation in which they focus on improving the efficiency and profitability of the business operations. For many this second stage will be brief before they embark on further expansion of the business. For others this stage will last much longer as they opt for gradual and steady growth, or where they have to use the profits of the business to fund future growth. In some other cases, notable with self-employed individuals and what we call lifestyle businesses, they choose never to go beyond this second stage.

Some business owners find it hard to break out of the second stage, having become too focused on operational aspects of managing the business. Part II of this book is therefore about making the transition from operational to strategic thinking, and about the development of the necessary skills and knowledge that will facilitate the subsequent long-term growth and sustainability of the business.

The chapters in Part II also draw on some aspects of best practice defined in the SFEDI (Small Firms Enterprise Development Initiative) National Occupational Standards for Business Development, including the process of carrying out the business health check to complement the conventional methods of strategic business analysis as a precursor to preparing the growth and development strategy. The self-assessment questionnaire in Appendix was developed from SFEDI materials, and is a useful tool in this process that examines and self-evaluates aspects of performance across seven operational areas of the business. So, having identified the need for the culture shift – the reincarnation of the former operational owner-manager as a strategic entrepreneurial thinker is equipped to take the business forward.

CHAPTER 13

The culture shift

During the past 30 years there have been a number of attempts by academics to describe and explain in a concise (but not simplistic) manner, how small firms develop and grow, and those efforts have mostly used the life-cycle model, which presumes that the small business development follows a pattern akin to that of product or human life cycles. Every business does have a point of "birth" or inception, but by no means all of them follow a subsequent pattern of development, maturity, and decline. Government statistics show that a fair proportion die off, i.e. fail in the early stages, others develop in different directions and to different extents, and a proportion go on to grow into much larger and long-living business institutions, where as quoted public companies, their existence as corporate entities, are in theory able to allow them to continue well beyond any human lifetime, and if the markets permit and their management is consistently could, they could persist almost indefinitely.

My personal view is that there have been two main reasons for academics and analysts failing to understand the development of small- and medium-sized enterprises (SMEs) in the past. The first is the tendency to view and analyse them as scaled-down versions of large organisations, resulting in the application of big-company principles of management in the wrong context, and a consequent failure to recognise fundamental differences in entrepreneurial motivation. The second is their lack of direct experience of starting and managing small firms, and of experiencing at first hand the pressures, practical problems, and emotions that go alongside that experience, and that influence and shape the thinking and approach of owner-managers to their businesses, particularly in terms of direct personal and financial involvement, and the associated risks of that. Until businesses are able to grow sufficiently large to take on a corporate existence of their own, independent of their entrepreneurial creator, the entrepreneur's personality, and personal objectives will have been a significant influence in the direction of their growth. It is not so much a lack of understanding of that, more a lack of appreciation of its real significance, that has caused the tendency to oversimplify some of the theoretical models and explanations of the small business life cycle. We will consider three examples of conventional models of the small business life cycle:

1. Churchill and Lewis (1983) explains it as a five-stage process:

Existence – Survival – Success – Take-off – Resource Maturity

The business comes into existence, goes through the start-up stage in which it often struggles for survival, but gradually succeeds in breaking even, progressively becoming more successful but eventually maturing at which point it ceases to grow any further. They do in fact acknowledge that some firms will not proceed beyond the success stage in that they distinguish between those that succeed and grow, and those that succeed but then "disengage" growth to become lifestyle businesses, however the presumed norm is still for firms to follow through the five-stage process.

2. Gibbs and Davies (1990)

Initiation – Development – Growth – Maturity – Decline

This has some similarities to the Churchill model, going through the start-up phase, developing and growing until it matures and subsequently declines – but we must ask why the inevitability of decline?

3. Burns and Dewhurst (1996)

Start-up – Incubation – Growth – Maturity – Decline and Failure

This is a refinement of the two previous models recognising the start-up stage, incubation to the point at which the business begin to make a profit, subsequently growing and maturing, but eventually declining and failing – again we must challenge the presumption of the inevitable decline and failure.

It seems then that conventional thought is based on a number of (unjustified) assumptions:

- That entrepreneurs all want continuous growth.
- That firms will continue to grow until they reach a stage of "maturity".
- That at some stage the firms will inevitably stagnate or decline.

There is no allowance for firms to jump a particular phase, or to regress to a previous phase, or even to hybridise or exhibit characteristics of more than one phase at the same time (Deakins & Freel, 2005).

Furthermore, not only do they presume development to maturity prior to decline – a stage that is by no means inevitable amongst new and small firms, as much as we are constantly referred to government statistics that "prove" that two-thirds of new firms close in the first 3 years of their existence – they also ignore one fundamental and highly relevant factor, i.e. the motivation of the individual entrepreneur or owner-manager. Irrespective of government policies, the provision of business support agencies, and incentives to encourage small firms to survive and grow. The bottom line is that a significant proportion of those firms will only achieve growth if it suits the owner-managers to do so. Closure can result as much from positive choice of the owner to close or sell (e.g. for retirement, health, or personal reasons), as from decline. To fully appreciate the development of small firms, the entrepreneurs and motivations need to be factored in, and when we do that, the emerging model (Figure 13.1) become more akin to a decision-tree rather than a linear process.

Another model proposed by Greiner (1972) does accept that owner-managers may positively decide not to progress from one stage to another, but suggests that progression where it does occur, happens more as a result of crises facing the business which trigger a move to the next stage, rather than from any positive choice or action by the owner-manager. In

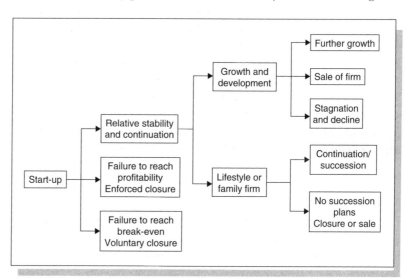

Figure 13.1
An alternative view of the small business life cycle.

some ways this almost labels entrepreneurs as reactive and underestimates their capabilities of being proactive or to think strategically. Whilst strategic thinking may not be a strong point of many owner-managers when they first start the business, it would be wrong to generalise that they are all reactive rather than proactive, and that they cannot normally progress the firm without an external trigger.

In reality then, the pattern of growth depends not just on the ability to survive the early stages, or on crises that trigger changes, but on the owners' personal ambitions and objectives in subsequent years:

- Whether or not they want to expand and grow/to create greater wealth or a personal empire/legacy for next generation, etc. In some cases the desire to expand and grow may be tempered or delayed by unfavourable economic or market conditions, until such times as the incentives to grow become stronger, or the market situation improves. This is where it becomes so important for governments to create the right conditions if they want small firms to become the employment creators of the future.
- Whether or not they want a good steady income and comfortable standard of living/balanced work-life situation. Some firms will fail in the early stages, others will grow to the point of profitability, but as the result of the owner-managers personal objectives will take the form of "lifestyle" businesses growing no further because the owner-manager is happy with the profit and return they generate in proportion to the effort incurred in operating the business. Others will be sold or merged with larger firms in particular those started by serial entrepreneurs, some will exist for many years but will cease to trade or be sold for lack of family succession when the person who created the business reaches retirement age. Others will grow rapidly into medium or large businesses – ceasing to exist as SMEs by virtue of their increased size.

The early stages of business development

From my observations and experience as an owner-manager and in training and advising other owner-managers over the past few years, I have observed a three-phase pattern of development in small businesses during the early years of their existence, after which the developmental stages they go through will be largely influenced by the objectives of the entrepreneurs who are driving the business. This is by no means proposed as a universal model but it does help to understand the development process. In some cases new firms fold or their owners withdraw or give up before even reaching the end of the first phase and in others the business is only started when an established and growing market is already in place – effectively skipping straight to the third phase. Some others with less ambitious objectives simply decide to stop at the second phase. However, I would estimate that the vast majority, perhaps 70% or more, move through these phases during their development. A summary of the three phases is shown in Figure 13.2 and will hopefully explain or contextualise some of the owner-manager decisions shown in Figure 13.1.

Phase 1: Business start-up

In the initial start-up phase of a new small business, the emphasis is primarily on survival and the struggle to reach break-even level and profitability before the limited working capital runs out. Typically this phase will last between 6 months and 3 years, although in extreme cases some small firms will struggle on for 5 years or more before reaching stability. The entrepreneur's personal objectives are focused on the need to achieve profitability at the earliest possible opportunity to reduce personal financial exposure or risk – especially if the family home has been offered as security against borrowing, or where levels of borrowing or investment have been substantial – but there is also the desire for a sense of achievement or accomplishment. This can create the tendency during the first phase is to accept any business which offers even the smallest contribution to overhead costs and profit. This marginal approach can often result in the owner-managers and staff running around like headless-chickens in the pursuit of marginal contributions to profit, resulting in a deleterious affect on overall profit margins without them realising it. (And the owner-managers ending up totally exhausted in the process – its no joke, I've seen it more than a few times!) What is essentially happening is that management decisions are being made at a purely operational level on the basis of short-term returns, and with little or no strategic thinking. Then as the owner-managers probably have few staff if any, to delegate the marginal work to, they end up working extra, and relatively unproductive hours, doing the work themselves, to the neglect of the overall quality of the management and operation of the business. Whilst such activity may keep the cash flow going, in reality because the profits can be so marginal, it requires the expenditure of a disproportional amount of effort to reach the break-even level of trading that is critical to reduce the owner-manager's financial exposure.

Development phase	Duration	Primary business objectives	Entrepreneur's personal objectives	Typical behavioural characteristics	Decision-making processes
Start-up	6 months to 3 years	Survival of the business To reach break-even level before working capital runs out	To achieve profitability at the earliest opportunity to reduce personal financial exposure Sense of achievement/ personal satisfaction	Accept all available business Focus on gaining extra marginal contribution to costs rather than overall profitability Tendency towards headless-chicken syndrome: much activity and effort generating relatively low-profit margins	Primarily operational Tendency for tactical decisions to be subsumed by chance of marginal contribution Focus on short-term returns with little strategic thinking
Relative stability	1 to 2 years	Consolidation Review and revise the operational processes of the business	To increase profit to ensure the long-term survival and stability of the business (and to reduce personal financial risk in the process) Move towards achieving return on capital investment, and repay personal effort.	Consolidation of activities, more focus on profitability/ profit margins More selective attitude to customers, e.g. rejection of slow payers and low-profit business More attention to customer, needs, quality and long-term relationships Tendency to stagnation and complacency in some firms if this phase lasts too long	Switch from operational to tactical thinking Initially not much strategic thinking, but this increases towards the end of the phase as a basic pre-requisite of the next phase
Growth and development	On-going in future years	Planned expansion to increase market share, turnover and profit Capital growth	Expand market share and sales turnover to generate and increase personal wealth Continue the reduction of personal financial risk (less urgent now) Expand personal power and influence	Confidence and stability achieved in the second phase provides the basis for a more adventurous attitude towards the market place Future growth financed from profits, and external funding now more readily available Importation or development of more specialist management skills, and increased delegation of responsibility	Primarily strategic and tactical Operational decisions tend to be increasingly delegated as business grows

Figure 13.2
Development stages for the majority of small firms.

Phase 2: Relative stability

Once a new small firm has consistently achieved a level of trading above that of the break-even level for a few months, a sense of relief occurs with the owner-managers. A major hurdle has been jumped, and there is now the opportunity for a period of stability and consolidation within the business. Typically this phase will last between 1 and 2 years, by which time most spirited entrepreneurs, will be looking to further growth. The key features of this stage involve the review at operational level of the processes of the business. The owner-manager is concerned with improving profitability, reducing operating costs and waste, and is now for the first time, in a position to make decisions about which customers to retain, and which (e.g. the bad or slow payers) to relinquish.

The emphasis is now less on survival and more on the increase of profit and the reduction in personal financial exposure. The owner-manager is looking for a return on capital invested plus a premium for the personal effort which has been put into the business. As a result, there is much more focus on profitability and the maintenance of healthy profit margins, coupled with a more selective attitude towards customers. This heralds the first opportunity to say, "No, I don't want or need your business or the aggravation associated with it" – at last slow or bad payers can be rejected in favour of good steady customers, or low-profit work can be turned down. There is also a focus on customer needs to ensure the long-term retention of regular customers, and along with this goes a positive effort to improve standards of quality within the business.

Unfortunately for some small firms, this stage becomes their primary objective, and in some cases a sense of complacency ensues. I am not saying that there is anything wrong with not wishing to expand a business beyond a basic level of comfort, but for most modern cultures there is a desire to push beyond this stage. It is also argued that in a constantly changing technological and economic environment, no business can afford to stand still without the risk of losing its place in the market. I would suggest, however, that at the bottom and of the SME spectrum there are many micro-firms and self-employed individuals who simply do not wish to continue expanding, particularly if they are personally financially stable.

What really characterises the second phase is the progressive switch from operational to tactical thinking. There is still not a great deal of strategic thinking involved, but as the desire to expand becomes more predominant, then the switch to strategic thinking must occur as an essential pre-requisite of the next phase – basically, without ambition and forward thinking the next phase will not be achieved.

Phase 3: Growth and development

This is an on-going process for future years involving a planned expansion to increase market share, sales turnover, and profit. Apart from expansion, the other key objective will usually be that of the capital growth of the business. Both the owner-manager and the business (which by now may be a corporate entity) are looking for an expansion of market share and increased profits, and a consequent expansion of their personal power and influence. The entrepreneur's personal financial risk is less than an issue at this stage. The overall confidence achieved from the second phase provides for a more adventurous attitude to the market place – what other markets exist that have not yet been exploited? There is also much less financial pressure on the business as funds for future development are becoming available. Typically, the recognition of the need for change in management practices to facilitate future growth results in increased levels of delegation. This is one of the fundamental factors without which future expansion cannot proceed, and this is usually accompanied by the importation or development of new and additional management, and staff skills, giving the opportunity for improved systems of delegation. At this level, decisions are primarily strategic and tactical, with operational decisions being increasingly delegated to supervisory levels of management as the business grows.

The culture shift

This is the essential change in small business culture and owner-manager attitude that is the pre-requisite to the future growth and development of the business. Essentially, it is necessary for the entrepreneur to make a positive shift from just making tactical decisions and day-to-day operational decisions, into a proactive higher gear which will involve strategic planning for the future of the business. Unfortunately this is one of the hardest moves which owner-managers are faced with, as it involves relinquishing many of the "comfort-factor" management responsibilities which have evolved alongside them during the early days of the business. In the infamous Video Arts training video "The Unorganised Manager" John Cleese playing St Peter the custodian of the Pearly Gates, described this as the process of "growing up". Invariably it involves delegating some of the control and responsibility previously associated with the early growth of the business, which because of those associations can often be a painful process. For example, "I *want* to keep maintaining the sales ledger to keep in touch with the business revenue" – irrespective of the fact that an accounts clerk can do the job in half the time, with better accuracy, and at a significantly lower hourly rate! And whilst the manager is dabbling with the sales ledger, who makes the strategic decisions, are they left to the accounts clerk or do they just get postponed until he has some spare time, or until as Greiner suggests, there is a crisis in the firm? However, this is not a crisis that triggers a move to the next stage of growth; it is a crisis within the very first stage of the life of the business that threatens whether or not the firm will even complete that first stage.

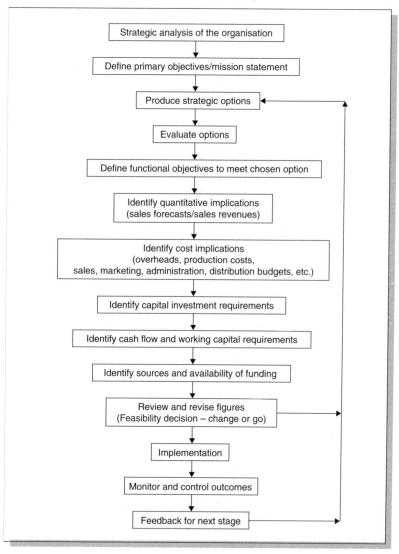

Figure 13.3
The strategic
planning process.

It is very easy for owner-managers to underestimate the effects their own personalities have on their businesses and in particular on the staff they employ. The fact that they occupy such a singularly dominant and influential role within the business means that the culture that operates within the business inevitably tends to reflect their own attitudes and personalities. In turn, that reflection is projected to the outside contacts, the customers, and suppliers. An aggressive and autocratic style can often evoke a defensive attitude or blame culture amongst the staff, and conversely, as caring and democratic style can generate a positive and congenial attitude in staff. Such attitudes and cultures are more than visible to any outsiders who come in contact with the business, and naturally, many of those outsiders are customers. Part of the culture shift therefore involves the owner-managers in becoming aware of the impact their own personalities have on the firm, and in ensuring that the impact does not have a negative influence.

The strategic planning process

The key to future growth and expansion requires a basic change in attitude and thinking – a veritable cultural shift – by owner-managers. It is the transition from direct involvement in all aspects of the operational control of the business, to a position and attitude of more senior management responsibility; wherein the operational aspects are delegated to allow more time to focus on the strategic planning, and development of the business. By working through the various stages of the strategic planning process shown in Figure 13.3, the owner-manager can make the necessary culture shift to improve the performance and focus on the direction in which the business is to go. Following this process does not imply total loss of contact with the operational side of the business. It should rather be seen as a move to optimise management resources to improve the tactical and operational performance of the business.

References

Churchill, N. and Lewis, V. (1983). The five stages of business growth. *Harvard Business Review*, **61**.

Deakins, D. and Freel, M. (2005). *Entrepreneurship and Small Firms*, 4th edition. McGraw Hill, Maidenhead.

Greiner, L. (1972). Evolution and revolution as organisations grow. *Harvard Business Review*, **50**.

Further reading

Bolton Committee (1971). *Report of the Committee of Inquiry on Small Firms*. HMSO, London.

Hall, G. (1995). *Surviving and Prospering in the Small Business Sector*. Routledge, London.

Institute of Management (1996). *Developing Managers in Smaller Firms*. IM, London.

Kirby, D. (1990). Management education and small firms development, and exploratory study of small firms in the UK. *Journal of Small Business Management*, **28**.

Storey, D.J. (1994). *Understanding the Small Business Sector*. Routledge, London.

Wickham, P.A. (2004). *Strategic Entrepreneurship*. FT Prentice Hall, London.

CHAPTER 14

Reviewing the performance of the business

The purpose of this chapter is to describe the processes which can be used to analyse the past and current performance of a business – the where-are-we-now scenario. In effect, this is the first stage of the quantum leap from operational to strategic thinking. The process will enable us to systematically examine and critically review the key aspects of business performance, and to identify areas where actions are needed to improve or strengthen current systems and procedures. This goes beyond an analysis of the strengths and weaknesses of the business, and the opportunities and threats it faces – that was okay for the start-up stages of the business but now we need to examine the needs of the business in more detail. It is in effect an audit of each facet of the business and the way it operates. It attempts to answer the first of the three key questions asked by the strategic planning process – where are we now, where do we want to go, and how do we get there? The chapter also relates to Small Firms Enterprise Development Initiative (SFEDI) National Occupational Standards for Business Development, and the self-assessment questionnaire shown in Appendix is based on the principles of the Business Health Check process in the SFEDI Standards.

Lasher (1999, p. 8) makes the distinction between corporate strategy as the process which takes place in large organisations to optimise the performance of their diverse activities, and competitive strategy which takes place in smaller companies, or larger ones in single lines of business activity. There are a number of well-established strategic analysis models that can be used for performance review, although they are primarily designed for use in that big-company corporate strategy context. For example, the McKinsey 7S analysis (Waterman & Peters, 1982) which examines the business in terms of its structure, systems, style, staff, skills, strategy, and shared values – picture six circles in a rose pattern with the seventh (the shared values) in the centre of them:

1. *Structure*: It represents the formal organisation of the business, lines of authority and responsibility, and the resources at its disposal, how the organisation breaks down its activities into distinct elements and how those elements are co-ordinated.

2. *Systems*: They are the formal and informal communications, processes and procedures that link the various parts within the structure to each other to facilitate co-ordination and control.

3. *Style*: It is concerned with the way the managers operate within the business, the philosophies, values and beliefs adopted by them in exercising their authority and achieving results.

4. *Staff*: They are the human resources within the business, the quantity and quality of the people employed.

5. *Skills*: These are the competencies (both available and required) in order to perform the various tasks to a sufficiently high standard.

6. *Strategy*: The strategy of the organisation is the summary of its key objectives and activities, and long-term policies. It includes the actions (proactive) and reactions (reactive) to developments in the external environment, e.g. the route to profitability or success.

7. *Shared values*: They are the aspects of organisational culture which are common to the various parts of the organisation and which overlaps with each of the other six. They are the values (written or unwritten) which underlie the stated objectives of the organisation and which *should* be shared by all of its members. These are often referred to as the "super-co-ordinate goals", e.g. ethics, standards of performance and behaviour, attitude to quality.

The McKinsey 7S framework can be useful in helping with identifying and understanding how the business operates. It is really better suited to larger organisations where the functional departments are more remote from each other, but I have come across some firms with 20–50 employees that have found it to be a useful tool to understand and evaluate how their business operates. In a small business this is rarely the case, although the 7S headings may assist the owner-manager to describe and comprehend how his or her own business works.

The Johnson and Scholes (2003) model of strategic planning employs the three key stages of strategic analysis, strategic choice, and strategic implementation.

1. *The strategic analysis:* This examines the environment in which the business operates by auditing the environmental influences on the organisation. It further analyses the expectations objectives and power, – the organisational structure, culture, management style, and its ability to implement its objectives. Finally, it looks at the resources at its disposal (physical financial and people resources), and how they are balanced to contribute towards the strategic capability of the organisation, i.e. how it will be able to sustain its policies in the future.

2. *The strategic choice:* It is concerned with generating and evaluating the strategic options available to the organisation, and selecting the appropriate strategy for the future needs of the organisation, e.g. maintain the status quo, go for expansion, develop new products or export markets, or to diversify the range of products and services offered by the business.

3. *The strategic implementation:* This looks at the three key areas of planning and allocating the resources, the organisational structure, and the people and systems; and how these factors must be changed and developed to enable the strategic choice (the chosen option) to be implemented successfully.

It is interesting that Johnson and Scholes point to one of the major obstacles that inhibits successful strategic planning as the tendency of big-company managers to focus too much on their own functional areas (production, finance, marketing, etc.) whilst failing to take a more holistic overview of the business. In theory, this ought to be one area where owner-managers score highly by virtue of the need for them to be competent in a broad range of management skills to run the business, particularly in the earlier stages of its existence. However, as discussed in the previous chapter, the various pressures and stresses of running a small firm usually contrive to keep the owner-manager thinking at the operational and tactical levels and rarely having time to aspire to the holistic or strategic perspective. In practice, the owner-managers of small firms and the functional managers of big organisations both need to be kicked into strategic gear; but in the case of the small firm it is usually only the owner-managers themselves (or occasionally their spouses or bank managers) who are in the position to do the kicking!

The big drawback with big-company models of strategic planning such as these is that they cannot always be easily applied or related to the small business situation. This is simply because of the nature of this nefarious beast "the owner-manager" whose role of jack-of-all-trades and sole decision-maker is incongruous alongside the big-company model wherein that role is spread across a range of specialist or functional experts who all congregate and contrive to contribute towards the decision-making processes. Mintzberg (1994) suggests that "effective strategists are not people who abstract themselves from the daily detail, but quite the opposite: they are the ones who immerse themselves in it whilst being able to abstract the strategic messages from it". There can be no doubt that owner-managers are good at immersing themselves in their businesses, the hard part is getting them to take a step backwards to be able to see the strategic messages.

The organisational environment

Before we can consider expanding the business we need to ensure that the various aspects of the business are operating efficiently or at least as well as they can within existing financial constraints and management

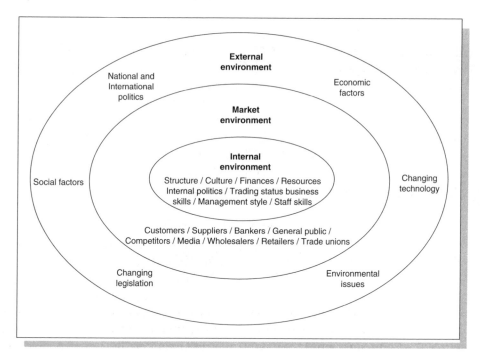

Figure 14.1
The organisational environment.

abilities. The process of performance review involves analysing in detail the organisational environment in which the business operates as shown in Figure 14.1. That is, the internal environment within the organisation itself, the trading status of the business, its finances, physical resources, staff and management skills, operational and control systems, policies and procedures, stakeholders' interests, etc. These are essentially factors which are or should be, within the control of the business. The market environment in which the business operates is an area over which the owner-managers have some influence but not control, e.g. the customers, suppliers, competitors, media, etc. The external environment consists of factors which are outside of the control or influence of the business but which can still have a major impact on the way in which it operates, e.g. changes in legislation, social and political policy, economic trends, etc.

The analysis involves finding answers to a whole range of detailed questions relating to the management and operation of the business under these three headings. By working through the questions we should also be able to identify necessary changes that must be undertaken in order to create the right conditions for further development of the business.

The internal environment: within the business itself

The first stage requires an investigation of the business itself and its internal operational systems, communications, and management and decision-making processes.

The trading status of the business

What is the current trading status of the business – sole trader, partnership, co-operative, or limited company? Is this satisfactory at present? Is it likely to be satisfactory for future needs? If not, what alternative options exist that might meet the needs of the business? For example, a sole trader or partnership that has been operating successfully in a small local wholesaling business, but now wishes to expand, may need to reconsider its status. If the expansion is to be substantial, e.g. opening new branches or substantially increasing the number of credit customers, this could leave the owners vulnerable to substantial exposure and risk from bad debts in the future. Limited liability status might reduce the extent of the exposure, although it might also reduce the borrowing capacity of the owners unless they are willing to offer personal assets as security against borrowing. The trading status may also be affected by interpersonal factors, e.g. partners who wish to develop the business in different directions. Alternately, it may be that a sole trader is looking to take a partner on-board to inject capital into the business, or to assist with its expansion and development by increasing production capacity.

The management skills within the business

The capacity of the business for future expansion is usually thought of in terms of available finance and the ability to expand the markets. But even if these factors are available, the future expansion can still be inhibited by deficits in other management skills – staff management and leadership, financial planning and control, operations management, and information management. Therefore, before we look at expansion, we need to know the current position in terms of management capabilities. What business and management skills or knowledge currently exist within the business? Are these being used to the full? Are these sufficient for the current needs of the business? Are they likely to be adequate for the future needs of the business or will other skills need to be imported or developed? What are the particular skills that are lacking? Are there any staff within the business who could be trained in these skills? What would the cost of training in terms of money and productive time lost from the business? Is suitable training available? Is training viable or would it be easier to recruit skilled staff or to buy in the necessary skills from an external provider? Can we afford to buy in the skills? What would be the cost and operational implications of not having the necessary skills, i.e. can we afford not to have them?

Current policies and the decision-making processes

The current policies within the firm may not even be specified or written down, as with relatively young firms these tend to evolve as the business establishes itself and starts to grow. As explained in Figure 13.2 these will also be initially influenced by the simple need to survive and to reach break-even level before the working capital is exhausted. Only after that stage is reached can proper forward planning begin. So, what exactly are the policies or strategies currently being utilised? Initially, they are likely to relate to maximising sales and revenue and subsequently to improve the profit margins within the sales revenue, and the marketing policy will tend to follow these rather than to lead to new opportunities. In fact as we have discussed in the previous chapter, in the early months of the business the owners will tend to employ tactics as opposed to strategies. In a similar vein, the decision-making processes will have been reactive rather than proactive. Ask yourself the questions then: what do I currently want from my business and am I achieving that? What key decisions have I made that have helped me to achieve my objectives and how were those made? Who else did I involve in the process? Were they spur of the moment decisions or carefully considered? What bad decisions have I made and what were the consequences? What mistakes have I made? How can I avoid repeating them? The reflective process may be uncomfortable or even painful to face up to, but it can be most valuable in planning for the future.

Stakeholders' interests and objectives

Who are the stakeholders in the business? Most obviously they are the owners or shareholders who have invested in the business and have risked their personal assets, but also the providers of loan capital whose repayment will depend on its success. The employees are also dependant on it for continued work and their own families for the income, the suppliers for continued custom, and the customers for a reliable source of goods or services. (Not forgetting the Chancellor for all the unpaid tax collection that small firms do on his behalf!) There may well be others that you can identify. What do these stakeholders think of your achievements so far? Are they satisfied with your performance? Have you met their expectations or let them down? Your own family or dependants are also stakeholders – what do they think of your enterprise, and has it met with their expectations both in terms of the business and you as a person? The direct families of owner-managers can easily become the most neglected of stakeholders as business demands take priority over the needs of the family. Theorists are divided on this subject, some (e.g. Carlock, 2001) arguing that for a new business to succeed and thrive the entrepreneur requires sound support and commitment from family members and that business and family objectives should be in alignment, whilst others (such as Fleming, 2000 and Fachler, 2003) claiming that to expect such total support from the family is unrealistic as family members have their own diverse priorities that do not necessarily coincide with those of the business.

The financial resources, capitalisation, working capital, and cost structure

Firstly, we need to examine the capitalisation – is the business funded predominantly by equity, long-term borrowing, from reserves generated by previous years' profits or a combination of these? What is the current borrowing capacity of the business, and is adequate security available to support further borrowing? Does the company need to consider selling shares in the business to rise more capital? Secondly there is the question of working capital – is it adequate for current needs, or are we relying on overdraft facilities and credit from our suppliers? Is the working capital adequate to allow for planned growth without further borrowing, or would we run the risk of over-trading? Thirdly, how do our operating costs compare with those of our rivals in terms of higher or lower overheads, variable production costs (Can we buy components cheaper than them?), and profit margins. Are these acceptable and sustainable in the long term?

The financial systems

These are the controls and record systems currently used within the business, and rarely have they been designed specifically for the operational requirements of the small firm. They tend to have evolved on a needs basis, with extra bits being bolted on as the business changes or expands, or as more demands for financial information are requested by lenders or the company auditors. In terms of financial records they will include sales, purchase, nominal ledgers, sales invoicing, customer statements and accounts, payroll and pay as you earn (PAYE) returns, value-added tax (VAT) records, and petty cash payments and receipts, etc. The main questions are, how efficient and time consuming are these to operate, and do they give us the information we need when we need it? In terms of financial controls we are looking at the monitoring of cash flow, collecting debts on time, paying our suppliers on time, and controlling and reconciling cash and bank figures with the ledger system. Are we managing our cash flow efficiently or having to use valuable time chasing debts to enable us to pay the bills? Do our customers keep within agreed credit terms or do we allow these to slip? Do we tend to stretch our suppliers' credit to the absolute limit? Is this adversely affecting our relationships with the suppliers? In terms of financial planning, do we regularly monitor our sales and expenditure figures against planned budgets to identify variances and potential problems, or do we just react to the crises when they hit us?

Past financial performance and profitability

In an ever-changing business environment, past records of profitability and performance may not be directly relevant to the current trading position, especially if the business has turned the corner from loss-making to a positions of steady profit. The accounting records are the tangible evidence that the business and its managers have (hopefully) shown a trend of progressive growth and profitability that would justify the interest of a potential lender or investor, and answer their key questions. Has the business made a regular profit in the past? If not, what are the reasons for this, or the main barriers to profitability? What has happened to make us believe that this will change in the future? The past performance may not necessarily relate to what is happening within the business right now, particularly with relatively young businesses, so we must ask: is the business trading profitably at present, and is it likely to start trading profitably and to continue to do so in the future? Which business activities generate the most profit and which generate the least? Bearing in mind that even low profit sales still contribute towards overhead costs, can we justify any changes to these activities, or should we concentrate on high profit-margin activities? Are our profit margins above or below the industrial average, or those of our competitors, and do we know why this should be the case? If they are lower than average, are the current profit levels still acceptable to the owners or stakeholders in the business? It may be the case that the owners rate long-term stability and survival above maximising short-term profits, or that they are still in the process of gaining a foothold in the market and are currently working on reduced margins. The emphasis here should be on understanding the reasons behind past performance to help plan future policies.

Monitoring and control systems

These will be largely determined by the nature of the products or services which the business is offering. In a manufacturing output they will relate to control of materials usage, standard costs, production outputs, product quality, etc., whereas in a wholesale or retail operation they may involve stock ordering and rotation, meeting delivery deadlines, and achieving sales volumes. In service industries, there may be more emphasis on customer care and retention, and minimising complaints. In either case the systems need to be in place to ensure the on-going provision of consistent and high quality goods or services that will keep the customers satisfied as described in Chapter 11. The questions arising then are – what monitoring and control systems do I currently have in place, and do they work? Is the information generated by them of practical use to me? Is the information up to date? What other data do I need to make my business work better? Are there any gaps in the present systems, perhaps highlighted by recurrent problems? What changes could be made to make the current systems more efficient and cost-effective?

The staff resources and their deployment

The review of staff resources if done properly can be a lengthy but useful process, although ideally it is something that should be carried out at regular intervals to monitor the changes that have occurred both in business and personnel terms since they were recruited. First, who are the staff and management, what are their roles in terms of their job descriptions, and what do they really do? Are any of them under-utilised, or could they be better deployed elsewhere in the business? Are there any that we could dispense with because they are superfluous to requirements or because they are no longer compatible with the needs of the firm (but beware of the risk of unfair or constructive dismissal)? Do any of them have skills or expertise not currently being used to the full? Do we actually need them all, or do we in fact need to employ more staff to improve our efficiency? In an ideal world the business would have two matrices – one of the ranges of technical and business skills needed to operate the business efficiently and profitably, and the other covering the staff employed and the respective skills they can offer. Unfortunately, owner-managers do not live in ideal worlds, and these matrices tend to be luxuries found in bigger firms who can afford to employ specialist training and personnel staff. In the real world the value of a member of staff tends to be noticed most when they are sick or on holiday and either you don't miss them at all, or you are desperate for their return.

The physical location and premises

Premises are an expensive overhead and often a long-term commitment, and if they are in the wrong place, or are too small, or are used inefficiently, they can become a major drain on the profits of the business. The factors that were relevant to the choice of premises when the business was started may have changed significantly as the business has developed, and rather than facilitating expansion, it is possible that as time has passed, the premises may in fact be constricting the ability of the business to grow further. So, we need to reconsider some of the questions asked earlier in Chapter 8. Where are the premises currently located? Are they sufficiently close or convenient to the customers or markets supplied by the business? If the business is involved in physical deliveries, are the premises located conveniently close to major road or rail networks? Are they adequate in terms of size, or do they currently restrict the capacity of the business? Is this because they are too small or because they are not being used efficiently? How much are they costing us at present? Will the premises be adequate to accommodate possible future expansion? Are alternative suitable premises available? These are the main issues that must be considered in the review of the current business performance, but they will also have implications for future planning. What would be the cost of moving premises and the associated costs of disruption to production and customers? Would these costs be justified by the extra potential capacity for production or storage? Should we consider renting, leasing or buying alternative premises? How would the additional overhead costs affect the profitability of the business? Can we afford to move to new premises? Again, can we afford not to make the move if we wish to expand and grow?

Physical resources, plant and equipment

When planning a new business the potential entrepreneurs are usually advised to produce an inventory of physical resources which inevitably includes all of the ideal equipment and materials, but which is abruptly revised once costs are identified. The second attempt usually divides the list into essential items and those which can be acquired as and when funds permit, also described in Chapter 8. Looking back at the required inventory, how far down the line have you gone with these? Do you now have a full inventory of plant and equipment covering all items that are regularly used? Do you have an active policy of maintenance and replacement or do you just buy new items when the old ones are beyond repair? Are you making full productive use of your inventory or is machinery sitting idle and costing you money for the space it occupies and the interest on the loan that paid for it? What other resources do you currently lack and do you have a plan to acquire them? How essential are they to the future of your business? The costs of future acquisitions will need to be incorporated into your financial plan, and once you start thinking strategically, you should be examining the returns you are achieving on the capital invested in your inventory.

Stockholding policies

These questions are primarily for retail and wholesale businesses, but also of interest to manufacturing firms holding stocks of raw materials and finished goods. What is the average value of the stock you are holding and in terms of days how does it compare with your sales revenue, i.e. is the stock being turned over at an acceptable rate, and how does this compare with the industry average? The average supermarket expects to turn over the tins of baked beans on its shelves every couple of days, and would be worried if that figure crept up to every 2 or 3 weeks. Do you have a realistic stock management policy? Are you always running short of stock, or are you holding too much? Have you established suitable re-order level to accommodate your suppliers' delivery lead times? Are you rotating perishable stock? Do you have a control system that monitors receipts, issues, and current quantities of each item? Can you monitor stock for theft or wastage? Do you have a system of stock valuation that links in with your financial accounts? Do you keep your records up to date? Stock control can be a major headache and a major loss of profit if it is not organised and maintained properly.

Current and recurring problems within the business

Problems occur within business with annoying regularity, and are usually dealt with quickly and forgotten until they occur again. They may well be treated as isolated incidents, when in fact they may be indicative of recurrent or more serious underlying problems. Do you have any minor difficulties that seem to arise with annoying regularity? What are they really costing you, e.g. how much time do you or your staff spend on rectifying these in an average day, week, or month? Would spending time to find a permanent solution be cheaper in the long run? How do the recurring problems affect staff morale? Do they affect your customers and their perception of your products or services? Are minor problems indicative of changes that need to be implemented in the business?

Changes within the organisation

Managing change is always a problem for any business, and more so if the change has resulted from a reactive decision rather than a proactive policy. What major changes have taken place in the business over the past year or two, and what changes are taking place at present? Were these changes planned in advance or were they the result of the need to respond to problems or new circumstances? Did they have any adverse effects on customers, staff or productivity levels? Were they implemented efficiently or could they have been done better? Would you do things differently a second time around? What changes are you aware of that your business should seriously be considering? How urgent or threatening are these? What would be the costs, risks or negative effects of ignoring or deferring them, and can you really afford to take a chance with them?

Capacity for engaging change

It is also important to consider the capacity that the business, its owners and its staff have to be able to engage the inevitable changes that will result from growth or diversification of the business. Does the owner or other managers have the attitude and expertise to handle the substantial changes that could result from growing the business? Do they have the necessary skills to project-manage the growth and development process? How well does the owner-manager communicate ideas and information to staff? What are likely to be the main barriers to change from employees and other stakeholders? How will the staff react to potential change and will their reaction be positive or negative? Are they likely to try to resist or fail to co-operate with the proposed changes? What would be the impact of that? How can the managers best implement the changes to avoid any problems? Further issues relating to the management of the change process are discussed in Chapter 20. It is certainly a topic that the entrepreneur needs to be aware of and needs to be able to put into practice if the firm is to grow efficiently.

The above points represent a fairly demanding and comprehensive series of questions about the performance of the business to date. By the time these have been examined the entrepreneur should have a critical and honest view of the business and its strengths and weaknesses which can be used as the basis for future actions and improvements. However, the real value of the process depends essentially on the owner-manager giving honest and realistic answers to the questions, and not hiding from questions or facts that might be uncomfortable to face up to. The questionnaire in Appendix has been specifically designed to assist the entrepreneur to carry out an objective evaluation of the current business performance across seven key areas – management competence, sales marketing and customer relations, business operations, finance, managing staff performance, innovation technology and Intellectual Property Rights (IPR), and managing for the future. Each section offers a series of descriptor words and relevant questions to prompt appropriate lines of thought, and can be graded in terms of performance to identify strengths and weaknesses.

The market environment

Who are our customers?

This may seem like a ridiculous question but it is often surprising how little some businesses really know about their customers. For example, do they fit into stereotype groups (usually described as market segmentation), or do they share common characteristics in terms of their size and types of organisation? How many customers of each type do you have, and which types generate the most profit for your business. What do you know about their buying patterns, e.g. the products they select, the volume of purchases and the frequency or regularity of orders? Have these patterns changed recently, and are the changes positive or negative? What are their key criteria for buying from you, as opposed to another supplier, e.g. low price, quality products, or reliable service? Do you actually know who the decision-makers are in the businesses that buy from you, and when did you or one of your staff, last speak with them?

Customer base and customer loyalty

Are you able to retain customers or do they tend to turnover or move on frequently? Of your total customers, how many of them trade with you on a regular weekly or monthly basis? How many of them have been trading with you for more than 12 months? How do these various patterns compare with those of your competitors or other firms in the same industry? Are your customers loyal out of choice or because there is little competition for them to turn to? Would they still trade with you if there was an alternative local supplier? Do you think that they would be likely to recommend your good or services to others? How do you think your customers perceive you and your business – with respect, admiration, as reliable and honest, as someone they enjoy doing business with; or as a temporary stopgap, perhaps a cheapskate or necessary evil, or simply just convenient, or because there is no current alternative?

The key to long-term retention of customers lies in ensuring that you are aware of their perceptions and expectations, and particularly of changes in these. Unless you are aware of changing perceptions and expectations, you cannot respond to them by modifying your products or services and the way they are provided, to keep the customers satisfied.

Market share and recent trends

The answers to the questions in this section will depend very much on the size and nature of the market in which the business operates, e.g. whether it is local, national or international. Some markets are easy to break into whilst others may have substantial barriers in terms of capital investment, heavy competition, or the market being largely controlled by a few major players. The first task then, is to define the market in which you see yourself operating, e.g. you may be a major operator in the local market but small in relation to national operators. A good example of this is the UK real-ale brewing industry where there are multitude or quite new local micro-breweries, about a sixty established regional brewers (Wadworths, Shepherd Neame, Samuel Smiths, Banks, Theakstons, etc.) and a just handful of major national conglomerates which have resulted form a progressive series of mergers and take-overs (e.g. Scottish & Newcastle/Courage, Interbrew, etc.). The key question then: just what market am I operating in? What is the total size by volume of output or financial value, of that market? What proportion of that market do I control and has this increased or decreased recently? How easy is it to increase market share? What proportion of the market could I potentially control, and would the cost and effort of achieving the extra market share justify the increased profits? Most of these have been asked previously in Chapter 6 at the start-up stage, but they now need to be reconsidered particularly in respect of market changes that will invariably have occurred since that time.

Quality standards and policies

Quality management is meant to be a continuous and on-going process, but with the numerous demands and pressures which face owner-managers of small firms, it is hardly surprising that those standards are often allowed to slip, and once this has happened it is much harder to re-establish them. So, do you currently have established written quality standards or policies? Can you remember what they are or when they were last reviewed? Are your employees aware of them? Are your customers aware of them? How do you promote the benefits of quality to your staff? How do you monitor and ensure the consistent achievement of quality standards within the business? What proportion of your outputs result in complaints or goods returned? How much time do you, or your staff waste chasing problems that should not have occurred in the first place? What systems do you use to get feedback from your customers about the quality of your products or services? Is that feedback generally positive or negative? Finally, when you get negative feedback, how rapidly do you respond, and what do you do to rectify it?

Current methods of advertising and promotion

Unless you are a marketing expert, advertising and promotion can be an expensive and time-consuming business. Once you find an advertising medium that works reasonably well, it is all too easy to continue using it without subsequent review or revision, until it sometimes becomes outdated and ineffective without you having realised the fact. Sales are promotion activities need continuous revision and monitoring to keep you ahead (or at least, alongside) the competition. It is particularly important to monitor your advertising expenditure against the results it generates. So, what are your main methods of promoting and selling your goods or services? Are you happy with these, or do you just regard advertising as a necessary expense which must not be allowed to encroach too much on your profits? Have you changed your advertising recently? How often do you review its effectiveness? What methods do you use to monitor the returns on your advertising, e.g. by measuring levels of response to advertisements against the costs of these, the numbers of telephone enquiries converted into sales, or your sales staffs' call rates and sales figures? How do your competitors promote their products? Do you compete head-on with these, or do you use different methods to sell your goods? What proportion of your sales revenue do you spend on sales and promotion, and do you think that this is adequate for current needs? Will it be adequate for future expansion? Do you think you could increase your sales if you could afford more advertising? If so, why haven't you tried it?

Competitors and their activity

Some industries or commercial activities are intensely competitive, particularly in areas such as research and development. Others, whilst still competitive, still co-operate to a certain extent with their rivals, often as a matter of efficiency. For example, licensed trade wholesalers compete heavily for customers, but still frequently work with each other to cover short-term stock shortages of particular products knowing that the favour will be reciprocated at a later date. They also often exchange information about bad and slow payers who may try to exploit the competitive nature of the market by playing them off against each other. In this situation it makes sound business sense to treat competitors as an additional resource for the business, as it is often better to co-operate with a rival than for both parties to lose business. So, who are your competitors and where are they located? Do they pose a threat to your business, or can you all co-exist within the overall market? Do you have contact with them, or share information about difficult customers? Contact with competitors can also increase your market knowledge – to put it in a military context: if you can see the enemy then at least you know what he is doing; but when you can't see him, that is the time to start worrying! You should treat your competitors with balanced respect – as friends when you need information from them but as potential enemies when you are competing directly against them.

Competitive advantage

This concept is concerned with identifying the competitive advantages one business has over another and how these can be sustained. Lasher (1999, p. 51) claims that "few firms have been able to achieve sustainable competitive advantage", i.e. to stay at the head of their market for a long period of time. So what? There may be a great deal of prestige in being the market leader, particularly in major international markets, but the average small business is not in that league, and its primary concern is that of achieving profitability rather than market share. However, the concept should not be passed over without first asking a few basic questions. First and foremost: What is it about my products and services that make them stand out from the competition? What unique features do they have that makes people want to buy them as opposed to the alternatives? How can I ensure that this uniqueness persists? If that is not possible, what else can I do to keep ahead of my rivals? What can I do that will make my customers remember me and come back for more? The answers to these questions will start to form the options for the strategic marketing plan.

The external environment

There are six main factors which normally for the analysis of the external environment: political, economic, social, technological, legislative, and environmental, and these are often referred to as a PESTLE analysis after their initial letters. Inevitably there is always some overlap between them because e.g. political decisions are often based on economic factors and are implemented via the legislative process. The fact remains that the PESTLE analysis is a useful tool to examine the external environment affecting large and small organisations alike.

Political influences

These tend to be issues which are generated at government (or increasingly at European Union (EU)) level, and which may have a direct impact on the day-to-day operation of the business. Some typical, recent examples might be the Statutory Minimum Wage which guarantees a minimum hourly rate of pay for employees; or the Working Hours Directive. This was a politically motivated move which was imposed in the UK in 1998 on the grounds of "health and safety" to ensure that British workers could not work more than specified hours, and thus render their employers more competitive than their continental rivals! The end result is that a major administrative burden has been placed on businesses which now have to monitor the working hours and overtime of all staff on a rolling basis to ensure compliance with the directive. Naturally this places a disproportionate burden on smaller firms that are less likely to have the administrative capacity. Similarly, the political move towards a single European currency will involve many small firms that will find themselves having to invoice their customers in euros or risk losing the business to competitors. This is yet another example of political objectives which add to the financial and administrative burdens of small firms. Another current political issue is whether or not country sports such as fox hunting should be banned. The contentious proposal to ban blood-sports is popular with many town-dwellers, but is seen as a threat to employment and small businesses (kennels, stables, blacksmiths, saddlers, etc.) in rural communities where jobs are harder to find. Other examples include such things as government policy on transport, unemployment, regional development, education and training, etc., e.g. there may be financial incentives to locate a businesses in a development area; or perhaps on a site close to where a new motorway junction is to be built. Foreseeable changes in policy may also present a threat, such as the heavy taxation of petrol and diesel to persuade people to use public transport, that will obviously create an ever-increasing overhead cost to any business which is involved in producing or transporting bulky goods over long distances. Which political issues can you identify that have recently affected your business, or may do so in the future? Were these favourable or unfavourable to your business? What long-term effects are they likely to have?

Economic factors

These can take on many different aspects, and can be hard to forecast in the longer term, as the international economic situation is influenced by a multitude of national policies, changes in demand, recession, inflation, etc. Currently, e.g. we are seeing the rapid growth of the Chinese economy offering cheap imported goods against which UK producers cannot compete. The year 2005 also saw rapid rises in oil and gas prices that had a major impact on the cost of fuel and energy. Economic cycles of high growth and prosperity changing to recession and vice versa, are largely influenced by factors which are determined at national or international levels, e.g. exchange rates between international currencies, the key financial markets in London, Tokyo, and New York. The government fiscal policies on inflation use interest rates as the primary control mechanism, but high interest rates push up currency values which make imports cheaper and exports dearer, pushing down profit margins. Again it is the smaller businesses with lesser resources which are most susceptible to the economic forces beyond their control. The question then, is which of these economic influences might be relevant to your particular plans for expansion, if not immediately, then over the next few years? How often do you take notice or show interest in economic forecasts? What recent or current issues have affected your business and how did you respond to these? What issues are you aware of that may affect you in the future and how have you prepared for them? Will you be proactive about facing them, or will you wait until they happen before you respond?

Social influences and trends

These include changing social trends and demographic factors such as the growth in single-parent families, ethnic minority influences, feminism and human rights, etc. Over the past 30 or 40 years there have been major social and demographic changes in the population, including a higher proportion of the population who are living longer in retirement, a larger proportion of younger people who stay in education to a later age, and a social structure that has seen the demise of the old social classes and a major increase in ethnic groups. For example, the ageing population and longer life expectancy are impacting on pensions, particularly for businesses with company pension schemes. Most social changes occur relatively slowly and their impact on businesses is not always obvious at first, and a good example of this is the issue of Sunday trading. Thirty years ago only a few newsagents, corner shops, and off-licences opened on Sundays and then for very limited hours and the Lord's Day Observance Society was most vociferous that this should stay the case. Today only a very small percentage of the population actively follows the Christian faith, and for those who follow other beliefs, Sunday trading is quite natural, and for people with fast or busy lifestyles it is highly convenient. What social or demographic factors influence your business or affect the range of goods or services you offer to your customers? Are you making full use of the opportunities available to you? Do you actively target potential customers from other ethnic groups or are you missing out on a possible new market. Are you aware of any social factors that could influence your business in the near future, and what effects would these have on it? Are you ready for them?

Technological factors

The fastest changes of all are occurring in technology and no small firm can afford to ignore it or live without it. In 1983 a 1 Mb computer with a basic accounting package would cost well over £5000, but now a highly sophisticated system with a full range of accounting and office software costs barely 10% of that figure. As we discussed earlier, changes in technology have not created a leisure age but have instead created the need for people to constantly upgrade their skills to remain employable. Similarly, if businesses do not constantly embrace and engage in new technologies the risk being left behind by rivals who do so. People increasingly work from home, or away from the central business locations, using electronic communications systems. Small firms use extensive e-commerce and Internet marketing. The point is that technology changed much faster and in different directions, in the past 20 years of the 20th century, than had ever been envisaged. Is your business making full use of current technology at the present time? If not, what plans do you have to improve its use? What applications do you currently operate? Could your systems be developed to provide you with better (i.e. more accurate or useful) financial information? Could they be adapted to provide better communications with you customers? Are you and your staff adequately skilled to make the best use of technology? If not, what do you have to do to rectify the situation?

Legislation: current and future

The range of legislation affecting businesses is constantly changing and increasing, now coming from both the British government and the EU. In the eyes of the law ignorance is no defence, so it is the responsibility of the owner-manager to keep abreast of changing legislation and the implications for the business. This applies both to general legislation affecting all organisations such as health and safety regulations, pollution control, disability discrimination, and employment law; and to industry-specific regulations such as controls over abattoirs, and food storage, processing and handling that have affected the food industry in recent years. Are you aware of the changes in legislation which have taken place over the past 2 or 3 years? How do these affect your business? Are you sure that you are already fully compliant with these and the possible consequences of non-compliance? Are there any new regulations in the pipeline with which you must comply in the future? What will be the cost implications of complying with these? Is there a possibility that a business you may be thinking of buying could be faced with substantial costs arising from new legislation?

Environmental issues and controls

In some ways this overlaps with legislation in that increased awareness of environmental issues have generated some valuable legislation, e.g. the Clean Air Act, and the Control of Pollution Acts. These are constantly being modified and standards upgraded to improve the environment. In recent years there has been a steady stream of environmental legislation to complement the increasing public awareness of environmental issues, and this will not go away. Most of it does benefit the environment but inevitably these have a financial impact on businesses both large and small. One of the most recent positive examples is the regulation requiring that a specific minimum proportion of all packaging should be recycled. A less enthralling example is the current political objective to reduce pollution by imposing high taxes on road fuel may seem environmentally friendly (or Is it really just an excuse to rise indirect taxation?) but as fuel prices increase motorists naturally look for the lowest prices. These lower prices are typically found in service station run by the multinational oil companies and the major supermarket chains, against whom small local independent garages cannot compete. As stated above, environmental issues and regulations will not go away, so the businesses that will best be able to handle them will be those which take a proactive stance and prepare to work with them. What environmental changes or issues are you aware of that might affect your business? What impact are they likely to have on your operations and your profitability? What preparations have you made to accommodate these and what are the cost implications?

The SWOT analysis

Invariably any strategic analysis of a business, particularly where lending banks are concerned, must contain a SWOT analysis – where the Strengths and Weaknesses of the business are listed (i.e. the internal factors – staff and management skills, gaps which need filling, etc.), and the Opportunities and Threats (the external factors) are identified, and frequently underestimated. The SWOT analysis can be a very valuable and useful tool but it must be used in a positive and productive manner. The strengths and weaknesses should really reflect the answers to the questions that have been posed in the analysis of the internal environment, e.g. by using the questionnaire in the appendices or a similar tool; and similarly the opportunities and threats will relate to issues which have been identified in the analyses of the market and external environments.

The process is basically the same as for the SWOT used in Chapter 5 to assess personal skills, but in the strategic planning process it is applied to the business as a whole rather than individuals or business ideas. All too frequently the SWOT analysis is treated superficially and is insufficiently checked or validated, therein wasting a useful opportunity – simply going through the motions of preparing the analysis may keep the bank manager happy but it does not really do justice to the potential future of the business. If there should be any major gaps or areas of deficiency, these would almost certainly affect the successful implementation of the business strategy. In the same way that a personal SWOT should be checked and validated by another (informed) person's opinion, any SWOT that examines the performance of the business should ideally be independently reviewed, or the owner-manager should ensure that each item within its four sections could be supported by appropriate evidence if challenged. So, when did you last carry out a SWOT analysis on yourself and your business, and isn't it about time you made a start?

References

Carlock, R. S. and Ward, J. L. (2001). *Strategic Planning for the Family Business*. Palgrave, Basingstoke.

Fachler, Y. (2003). *My Family Doesn't Understand Me: Coping Strategies for Entrepreneurs*. Oak Tree Press. Cork, Ireland.

Fleming, D. (2000). "Keep Family Baggage out of the Family Business". Simon & Schuster, Cambridge.

Johnson, G. and Scholes, K. (2003). *Exploring Corporate Strategy*, 6th edition. Prentice Hall, London.

Lasher, W. (1999). *Strategic Thinking for Smaller Businesses and Divisions*. Blackwell, Oxford.

Mintzberg, H. (1994). *The Rise and Fall of Strategic Planning*. Free Press, New York.

Waterman, R. and Peters, T. (1982). *In Search of Excellence*. Harper & Row, New York.

Further reading

Bennett, R. (1998). *Small Business Survival*. NatWest/Financial Times, London.

Bowman, C. and Asch, D. (1996). *Managing Strategy*. Macmillan, Basingstoke.

Jones, O. and Tilley, F. (2003). *Competitive Advantage in SMEs*. Wiley, Chichester.

Wickham, P. A. (2004). *Strategic Entrepreneurship*. FT Prentice Hall, London.

CHAPTER 15

Identifying growth and development options

This chapter is concerned with the fundamental decisions about where the business is moving and how it will develop in the future. It sets the context and defines the objectives for the business to set the scene for subsequent chapters that will focus on the specific policies and strategies (marketing, finance, resources, personnel, etc.) which will facilitate the achievement of those objectives, and first and foremost is the issue of just what the business is all about.

Mission statements

Over the past 10 or 15 years much has been made of the need for every organisation to have a vision or mission statement which specifies (frequently in a grandiose fashion) the key objectives of the organisation. The mission statement is heralded for all to see as a proud emblem of the organisation's customer focus and an inspiration for the employees and almost becomes an aspect of competitive pride between organisations – almost a case of "my mission statement is sharper than yours!" Lasher (1999, p. 31) summarises mission statements quite well: "The vision (of a company) is reflected in a mission statement which summarises the overall goals and values of the organisation as succinctly as possible. The purpose of the mission statement is to communicate these ideas to interested parties, especially the employees". Cole (1994, p. 18) defines it as "a public statement on behalf of an organisation which sets out its raison d'etre in terms of the customer needs it intends to satisfy, the markets in which it will meet those needs, and the manner in which it will meet them".

In many organisations, the mission statement does have a useful and positive function, typically those that regard it as a working tool against which achievement is measured, and which is itself periodically reviewed, and where both the objectives and the measurement of achievement are communicated to the employees. In others it is a "must-have" (because all other important and successful businesses have one, don't they?) that bears little relevance to the on-going operation and long-term development of the business. At the risk of stating the obvious, there is little point in having a mission statement if you do not intend to implement what it says.

The point to be drawn from this is that if you intend to summarise or formulate your primary objectives in such a format, then there must be some practical and measurable purpose behind it, and it must be realistic and achievable. For example, a local butcher might dream to aspire to become "The largest and most profitable butchery business in the UK" and perhaps in 20 or 30 years this might be achieved, but the strategic plan for the business cannot practically look 20 years ahead. The key to successful growth and development of small firms lies in their ability to respond flexibly and rapidly to market change and customer needs. Therefore, the strategic plan for the small business can only realistically focus on what can be forecast as likely to happen over the next 2 or 3 years, or 5 years at the most; as distinct from large conglomerates which can plan their strategies over 5 to 10 years because they are sufficiently large to be able to exert some influence over the market in which they operate. In the smaller market, the chances are that within 3 years local circumstances will change, and when the changes occur, the policies and ambitions of the owner-manager will have to change to meet them. Back to our butcher then, a more realistic mission statement might be "to become the first-choice supplier of high-quality fresh meat and produce in the district" which would be a perfectly realistic and achievable objective within 2 or 3 years. In the longer term the strategic objective might be extended with the opening of other shops "to become the first-choice local butchery service throughout the county". Alternatively as pressure from the large out-of-town supermarkets increases the objective might be modified so as "to maintain a profitable chain of independent high street butchery shops represented in each major town in the county". This recognises the changes in purchasing patterns of the general public where the convenience of shopping in one location often outweighs quality produce and individual service. More to the point, it illustrates that mission statements are not written in stone and will change over the years in response to external and market influences.

What do you personally want to achieve?

This is the first question the owner-manager must consider, as in most small businesses his or her personal ambitions will be integral to the direction the business will take. In its earlier stages, the culture of the business will often be a reflection of the attitudes, management style, and values of the entrepreneur who created it, at least until it has grown sufficiently large to employ other managers who can add their own influence to the firm's culture. An entrepreneur with great personal ambitions for wealth and prosperity will want to see the same attitude in the business, for the business will hopefully become the vehicle that delivers that wealth. Another person who is just running the business as a hobby, perhaps earning some extra cash by doing something they enjoy, will have far lower personal and business expectations that will again be reflected in the approach to future growth and development, or lack thereof.

The ambitions which individuals hold for themselves are often determined by their own personal parameters – their financial circumstances and family responsibilities, their background and previous experiences, etc. – and here we are touching on the realms of psychology, Maslow's Hierarchy of Needs, and Hertzberg's hygiene factors. The entrepreneur with a dependant family will want to create sufficient income and wealth to provide them with a comfortable and safe environment. However, the extents of their ambition over and above that, may well depend on other motivations and possibly behavioural factors. For example, the extent of their own competitive nature, whether or not they have experienced former wealth or deprivation, whether their ambition and drive is linked to the need for prestige and esteem. As we discussed in Chapter 13, the extent of personal financial exposure can also be a big influence on the entrepreneur's objectives, at least until that exposure is moderated or removed, at which stage the motivation and objectives may change. In the example of the hobby-business mentioned above, a person with adequate income (perhaps from a spouse or partner) the primary motivation is personal satisfaction rather than the generation of income. So what are your personal ambitions, financial needs and motivations? Are you in business purely to make money? Are you looking for job satisfaction? Is status and recognition important to you? Do you feel that you have a responsibility for the employment of your staff? Or are you motivated by a combination of these? How will these personal ambitions affect the way you operate your business? The answers to these questions will largely determine what you personally want to achieve, which will in turn decide whether the business stays as it is, changes direction, or proceeds to develop and grow.

What long-term objectives do you have for the business?

Once you have considered the personal issues and questions in the previous section, you should be able to start to synthesise from your personal objectives some form of overall direction for the business that can subsequently be translated into a key objective or mission statement for the business itself. Using the earlier example: "I want to develop and expand my butchery business to provide a good level of income for myself and my family, and a long-term investment and legacy for my children", becomes: "I want the butchery business to survive and prosper in the long term and to generate good profits on a regular basis". In turn translating this into a more customer-focused mission statement, this becomes "Our objective is to maintain a profitable chain of independent high street butchery shops, supplying quality produce, in each major town in the county".

It is quite interesting that an analysis of the growth aspirations of smaller firms conducted by the Cambridge Small Business Research Centre (Storey, 1994, p. 120) revealed that of the sample population interviewed approximately 64.3% of small and 65.7% of micro-firms were interested in moderate as opposed to substantial growth, and 10.4% of small firms, and 13.2% of micro-firms wanted to stay the same size. 1.7% and 2.7% respectively wanted to grow smaller, whilst a quite modest 22.9% and 17.0% respectively were looking for substantial growth. As we have seen in Chapter 13, growth for the creation of wealth, particularly for its own sake, is by no means the most significant focal point or objective for owner-managers. The creation of a satisfying lifestyle or of a business legacy for the next generation can be of equal important to some of them.

What options are available to achieve the objectives?

This question rises the key issues of defining the strategic options for the business. Johnson and Scholes (2003) argue that strategic options need to be examined in terms of generic strategies, directions and methods:

- Their generic strategies consist of three alternatives. First, cost leadership, which is the strategy by which businesses maintain competitive advantage in the marketplace by planning and managing the cost structure (comparative price) of their goods and services in relation to that of their competitors. Second is the differentiation strategy, which focuses on product choice, quality, service, and perceived value in the eyes of the customer. For small firms this is often more feasible than the cost leadership option where as new entrants to the market, they may not be able to achieve the same economies of scale available to established competitors. Third, is the focus strategy whereby the organisation targets its efforts towards one or more specific niches in the market; and this in particular, is a frequently used means by which small firms can achieve market share in the face of competition from bigger rivals. The drawback however, is that too much success by a small firm in a niche market, can attract unwelcome attention from powerful and more wealthy competitors. There is an additional hybrid strategy proposed by Lasher (1999, p. 87), that of best-cost provider, which combines cost leadership with differentiation, e.g. providing a high-quality product at a mid-range price.

The directions in which organisations can move are quite varied. The most obvious is the "do-nothing" option which, whilst it may be unthinkable in the majority of larger businesses, is often perfectly acceptable to the small firm owner-manager particularly if the current business situation accommodates their own personal lifestyle requirements and aspirations. Johnson and Scholes cite the "withdrawal" option as being one that is often overlooked. In some cases, it is the owner-manager's specific intent to develop the business to a certain size and then to sell it as a going concern. In other cases, if the future prospects are looking grim then a strategic withdrawal from all or part of the market may be the soundest decision to make. A stage of "consolidation" may be chosen wherein the firm makes no move to expand or grow, but prefers to focus on its internal operations to improve its efficiency and profitability. More positive options include moves which increase "market penetration" to sell greater volumes of current products or services in the existing market, "market development" to sell existing products in new segments of the market; or alternatively "product development" to expand by developing new products for the market. Another option is to diversify the product range. "Related diversification" is the process of expanding the product range beyond the current situation but remaining within the same industry, e.g. where our butcher friend from the earlier example decides to start making and selling meat pies. "Unrelated diversification" occurs when the business moves into a different line of products or services, e.g. when our butcher decides to expand his shop to sell fish, or fruit and vegetables. The latter would be an example or horizontal integration where the butcher is selling complementary products, but the diversification process could also involve backward integration, e.g. where the butcher acquired a live-stock farm or an abattoir, or such as the Shepherd Neame brewery in Kent (claimed to be the oldest independent brewery in the UK) which owned its own hop farm to ensure the supply of quality hops for its brewing process. The integration could also move forwards, e.g. if a small independent brewery decided to acquire one or two pubs through which its products could be sold, or a market gardener opened a farm shop to sell the produce it was growing direct to the public. In the case of Shepherd Neame, the firm also kept pigs and cattle on its farm at one time, to utilise the spent hops and barley from the brewing process.

▨ Johnson and Scholes identified three main methods by which organisations could develop. The first of these is "internal development", i.e. growing from within, using its own or borrowed resources to expand or to develop new products, particularly if it does not have sufficient resources, e.g. to buy another business to facilitate rapid growth. Second, by "acquisition" wherein the business buys or takes over another business either in its own market to increase market share or economies of scale; or as part of the diversification process to gain a broader product base. This is often the easiest and fastest method of expansion or diversification when resources are not limited, or when the barriers to entry into a new market are substantial. Third, by means of "joint development" where for example, two or more businesses co-operate in the development of a new product or venture. This consortium approach is more likely to occur between large organisations involved in major projects (e.g. civil engineering or aircraft design), but in the small firms situation the joint development may take the form of the franchising of products or services to achieve growth.

Moving back to the original question (where do you want your business to go?), the key questions to be asked are:

▨ Do I want to keep the business or to sell or liquidate it?
▨ If I keep it, do I stay as I am or do I wish to change or grow the business?

      ▨   If I do not change, do I continue to trade as at present, or do I consolidate, i.e. focus on improving efficiency and profitability?

      ▨   If I decide to develop the business, do I want to:
- grow it by being more competitive,
- grow it by developing, or diversifying into, a wider range of products or services,
- grow it by focusing on niche markets?

      ▨   If I opt to increase market penetration, do I achieve this by increasing my own sales and marketing activities, or do I seek to acquire another business and its share of the market?

      ▨   If I decide to develop my market share by offering a wider range of products or services, do I develop this within the business using my own or borrowed capital? Do I develop these in co-operation with another business, perhaps in a foreign market that is not in direct competition with my own? Or do I buy them in from another supplier, perhaps under licence or in a franchise arrangement?

      ▨   Is there any advantage to be gained by integration, backwards forwards or horizontal, e.g. by developing subsidiary parts of the business or buying a related business? Will the cost savings or extra profit from this is comparable with what could result from an alternative strategy, e.g. market development or penetration?

Case study 15.1

Folkestone whelks

For many years, Folkestone Harbour has reputedly sold the best whelks in England, with an almost perfectly competitive market situation operating between the vendors. Five small seafood stalls and a wet-fish shop sell their whelks of similar quality, at broadly similar prices, with similar trimmings, in similar containers. Two or three open every day, but several open just at weekends or daily in mid-Summer. They compete with each other but co-exist, and have done so for scores of years; visited by generations of day-trippers from London, with their children and grandchildren.

    However, traditional taste are changing and in recent years day-trippers have wanted more than just a bowl of whelks, winkles, shrimps, cockles, mussels, or jellied eels, all liberally doused with chilli vinegar. But behind the seafood stall lies an interesting pattern of generic strategies. Although none have opted for a cost leadership approach, two have achieved backward integration with boats moored nearby to catch their own produce. One of those has also integrated forwards as a wholesaler supplying other stalls and wet-fish shops in nearby towns. One has opted for market penetration by acquisition, now owning two of the outlets. One has chosen market development by diversifying, i.e. by purchasing wet fish from other trawlers and selling it to the general public. The final stall holder has chosen product development by offering hot and spicy cooked seafood, dressed salads and escargots alongside the conventional fare (well, he is French); and horizontal diversification with an adjacent stall selling burgers and hot-dogs to the day-trippers' kids.

They continue to co-exist side-by-side, the day-trippers still flock to the harbour at weekends and summer holidays come sun, rain, wind, or hail; and the whelks are reckoned to be as good as ever – if you like whelks that is!

The range of questions we have just considered are those which decide the fate of businesses in terms of their progress, or lack thereof, along the routes in the model shown in Figure 13.1.

Which option is best for my business?

Finding the answer to this question requires a systematic evaluation of the strategic options, i.e. the process of answering the questions rose in the previous section but in the context of the strategic analysis of the organisation. Again, Johnson and Scholes (2003) have come up with a suitable method based on three main factors:

1. *Suitability*: To what extent the strategic options are compatible with the strategic analysis of the organisation, its operating environment, and its strengths and weaknesses. Would a particular option make full use of the organisations strengths whilst at the same time avoiding any adverse impact by its weaknesses or any foreseeable external factors such as changes in legislation or government policy?

2. *Feasibility*: This examines how and whether or not the strategy might work in practice. For example, an option to expand into export markets might not be feasible if the business had no knowledge or experience of exporting and lacked the economies of scale to compete on price against the local suppliers in those markets. Similarly, the option to grow market share by acquiring another business would be totally unrealistic if the business had little or no spare capital and borrowing capacity to finance the acquisition. In the case of the small firm, the feasibility of any option in terms of the firm's capacity and resources, will always be the limiting factor.

3. *Acceptability*: How acceptable and compatible it will be relative to the needs and objectives of the stakeholders in the business. An option that appeals to one stakeholder may be totally unacceptable to another. This is a situation that can frequently arise in

partnerships and small family firms, when one partner wants to grow and expand whilst another wants to avoid risk and just consolidate the business. A similar situation might be where one director wants to focus on market penetration for current products or services, and another wants to diversify the business. In an ideal world, the business might be able to follow both strategies, but in small firms the financial resources rarely permit such luxuries.

In terms of practical decision-making methods that can be used to evaluate alternative options there are a wide range of models, tools and techniques available. These range from the ever-popular SWOT (strengths, weaknesses, opportunities, and threats) (see Chapters 5 and 14), through a range of financial methods such as cost–benefit analysis, payback periods, liquidity and financial ratios, return-on-capital-employed calculations, net present value, cash-flow and profit forecasts; to more complicated models, which are designed to forecast market share, analyse the sensitivity of the market, and evaluate stakeholder support. It is not intended to describe these individually here as they could fill a book in their own right, and they are more than adequately described in books dedicated to the subject, e.g. Gore *et al.* (1992). The choice of appropriate methods will be largely determined by the nature of the primary objectives themselves. For example, a business objective relating to long-term profit generation will most likely use financial techniques to evaluate available options: profit forecasts, return-on-capital-employed, etc. Whereas an objective based on expansion and market share might use statistical models or techniques to compare potential growth rates, sensitivity, or an analysis of market trends and opportunities.

The biggest problem for an owner-manager is to identify the right method for their particular needs, and this is where specialist advice may be well worth paying for. Potential sources of advice and guidance might include chartered accountants or management consultants (both relatively expensive), bank managers (with a possible tendency to focus on your borrowing capacity or matching it to what they have to offer), marketing consultants, local enterprise agency business advisors, and local business links. The latter two may be the most appropriate for smaller businesses because they are more impartial, and tend to cost less, often offering a free initial consultation and fixed fee advice, although business links are sometime criticised for preferring to focus on the medium-sized or larger firms where results attract more publicity. The UK government introduced the Small Business Service (SBS) in 2001 to supposedly co-ordinate the activities of the various support agencies to provide better support small firms, but the efficacy was somewhat diluted with much of the support agency funding also being directed through the newly established Regional Development Agencies, and indeed these are to become responsible for the business link network in future years. It could be argued that the biggest weakness in the provision of support to small firms in the UK results from the dissipation of funding through three separate government departments – the Department of Trade and Industry which funds the SBS and expert trade advice, the Department for work and skills which funds business training via the local Learning and Skills Councils, and the Department for Environment and the Regions which funds support via the unelected Regional Assemblies and their corresponding Regional Development Agencies. In view of the significance of small- and medium-sized enterprises (SMEs) to the UK economy, there is a strong argument for a single stream of funding (perhaps a government department for small business) to remove duplication of provision and to ensure that business support and train-ing is channelled as simply as possible to the firms that need it, instead of wasting so much through the use of parallel channels of funding from which the duplication of administrative functions removes so much of the funding that could be used to provide better quality sup-port for small firms.

Whatever source of advice you choose, any objective factual analysis of the pros and cons of the various options should also take due account of your own personal objectives as owner-manager of the business, because you have to be comfortable with the final choice to make it work. Remember that the strategy of the business should aim to match its inter-nal strengths and resources to the needs of the marketplace, whilst remaining within the parameters defined by its stakeholders.

So, in order to evaluate the various options that have been identi-fied, we must ask a further range of questions:

- Which of the selected options are most compatible with the strengths and weaknesses that were identified in the strategic analysis of the business? Do they build on the strengths? Do they avoid or overcome the weaknesses?
- How do the options relate to the opportunities and threats that have been identified, and do they take full advantage of those opportunities? Are they robust enough to withstand any obvious threats?
- What external factors (changes in government policy, legisla-tion, economic trends, etc.) could influence the various options, and would the effects of these factors be positive or negative?

- Are the options compatible with the objectives of the owners of the business; and if this is not the case, are the differences minor, substantial, or critical?
- Are there any factors within the options which might be regarded as unacceptable by other stakeholders such as suppliers, financiers, or bankers?
- What risks are associated with each of the options, and are these regarded as acceptable by the owners and stakeholders involved in the business?
- Is the business capable of accommodating or implementing any changes implicit in the various options?
- What are the current limiting factors that might inhibit the options? For example, financial resources, borrowing capacity, physical space, management skills, staff availability and skills, market size and accessibility. How might these limiting factors be overcome?
- Given current resources, which of the proposed options could realistically be achieved by the business in the next 3 to 5 years?
- What returns (in terms of increased revenue, cost savings, improved profits, etc.) might we expect from the respective options, and what levels of investment would be required to achieve those returns?

Defining the business objectives to meet the chosen option

The mission statement and primary objectives of the business are insufficient in their own right to provide a practical basis for growth and development. The broad strategic or primary objectives of the organisation need to be broken down into a series of subsidiary objectives relating to specific functional areas, operational areas, or management units within the business. These specific objectives should be compatible with each other and should compliment the primary objective. Lasher (1999) describes this as the process of upward support, essential to ensure the co-ordination of the subsidiary objectives to avoid management and strategic problems, conflicts between operational areas of the organisation, etc.

For example, a primary objective "to grow the business by 20% per annum over each of the next 5 years" does not mean that each functional area of the business must grow by no less (or no more) than 20% per annum. The specific objectives for each department may be totally different for practical reasons. The sales department may have a target to increase output by 30% in year 1, although the cost of doing so may only raise sales revenue by 15% in the first instance. The production department may need to double its capacity in year 1, and again in year 4 to meet the overall target, as this may be less disruptive, and more practical and cost-effective than increasing output by 20% each year. For the finance department the target may be to implement a new invoicing and customer-accounts system within 6 months, and for marketing there may be a need to design a new image for the company's products within the next 3 months. Personnel may need to recruit and train new staff in readiness for the expanded production capacity and staff in the retail customers' outlets will need product training. Some of these objectives are longer term (i.e. strategic in their own right), whilst others are tactical and relate to the shorter-term implementation of the strategy.

For objectives to work effectively they need to meet a number of criteria:

- They need to be challenging, i.e. achievable but stretching performance beyond what is currently achieved, or what could be easily achieved. However, the resulting increase in performance may need to be rewarded in some way if the motivation of staff is to be maintained, and if further increases in performance are subsequently sought.
- They must be SMART. *Specific*, so as to define targets in a manner that can be clearly understood. *Measurable*, to enable their achievement (or otherwise) to be accurately assessed. *Achievable* in terms of the capabilities of the staff or business units assigned to meet them. *Realistic* in terms of the resources made available to achieve them. *Timely* in terms of defining the target period or deadline within which they must be achieved.
- Within the objectives, we must build in key success factors or performance indicators that provide a measurable indication that the key stages of the objectives are being achieved to an acceptable standard.
- At a less strategic level, Cole (1994, p. 17) states that explicit goals and objectives provide standards of performance which can be used to motivate staff; and objectives (p. 29) are "the short-term and specific intentions of the various operational units of the organisation. They are often called targets and are key elements in the tactical plans" of the organisation as they provide a focus for the day-to-day output and efficiency of the business.

- Objectives should compliment each other, and should not conflict with each other. This seems to be a case of stating the obvious, but whereas the objectives themselves might appear to be complementary, it could be that the implications of them or the ways in which they might be implemented could create conflict, particularly when resources within the firm may be limited.
- The objectives should be explicit so that they can be easily understood. They should be "sold" to staff to ensure that the form's staff take ownership of them to improve the prospects of their achievement. If the employees do not understand or relate to the objectives, or the importance of them to the organisation, then there is no guarantee that they will co-operate with their implementation. Indeed, if they are not sold on the importance of the objectives to the organisation, they may well positively interfere with their implementation.

Questions to be asked when formulating the functional objectives that support the chosen policy for development of the business:

- Are the defined objectives compatible with and supportive of the primary objective of business development?
- Are the objectives of the various functional areas compatible with each other, or do they contain conflicting elements?
- Do the objectives meet the SMART criteria?
- Will they stretch the functional departments of the organisation and their staff?
- Are the staff aware of, and do they understand the firm's objectives?
- Do the employees of the firm accept the relevance and importance of those objectives to the future of the organisation?

References

Cole, G. A. (1994). *Strategic Management.* DP Publications, London.

Gore, C., Murray, K. and Richardson, W. (1992). *Strategic Decision Making.* Cassell, London.

Johnson, G. and Scholes, K. (2003). *Exploring Corporate Strategy,* 7th edition. FT Prentice Hall, London.

Lasher, W. (1999). *Strategic Thinking for Smaller Businesses and Divisions.* Blackwell, Oxford.

Storey, D. (1994). *Understanding the Small Business Sector.* Thomson Business Press, London.

Further reading

Bowman, C. and Asch, D. (1996). *Managing Strategy*. Macmillan, Basingstoke.

Porter, M. E. (1985). *Competitive Advantage: Creating and Sustaining a Superior Performance*. Free Press.

Jones, O. and Tilley, F. (2003). *Competitive Advantage in SMEs*. Wiley, Chichester.

Wickham, P. A. (2004). *Strategic Entrepreneurship*. FT Prentice Hall, London.

CHAPTER 16

Additional resource implications of growth

Once the strategic choices have been made, and the objectives have been determined and agreed, the next phase involves the tactical decisions, that is how to plan the details of the staged implementation of those strategies in the medium term. The first question that springs immediately to mind is "What resources will we need to do it?" Broadly speaking we are talking about premises, space, plant and equipment, transport, office equipment and computers, communications equipment, raw materials or stock, packaging, advertising materials, staff and managers to make productive use of it all, and of course the money to pay for everything. However, before the acquisitions can begin there are still a large number of crucial decisions that have to be made, as many of these purchases will involve substantial long-term capital investment, and few businesses (particularly smaller ones) can afford to make expensive mistakes. Some of these decisions rise the same questions and issues that are covered in Chapter 14 and in the performance review questionnaire in Appendix, as this is the stage at which you need to plan for the resources and associated costs of implementing improvements.

Premises

Many of the aspects relating to the criteria for the location and selection of premises have been covered in detail in Chapter 8, but the premises needed at start-up stage are often selected on the basis of short-term priorities, such as:

> ■ *Affordability*: Premises are often selected in line with short-term budget restrictions, limited working capital, unpredictable cash

flow – opting for the cheapest rather than the most suitable for the business.

- ▪ *The desire to minimise overheads*: To keep down the break-even level of trading to give the business the best chance of survival before working capital runs out.
- ▪ *The need to keep expenditure down*: To cover what is needed for the immediate future rather than have unutilised space available for the future. The entrepreneur may have been fully aware of the costs and disruption involved in moving premises at a later date but willing to finance that from profits (if they occur) in preference to overspending in the short term.
- ▪ *The reluctance to take on long-term commitments*: In particular the risk of signing long-term lease or mortgage agreements when it is not known if the business will or will not succeed, possibly leaving the entrepreneur exposed to financial penalties or debt.

When an established business is contemplating growth, those criteria will invariably have changed:

- ▪ The firm may want to find premises that offer a long-term location (possibly even for purchase) and ideally with sufficient capacity to facilitate all foreseeable long-term growth.
- ▪ The firm may want to optimise its position on the market, e.g. by finding a prime high street retail location, or a site that projects an image of success and professionalism alongside with other high-growth firms.
- ▪ The firm may be considering arrange of other geographical locations to expand its distribution coverage or network.
- ▪ The owners may simply want to relocate to another area that offers a better location from the point of view of access or security.

More detailed questions that need to be considered are as follows.

What space or premises do I currently have available, and will these be adequate for the future?

As stated above, most new firms start their existence by selecting the premises that match their immediate needs at the lowest affordable cost, so as not to eat into valuable working capital. They can seldom afford space for future expansion and in consequence often find themselves faced with moving premises at least once in the first 2 or 3 years, which is an expensive and disruptive process. Faced then with the desire or necessity to expand, the obvious first step is to review the current premises. Very often, what looks like an over-crowded building is one in which space is simply being utilised badly, in particular vertical space. So, can a move be avoided by better use of existing space? Is there an opportunity to use storage racking, or perhaps to install a mezzanine to free-up floor space? Is there an opportunity to extend the building in any way? If the answer is no, and a move is essential then you must move onto the next question.

What space or premises will I require for the future?
Well, just how far into the future are you looking? If you have completed a strategic analysis of your business and identified the direction(s) for your growth, along with some realistic and quantified objectives, this should not be too much of a problem. For a service business, for which the moving process is usually less complicated than a manufacturing or distribution business, the size of premises may be of less significance than their location in relation to the market community. But for a manufacturing firm, the growth objectives may require substantial capital investment in production machinery and storage space.

How much extra space will I need?
The chosen site will need to be sufficiently large to accommodate the extra plant and equipment for a number of years, and ideally having sufficient surrounding area to accommodate further expansion at a later date. With the high costs of relocation, measured in terms of disruption to output as well as the cost of physically moving, it is realistic to look for premises that will be adequate for at least the next 5 years and ideally 10 years, otherwise your surplus profits and reserves will be swallowed up by repeated relocations. This may mean that you are paying for space which is not being fully utilised in the earlier stages, but you can always consider sub-letting it until you need it for your own use (and in doing so you may generate some extra revenue). It may be easier to lease a site that is initially too large, than to have to try to buy out the leases of your immediate neighbours at a premium, in order to expand a year or two later. If you have sufficient capital, you may look to buy a site with adequate space to add additional buildings, as you need them. Remember, you are in business to make a profit for yourself and your shareholders, not for the benefit of estate agents, solicitors, landlords, and mortgage lenders!

How soon will I need to expand and what sort of lead-time is involved?
It is often the lead-time that determines the how-soon. If you are aware that your premises are becoming tight and will be inadequate within a year, then the time to look is now. It can often take months of searching to find the right place and to negotiate the right deal for its lease or purchase. The more time you have available, then the more chance you will

have of negotiating terms to your own benefit. For example, it is quite common for a landlord who has been sitting on empty premises to agree to an initial rent-free period of 3 to 6 months, which can be a great help towards recovering the costs of relocation and refitting the new premises. It can also facilitate the ease of relocation by enabling you to prepare the new premises so that you can relocate with minimal disruption to your customers. In terms of lead times, it can sometimes take months to find the right site. Subsequent to finding the site, it is also quite common for solicitors to take a further 3 months to negotiate and complete the terms of a lease, especially if you require finance from a bank of commercial mortgage lender.

Should I relocate to another area?
The answer to this question will depend on several factors: the location of your customers, the location of your competitors, and any incentives that might influence your relocation. As discussed previously, if your customers are very local, then there will be nothing to be gained by moving away from them, and you should be thinking in terms of locating your business at a site where you will be readily accessible to them. If your customers are remote, e.g. supplied by mail order or delivery service, then you stand to benefit by any cost savings gained through relocation. Certainly, you should not consider relocation if it puts you at a disadvantage in relation to your competitors, unless of course, there are compelling financial gains to be made. Regional Development Agencies are often able to offer substantial financial incentives to move into designated development or regeneration areas. The main objective of these incentives is to generate local employment opportunities, so you must first ask yourself if such a move would create problems in finding suitably skilled or qualified staff in that area. Think about it – will there be many precision engineers or software programmers to be found amongst the local shepherds or potato-pickers?

What sort of a contractual arrangement should you be thinking about?
The three most common options are to rent, lease or buy. Renting usually requires relatively little outlay up-front, typically 3 months' rent in advance. The duration of the rental agreement is usually negotiable but if you hope to get an initial rent-free period that some landlords occasionally offer to tempt customers, the duration of the contract is unlikely to be less than 2 or 3 years. If you think that there is a chance you will outgrow the premises, say after 5 years, you may sign up for such a period with the option to extend the rental period after that date. The landlord will invariably insist on regular rent reviews, and reviews always go upwards, so be sure to use an experienced solicitor or

agent to negotiate on your behalf to avoid any commitments that might adversely affect your profits. Long-term leases on premises avoid the spiralling costs of rent reviews and provide a known fixed level of future overhead costs (ground rent, council business rates, etc.), but do require an initial capital outlay to buy the lease. On a long-term lease the capital outlay can probably be recovered by selling the lease at a later date, often showing a profit. There is however, the drawback under English law whereby if a subsequent purchaser of the lease should default on ground rent then the liability will usually revert to the previous leaseholder. In the past this has left some businesses finding themselves liable for overhead costs on premises they no longer occupy, and which cannot be sold because of legal distraints on assets, or charges against the site held by mortgage lenders. If you are in the fortunate position of having surplus capital, or the private resources to offer a second guarantee against a commercial mortgage, then it might pay to consider buying the freehold of suitable premises. This would offer the benefits of regular and foreseeable future outgoings coupled with the prospect of capital growth, although to gain the full benefits it would probably be necessary to stay on the site for at least 5 to 10 years. Whatever option you choose the key factor to remember is that you should never deplete or use your working capital to pay for fixed assets.

How much will each type cost?

There is no easy answer to this question. Relative costs will vary from month to month according to interest rates and local demand for commercial property. Costs of similar premises may vary widely between districts just a few miles apart depending on availability, local services, and accessibility to road networks, etc. A cost comparison of the various options is essential but cost should not be the only consideration, as it is no good having cheap premises if they are not accessible by your customers, or not located near your markets, or in an area where security could be a problem.

What options are available to fund the expansion?

There are always costs attached to moving premises, and if these cannot be financed from profits or reserves, then medium or long-term bank loans (3 to 5 years) may be the answer, although some form of security will invariably be required for these. Commercial mortgages are available to finance leases or to buy property, typically over 10 to 15 year periods, but the lender will require a deposit, typically 20% to 25% of the full cost to be provided up-front by the borrower. The precise figures will depend on the age and value of the premises, or the residual period of the lease, etc., and legal fees and expenses will also be incurred in the process. Some of the options for acquiring and financing premises are considered in Chapter 8.

Plant and equipment

What do I have at present and is it adequate for my current needs?
It is necessary to start with a critical and objective assessment of the current inventory of plant and equipment. How old is it, and how much useful life does it have? Is it paid for or is there still outstanding finance due? Is it currently reliable or are we losing money as a result of frequent downtime for repairs and maintenance and if so what is the frequency and average cost of breakdowns? It may well be that the cost of repeated repairs and maintenance may be less per annum than the cost of leasing of buying new equipment. Are there alternatives available that offer higher rates of output or a better potential return on their cost? Do the manufacturers have anything new in the pipeline that could be worth a few months' wait? Are our competitors gaining a march on us by using better or more cost-effective machinery? Before you think that you have all of the answers to these questions, just check back with your members of staff who actually use the plant or equipment, and ask them for their honest opinions, as these may surprise you. They will often be able to identify problems (or potential solutions) of which you yourself are not aware.

Is it likely to be adequate for your future needs, or do you need more production capacity?
Those future needs will have been largely determined by the strategic choices you have made. If you are planning to adopt a policy of expansion by market penetration, and still have spare production capacity available, then further capital outlay may not be necessary. However, if you plan to expand by diversifying your product range then current equipment may be of little use beyond that of maintaining output of current product lines. This is where the need for accurate sales and marketing forecasts become critical, as you must decide on the right amount of capital investment to match your long-term production plans. If you invest too little there is the risk or running out of production capacity far too soon, and facing further investment before adequate profits are available to pay for it. If your forecasts are too high, you risk having expensive plant and production capacity laying idle and burdening you with disproportionate overhead costs. The ideal compromise is to plan your growth in progressive stages which can be financed out of on-going profits, however where high-tech manufacturing equipment is concerned this is

not always practical, as to buy several smaller installations of plant may prove far more expensive than a single large installation.

Can I afford not to invest in new plant or equipment?

There always remains the "do-nothing" option, but sooner or later, current equipment will wear out. Even if the owner-manager has no ambitions for expansion there is always a need to keep pace with changes in customer demand over a period of time, and even traditional craft industries have to modify their practice and methods occasionally to keep themselves competitive and their products affordable. Perhaps the question should be supplemented with another: how long can I expect to stay in business if I don't invest in the business at some stage? It was systematic lack of investment in new steel and shipbuilding technology that contributed to the decline of these industries in Britain in the latter half of the 20th century.

Should you be investing in new technology?

The answer will depend on what possible advantages the use of technology can provide over your competitors. New technology can make a great contribution towards competitive strategy, for example, if it gives you a cost advantage such as a cost saving, compared with what your competitors can achieve, then this may assist with your cost-leadership strategy. The advantages could lie elsewhere in terms of increased quality or more flexibility in product design, enabling some diversification of your product range. There really has to be some tangible and measurable advantage to be gained from employing new technology, rather than just using it for its own sake; and in some markets in which customers value traditional craftsmanship, technology can be a disadvantage. The important issue then is whether or not the use of technology will complement and help the firm to achieve its strategic objectives.

How do you assess the best option?

This is where you must decide on a policy against which you can evaluate the relative costs. Are you going to look for the quickest payback, i.e. the fastest recovery of capital invested; or will you seek the highest percentage return on the money invested, which may take longer but could offer a higher total profit? When you are examining these options, remember to include all of the costs involved and not just the basic cost of the new plant or equipment. You must include the costs of financing the purchase, not just in terms of interest paid, but the investment income you may have lost by using your reserves. You must also try to calculate and include all of the other costs that relate to the purchase and installation of new equipment, including lost production caused by disruption, physical installation costs, staff training and the commissioning period until full output is achieved once again. Finally, what if any, is the cost of disruption, in terms of lost business?

Transport and distribution

Do you need to operate my own vehicles?

The first question: why do you operate them now? If your customers are local, i.e. situated within a reasonable driving distance, and need regular and reliable deliveries then it is probably more cost effective to operate your own vehicles. For example, wholesalers who supply local retail outlets (shops, restaurants, pubs, leisure facilities) on a regular and frequent basis will usually choose to deliver direct and indeed the contact with customers during deliveries can be a valuable part of the sales process. Less frequent direct deliveries may also be viable given sufficient value or volume of goods being supplied. Furniture manufacturers will often have regular fortnightly or monthly delivery runs to customers in specific parts of the country, and lead times are built into the order process to tie in with these deliveries to make them cost effective. However, for the majority of small items and one-off sales over long distances, it is seldom profitable to use direct deliveries.

What are the alternatives?

For small items and infrequent orders mail order is often the easiest method. For high-value or fragile items, contract courier deliveries (Business Post, TNT, UPS, DHL, Amtrak, etc.) which use a network of international and local depots offering an overnight service throughout the country, are relatively cheap and efficient. By making prompt and efficient deliveries to your customers, they aim to retain you as one of their customers, so the interest is mutual. Consider the cost of running just one delivery vehicle for a year: the capital outlay and depreciation, interest on finance, road tax, insurance, breakdown cover, fuel, tyres, repairs and maintenance, delays caused by traffic jams and breakdowns, hiring replacement vehicles, the drivers' wages, their national insurance, sickness and holiday pay, cover for lateness and absence; the cost of the supervisor who plans the deliveries and organises and administers the vehicles. It might pay to total up all of these costs and then divide them by the number of packages or items delivered by that vehicle in a year. How then, does the unit cost of those compare with the postal or contract delivery alternative?

What sort of transport do you need?

The obvious answer is to match the vehicle to the weight, size, volume and numbers of items being delivered. Usually the larger the capacity (volume or payload) of the vehicle, the lower the unit cost of the deliveries, although the final decision may also be affected by where the goods are to be delivered and how they will get there. Consider Case study 16.1.

Case study 16.1

Kent & Sussex Ales

Kent & Sussex Ales was a small real-ale, beer and mineral wholesaler supplying pubs clubs and restaurants in a relatively rural area. It used three transit-type vans for deliveries. Most of these involved just two or three casks of beer delivered to pubs typically spaced about five miles apart in country areas using minor roads. Some journeys involved round-trips of 80 miles per day. A few customers (about 10%) placed larger orders of 8 or more casks.

As the business grew, a decision had to be made about acquiring additional delivery capacity. Two options were considered:

Option 1: To sell one of the existing transit vans (payload 1.5 tonnes) and buy a 7-tonne truck (payload 4 tonnes) and to employ an additional driver/delivery man.

This option offered more capacity overall (an additional 1.0 tonne or about 18 small casks of beer) and would save on road tax, insurance, MOT costs, etc. The fuel consumption was slightly higher but because of the extra volume and payload, the larger vehicle could undertake longer journeys. Loading and unloading was slightly slower due to the curtain-sided access.

Option 2: To buy an additional transit-type van (payload 1.5 tonnes) and to employ an additional driver. This option would incur extra capital expenditure and overhead costs (tax, insurance, MOT, etc., compared with option 1, amounting to some £8,000 per year.

The larger vehicle was the obvious choice on the grounds of cost savings, and appeared to be more efficient as it could handle larger quantities of goods and make longer journeys. It raised the overall delivery payload of all vehicles to 7 tonnes, whereas Option 2 offered only 6 tonnes. However a 4-week trial of the options using rented vehicles threw up several major issues:

- First, the majority of pub customers were not early risers and wanted deliveries between 9.00 a.m. and 3.00 p.m. when they closed for the afternoon, and the longer journeys could not be fitted within that time scale.
- Second, until the larger van was tried, the drivers had not realised that most of the short-cuts used to ensure deliveries used narrow country lanes, many of which had width or weight restrictions that the larger truck could not meet.
- Third, by planning small van routes carefully so that one of the four vans was retained for closer deliveries, the short-haul van was capable of a second daily run which made up for the lower delivery capacity of the four small vans.

The extra capital and operating costs of Option 2 were more than outweighed by the flexibility gained, and in keeping the customers happy by delivering on time. However, in a more urban area with closer delivery points, better roads, and possibly larger delivery drops, the reverse might have been true.

Should you lease or buy my vehicles?

In the early days when a business is first established profits are small if any, regular outgoings must be minimised, and there is often a preference to maximise the tangible assets shown on the balance sheet. For this purpose, hire- purchase is ideal, as once the initial down-payment is made the regular payments are relatively low, and the net value of the purchase can be shown on the balance sheet as the buyer will eventually own it. The less attractive tax relief offered by the capital allowance system is not seen as a problem as taxable profits are usually modest. However, by the time an owner-manager has consolidated the business and is thinking of expansion this situation should have changed. With trading profits coming in there is less need for assets to be shown on the balance sheet, but there is a need to minimise tax liabilities, and here leasing is a better option. As the business does not and never will own the leased vehicles, they cannot be treated as an asset, but on the other hand, they do constitute a tax-deductible operating expense of the business. In simple terms then, hire-purchase is a better option than a bank loan, as it does not have to be secured on anything more than the purchased item itself; but for companies in profit, leasing is more tax-efficient than hire-purchase.

Administration, information technology, and communications

Are my current information systems performing to meet my needs?

This is not just an issue of information technology, it is also about the basics of organising your administrative systems, i.e. can you find something when you need it? There are some records that must be kept for tax or value-added tax purposes and others like customer records that are important for the running of the business. However, there is other information sitting in your filing cabinet and taking up space that you will never use again. If these information being held within your systems that is unnecessary and needing deletion in order to comply with the Data Protection Act, that could create free space? When did you last review your information systems to determine what information is essential and what is just cluttering your systems and filing space, out-of-date trade brochures, etc.? The point of all this is that if you are planning a substantial expansion of your business, then the administrative systems will need to be able to support that growth.

So, where are the shortfalls in the current systems?

Do you waste time because you have trouble finding papers that have been filed? Do you have piles of papers waiting to be filed? Are you keeping paper records when electronic data storage would be more efficient? With the cost of PC storage currently lower than it has ever been, there is no longer any excuse for cumbersome paper-based systems for anything but the most basic business, but the use of computerised accounting, database and word-processing systems does require a modicum of discipline. In particular, the accessibility they offer in terms of fast and accurate data recovery will only work if data is backed-up regularly and stored securely. For many owner-managers that is a task too far in the light of other priorities.

The type of electronic data storage and communication systems you choose should not just be determined by your own current and prospective needs, they should also be considered in relation to those of your customers. What preferred systems of communication do the customers use, e.g. telephone, fax, e-mail, etc.? Can you be sure that they can all make contact with you easily? How many orders might you be losing because customers cannot fax or e-mail their requirements to you, or speak to anything other than an answer phone? What is the cost to you of those lost orders in an average year? That is a hard question to answer, but you only have to lose one order each week to make a big hole in your annual profits, and once a customer is lost it is much harder to win them back. In this context, it is not too hard to justify a modest investment in computing and communications systems.

Raw materials, resale stock, and packaging

Issues of stock management are of less interest to, service-provider businesses, but they can be critical to retailing, wholesaling or manufacturing firms, particularly if the firm is in a competitive market where profit margins are tight, or where it has adopted a strategic policy of cost-leadership. It does not take a great deal of lost or damaged stock to knock a big hole in the firm's profit. For example, if you are buying items in at £80 to resell them for £100, then on the face of it for every lost or damaged item you will need to sell an extra four just to cover the cost of the lost item. In reality the figure is higher as there will be variable costs (distribution expenses, etc.) associated with each of those sales. Efficient stock management is important, so we will look at a few of the questions that must be asked. These issues should have been considered when carrying out the review of the performance of business (Chapter 14 and Appendix), but as part of the additional resources requirements, it is necessary to go beyond an assessment of the current weaknesses and to actually plan the actions and implications of the improvements in terms of time and costs:

What improvements could be made?
First, you have to identify the problems by asking the question are you managing your stocks properly. There are a multitude of things which can go wrong in handling stocks: loss through damage or theft, waste caused by poor rotation or over-stocking beyond use-by dates, over-purchasing resulting in too much working capital tied up in stock too much stock re-order systems. Problems can also occur in paperwork systems, e.g. where incoming stock is not checked against delivery notes, or the quantities, prices and discounts are not checked against the suppliers' invoices. Outgoing stocks must also be monitored particularly where urgent deliveries or collections are involved outside of normal working hours. It is very easy to help a customer out by staying open late for a collection, but will the accounting system pick up that collection and invoice the customer for it. If the stocks are eminently "desirable" e.g. alcohol, cigarettes, or electronic consumer goods, be watchful of slippage, i.e. theft by warehouse or distribution staff whose ingenuity at theft will certainly outstrip their initiative and creativeness demonstrated within their regular jobs.

Are you managing my purchases properly?
It pays to carry out a periodic review of the terms of trade offered by suppliers, e.g. the relative discounts offered by various suppliers, delivery charges incurred, credit terms, reliability of supply and delivery, etc. Very often, this review is best carried out together with suppliers, and with a bit of imagination or lateral thinking it can generate benefits for both parties. For example, there may be an optimum order or delivery size for the supplier that will result in cost savings that can be shared by both parties – "if you can take a whole truck load in one drop, I can give you a better unit price". It is easy to forget that our suppliers are in business to make a profit as well as you, so the relationship has to be mutually acceptable. It is as much in the suppliers interest for you to make a profit and to continue buying, as it is for the supplier to make a profit and stay in business to supply you.

How would you describe your relationship with my suppliers?
Perhaps a more appropriate approach would be to ask the question – what do my suppliers really think of me? Would they describe me as a good customer? Do they welcome my orders or am I tolerated as a necessary evil? Do they always have to chase me for payment or can they rely on me to pay on time? There is much to be said for sustainable supplier relationships, and reliability and quality service can prove more important

in the long-term than squeezing the last per cent of discount from them. The relationship should work both ways, so that if you need a bit of leeway e.g. a few extra days' credit to cover a cash-flow problem, there should be no embarrassment in asking. Similarly, the suppliers should feel able to ask you for payment a few days early if they have similar problems.

Over-packaging, particularly on food products, has become a major problem in recent years. The average Kit-Kat bought in a multi-pack at Tesco used to have three layers, and sometimes four, but the British government is now forcing businesses to have a positive policy of re-cycling a large proportion of packaging that has reduced a large proportion of over-packaging. Can I reduce my packaging costs then? This will depend on what the packaging is for, e.g. to protect the goods during consignment, or to sell the products to the end-user, but as a part of the stock-management review process, the question must be raised: Is all of the packaging on my products really necessary?

Staff resources

Strategic Human Resources Management (known to lesser mortals as manpower planning) is all about getting the right people, with the right skills, in the right place, at the right time; and then providing the right structure and balance of motivation and reward, to keep them there. This is hard enough to achieve in a large organisation that has the resources to employ human resource professionals that can afford the necessary reward structures and opportunities for promotion or career development, and that can make use of highly specialised skills. However, as we have discussed a number of times in previous chapters, the average small firm does not have these luxuries, often lacking or possessing only limited resources, relying on the limited personnel knowledge of the boss, and the willingness of the multi-skilled staff to be flexible in their work.

Workforce planning

At a strategic level, this involves matching the skills of the key executives or managers to the needs of the strategic plan by identifying those management skills that are needed to achieve the long-term objectives of the business. For example, a policy of substantial growth that involves exporting as part of the process would normally require the business to have someone at policy-making level that possesses substantial skills and experience in international marketing. The strategic aspects would also involve the monitoring and appraisal of performance to ensure that (a) the managers are performing at a level that will enable the business to achieve its strategic targets, and (b) that skills are modified or developed on an on-going basis in line with the changing needs of the business.

On a tactical level, manpower planning involves designing and creating a reward system that will provide and retain a stable and motivated workforce. It will involve anticipating future problems of surpluses or deficits of staff skills; possibly requiring the development of a more flexible workforce with a core of regular key staff supplemented by peripheral staff: temps, agency staff, part-time, or seasonal workers. The tactical aspects are also concerned with medium-term staff development, career development, training plans, etc., as a means of reducing the dependence on external recruitment when skills are in short supply.

On an operational level, manpower planning is about the day-to-day recruitment and selection process, induction, staff training to facilitate immediate needs, and to create multi-skilled staff to provide more flexibility, and to make the best (most productive) use of available human resources. It is also concerned with performance appraisal, administration, and the monitoring of reward structures and on-going motivation.

The owner-manager as a human resource

Throughout this text the term owner-manager has been used as interchangeable with the term "entrepreneur" as in the 21st century there is little practical difference. Whereas the "entrepreneur" has an almost flamboyant connotation which is often perceived as the progenitor of larger high-flying companies, there are still some public perceptions of the owner-manager as the small garage owner wearing a grease-covered boiler suit, working in a lock-up with rain leaking in through holes in the roof, which somehow doesn't quite match up to the description of "entrepreneur".

Perhaps "owner-manager" just appeals to the English sense of understatement. In either case, whilst the "owner" part of the label may be the case, the "manager" part does not imply the automatic presence of any management skills, the title often being bestowed by virtue of position alone, rather than from knowledge or experience of managing a business. Just imagine if the French philosopher, Rene Descartes (1596–1650) had been an owner-manager, the whole meaning of his justification of personal existence would have been transformed: "Cogito ergo managum, – I manage therefore I am", and "Sum res managans – I am a managing thing"; and his theory of Dualism could be expressed as the mind of the manager is like a ghost in a machine! Apologies to Descartes but perhaps this isn't so far away from the thinking (or actions) of some managers after all!

As we have said before, when the business first starts up, the owner-manager must be all things to all men: the decision-maker, the salesman, the accountant, the buyer, the production manager, the debt collector and sometimes the labourer and toilet cleaner. As the business grows the specialist management functions become more essential and more affordable (or perhaps no longer avoidable), so specific roles can be allocated to other staff or specialist services can be bought in, e.g. the sales agent, or the part-time book-keeper. However, no matter what specialist or technical skills the owner-manager can purchase or employ, there are three key skills which he or she must master: the ability to organise oneself, the ability to organise others, and the ability to delegate. So, at the risk of repeating some of the questions asked in Chapter 14 are as follows:

- How well do you organise yourself?
  - Do you plan my time carefully to make full use of the working day, or do you flip from one job to another in response to calls or demands?
  - Do you use a diary or planner to schedule regular activities, and allocate time around these for other work, or to respond to urgent items?
  - Do you prioritise my work to take account of relative urgency and/or importance?
  - Do you plan my travel efficiently to avoid wasted time or unnecessary distance?
- How well do you organise my staff and their work?
  - Is the work planned in advance to meet customer orders or requirements, or do they always seem to be responding to "emergencies"?
  - Do you have a good working relationship with your staff?
  - Do they think that you have a good relationship with them?
  - Do they like or dislike you?
  - Do you care about that?
  - What style(s) of management do you use?
  - Does your management style have a positive or neutral effect on them, or is it de-motivating?
  - Can you handle staff problems or conflict comfortably?

- Do your staff feel that you are approachable when they have a problem?
- Do you delegate work effectively to others?
  - Do you match the person to the task, or just give the job to the nearest one, or to your favourite?
  - Do your staff welcome responsibility or shy away from it, and why is this so?
  - Do you explain what you want them to achieve, how it is to be done, and what responsibility and authority they will have to complete the task?
  - Do you provide the necessary training, support, and resources to enable them to achieve the task?
  - Do you keep in touch to monitor progress with new tasks?
  - Do you give feedback and praise on their performance?

There are plenty of both long and short training courses to improve any of the above skills, but self-management and delegation skills are only really developed by practice, by doing them on a regular basis. Organising and managing other people can be learnt from a book or a training course, but how effective that learning really becomes also depends on learning how to observe those people. By observing how they respond and react to your instructions or requests, by the verbal and non-verbal feedback they give, by watching their body language, by listening to what they tell you, and by monitoring their output or productivity.

The costs of employing staff

As described in Chapter 9, when you buy a computer, a car, a van or a piece of production machinery, you or your accountant can perform some simple calculations to identify the outputs or benefits you will gain from the investment, how long it should last, the cost per annum over its lifetime, and the payback or return you will achieve on the investment. A delivery van might be good for 5 years, or a production machine for 10 years. Either way, you can be fairly sure that if you make the right choice in the first place, you will get a return on your investment. Unfortunately, people are not like that, and employing them can be both risky and expensive. So you advertise for a skilled member of staff, you carry out a series of time-consuming interviews, select the person you want, and wait until they have worked their notice from current employment. When they start, you provide them with induction training, and perhaps product or job training, all this time running at less than optimum efficiency. Then 3 months later, just as your business is returning to full efficiency, they up and leave; and you have to go through the whole time consuming and expensive process all over again. People are expensive to find, expensive to train, expensive to replace, and inherently unreliable; that is unless you have the right motivation and reward structure to retain them.

Even if you do have the right structure in place, the on-costs of employing staff in terms of national insurance and pension contributions, sickness and maternity entitlements, annual holidays, cover for absence, training, uniforms or protective clothing, etc., can still add 30% to 40% on top of the basic wage (and more if you run a business in parts of mainland Europe). The moral of all is that it is imperative to make the right decisions about your recruitment and staff development policies, as mistakes can be very expensive.

Symptoms of poor staff management or reward systems

The most obvious sign of a problem can be easily checked by measuring the annual rate of staff turnover within the business. There will always be some degree of natural staff turnover, e.g. resulting from retirement, staff moving to another area, health problems, or family commitments. The acceptable level of staff turnover will vary from one area to another, dependent on the stability of the local population, the supply of labour, and the competing demands for that supply. In a rural area where people tend to be less mobile, and jobs less available, the percentage may be low, say 4% or 5%. In an urban area where there are more jobs around and the population is probably more mobile, 10% may be nearer the norm. But in either case, if the annual staff turnover (i.e. the percentage of leavers compared with the size of the total workforce) is above 15 or 20%, then there is a clear problem. This may possibly be due to low levels of reward, or to poor working conditions, or unpleasant or repetitive work. On the other hand, the problem might also lie elsewhere, perhaps in the recruitment policy of the business, resulting in the wrong type of staff being recruited for the work, or inappropriate methods of selection being used.

Other symptoms of problems include rising rates of sickness or absenteeism, poor motivation resulting in reduced output, disruption of output, and most obviously, industrial action. It may well be the case that there is simply a shortage of suitably skilled workers in the geographical locality, in which case the firm must consider transporting them in from

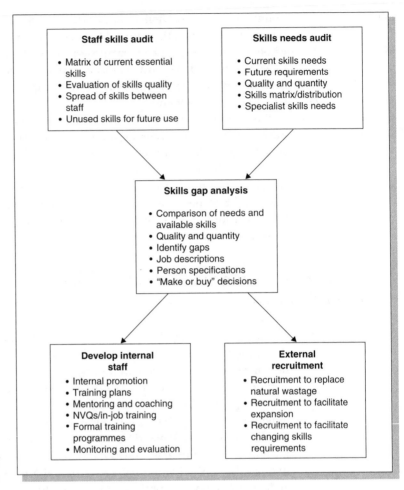

Figure 16.1
Skills gap analysis

further afield, of introducing a training programme to develop them in house. This is often described as the "grow-your-own or buy-in dilemma" (see Figure 16.1) arising from the skills gap analysis.

Carrying out the skills audit

The *first stage* of this activity is concerned with identifying precisely what skills are needed, and the normal way of doing so is by drawing up a skills matrix. On one axis, you need to establish the jobs that are already occupied, and those which will be needed to accommodate growth or diversification. Remember that these must relate to the jobs themselves, and not the persons who occupy them. On the other axis the range of skills needed for each of those jobs are listed. Sources of information for this process include the job descriptions for the essential and desirable qualifications and experience needed for each post; and if they don't exist, now is the time to remedy the situation. Standard Operating Procedures, product specifications can indicate the need for specific technical skills. Work or shift rotas can indicate gaps in secondary skills such as first aid training, to ensure that there is normally a qualified first-aider on each shift. Minutes of meetings and reports can help to highlight deficiencies in skills that are causing problems for the business, and new product development information can point to future needs. Identifying those future needs is particularly a critical part of the process, as without having the right skills available in readiness for any planned expansion, the whole strategic plan for the business could be disrupted.

The *second stage* asks the question: who has the skills we need? It involves comparing the actual skills of those persons occupying the positions against the skills requirements of the jobs. The necessary information can normally be gathered from *curriculum vitaes* and staff records, training records, and appraisals, or by checking on previous qualifications and experience, courses attended, in-house training sessions completed, etc. If in doubt, you can always ask the supervisors or the staff themselves, and at the same time you can find out if they have any skills that you are not currently aware of, that might be useful in the future. It is always surprising how many people can offer useful transferable skills gained in previous jobs in the past.

The *third stage* involves matching the two against each other in order to highlight gaps between the ideal skills required to adequately perform each job role, and the actual skills that the occupants of those roles can demonstrate. This is what we mean by the skills gap analyses, i.e. what gaps have to be filled? The uncovered skills denote either areas for training and development, or roles for which external recruitment will be needed to provide the essential skills. Some of the gaps may already have been picked up by the firm's appraisal process, if there is one in place. The two stages can be combined on a simple spreadsheet for each section or department of the business, as shown in the example in Figure 16.2.

Lead-time

The gap analysis should not just focus on current staff and existing vacancies. It should also be carried out for all employment needs in the foreseeable future. This will mean looking closely at the resources that

JOB ROLE	Ref.	Induction	Health & Safety	Manual Handling	OND Engineering	NVQ3 Management	NVQ2 Team Leader	F-t Driver course	Driving licence	First Aid Cert.	Assembly training	Packing & despatch	Customer service	Basic IT
Assembler 1	A1	#	#	#			#			#	#		#	#
J. Jones		Y	Y	Y			Y			Y	Y		N	Y
Assembler 2	A2	#	#	#							#			
F. Smith		Y	Y	Y							Y			
Assembler 3	A3	#	#	#							#			
J. Davies		Y	Y	N							Y			
Assembler 4	A4	#	#	#							#			
R. Johnson		Y	Y	N							Y			
Assembler 5	A5	#	#	#							#			
Vacant														
Assembler 6	A6	#	#	#										
Vacant														
Packer 1	P1	#	#	#						#		#	#	
E. Elpus		Y	Y	Y						N		Y	Y	
Packer 2	P2	#	#	#								#	#	
D. Appy		Y	Y	Y								Y	Y	
Maintenance Engineer	Engr	#	#	#	#									
A. Bodger		Y	Y	Y	Y									
Fork-lift driver	FD	#	#	#				#	#					
R. Ammer		Y	Y	Y				Y	Y					
Supervisor	Sup	#	#	#	#	#				#	#	#	#	#
V. Bossy		Y	Y	Y	Y	Y				Y	Y	Y	N	Y
Storeman	St	#	#	#									#	#
S. Tackit		Y	Y										N	Y
Van driver	Dr	#	#	#				#	#			#	#	
S. Peedy		Y	Y	Y				Y	Y			N	Y	
Cleaner	Cl	#	#											
Mrs Mop		Y	Y											

= skill needed, Y = training done, N = training needed

Figure 16.2
An example of skills gap analysis.

have been identified as essential to meet the organisation's strategic development, and what staff will be needed to operate or support those resources. Furthermore, it must examine the various stages of phases of growth, to ensure that the staff will be available in readiness for when they are needed. No business wants to have staff standing around idle, waiting for work to come in, but equally, no business can afford to be understaffed when that work does arrive. Irrespective of whether the staff are developed internally, or recruited externally, there will inevitably be a lead-time before they are fully operational, because both the training and development process and the recruitment and selection process can be extremely time-consuming.

Grow your own or buy in?

The gaps that are identified by the matching process will form the basis for the development strategy of the business. That is, whether the business decides to plug the gaps by means of training and developing existing staff, or to recruit or buy-in ready-trained staff from the labour market. Recruiting staff who are ready-trained can be very attractive to a growing business. True, the advertising and selection process does cost time and money, but there can be equally significant savings elsewhere. For example, training costs can be high. Ready-trained staff provide an immediate saving on the cost and time required for training, and can quickly achieve a high level of efficiency or productivity in their jobs; whereas trainees may have to work up to that level over a period of time. It is also much more attractive from the owner-manager's perspective, to buy-in ready trained staff, rather than to train them yourself, raising their career expectations as you do so, and then seeing them move to a competitor a few months later. Is it not much better and cheaper then, to poach the trained staff from your competitor in the first place? Perhaps, but it can also be short-sighted in that two or more firms competing for a limited number of skilled staff in a small locality, can just end up creating a wages spiral for themselves.

We have said that internal promotion can take time and cost money, however it also has its advantages, frequently in terms of the loyalty it can generate from promoted staff, who appreciate the promotion or development opportunities. Internal development also has the advantage of familiarity, in that existing staff are already comfortable with current systems within the business. The time needed to recruit externally can be particularly problematic if there is a fairly low level of local unemployment when local staff may be hard to find, or may cost above-average rates, or may have to be transported in from further afield. This is where internal development scores much higher than external recruitment. Equally, when there is a shortage of skilled labour in the locality, there simply may be no alternative other than to develop current staff, and then recruit less-skilled replacements to fill the gaps at the bottom.

Barriers to training uptake in small firms

In Chapter 5 we looked briefly at the organisational skills needed by owner-managers, the need to be able to organise others, to organise their own time and prioritise their work, and to be able to delegate work to others. We also mentioned the broad range of business skills that owner-managers need, especially in the early stages of the business. However, when it comes to self-development, owner-managers are often their own worst enemies, frequently putting the short-term needs and pressures of work ahead of the need to enhance their own management capabilities and competence. There is also a core of owner-managers who are blind to their own shortcomings and do not even recognise that there is a need for self-development for themselves or their staff. Staff development is an interesting area for consideration, not least because of some of the opinions expressed by owner-managers:

- "If I'm going to spend money on training for anyone it will be for me!" – fortunately this view is not heard too frequently nowadays, but it was a view that tended to run alongside the view that the best (and cheapest) way of staff training was "sitting with Nellie" – observing experienced staff for a period of time to learn the job from them, and quite frequently learning some aspects or poorer practice as well as the dodges, particularly in industrial environments where piecework was involved.
- "What's the point of training staff when they just leave for another job?" Of course they will if other employers recognise and are willing to pay for their skills.
- "It is cheaper to buy-in skilled staff". Perhaps that is so in the short term, but the longer-term higher wages costs plus the de-motivation for other staff on seeing both a lack of opportunities and differential pay for new staff will outweigh the short-term benefits.

In the early stages of a business when the money is tight, many owner-managers will only pay for staff to attend short (and preferably inexpensive) courses to acquire essential skills that they cannot manage without, but otherwise, staff development tends to be kept to the minimum. This is because it is regarded as being either not absolutely essential, or a necessary evil which just adds to overhead costs, and takes up valuable working time.

Much research has been carried out into the barriers that affect the uptake of training in small firms, and the findings from these reveal that owner-managers are looking for four key factors when they consider training or development (Butler 2004):

1. Training programmes must offer a tangible and measurable payback on the time and money invested. The substantial time commitment involved in attending conventional training courses that often span 1 or 2 academic years is unattractive to small firms who want to be able to apply the learning immediately, and see corresponding quick results and improvements in business practice and performance.

2. Courses must be available at convenient times, i.e. outside of the main working week. For most small firms but for micro-firms in particular, neither the owner-managers nor staff their can be spared from work to attend training during core working hours. This may be due to the shear pressure of work, or to the lack of cover for key staff who are absent. Unfortunately, the bulk of available training opportunities tend to be offered within that same core of working hours, and the immediate demands of work inevitably take priority. Any experienced management trainer will be able to recount plenty of examples of staff from small firms who send apologies or back out of training days at the last minutes due to work priorities.

3. Courses must be reasonably priced. The high cost of conventional accredited management development programmes normally runs into hundreds of pounds, at lower levels, and thousands for higher-level programmes, DMS, MBA, etc. These prices are simply unaffordable to many new and developing firms which may only be making small profits in the early stages, and who need to reinvest those profits to keep the business going and growing.

4. Training must be available locally, where it can be accessed quickly and easily without wasting core working time travelling around the countryside, when working time is at a premium. One of the other interesting side issues of the research was that a large proportion of owner-managers were often totally unaware of just what useful business and management

training was available in their locality. This was partly because they had not looked around properly, but largely because of inadequate or low-levels of marketing by the training providers, especially further and higher education institutions that tend to target larger organisations for business and management training.

As the firms start to grow, these old attitudes and inhibitions still pervade, and new management skills are introduced only when really required. It seems as if there is some unspecified and unidentifiable critical mass, beneath which staff development is treated as a necessary expense; but once that mass or size is reached, the owner-managers seem to become enlightened and start to welcome the development. This may well occur when the firm reaches a size in terms of numbers of employees, where other specialist staff or managers are brought on board, particularly in the human resources role. It may also be due to a realisation that staff training and development can be cheaper in the long-term, and more motivating to existing staff, than recruiting skilled staff from external sources.

The financial implications of manpower planning

In reality, the manpower planning strategy will not specifically choose to follow one or other option, but will select an appropriate combination of both, by selecting some staff for development, and recruiting others from outside. The key factor is to ensure that the chosen methods will enable the firm to get the right skills in the right place at the right time, to enable it to meet its strategic targets and objectives; whilst keeping costs down to an acceptable level.

As we have stated above, staff can be an extremely expensive but notoriously unreliable resource of the business. Once the staffing levels and skills requirements have been identified, the costs of these need to be fed into the financial plan for the business. As we mentioned above when considering the costs of employing staff, those costs do not just relate to the basic salary or wages. The on-costs of National Insurance, pensions, uniforms, annual leave, cover for sickness, absence or maternity leave, etc., can easily add another 30% to the annual bill for each member of staff. There is also the added cost of administering the payroll systems, tax-credits, stakeholder pensions, etc., which small firms are now obliged to provide and administer. Advertising costs, staff time for sifting applications and interviewing potential candidates all has a cost, particularly if the owner-manager is having to forego potential sales activities to attend interviews. Recruitment agencies can reduce that time commitment, but they themselves may charge up to 20% of the first year's salary as their commission. Pre-expansion training for current staff, and induction training for new staff will also add to the costs. So when preparing the budgetary and cash-flow forecasts for expansion programmes, it is essential to build an allocation within the budget for these indirect costs, many of which will be incurred up-front. It is easy to see why many modern businesses, particularly those involved in manufacturing, prefer to use robotic systems – they don't answer back, or "throw a sickie" on a busy Monday morning, and you never hear of a robot claiming sexual harassment in the office!

Good selection and carefully planned staff development policies are an essential pre-requisite for efficient business performance, but are still ineffective unless backed up by carefully designed reward systems. This is where many organisations go wrong, by putting the recruitment and training in place, only to cut corners by offering minimal wages or very basic other benefits; and then experiencing enormous levels of staff turnover which push their operating costs through the roof. The reward system is the final link in the chain. Rates of pay and other conditions of employment must be sufficient to attract staff, to retain them, and to motivate them to willingly contribute to meeting the objectives of the organisation. The system must be capable of influencing the internal culture of the business, to encourage initiative and innovation; and it must reward responsibility within the structure of the business.

There is no golden rule or formula to get this right, as the optimum system will depend on the nature of the business. Job-based pay with annual reviews, if set at the right levels can encourage loyalty and stability in the workforce, but motivation and performance may be enhanced by team bonuses or profit share systems. Individual bonuses or performance-related pay (PRP) is highly motivating for individuals and encourages initiative, but can be a nightmare to administer when all staff are on different rates. PRP can have a negative effect on less able staff, and can often encourage competition rather than co-operation between staff. Financial reward can also be of particular significance to staff of small firms where there may not be any opportunities for advancement due to the small size of the firm.

It is particularly important for the owner-manager to keep a weather-eye on local wage rates and the supply and demand for skilled labour in the area. If these rates are high due to relatively low levels of local unemployment, then cost-cutting exercises to save on wages costs will only be counter-productive, and will result in staff leaving for better pay elsewhere. This goes back to what was said earlier about staff turnover levels, with the costs of replacing staff outstripping the marginal extra cost of retaining them in the first place, but more important than the cost, is the disruption it can cause in achieving the strategic objectives. In summary then, the reward structure is the key to successful man-power planning, and getting it right is just as important to the business as the recruitment, retention and development of staff.

As a footnote to this chapter, back in Chapter 1 (The political context) it was mentioned that for the past 20 years or so, government has finally recognised the importance of small firms as the major source of employment opportunities for the future. In consequence, successive governments have introduced a range of support services to assist and encourage Small and Medium-Sized Enterprises (SMEs) to help them to reduce the impact of politically embarrassing unemployment statistics. Smallbone & Wyer (2000) argue that "one of the issues that need to be recognised in any discussion of small business growth is that not all owners see growth as an important business objective". They argue that "although employment generation may be an appropriate growth criterion for public policy, for most SME owners and managers it is a consequence rather than an important business objective". This is an interesting and very true observation. The fact is that growth in the small firms sector is frequently driven by the objective of increasing the owner-managers' personal profits, as opposed to the view many large organisations that growth should be an objective in its own right. The growth of employment potential as the business expands is very much incidental, and is rarely seen to be of major consequence to the strategic objectives of the average owner-manager, who most certainly does not see his or her self as the key facilitator of government employment policy.

Furthermore, the heavy burden of red tape imposed by government on all employers in recent years has fallen disproportionately on smaller firms. This has resulted in the inevitable attitude from owner-managers that employing extra staff is just a necessary evil that must be accepted when they need those extra staff in order to grow their businesses. As long as successive governments continue to nurture the vision of small firms as the major source of employment, presumably the small business support organisations will endure. However, one wonders what would happen if the Whitehall mandarins suddenly woke up to the fact that whether or not employment continues to grow in the small firms sector, is not so much a consequence of their intervention and support policies, as the personal objectives and individual actions of some 3.7 million owner-managers, many of whom would gladly stick their fingers up to Whitehall at the first opportunity. Could it be that the concept of employees as an expensive and unreliable resource obviously does not ring any bells amongst Whitehall mandarins, or is it just that they have never tried to run a small business?

References

Butler, D. (2004). "Breaking down the barriers to training uptake in small firms" ISBE Conference, Newcastle.

Smallbone, D. and Wyer, P. (2000). In *Enterprise and Small Business, Principles Practice and Policy* (Chapter 23). (S. Carter. and D. Jones-Evans, eds) FT/Prentice Hall, London.

Further reading

Armstrong, M. (2003). *A Handbook of Personnel Management Practice*. Kogan-Page, London.

Gibbons, B. (1999). *If You Want to Make God Really Laugh, Show Him Your Business Plan*. Capstone, Oxford.

Lasher, W. (1999). *Strategic Thinking in Smaller Businesses and Divisions*. Blackwell, Oxford.

Stokes, D. (2004). *Small Business Management*, 4th edition. Thomson, Harlow.

Thomson, A. and Thomson, R. (2002). "*Managing People*," 3rd edition. CMI/Elsevier, Oxford.

CHAPTER 17

Financial planning for growth

In the same way that in the foregoing chapters we have examined and systematically evaluated the performance of the business in relation to its operating environments, its resource requirements, its sales and marketing performance, its managerial capabilities, and its staff management; we now have to look more closely at the financial performance to date, and the financial systems the business currently employs. This chapter is also concerned with forecasting the costs of implementing the strategic objectives, and ensuring that sufficient funding is available to enable them to be implemented efficiently and effectively. It will also look at the sources of finance available to expanding businesses.

If anything, financial performance has got to be one of the easier areas to evaluate, because it is measured against what is essentially factual information, but in practice this is not simply a case of just comparing the factual data on a year-on-year basis. Such comparisons only tell the analyst about what is happening within the organisation over a period of time, and not what is happening in a wider context, i.e. how the business is performing in the market environment, and how it is performing in the light of changes in that market. Achievement cannot just be assessed by actual performance alone; it has to be assessed in relation to the market environment in which the organisation operates. For example, a business that has sales of £1 million in a market worth £10 million in 2005 has a 10% share of the market. However, if in 2006 the sales increase by 10% to £1.1 million, but the overall market size grows by 20% to £12 million, then although the company's sales have grown significantly, its overall market share has decreased from 10% to 9.17%; as rival businesses must have gained a greater market share during the year.

In the 1990s there was a popular move towards benchmarking as a means of evaluating organisational performance, particularly in the public sector. The benchmarking process aims to assess the relative efficiency of service provision, in public sector organisations (where profit is rarely regarded as a relevant performance indicator, and for that matter, neither is break-even), by comparing their achievements with other organisations of a similar type and size, that provide the same or similar services. The key to the comparisons lies in first identifying areas of "best practice" against which the performance of others can be matched, based on the principal that no one organisation has the monopoly on best practice. Whilst this process may be fine with the relatively well-resourced larger public sector bodies, such as local councils and health authorities (although they would probably refute that they are well resourced, even compared with small firms), in the small firms context benchmarking is a less attractive and less practical option. Similarly, larger private sector organisations are able to "benchmark" themselves against the performance of their rivals, perhaps by comparing the data in published annual accounts, or against market research data for specific industrial or service sectors. Other sources of comparative data might include Government-published statistics, trade or professional journals, business journals (e.g. the *Economist,* or *Fortune* in the USA), but again these are of little direct relevance to the small or medium-sized firm.

Benchmarking is also employable in the private sector, and not just for service industries, although the emphasis is on comparison with the performance levels of other similar organisations rather than comparison with best practice. After all, best practice in competitive commercial terms is all about optimising performance to maximise profit. International Computers Limited (ICL) was said to benchmark itself against 20 rivals in the computer industry on four main points: the ratios of average debtors and creditors to sales turnover, the spending on research and development compared with sales turnover, the return on capital invested, and the sales revenue per head of employees. When it comes to benchmarking the average small firm hits three major obstacles. First, it rarely has the resources to devote to surveying and analysis the data; and second, that as most of the data is collated from information relating to big companies, its relevance to the small firm is questionable, or at very least, hard to accurately evaluate. Can a small personal computer (PC) assembly company, or a local software sales and support business gain any genuinely applicable market intelligence by benchmarking itself against a long-established international player and its 20 major rivals? Third, there is still relatively little comparative performance data about small firms in specific industries, although that situation is slowly improving.

Accounting ratios

Given the inherent shortfalls of benchmarking in the small forms sector, the standard and established alternative method of evaluating financial performance lies in the use of accounting ratios. These compare facts and figures gleaned from the annual accounts of businesses, and provide year-on-year data about performance in key areas for comparison. But, as stated above, this data is essentially concerned with internal performance, and does not make comparisons with the overall market environment, although it does facilitate year-on-year comparison. Accounting ratios are primarily tools that can be used to assess the performance of the business, particularly in term of solvency and liquidity. There is a range of ratios that can be applied to test different aspects of business performance, but we will just concentrate on some of those that are of significance to the small business.

Liquidity ratios

- The working capital ratio (also called the current ratio) tests the short-term liquidity of a business. It compares the current assets (cash, stock, debtors, work in progress) to the current liabilities (bills falling due for payment). Ideally the current assets: current liability ratio should be 2:1. If the ratio is less, then stock levels or credit facilities given to customers may be too high.
- The liquidity ratio (also called the acid test or quick ratio) is a more precise measure of liquidity, as it compares the liquid assets of the business (current assets less slow-moving stock or bad debts) with the current liabilities. The liquid assets when compared to current liabilities should show a ratio of at least 1:1 to demonstrate that the business can meet its current obligations, i.e. it can pay its creditors on time.
- The other way to check on solvency is to compare the average credit given with the average credit taken. In the first case we take the average outstanding debtors figure × 365, divided by the sales turnover. For example, an average outstanding debt of £20,000 compared with an annual turnover of £240,000 is one-twelfth of 365 days, which equals approximately 30 days. An average credit taken of £24,000 compared with the same turnover equals one-tenth of 365 days, i.e. 36.5 days. It is obviously more advantageous for the cash flow and working capital

of the business to give 30 days' credit to customers, and to take 36.5 days' credit from suppliers.

Borrowing capacity

- The Gearing ratio is more concerned with solvency, as it compares the equity (or share capital) and reserves of the business with its long-term liabilities (loans, mortgages, and preference shares), to ensure that loans etc., can be repaid if the business should cease trading. In simple terms, it compares the resources supplied by the owners with the resources borrowed from others, to ensure that the first exceeds the second. The Preference shares are lumped in with the long-term liabilities simply because the dividends on these have to be paid before any ordinary share dividends can be considered. This ratio is regarded as a good measure of the borrowing capacity of the business, as the higher the ratio, the better the borrowing potential.

- The asset cover ratio compares total assets with total debt to determine how many times the debts of the business are covered by its assets. This again reflects the borrowing capacity of the business, as the higher the ratio, the more it is likely to be able to borrow, because it is seen to have the surplus resources to cover further debt. The borrowing capacity is of interest not just to providers of long-term liability funds (bankers, debenture, and mortgage lenders, etc.) but to the "current liabilities", the ordinary suppliers and creditors who want to be assured that their credit is adequately covered by assets.

- The net asset value compares the ordinary shareholders' funds (capital and reserves etc.) with the number of shares issued. This measures the value of the assets of the business that are attributable to each share. So, a business with assets worth £4.00 for each £1.00 share issued would generally be regarded by a lender as being a better risk than one with assets worth just £1.50 per £1.00 share.

Profitability ratios

- The Return on Capital Employed (ROCE) compares the profit received from ordinary trading activities before interest, with the sum of the capital employed in trading. It is expressed as a percentage. For example, if the company employs capital of £100,000 and produces a profit from ordinary trading of £30,000 it has made a ROCE of 30%. This ratio is of key interest to potential investors. It is also important to remember that if the ratio falls below the average level of interest paid on bank deposits or investments, then the business would be better off not trading, and just leaving its capital on deposit at the bank. In the case of owner-managers, this means that they would be better off shoving their money in the building society or some other form of investment, and getting a job working for someone else. The reduction in stress would probably also increase their life expectancy in the process! The point of this is that if you are working for yourself, you should expect a reasonable return on the time, money, and energy you expend in running the business, and that the level of return should be demonstrably greater than that which could be achieved by leaving your money in the bank, and working for someone else (job satisfaction aside). The ROCE provides the means of comparing your results with the softer option.

■ The Earnings per share ratio compares the net profit after tax, less preference share dividends, with the number of ordinary shares issued. In very simple terms, the amount of tax paid profit that could possibly be distributed amongst shareholders, divided by the number of shares eligible to receive it.

■ Gross profit compared to turnover is another good indicator of profitability, especially on a year-on-year basis, as is also the operating profit to turnover ratio (gross profit less distribution and administration costs divided by sales turnover). However these do not always necessarily correspond with each other year-on-year, if changes have occurred in distribution and administration costs during the year.

■ Another measure of profitability is the comparison between sales turnover and the number of employees in the organisation, usually expressed in terms of £000's per head. Variants include comparisons of operating profit to turnover and net fixed assets to turnover. These ratios tend to be more popular in the USA than the UK, and can influence stock exchange values on the US stock markets. Whilst not particularly relevant to the small firms sector, these comparisons do actually influence the employment policies of large multinationals. Pfizer Pharmaceuticals e.g. employ large numbers of permanent contract staff in their UK locations for security and administrative duties, in order to maintain the ratio to their advantage in overseas stock markets. Those contract staff simply appear as an expense item on the profit and loss account. There is of course, nothing illegal or improper about this practice, and it creates a lot of opportunities for the smaller local contract companies that supply the staff. However, employment policies such as these might create a false impression amongst individual US investors who had not taken the trouble to familiarise themselves with the details of the policies, or any relevant disclosures in the published accounts.

Efficiency ratios

- There are quite a few of these to choose from, e.g. the working capital (current assets less current liabilities) to sales turnover ratio tests the number of times the working capital is being utilised each year. This is a measure of how well the business is using its resources, although obviously what is deemed as a satisfactory or good ration will depend on the market in which the business operates. A wholesaler or retailer of foodstuffs will turn over its stock rapidly, so in turn the working capital will have been used on a regular basis, perhaps weekly. In contrast, a manufacturer of specialist engineering machinery that cold take 6 months to build, install, and commission, may only turn over its working capital a few times each year. This is the contrast between a low-profit-high-turnover business, and a high-profit-low-turnover business.
- The same comparison can be made using the whole capital employed by the business in relation to sales turnover to determine how frequently that is being utilised, but again, the outcomes must be reviewed in the context of what is satisfactory or good for the market in which the business operates.
- By comparing the ratio of the average stock held against the total value of stock purchased in the course of the trading year, it is possible to determine how fast and how efficiently the stock is being turned over. For example, an average stock of £10,000 compared with a total annual purchase of £730,000 over 365 days, would indicate that the stock is being turned over, i.e. sold, every 5 days. This figure in itself is not particularly helpful unless compared or benchmarked in some way with an industrial average. For example, a branch of Sainsbury

or Tesco supermarkets might expect to turn their stock of baked beans over every couple of days, and their bread almost daily, but a furniture retailer such as DFS, would no doubt be more than happy to turn all of their stock over once each month.

- It is also possible to evaluate a whole range of specific costs as a percentage of sales turnover, e.g. sales costs, marketing costs, production costs, distribution costs, administration costs etc., in the same way. In their own right, these are not necessarily immediately useful, but when compared year-on-year that can be a good indicator of changing patterns of performance within the business. For example, they may highlight how one cost area might be rising disproportionately in comparison with others, or perhaps to explain why the ratios of gross profit to turnover, and operating profit to turnover may not be moving in the same direction or at the same rate, as mentioned earlier.

Cash management

The key to the survival of any business is cash flow, because if cash does not flow into the business at an adequate rate to maintain the level of working capital, then the business will struggle to survive. The working capital is defined in terms of current or short-term assets (petty cash, cash in the current account, stock, work in progress, and cash owed to the business) minus the current liabilities (overdrafts, money owed to suppliers or other creditors etc.). If there is not a positive difference between the two, then the business cannot pay its bills on time. If cash flow is poorly managed or if the rate of expansion outstrips the size of the working capital (a situation known as over-trading), then only the goodwill of the banks and the creditors will keep the business going. In reality, neither of those groups can afford to be philanthropic when faced with repeated late payments which are a sure sign of a potential risk; well, perhaps a little philanthropy from the banking sector would not go amiss at times.

Any business that is planning to diversify or grow must first ensure that it has adequate working capital in place to facilitate the expansion, and second, that it has suitable systems in place to monitor and control its cash flow. Unless the business operates in a strictly cash environment, any expansion will require the giving of a higher volume of credit than is currently the case. Whilst corresponding increased credit can usually be obtained from its suppliers, there will always be a gap between the two, i.e. the cost of the added-value, and the profit margin which the business must make. It is the added-value part, the staff wages, the overhead costs, distribution expenses etc., that the working capital must bridge until the goods or services are paid for, and the more i.e. sold, the more the funds that are needed to bridge the gap. Without the working capital to bridge this gap, the firm will end up over-trading, which apart from being illegal (in that it is trading insolvently because it cannot pay its creditors when due) is a straightforward recipe for disaster. Many highly profitable firms have gone under because they have attempted to expand faster than their working capital would allow, and have simply run out of money with which to operate the business on a day-to-day basis.

Main factors that influence cash flow

These have already been examined in detail in Chapter 10, but to summarise, they include:

- Increases or decreases in the net profit from trading.
- The sale or purchase of fixed assets.
- Receipt and repayment of loans.
- Injections of share capital, redemption of capital and payment of dividends.
- Changes in the average balance of debtors and creditors.
- Increases or decreases in stockholding.

Each one of the above aspects needs a definitive policy and careful management if the available working capital is to be optimised, because it is easy for any one of them to get out of control and to wreck the effects of careful cash management in the other areas. For example, the benefits of a tight credit control policy can easily be wiped out by the loss of available spare cash due to overstocking or by not making best use of available credit from suppliers.

Credit management

How can we develop an effective credit control policy that will make a positive contribution to the business? The first objective must be to ensure the correct balance of debtors and creditors, i.e. that the overall level of credit given to customers does not exceed the overall level of credit received from suppliers. As described earlier in Chapter 10, this is easily checked by comparing the average debtor-days with the average creditor-days. However, that comparison alone will not suffice. Consider the situation where we take an average of £50,000 of credit on an average of £100,000 of purchases per month, resulting in a figure of 15 creditor-days. At the same time, we give our customers an average of £60,000 of credit on sales of £150,000 per month, which works out at 12 debtor-days. On the face of things, this looks good in that we are giving 12 days' credit but receiving 15 days' credit. But in reality we are giving an average of £60,000 credit each month but only receiving £50,000 which causes a net outflow of working capital. In a situation where the business is seeking a rapid expansion of trade, this is likely to be a common occurrence, and the actual cash figures should not be ignored just because the ratios look to be acceptable.

Getting the right balance involves ensuring that both the periods of credit and the total sums involved are both in our favour. The above imbalance might be addressed by offering prompt payment incentives to reduce the debtors' figure. Alternatively, we could negotiate with our own creditors for longer payment terms, so that the average outstanding payments owed to them were larger that the debtors figure, say 60-day payment terms rather than 30-day. If the business is growing, the trade-off incentive to the suppliers might be the opportunity to deliver larger consignments of goods in one drop, requesting improved credit terms as an alternative to bulk quantity discounts. Remember there has got to be something in the deal to make it worthwhile to the supplier.

Another factor to bear in mind is that when trying to establish a balance between the overall debtors and creditors, it is not necessary for every single one of them to be in balance. For example, there may be one or two highly valued customers with whom you have negotiated special terms, e.g. extended credit for larger orders or long-term contracts. These could easily be counter-balanced by other customers to whom you give discounts for cash on delivery, or other prompt payment terms, such as within 7 or 14 days of invoice. It is the overall balance that is important to achieve.

As the business starts to grow so the management of credit becomes so much more crucial and it is also important to have a clearly defined credit control policy especially if the function is more likely to be delegated to staff. This topic has already been discussed in detail in Chapter 10. Many firms find that the most practical way to manage this is to outsource it to factoring companies, but if it is to be kept in house, then it is necessary for the sales or accounts staff (or whoever deals with outstanding debts) to have clear guidelines to follow. These might include:

■ Specified credit limits for each customer, which they cannot exceed without either payment, or the owner-manager's specific authority.

 ▓ Specified dates or points at which the various credit control activities are triggered, e.g. initial reminder telephone calls, reminder letters, warning letters, supplies stopped, legal action commenced etc. Once established, these should be adhered to firmly. Simply monitoring the aged debtors analysis generated by the accounting system at the end of each month is insufficient, there needs to be a designated person in the business who has the specific responsibility of monitoring payments due, on a daily basis.

 ▓ Clearly defined responsibilities for debt recovery and customer liaison. There is nothing worse than one person in the business chasing a customer for late payment, whilst the salesman is on the premises trying to get further orders. This happens frequently, and particularly in smaller firms where the financial and customer information systems are less likely to be fully integrated.

 ▓ Good working systems to ensure that the creditors of the business are paid on time, to ensure the maintenance of the supply chain, and to avoid the embarrassment of unavailable stock when your supplier won't deliver until your cheque is cleared.

 ▓ A contingency plan in case of emergencies, e.g. seasonal disruption of trade through bad weather. This is where the budgetary plan and cash flow forecast can help identify potential problems, and where e.g. temporary overdraft facilities can be arranged well in advance in readiness for any problems. Apart from the arrangement fee, an overdraft only incurs charges if and when it is used, although the fact that it is available should not tempt you to use it unless it is really required.

Budgetary planning and cash flow forecasting

I am assuming that any owner-manager-readers who are contemplating the expansion of their business, will have previously prepared at least one budgetary plan to satisfy a potential bank manager, and will therefore be fully familiar with the grief this process can cause us lesser mortals who do not aspire to the lofty elevations of qualified accountants. In the early stages of a new business, it is very easy to overlook, or at least to underestimate the importance of the budgetary planning process. Quite often owner-managers will simply use broad estimates for input data, or will just focus on major items of income or expenditure, failing to fully consider the detailed costs involved. At the outset this may be due to lack of awareness of all of the cost factors involved in running a business, but as the firms grows it can be also be due to a lack of attention to detail, or possibly a lack of the appropriate understanding needed to evaluate the full cost implications of running the business. However once the owner-manager is faced with making strategic decisions about the long-term future of the firm, the finer details can no longer be ignored, and every single aspect of income and expenditure must be considered in detail and incorporated into the budgetary plan. Once it has been established, we can start the really important part, that of identifying how the budget will be influenced and will need adjustment to accommodate cash factors:

- Cash-balances brought forward from the previous period.
- Payments due to suppliers (creditors) incurred in the previous period.
- Payments due from customers (debtors) owing from the previous period, and adjustments for bad debts.
- On-going credit being given and received during the year.
- Receipts of loan income or capital.
- Purchase or disposal of fixed assets, lease payments, loan repayments etc.
- In the case of sole traders and partnerships, the income tax liability for the business in the previous year, and with limited companies, the corporation tax liability for the previous period.

Faced with a period of expansion or diversification, there will inevitably be a number of abnormal pressures on cash flow, initially in the form of extra expenses incurred by the expansion, but subsequently by the credit-gap that can be the result of increased sales and credit given to customers. An example of the credit-gap, and the difference between budget-plan figures, and cash flow forecast figures is shown in Figure 17.1. This illustrates the negative cash flow resulting from a combination of increased sales and an imbalance of credit received and credit given, in spite of profitability. The sums involved would be hard to sustain over a period of time without substantial working capital, and the interest charges incurred in borrowing to bridge the gap would considerably reduce the profit margin.

Financial monitoring and budgetary control

It is a source of constant amazement that of the number of small business owners who are obliged to prepare an annual budget and cash flow forecast for their bank manager in order to renew their overdraft

Summary budgetary plan XYZ trading limited

	Month 1 £	Month 2 £	Month 3 £	Month 4 £
Sales income	150,000	160,000	170,000	170,000
Expenditure:				
Overheads	40,000	40,000	40,000	40,000
Stock purchases	75,000	80,000	85,000	85,000
Operating costs	30,000	32,000	34,000	34,000
Net income/expenditure	5000	8000	11,000	11,000

Assume:
- The previous 2 month's figures sales were £140,000 purchases were £70,000.
- 60 days' credit is given on goods sold.
- 30 days' credit is received on purchases.
- Operating costs and overheads are paid in the months in which they are incurred.

Summary cash flow forecast XYZ trading limited

	Month 1 £	Month 2 £	Month 3 £	Month 4 £
Sales receipts	140,000	140,000	150,000	160,000
Expenditure:				
Overheads	40,000	40,000	40,000	40,000
Stock payments	70,000	75,000	80,000	85,000
Operating costs	30,000	32,000	34,000	34,000
Net income/expenditure	Nil	−7000	−4000	1000

Difference between budget figures and cash balances

	Month 1 £	Month 2 £	Month 3 £	Month 4 £
	−5000	−15,000	−15,000	−10,000

Note how the deficit increases as the monthly sales figures rise, and the huge drain on cash reserves, in spite of profitability.

Figure 17.1
Budget and cash flow comparison.

facility, there are still some who shove it in the filing cabinet drawer and forget until next year, once the bank manager has approved it. The budgetary process in any business should be a constant cycle of plan, implement, monitor, and review. You plan the budget, start trading, monitor the actual income and expenditure by comparing it with the forecasts (at frequent and regular intervals), and review it to identify any problems and their causes and potential remedies. Every owner-manager knows that accounts and paperwork are an administrative pain in the neck, but the monitoring of budgeted figures against actual outcomes is the most critical pain in the neck of all, and if ignore, can easily turn into a terminal problem for the business if it is ignored for too long.

The importance of monitoring cash flow and budgets right from the start-up stage was mentioned in Chapter 10. Once again, the importance of an efficient budgetary control system comes to the fore when the firm is faced with expansion or diversification, because the budget monitoring system should form the yardstick for monitoring the effectiveness of the expansion. The monthly comparison actual versus forecast income and expenditure will give feedback on a number of key performance indicators against which the strategic plans for expansion can be measured. There are also a number of questions that must be asked in response to any variances in the outcomes:

- Are the actual levels of sales revenue in line with the forecasts? Are there any fluctuations and can these be explained to our satisfaction? If not, what has happened and how do we respond to the fluctuations?
- Are there any unforeseen longer-term changes or trends in the pattern of demand? What are the causes? How should we respond to these? Do we have the capacity to respond to them?
- Are the profitability and cash-flow figures acceptable? If not, where are the variances and what are the reasons for these? What action do we need to take to remedy the problem(s)?
- Are the changing costs of overheads, raw materials, labour, sales and marketing, transport and distribution, administration, etc., acceptable or do we need to look closely at specific items? What will be the impact of these changes on our profitability? Should we be considering changes to our mark-up or selling prices?
- Are our sales activities and advertising campaigns working? Are they having a positive effect on sales? If not, why not? Are we doing something wrong? Are we missing something? What else should we be doing to make the advertising work better?
- Is our current working capital sufficient for our future requirements, or are we likely to hit cash flow problems? How soon will these problems occur? Do we have sufficient reserves, or do we need to arrange additional finance? Is the problem temporary, requiring a short-term overdraft, or do we need longer-term finance to increase available working capital?
- Will any current or likely changes in interest rates and exchange rates affect our operating costs or profit (particularly if we are exporting our goods or services)? What action do we need to take to minimise the effects of this?

Monitoring the budgetary plans and the actual cash flow of the business is the most important process in assuring that strategic objectives are being achieved. Quite simply, the budgetary comparison will tell you whether or not you are making a profit on an on-going basis, and should enable you to highlight any problem areas if you ask yourself the right questions. Monitoring the cash flow situation will tell you if you are sufficiently solvent to continue trading, and if controlled closely, will alert you to potential problems. In this respect, whilst monitoring of actual against budgeted expenditure can be carried out monthly, cash flow monitoring does need to be carried out on a weekly basis, and in times of difficulty, on a daily basis.

The production of an accurate and realistic financial plan is fundamental to the whole strategic planning process, and as mentioned in the previous chapter, it is a task for which a large majority of owner-managers are not suitably equipped. The production of budgetary plans and cash flow forecasts is frequently seen as an unpleasant chore, an annual burden that detracts from the mainstream running of the business, and adds nothing measurable in terms of profit or productivity. This attitude leads to the tendency to get it over with as quickly as possible, and to use short cuts, rounded-figures and approximations, to save time and effort. In the back of the mind lies the view that attention to fine detail and accuracy are pointless when the actual income and expenditure figures will invariably differ right from day one.

Once again, this is where we see the need for another culture shift and change of attitude on the part of the owner-manager. When expansion or diversification is being considered then it is critically important to be as detailed and accurate as possible in formulating the financial plans for the business. Omissions or underestimates can leave the business with insufficient working capital that might restrict the rate of expansion that can be achieved. The rounding-up of cost forecasts and the building in of contingency sums might provide a safety margin, but if the budgetary plan is to provide the basis for variance analysis between planned and actual costs, those safety margins will distort and invalidate the comparison. Rounding-up of sales forecasts can be even more disastrous when revenue projections are based on over-ambitious figures. Obviously some figures must be based on a best-guess if no historical data is available. For example, it is hard to precisely estimate the annual running and maintenance of costs of vehicles, but in such cases the obvious tactic is to isolate such items and enter them in a separate line in the forecast, so that they can be monitored.

The culture shift that is needed for effective financial planning, is the appreciation of the importance of accuracy and attention to detail during the stages of preparing the financial plans. If the owner-manager remains reluctant to get directly involved in preparing the plans, then it will be necessary to pay or employ a suitably skilled person to do the job, and to be prepared to give them sufficient co-operation, time, and information, for them to achieve the necessary accuracy. This is not simply a task that can be delegated to the first available employee who has a bit of spare time, or who can use a calculator quite well.

The planning process

Figure 17.2 outlines the process that is involved in formulating the financial plan. The market research process will have identified opportunities in the market, the marketing, and sales plans will have identified the strategy for achieving the market share and forecasting the sales volumes and revenues, and the costs involved in doing so. The sales volumes will give the production side of the business information about the volume of output needed so that production and distribution costs can be identified. The output targets will also determine whether or not current capacity is adequate, and what additional resources are required. These may be capital items such as the purchase and installation of new production machines, staff training for these, new delivery vehicles, or the research and development of new product lines. Alternatively, they may be paid for out of the revenue budget (the working capital) such as raw materials and the wages of staff to operate the new machinery. The phasing of the expansion and the key aspects of its implementation such as the sales and promotion activities, and the installation of additional production capacity, will be reflected in the budgetary plan for the business that will incorporate both the revenue and capital budgets. That will in turn enable the production of a cash flow forecast which will identify any cash flow problems, i.e. where there is a deficit in working capital that must either be bridged by short-term borrowing such as an overdraft, or if the gap is substantial, by an injection of funds from such as additional capital or a bank loan. That, together with the capital budget items, will determine the total amount of longer-term borrowing and/or additional equity that the business requires, and the budgetary plan will have identified the points in time when the funding would be needed. All that remains is for the decisions to be made by the owner-managers about suitable types of funding and the sources of these.

The most appropriate form of borrowing will be determined by a number of factors, which in most cases are similar to the criteria for lending to small businesses as briefly mentioned in Chapter 10, but the main difference being that the established firm has the advantage of a

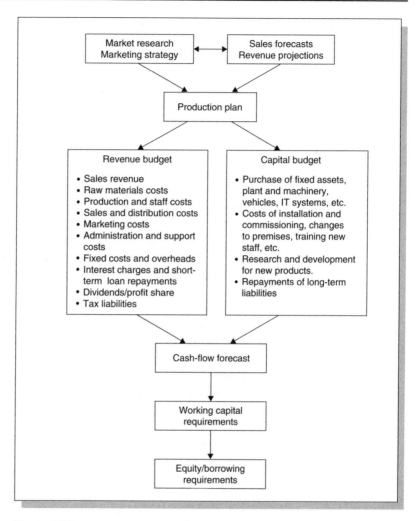

Figure 17.2
Formulating the financial plan.

proven track record, and hopefully some reserves of its own generated from previous profits:

■ The purpose for which the funds are required, e.g. whether it is to increase working capital, or to acquire a vehicle or an item of capital equipment. For the former, some form of short-term funding would be most appropriate, whereas to finance the purchase of plant and equipment, longer-term finance might be better, e.g. leasing, hire purchase, or a bank loan.

- The size of the borrowing requirement. Most bankers will only lend against security. A personal guarantee might be acceptable to cover a loan of a few thousand pounds, but for a more substantial sum, the loan will need to be secured by a legal charge on some property or other tangible asset. Borrowing small sums of money can also be quite expensive in that interest rates tend to be high for smaller sums, but reduce as the size of loan increases. Also, with small loans, the initial set up fees charged by banks or lenders, form a larger proportion of the total cost.

- The availability of security or collateral. Bankers will rarely lend against the full equity value of property, and will seldom offer lend more than 80% of the equity value, on the grounds that if property values fall, the borrower may be in a negative-equity situation. In fact, 50% is a more realistic figure for some high street banks, especially when the borrower is the owner-manager of a newly established small business; but in the case of established firms the banks may be willing to increase that percentage. As described in Chapter 10, if the net equity value of your home is £50k, then you may only be able to borrow £25 to £30k against it. An alternative is to offer the bank a fixed and floating charge against the book debts and assets of the business. This is an option for limited companies that own some measurable and tangible fixed assets, whereby a legal charge is registered against the company by the lender with the Registrar of Companies. In the event of insolvency, it gives the lender first call on all of the fixed assets of the business (the fixed charge) and on any current assets of the business including the debtors (the floating charge).

- The period over which repayment will be made. Short-term borrowing tends to incur higher rates of interest, often 5% above the base lending rate, whereas the interest rate is usually lower when spread over a longer period, e.g. 2% or 3% over base rate. Some forms of finance also have maximum repayment periods, such as commercial mortgages; or repayment periods that are linked to the size of the borrowing and the potential lifetime of the asset, as in the case of car loans.

- The rate of repayments that the borrower can afford. The important question when assessing funding options is "Can my business afford to make the required regular payments from its current or forecast levels of profit?" If not, then the whole viability of any expansion plans must be questioned; or the owner-manager must look towards raising more equity (e.g. by perhaps selling a share of the business), or finding some cheaper, longer-term finance, perhaps another lender who will consider lower repayments spread over a longer period.

In practice, one form of borrowing alone will not normally satisfy the needs of a growing business, and will probably not be the most cost-effective. The optimum borrowing pattern may combine several types of funding possibly obtained from different sources, and combining both long-term and short-term facilities. For example, the bulk of the expansion costs might be financed by means of a 5 or 10-year bank loan, with seasonal fluctuations in sales revenue covered by an overdraft arrangement, production machinery financed by hire purchase, vehicles on lease, and with the use of factoring to improve cash flow.

Short-term borrowing

This is really most appropriate to plug gaps in working capital requirements. Several options are available, each of which have already been explained in Chapter 10:

- Overdrafts to cover temporary periods when cash flow may be poor or to cover seasonal revenue fluctuations.
- Unsecured loans – typically from close friends or
- Short-term bank loans – suitable e.g. when a business is expanding and expects to have a consistent cash shortfall for perhaps the first 12 to 18 months of an expansion period, and a cheaper alternative to an overdraft facility because of the lower rates of interest.
- Factoring or invoice discounting involves the management of the firm's sales ledger by an outside organisation, typically the factoring division of a lending bank, with cash advanced against up to 80% of the value of invoices.
- Hire purchase to buy fixed assets that will belong to the firm.
- Leasing agreements as a more tax-effective means of acquiring fixed assets by renting them from a leasing company over a fixed period of years.

Medium and longer-term finance

From the owner-managers viewpoint, the best form of longer-term funding is the use of reserves that have accrued by the retention of previous profits from trading. Failing that, the next best option is equity in the form of investment capital, because it does not incur interest charges, and dividends or profit shares are only paid out when the business makes a trading profit, and not always then if the owners want to use the money for expansion. Raising capital for expansion can be hard for owners of small firms unless they have rich relatives or plenty of cash slopping around. The easiest option is to utilise any equity in the family home or other property, e.g. by means of a second mortgage. However, this still has to be funded, which usually means that the owner-manager has to draw extra money (which is taxable) from the business to meet the mortgage payments. An alternative is to sell part of the business to a third party, but that can result in loss of control or interference with the way in which the business is managed, and finding potential investors can be quite hard.

Unless the owner-managers have access to substantial financial resources through family or personal connections, then the expansion programme will almost certainly have to be funded by some form of borrowing. There are various options available:

■ Venture Capital is one source of extra equity that can be achieved without losing control of the business. Venture Capital organisations are specialist companies whose primary activity is to invest in new businesses and unquoted companies to help them expand and grow. Investments can take the form of loans or minority shareholdings, but typically, venture capitalists are usually only interested in investing sums exceeding £500k. They generally seek investments that offer them potentially high returns, with 20–40% of capital investment as a typical minimum expectation over several years, from dividends and capital growth to justify the investment risks that they take. They usually seek Boardroom representation, they require regular and detailed reports and information, and will normally expect the business in which they have invested, to buy out their share after a specified period of time. Venture Capital companies can provide the levels of investment that might otherwise only be obtainable via the Stock Exchange, but without the massive cost of achieving Stock Exchange listing. They also impose structure and regulation on company affairs, and can provide valuable management expertise. On the negative side, they can limit the owners' ability to make decisions, their expectations are high, and the owner loses a good deal of strategic control over the business. The owner must also pay for the initial legal and accountancy charges incurred in the process of setting up the contracts to facilitate the capital injection. On balance, they do offer a great opportunity to finance the expansion of small firms in high-growth industrial sectors.

- Medium to long-term loans from banks. High street banks will make medium and long-term loans to businesses, typically on over 5 to 10 years, on a secured basis, and with interest rates around 3% over the base lending rate (or 5% for a new business without a trading record. Beyond that period, the loan is more likely to be treated as a mortgage, being secured by a specific fixed asset belonging to the business or one of its proprietors. Again, arrangement fees are charged and there may be some solicitor's costs incurred in setting up legal charges on property.

- Debentures are a special type of fixed-term loan, often guaranteed by a charge on the assets of the business, and sometimes linked to an option to convert into share capital. They differ from conventional loans in that during the lifetime of the loan, only interest is paid. The capital sum does not fall due for repayment until the period of the loan expires, when it must be repaid in full. Interest rates are agreed at the start of the term either at a fixed level, or linked to commercial lending rates, with a minimum specified level. Debentures will often be arranged between one company and another, or by financial institutions, particularly to assist with expansion of a business. They can therefore be particularly useful and attractive to small firms that are looking to expand. How do you find another firm that might be willing to loan the money? Well, look first to your own suppliers and customers. It may be that you have a supplier that is fairly large and well established, that might welcome the opportunity of a fairly safe and secured investment that would both consolidate its relationship with one of its customers, and at the same time to increase its sales to that customer. Similarly, if you have a large customer that depends on your supplies, a debenture can cement the relationship, guaranteeing both their source of supply (possibly on favourable terms) and a proportion of your sales.

- Mortgage debentures, as the name suggests, these are debentures which are mortgaged to a specific fixed asset of the company, e.g. a piece of land or a building. Otherwise they work in the same way as a debenture.

- The availability of grants to assist with business expansion can depend largely on the location of the business. Some relocation grants are available for businesses starting up or moving to development areas, particularly in more remote rural areas, e.g. in Wales. Local authorities in strategic regeneration areas often have access to European Social Fund monies, which are sometimes issued in grant form to assist small firms. Local councils or chambers of commerce can often advise on the availability of these, as they will differ from area to area. Grants to subsidise training for employees can also be obtained from some local authority economic development units, and from most business links, particularly if your business is working towards investors in people status.

- Commercial mortgages are used to buy business premises, or to expand premises that are already owned. A commercial mortgage arranged through a bank, insurance company or financial institution is basically the same as a mortgage used to buy a private home. It would normally be repaid over 10 to 15 years, as opposed to the typical 25-year repayment period for a domestic mortgage. Commercial mortgages for licensed premises can also be obtained from some of the regional and national breweries, linked to a contract to buy their products (a barrellage loan). For owner-managers in the public trade, or hotel and tourism industries, these arrangements can be useful if the target for expansion involves acquiring multiple outlets.

- Treasury fixed rate loans, available through the main high street banks, these are available for sums in excess of £100,000 and can be repaid over a period or up to 25 years, so they are ideal for the purchase of major fixed assets, or for business expansion. The interest rate is negotiated and fixed for the full term of the loan (and so will incur penalties for early repayment), and security is normally required.

- The Loan Guarantee Scheme (LGS) was introduced by the government in the early 1980's to encourage banks to lend to new and small firms whose proprietors could not offer any conventional security. The idea was that the government, in return for a percentage charge, would guarantee up to 85% of the value of the loan. The banks, in return for a higher rate of loan interest, would stand the risk of the other 15%. Loan guarantees can still be found, but the scheme as a whole is generally viewed as a failure. Apart from the high cost of interest and fees, banks simply don't like to risk lending even as little as 15% or 20% to a small businesses on an unsecured basis, and so were only willing to advance money to established firms with a proven track record. Home-owning applicants were told that as they had potential security, the LGS was inappropriate.

Applicants with no assets were asked why the bank should risk backing them, when they had nothing at risk themselves. Loans are available for anything between £5000 and £250,000 over 2 to 10 years, and for most business purposes (although not for licensed premises), but they must not be used to replace existing finance. The idea sounds very attractive to owner-managers as a low-risk means of raising money for expansion, but the loans can prove to be a very expensive form of borrowing. Interest rates are high, often about 5% over base rate to reflect the risk that the banks are sharing. On top of this, there is a Department of Trade and Industry (DTI) premium of 3% for the government's guarantee, and arrangement fees have to be paid at the outset. The loans can also take time to set up as if they exceed £30,000 they need both bank and government approval, but below that figure the banks can approve them quite quickly. Having highlighted the drawbacks of the LGS it must be said that since 2005 the government has been trying to encourage the lending banks to be more proactive with the provision of LGS finance to small firms by restricting LGS to firms under 5-years old, and by raising the previous balance sheet value of the firm for eligibility purposes to £5.6m. The target is to reach more start-ups but the focus remains on high-growth firms. This is almost a self-contradiction in practical terms of the banks' lending criteria, and it still seems more likely that any growth in the issue of LGS loans is more likely to be for expansion of businesses with an existing track record rather than those in a start-up situation.

Further funding options more suited to larger organisations

These are really mentioned in passing, just to draw the reader's attention to the fact that they exist, as they would certainly not be relevant to most small firms. Taking those firms at the top end of the government's definition of "Small and Medium-Sized Enterprises" which employ between 100 and 250 staff, some of those would be more likely to consider using the following options. However, for the 97% of firms in the UK which only employ less than 20 staff, they are largely inappropriate:

- *Loans from merchant banks*: It is often said, that it is easier for a business to borrow £10 million than just ten thousand. Most of the merchant banks and financial institutions that specialise in providing business finance have little interest in setting up long-term loans of less than £250k, as the time and effort involved does not justify the potential profit. This policy does leave small firms very much at the behest of the high street banks, as the bigger institutions have no interest in lending to them, so that type of borrowing is really best suited to companies that are already well established and which are looking for six-figure sums to finance substantial growth. Loans from merchant banks are invariably secured, if not by property or assets, then by a debenture, probably supplemented with directors' guarantees. Interest and capital repayments are made monthly or quarterly, with interest rates set at pre-arranged levels. Arranging the loans will incur legal costs, and larger loans can take several months to negotiate and set up if appropriate information about financial performance is not readily available.

■ *Flotation on the Stock Exchange or Alternative Investment Market (AIM)*: This can be a very expensive process, and is generally regarded as not being justified unless the floating company intends to raise at least £5 million. The company has to prove that it can meet specific accounting, operational, and capitalisation standards in order to find a merchant bank willing to underwrite the floatation (i.e. to buy up all of the surplus shares if no one else likes the look of them). Once listed, its shares can be sold to the public, and the capital raised can be used for expansion. Flotation has become very popular amongst small high-tech and e-commerce businesses (the so-called Dot-Com companies) but as the result of a number of failures, investors are becoming increasingly wary about buying shares in these types of business. Floatation also places the business under public scrutiny and reduces the autonomy and control of the owner-manager, who becomes an employee accountable to the shareholders.

■ *Convertible loan stock*: This takes the form of an option to buy shares in a company, which is issued against loans, typically from financial institutions or investment companies. The company that issues the shares receives a loan, usually at quite low-interest rates, with no capital repayments until the settlement date, and with the interest being paid out of pre-tax earnings; so this amounts to a very cheap form of finance. The lending company, as well as receiving interest on the loan, has an option at the end of the loan period. If the borrowing company's shares have performed poorly, the loan can be repaid in full and return the share option. Alternatively, if the shares have increased in value in the meantime, the lender can exercise its right to buy them at the original price then in lieu of repayment of the loan, (i.e. "convert" the loan into shares) and sell them for a capital profit. How does this fit in with the expansion needs of small firms, particularly if, as is highly likely, their shares are not publicly quoted? Irrespective of a lack of stock exchange listing, there is nothing to stop a small company from selling its shares privately, so as with the debentures, look towards your supply chain for potential financiers or investors.

- *Commercial bonds*: These are way out of the league of small firms, as they are usually issued by large blue-chip companies. The company issues (sells) a negotiable bond with a guaranteed redemption value of perhaps £100k payable in 5 or 10 years' time. The initial selling price is less than the face value, but as time progresses towards the redemption date, the value will increase. Dealings in the bonds take place in the Stock Exchange.

- *Bills of exchange*: Usually with a value of at least £100K, these are a bit like post-dated cheques, but they are only payable when certain conditions have been met, e.g. the goods to which the bill of exchange relates have been delivered. However, they can be discounted to finance early payment, or money can be borrowed against them, subject to the reputation and status of the issuing company.

Summary

If the strategic objectives for expansion are to be achieved, the owner-manager must plan the finances of the business carefully to ensure that:

- The business has sufficient cash flow and liquidity to finance the growth without the risk of over-trading. Don't leave the business short of working capital at the time when it is needed most.
- The amount of funding is sufficient to do the job properly, i.e. to enable the business to achieve the desired level of expansion smoothly and without interruption. Build a contingency sum or safety margin into your figures, as you will invariably need it at some point.
- The terms of any borrowing (interest rates etc.) are commercially competitive so as not to adversely affect profit margins.

Don't be afraid to challenge the rates offered by potential lenders. Shop around and negotiate. The banks need your business as much as you need their money.

- The ratio of borrowing to security is not unfavourable. The banks might like twice as much security as the sum advanced, but this could limit any further borrowing at a later date. In addition, the amount of security that is provided by the owner-manager's private resources should not be so large that it constitutes an unacceptable risk or causes personal stress or family disputes. Running a business is stressful enough without adding to the problem.

- The repayment terms of any borrowing are within the capacity of the business, and do not over-stretch it. Any borrowing must be affordable otherwise it will eat into working capital and cause cash flow problems.

- The types of funding are appropriate to purposes for which they are sought, e.g. the use of overdrafts for short-term financing only, or the use of hire purchase to buy machinery or vehicles.

- The sources of finance meet both the needs of the business and the aspirations of the owner-manager in terms of ownership and control. For example, don't be forced into relinquishing control of the business by selling shares in order to raise money.

- Finally, make sure that you have an accounting system that enables you to keep full control of the finances of the business, and gives you the information you need, when you need it.

Further reading

Barrow, C., Brown, R., Burke, D. and Molian, D. (2005). *Enterprise Development.* Thomson, Harlow.

Broadbent, M. and Cullen, J. (2003). *Managing Financial Resources*, Elsevier, Oxford.

Harvey, D., McLaney, E. and Atrill, P. (2003). *Accounting for Business*, Elsevier, Oxford.

Vinturella, J. and Erickson, S. (2004). *Raising Entrepreneurial Capital*, Elsevier, Oxford.

CHAPTER 18

Sales and marketing for growth

In Chapter 13 we mentioned the headless-chicken syndrome, wherein small business owners have a tendency in the early stages of the firm's existence, to chase all sales opportunities that come their way irrespective of profitability, on the assumption that any sales that make a contribution towards their overheads must be good for the business. In consequence they often expend a great deal of effort chasing low-margin sales when a more planned and directed approach could have resulted in much more profit for much less effort. As the business matures the sales effort becomes directed towards the more profitable sales opportunities, but such opportunities are usually limited because of strong competition in the market. If the business is to expand and develop in the long term, it has therefore, to either expend a great deal of time, money and effort fighting for limited opportunities, or to focus on the market segments or niches where it can use its strengths to the full. This chapter will look at some contemporary ideas about the strategic marketing audit, the process of identifying suitable market segments, and the production of the strategic marketing plan, and how these apply to small and developing firms.

The marketing audit

The first stage in preparing your business for expansion is to carry out a review of the marketing processes presently in use, identifying areas of strengths and weaknesses, current spare capacity and/or overload, and in particular any major problems that need to be addressed. Some of the relevant issues will hopefully already have been picked up during the strategic analysis of the business.

Hooley *et al.* (1998) propose that the starting point of the marketing audit should be to examine the organisational assets of the business, covering the finances, physical assets, people, operations, intellectual property (patents and copyrights, etc.), systems, and marketing assets. Drummond and Ensor (1999) focus on the last of these as being particularly significant to marketing strategy, the marketing assets, which fall into four categories:

1. First, the customer-based assets are those which are important in the eyes of the customer: the image and reputation of the business in the marketplace, any brands which the business owns that are strong enough to generate customer loyalty (and therefore a potential competitive advantage over rival businesses). The customers' perceptions of the business as a market leader or brand leader are also significant in that in the case of fast-moving consumer goods, such perceptions can generate prime locations within retail outlets. They also mention the country of origin as being relevant, quoting as an example, the German car manufacturers BMW and Mercedes. Whilst this may be relevant to the international motor trade, I am not so sure of its importance to small firms unless they are producing or selling premium goods for the top end of the consumer market. It is certainly less applicable to service industries. The main features to focus on are the unique features of products and services which distinguish them from the competition, whether it by price, quality, design, or a combination of these.

2. The size and strength of the distribution network in key geographical areas, is a very and crucial valuable asset for the firm. This is not just an issue of the size of the area covered, or its depth of coverage, but the speed and efficiency in which the business can respond to its customers. The other aspect of distribution is whether or not the firm has any influence or control over the distribution network. The example quoted by Drummond and Ensor (1999, p. 53) is that of Coca-Cola using its global influence to keep the relatively small but popular Scottish Irn-Bru soft drinks out of MacDonald's restaurants. As a case in point, this illustrates well one of the major problems facing small firms in large international markets. Even where the barriers to market-entry can be overcome, it is very seldom the case that small firms can achieve any degree of market control, except of course with the approval of the large global organisations.

3. Cost structure advantages such as economies of scale or the application of technology can provide valuable internal assets to a business, although in small firms any economies of scale are much less likely to be as significant, as the ability to make use of innovative technology. Equally, the information systems used for market research are likely to be less significant to small firms, apart perhaps, from those working in the information technology markets.

4. The fourth type of assets are described as alliance-based, because they involve the advantages gained from external relationships with other organisations, and this is one area where small firms can potentially score highly. For example, many small firms gain access to larger markets via partnerships or contracts with other distributors or suppliers in those markets, sometimes involving exclusive supply agreements with major players in the market. Such relationships can also involve savings from shared product development. In this respect, providers of venture capital can count as an asset in terms of both the networking opportunities and the management expertise they can offer to their siblings.

Can you then, identify any of these internal assets which may exist within your business, or are there any possible areas which could be exploited for the future? Are there any other internal factors that could be regarded as internal assets, such as any specialist marketing knowledge or expertise relating to the firm's customers and markets? Most important, having identified your internal assets, are you making them work for you to their full potential?

Kotler outlines a five-stage model for the marketing audit process (Kotler *et al.*, 2004) which can help managers of both large and small firms to carry out an audit of their own organisations. The model is really designed to challenge any comfortable assumptions that all is well in the marketing context, as it highlights each of the possible areas where problems could have crept in over a period of time, since the marketing policies were formulated or last reviewed. This is especially pertinent to small firms where policy reviews are not automatic, often because of the singular and sometimes autocratic role of the owner-manager as the primary decision maker:

1. The *Marketing Strategy Audit* looks at the compatibility of current marketing activity with the overall marketing objectives of the organisation, and if sufficient resources have been allocated to allow the objectives to be achieved. Do the activities

fit with the strategies or have they diverged over a period of time? One would think that with the more specialised management resources available to big companies this would be less likely to happen than in a small business where the owner-manager may be more readily distracted from original policies. Have your marketing activities inadvertently diverged from the original plans over the past year or so? Are the differences just minor or has there been a major change in direction, and what impact has that had on sales volumes and revenues? What were the reasons for the change? Do the current activities now need to be brought into line with the overall strategic objectives of the business?

2. The *Marketing Structures Audit* looks at the role of the marketing function within the organisation as a whole, its representation within the management and decision-making process, and its relationships with other functional areas of the business. In theory, the sales and marketing function should be of prime importance to the owner-manager as they are the lifelines of the business, but in many small firms, they are relegated to a secondary position. This is a particularly common occurrence if the owner-manager comes from a manufacturing or technical background, when the "marketing" (or more often just the advertising) is often delegated to a secretary to arrange. Conversely, owner-managers from a sales background tend to place a strong emphasis on marketing, although with a strong awareness of the importance of the product itself in the marketing mix, the need for technical expertise is not relegated to a lower priority in the same manner. Where then, does the marketing role fit within your business, and have you got the balance right?

3. The *Marketing Systems Audit* looks at the planning and control systems used, and new product development. Are you able to monitor and evaluate the returns achieved by sales and marketing activities, for example, in terms of enquiries or actual sales generated by an advertising campaign, or by the regular activities of sales staff? Does the product development policy of the business follow from market information and research, or from the inspirations of the owner-manager and technical staff? There is nothing wrong with the latter, but the former does a great deal to validate its potential benefits and to guide it in the right direction. The systems audit should also include a review of the market research activities and capabilities of the organisation, in particular with an examination of the

depth to which research is carried out. Market research is not an activity that comes easy to many owner-managers and there can be a tendency, often driven by experience in a particular industry or service, to assume that there is little more to be learnt beyond that which the owner-manager already knows. This is more important prior to a period of growth or development, especially when diversifying into new markets, as it is all easy to underestimate the barriers to market entry because they have not been sufficiently researched. For example, there may be a big market out there waiting for you, but how much of it is tied up in long-term contracts with major competitors whose size and economies of scale, enables them to control and manipulate prices to keep out newcomers.

4. The *Productivity Audit* looks at the contributions made by the various products or services offered, their individual profit to cost ratios, and the cost-effectiveness of the various distribution channels and markets. Do you know which of your products or services (a) generate the biggest overall contribution towards profit and overheads for the business, (b) generate the best profit margins, (c) fail to cover their costs? Do you know which of your lines of distribution contribute the biggest profit to the business? Are any of the markets in which you operate, actually loosing you money? This analysis can provide useful data about products or markets on which to focus, and others to avoid or withdraw from in the future, and as an audit process it should be regarded as an aspect of basic good housekeeping, as most small businesses have the necessary data available to them to extract this information, but they don't always make time or take the trouble to find the answers to these questions.

5. The *Marketing Functions Audit* is a way of reviewing the marketing mix (product, price, place, and promotion, etc.), to investigate its on-going effectiveness. Are there any factors that have changed the relative significance of any of the components, e.g. an aggressive pricing policy or advertising campaign by a major rival? Has the demand for the product(s) changed at all? Most important of all, to link it with the strategic objectives of the business, what changes in the marketing mix are now needed? This last question will reflect the decisions made about the strategic options faced by the business (cost-leadership, diversification, market-focus, etc.), as it will tell you how far off the mark the business actually is.

Market segmentation

In the previous section we mentioned the importance of comprehensive market research, and one of the key focal points of marker research should be to identify the individual market segments which constitute the market as a whole. People do not simply drive cars, they drive saloons, estates, coupes, convertibles, sports models, roadsters, off-roaders, even Chelsea tractors, etc. The sports car options start at the modest and very basic self-build Caterham kit-cars, through MGs, Morgans and Jaguars, through to more expensive Porches, to the top-of-range Lamborghinis, and customised Ferraris. Every type of car and every price-variant of each type constitutes a different market segment within which it is broadly possible to stereotype the potential customers according to certain common characteristics such as income, type of employment, social class, family composition, etc. The average engineer, social worker, salesman, school teacher or college lecturer might aspire to owning a three or four bedroom house and a fairly new middle-range saloon car, but short of a lottery win that person could not hope to achieve the lifestyle and associated expensive cars enjoyed by Premier League footballers.

The purpose of identifying market segments is to evaluate and select those in which the business can achieve some differential advantage over its competitors. This does not mean the firm has to focus on just one or two segments, rather than it can build up a portfolio of segments that compliment each other in terms of generating income and contribution to overhead coverage and profit. Put simply, we are trying to identify various groups or types of customers who share common characteristics, or similar patterns of demand, so that we can focus our sales and marketing effort towards them. The market research enables you to select those that offer you the biggest potential in terms of sales volume or profit, in relation to the effort expended in achieving those sales. By virtue of the fact that they will have differential characteristics and criteria for buying, they will require different approaches, i.e. marketing mixes. In Chapter 6, Figure 6.1 shows an example of segmentation prepared for a small contract cleaning company. This shows examples of the types of customer, the typical value and profit margins of their contracts, their service criteria and requirements, their motivation in terms of price or quality of service, and finally the proportion of the firms' total sales that are likely to be derived from each type of contract.

Drummond and Ensor (1999, pp. 108–109) propose that market segments should be assessed in terms of both their market attractiveness of the various segments, and the ability of the firm to supply the needs of the particular segments. For the small business, this rises a number of issues:

- Should the firm focus on larger opportunities to gain economies of scale and to justify greater investment in market development, but run the risk of heavier competition from rivals, or should it focus on smaller niche segments that will not readily attract the unwanted attention of our rivals?

- What are the opportunities for growth within the segments? Are we looking at good profitable opportunities, or mature or even declining markets? The former would be preferable, but again might also attract the attention of competitors, the latter although less attractive, could still offer good short-term profits.

- Which of our competitors are already active in the segments, and will there be enough potential profit within them to justify the investment incurred in breaking into the market segments? Conversely, if we move into a segment where there is unsatisfied demand, what barriers or costs are there to stop our rivals moving in alongside, and reducing our profits?

- How sensitive is the population of the segment to price? A price-sensitive may mean working on low-profit margins, but less sensitivity could give an opportunity for good profits, so long as we do not attract too much attention from our rivals.

- What is the pattern of demand within the segment? It is unusual for any market to have a total level and consistent demand, as most markets are influenced in some way by seasonal factors (weather, Christmas or other festival dates, holiday seasons, etc.).

- What are the possibilities that a particular niche market will become a target for new alternative or substitute products that could render ours obsolete? Can we afford this risk? Are we in a position to develop innovative products ourselves?

The strategic marketing plan

The above questions will help to provide the criteria by which we can evaluate the relative potential of the various optional market segments that are available. If the chosen segments are compatible with our overall strategic objectives, we can move on to define the marketing plan, i.e. the policies and tactics we will use to address these market opportunities, and the competencies we will employ to gain an advantage over our competitors. The plan should develop a marketing mix for each of the target market segments that will make full use and advantage of the strengths of the business and its marketing resources. This is the process of getting the right product or service, of the right quality, to the place where the customer wants it, at the right price, and using the right methods of advertising and promotion to optimise profits along the way.

The strategic analysis and the resultant chosen options should have determined the organisation's policies for the pricing strategy of the products or services, as well as the plans for future product development in terms of the focus or diversification of the product range. The subsequent marketing audit and segmentation of the market will have determined the target market and its customers, and will assist in making decisions about our position in the markets in terms of our strengths, public image, brand awareness; as well as our ability to respond to changes in the markets, to develop new and innovative products or services advantages, etc. Remember, what we are looking at here are the strategies with which we will implement the overall policies and objectives of the business. Those strategies should compliment the objectives rather than diverge from them, or result in activities that compete with each other for limited marketing resources. In the case of the marketing plan this means that the strategies should be formulated in conjunction with the plans of other functional areas within the business (production, finance, sales, etc.) and not in isolation. This is to ensure that their respective activities are complimentary do not detract from each other or do not compete with each other for limited company resources.

Having then covered the Price, Product, and Place aspects of the marketing mix, the next chapter will look at the Promotion, that is, the long-term policies and tactics that will promote and sell the products or services, and the new opportunities currently emerging to achieve these policies.

The first part of this chapter is concerned with the tactical aspects of the marketing plan for the business. The Product, Price, and Place aspects of the marketing mix are essentially the policy decisions covered in the previous chapter, but the Promotion aspects (achieving the sales) are more tactical in that they relate to the methods that will be used to project and present the other three aspects to the market and the customers. In particular, there is a need to distinguish the "marketing" aspects of promotion, from the "sales" aspects. Advertising and promotion creates interest in a business or its products and services, and in the case of direct sales organisations, it is also the sales mechanism that takes the orders. However, for the majority of businesses, the marketing and promotion activities alone do not always generate sales orders. There needs to be a supporting mechanism in the form of staff who are actively selling to customers, or an order taking and processing system, to convert interest and enquiries into actual orders.

The chapter will also examine some of the issues associated with exporting and e-commerce, two increasingly overlapping areas. The first of these is an obvious potential opportunity for any firm considering expansion. The second is a subject that no modern business can afford to ignore, as Internet marketing offers small firms the opportunity to break into wider geographical and export markets hitherto inaccessible to them.

Developing an advertising and promotion strategy

It is very easy when running a small business, to go from year to year using the same tried and tested methods of advertising and promotion without giving thought either to whether or not they are still achieving satisfactory results, or to new or alternative options. The monitoring of sales and promotional activities, should be an on-going process, e.g. in terms of enquiries and actual sales per advertisement, of numbers of sales calls per day, conversion rates per sales call, the revenue sales volumes and profit margins generated by each sales person, etc. Sadly, this monitoring is often overwhelmed and subsumed by other business pressures until suddenly a major problem is identified. Sometimes the problem goes unnoticed until perhaps a salesman leaves and the replacement person swamps the business with orders, making the owner-manager suddenly aware that the former employee was ineffective and that this had gone unnoticed. So, the point at which the owner-manager is looking for growth and development within the business should also be the point at which the efficacy of the sales and promotion activities are reviewed, as they need to be fully efficient to facilitate that new growth. The review process requires the owner-manager to consider a further range of questions:

- What methods of advertising and promotion are currently being used? Does the business use a wide range of methods or does it just rely on one or two proven options? Has it chosen those methods because they are the most appropriate for the needs of the business, or were they simply the most convenient at the time?
- Are the current methods satisfactory, i.e. do they optimise the sales opportunities for the business? Are they cost-effective in terms of the profit they generate in comparison with the actual costs incurred? Are they generating the levels of sales expected

of them? What evidence is there to verify the answers to these questions? For example, if we choose a particular form of advertising, say adverts in local newspapers, we would expect the profit gained from the additional sales which result from the advertising to more than outweigh the cost of the advertising, and otherwise it has been a failure. If there were a choice of more than one local newspaper in which we can advertise, we would need to monitor the adverts in order to determine which of the two gives us the best results. This could be measured in terms of the number of enquiries that follow each advert, and/or the number of sales that result from those enquiries. We should also be monitoring these on an on-going basis to identify seasonal fluctuations or other factors which may be affecting the response levels, so that for example, we do not advertise at those times of year when we know demand will fall. If the business offers a multiple range of products or services, then it will be necessary to monitor the effectiveness of each form of promotion against each product, as particular methods will prove more efficient in selling to some market segments than others, and the business needs to be able to identify the best method to reach each type of customer for each product or service. This is just good basic common sense market research.

▪ Will the same methods be compatible with the plans for expansion? If the plans for expansion involve moving into new markets or diversifying product ranges then the answer to this question will almost certainly be no. It is imperative therefore, that you do not just assume that because your favourite sales and marketing methods has worked in the past, they will still work for your new services or new market segment customers. In the earlier chapters, we talked about identifying tactics that will enable us to implement the strategic objectives. Part of that process involves defining suitable methods of advertising and promotion that will enable the business to hit it sales targets in the new market segments, or for its new product lines.

▪ What actual methods of sales and/or promotion will be needed for the future? No business can rely on its reputation or on word of mouth recommendation alone to sell its goods or services, and it is rare that any single method of promotion will be adequate, so we are usually looking for a combination of methods from the most popular available:

– *Media advertising*: This using television, radio, posters and hoardings, etc., can reach large proportions of the buying public quite easily, and are particularly good for raising and maintaining brand awareness amongst household products, and for encouraging the public to buy those products. They are however, expensive and have relatively little use in selling specialist services to specific parts of the market. The television adverts might tell me what is the best beer to drink or crisps to eat whilst I am watching football, but they will not tell me who is the best supplier of contract catering in my locality, or where I can find a plumber that works for less than £500 per day.

– *Publications*: Local for local sales and services, a double-glazing firm does not want to be travelling all over the country if it can get enough trade within a fifty mile radius. National advertising for national markets, e.g. a company selling stair-lifts for the elderly will probably need to trade nationally to ensure it can get sufficient business to cover overheads and make a healthy profit, whereas to just trade on a county-wide basis would risk failure. Specialist publications are ideal for niche markets: suppliers of pigeon food for racing pigeons advertise in the Pigeon Fancier or Fur & Feather magazine; whilst manufacturers or waterproof waders prefer Trout and Salmon or other angling magazines. In each case, a general daily newspaper might offer a much broader readership but with far less likelihood of any sales.

– *Employed sales staff*: There are two main options here, to train up existing staff, which can be cheaper for younger businesses, or buy in or recruit already trained staff from competitors. Recruiting experienced sales staff tends to cost much more as you are paying for a track record of sales skills, experience in the industry, and usually a ready-made list of contacts and potential customers. The extra cost is often justified by the more rapid returns through increased sales, but there is always the risk that poached staff can be poached back by the offer of higher rewards elsewhere. "Home-grown" sales staff, if properly rewarded, can often prove the most loyal in the long term.

– *Sales agents*: They can provide a source of skills, experience and relevant industrial knowledge. They are relatively cheap usually being paid a basic retainer fee plus commission on results, but being independent they are not under your direct control, and you may find at times that there is a conflict between your priorities and those of the other organisations that use them.

– *Franchises*: The features that attract potential franchisees to a franchise opportunity in the first place are normally associated with the pre-existent brand image and reputation of the franchise opportunity. Classic examples are household name such as Body Shop, McDonalds, and more recent arrivals such as Starbucks, Kall-Kwik printing, and Snappy Snaps.

– *Licensed products*: Where the owner of the patent or copyright of a particular product issues licences for other businesses to produce and supply that product into specified market areas. There are normally only four reasons why a business would contemplate selling licences to allow other firms promote and distribute their products: a lack of capital to allow them to expand the market themselves, to break into an export market with the minimum of effort and investment, to stave off the risk of unauthorised copies of the product, or as the result of an offer too good to refuse.

– *Internet*: It has been the major growth area for cheap coverage of potentially world-wide markets, in terms of both consumer buying and business to business transactions. This is examined in more detail below, but with the rapid growth of e-commerce and the Internet as a source of product information.

– *Telesales activities*: This as a means of selling expanded at an enormous rate in the late 1990s, but have more recently been superseded by on-line buying on the Internet 5 years – as evidenced by the switch to on-line quotations for insurance cover. There are two basic formats: (a) the telesales answering services that respond to sales advertisements on TV and in the newspapers such as SAGA Holidays, and Direct Line Insurance, and (b) the cold-calling telesales typical of replacement window and conservatory suppliers. What always amazes me about the latter is that they always call you without fail, when you are in the middle of an evening meal – it is almost as if they have some secret device which links their telephone service with the cooker in your home! Cold-calling telesales is very much a numbers game, requiring a large number of calls to generate a few enquiries, and even less actual sales, but the frequency with which we receive such calls at home must be indicative of its cost-effectiveness.

Remember, the criteria for selecting the most appropriate method or combination of methods of advertising and promotion should not just focus on comparative costs or potential returns on outlay, they must also ensure that the advertising and promotion policies compliment the overall development strategies of the business.

Selling and exporting abroad

What is it that turns the heads of owner-managers to think about exporting? Paliwoda and Thomas (1998, p. 105) argue that in general this is rarely the result of planned or extensive market research. Sometimes it is an order or enquiry from a foreign country that arrives unexpectedly and prompts the sudden realisation that life (and business) exists beyond the Straits of Dover. Once the order has been met and the basic export procedures are in place, it is an obvious next step to make further use of these by searching for more export opportunities. In other cases, it may be the prospect of low-cost or low-risk entry into markets that are proving hard to penetrate, or are already saturated, in the home country.

The export markets may present an opportunity to expand production of current product lines, and to grow the business without the capital investment costs that may be incurred by a strategy of product diversification. This does not however imply that exporting is a low-cost option, as the costs of developing an export market can be substantial, in terms of preliminary market research and sales effort, and the funds tied up in goods in transit, or when payment is awaited from foreign distributors. In particular, the costs of replacing or servicing faulty goods can quickly wipe out profit margins, so the move into exporting should not be considered lightly.

The potential exporter must also make decisions about the extent of the involvement the business will have in the foreign markets, and a number of options exist here:

- If the business decides to utilise spare capacity at the home base, and transport the goods abroad, decisions still need to be made about the sales and distribution networks that will be used:
  - Do we set up a complete sales and distribution network from scratch, thus incurring substantial initial outlay and on-going overhead costs, possibly in a market where the true levels of demand for the goods are not yet assured? This could be both a high cost and high-risk strategy if we do not have good market knowledge and established contacts.

- Do we set up a foreign base but use sales agents who have better local market knowledge, as well as established contacts with potential users or outlets? This gives a measure of control over the issue of goods, but still incurs some capital outlay and overheads.
- Do we simply supply a foreign agent or wholesaler who would then undertake the whole sales and distribution process on our behalf? In terms of capital outlay and operating costs this is the cheapest option, but it does mean that once the goods have been despatched abroad, we have no control over them, and we are totally reliant on the efficiency and honesty of the agent.

- If there is inadequate spare production capacity at home, it may be more cost effective to set up production abroad, generating savings on the cost of transport or carriage between countries, and possibly achieving lower production costs with local labour:
  - Do we set up a new production facility with all of the capital and development costs? In some foreign countries, this might attract subsidies or incentives, although in others it may be necessary to grease a few palms to avoid problems or delays. Either way, capital costs may be well beyond the resources of a small firm without outside help.
  - Do we sub-contract the licence to an established manufacturer in a similar industry (if such exists)? An alternative option might be a joint venture with a local manufacturer, but such venture can present a great deal of risk and exposure, especially if there are problems or disagreements when local courts may favour the home player.
  - Do we franchise or licence the products for local production? This can be a practical proposition if the business holds patents or copyrights, although there are always potential problems of enforcing these on foreign soil. In some oriental countries there can also be problems arising from unauthorised copying of patented goods, resulting in the market being swamped with cheaply produced copies.

- A less common but often cheaper and more practical option is for the would-be exporter to join a consortium of other exporters that produce complementary products for the same markets. This can generate savings in shipping costs, storage, sales and distribution costs, whilst giving access to established distribution networks, and utilising established or shared administrative systems. The hardest problem here is in making the initial contacts with other exporters, but there are government agencies and advisory bodies that exist just to assist with such problems.

- Accessing overseas markets is becoming more and more easy via the Internet, with huge increases in person to person sales by post, by-passing export/import duties, and in many cases the associated Duty charges; but although export documentation can be in part completed on-line, there is not yet any easy and legal way to avoid conventional export processes for bulk goods.

The export business does offer the potential of high and sustainable long-term profits, but it is also riddled with risks, obstacles and potential problems for small firms:

- Identification of potential markets and customers. Apart from the practical difficulties and expense of carrying out market research from a distance, in many cases the date simply does not exist. In addition, small firms often have limited resources, both in terms of finance and management time, and invariably they also have little or no expertise in exporting. Paliwoda and Thomas (1998, p. 106) state that in consequence, the small firms tend to spend relatively little money on market research, and to focus their sales effort on trade fairs and exhibitions, and personal visits to major customers. Other than this, the majority of small firms seem to prefer to work through agents located in the target countries.
- The actual selection of reliable distributors or agents can be a problem in that although there are sources of information about available export agents through various government agencies and business support organisations, it is much harder to obtain information about the quality, honesty, and efficiency of the various agents. This may sound a bit xenophobic, but from the perspective of most owner-managers, there is an obvious risk in supplying goods on credit, to a person they may not even have met, who is thousands of miles away, speaks a different native language, has a differing cultural view of life, with possible different business objectives, and an unknown reputation. These are the same owner-managers who are often reluctant to trust their own secretaries to do the daily banking in their hometown!
- When dealing with foreign countries there are the obvious barriers of language, culture, and pace of life, where "urgent" means "some time this week", or where families take priority

over business. The cultural differences often prove frustrating and hard to comprehend, but the problem is compounded when they cannot be easily discussed due to different languages, and profit is at stake. The average owner-manager's time is at a premium, and foreign travel is both expensive and time consuming; so it can be exasperating to reach the end of a long journey only to find your destination is closed for 3 days due to a local religious festival or little-publicised public holiday.

- The economic aspects of foreign trade must not be ignored. Fluctuations in exchange rates between the dates of sale and dates of payment can often wipe out or minimise profit margins. Some countries still operate trade tariffs, taxing or restricting imports, and others have restrictions on the amounts of currency that can be taken out of the country. It is no good having a huge and profitable market opportunity if you cannot bring that profit back to your home country, or if the currency in which you are paid, has little exchange value.

- There is also the need to establish letters of credit from reputable banks to ensure that your customers or agents will pay you, and this is in itself can be a time-consuming process, especially as some banks have a minimum transaction level which may be above the average sale value of small exporters. Fortunately there are some government agencies and other bodies that can assist in these matters:

  - The Department of Trade & Industry in London, has an Export Market Information Centre (EMIC) which can be a useful source of data and statistics for various world markets; and can provide information on international trade fairs and events. Its Export Marketing Research Scheme (EMRS) also offers advice on how to get market research information for different products in different world regions. It also has information on country profiles and directories for various parts of the world.

  - The Export Credit Guarantee Department (ECGD) can offer advice on credit guarantees, and contacts with specialists in various parts of the world, but is primarily geared towards the needs of larger exporters.

  - The English Export Finance Association in Rochdale, is more suited to small firms as it handles smaller credit transactions than mainstream banks will normally touch.

  - The British Standards Institution offers a service called Technical Help to Exporters, which can provide date concerning rules and regulations in foreign countries. Similarly, HM Revenue & Customs can provide information on UK regulations affecting exports out of the UK. In addition, there are a number of trade associations and national export organisations that offer export advice to members, including the British Exporters Association, and the British Chambers of Commerce, which can be accessed via the Internet.

Internet marketing

The rapid growth of e-commerce in recent years has turned aspects of conventional marketing theory upside down, the Internet itself now being the Place part of the marketing mix, in a world wide rather than local context, and the distribution systems being postal or contract delivery services rather than direct deliveries by the producer to the customer. Because of the Internet, the physical location of the manufacturer or supplier is of much less importance, but the quality and efficiency of the communications system is now of paramount importance. In effect, the user-friendly website, the facility for secure payment, the convenience of armchair shopping, and the promise of prompt delivery, has become the new customer service system. The Internet has streamlined mail order purchase systems, particularly for CDs and electronic goods, etc., because in the time it previously took to post an order and cheque to the supplier, the goods have now been delivered. It has opened up the market size or customer potential for small firms supplying niche markets, and it has offered an affordable system of advertising and selling in those markets, when the cost of conventional sales activities would have prohibited entry into those markets.

Initially, small firms have responded better to the new opportunities of e-commerce than their larger counterparts. Big companies made good use of the Internet to dissipate knowledge and information, and to communicate with their global customers, but websites are used more for advertising and information sources, rather than to generate direct sales. However, in the past 5 years the floodgates have opened, with all of the major supermarket chains offering on-line buying and door-to-door delivery. The big companies originally tended to opt for more grandiose websites with colour photographs of impressive premises, products or achievements; but the ease of website design means that any size of organisation can develop quite sophisticated website for relatively low cost; and can link it with the facility to place orders in a financially secure environment, and to be able to track the progress of those orders during delivery. Businesses that were previously restricted to small local markets have suddenly become international traders, and both sales and profits have grown fast. E-commerce has given the small business wishing to develop end expand, a monumental opportunity to engage a huge marketplace at costs that were previously inconceivably low. This is also one way in which the small fry lacking any economies of scale can break into market segments that were previously inaccessible due to the cost-leadership advantages of large operators.

One of the biggest problems that befall new websites is that their owner-operators fail to decide exactly what they want to achieve from them. The creation of a business website in its own right is an insufficient objective, particularly if it is intended to generate profit, or to contribute towards the development and growth of the business. There are several questions that should be asked:

- Why are you on the Web in the first place? Is it a question of personal enjoyment, ego, self-satisfaction, or are you seriously contemplating a profitable commercial venture?
- Who are your target audience, or whom do you want your website to attract? This question is concerned with the demographic breakdown, activities, areas of common interest, and motivating factors of your prospective audience. The important thing to remember is that the structure and combination of these will provide the determining factors in identifying the target audience and the appropriate external links (on your Internet site home page) needed to make contact with that audience. The target audience will also influence the content of your site, and the ways in which you advertise it.
- What do you want your site to do? What do you expect to accomplish on-line that cannot be accomplished elsewhere? For example, "to increase annual sales by 10% through on-line marketing". The answer to this question entails the production of a list of specific objectives that you want to achieve with your Internet activities.
- On-line strategy decisions involve the process of reaching your target audience. When people are looking for the type of products or services, what are the key words that they will be likely to use for on a search engine? If you want to be on the first page of any search you must ensure that the most important words are prominent on your pages.

- Once the enquiries hit your site, you must provide a user-friendly and secure direct-response facility within site, i.e. to provide a registration form, on-line shop with descriptions, prices and options of goods, and a shopping basket and ordering service which they can immediately hook into, and don't forget the prominent display of special promotions.
- Pay-per-click options allow you to but prime advertising space and prominent links to your site when any web searcher uses keywords in a search. You only pay for the advertising when people click on the link to your site.
- Links can also be achieved at less cost by contacting media sources and journalists associated with your particular industry, and this can be easily and cheaply achieved by sending them an e-mail inviting them to visit your site.
- The "hits" you get on your website can provide invaluable market research information about both your products and services, but the market in general. Don't be afraid to exploit this opportunity by using questionnaires or surveys to gain further information about your prospective customers.
- The website can also form a relatively inexpensive means of providing your customers with backup service and support, in a format which can be much more convenient to you (and less exasperating to them) than on-line telephone services.

Back in the mid-1980s it was common to see in the reception areas of businesses, a large popular poster depicting a magnificent male lion with the declaration beneath "The Customer is King". Many employees would also add to this the subscript that the customer can be a pain in the butt, but such often-deserved observations can only rightly be made out of earshot of those customers. However, the supplier–customer relationship has changed somewhat in recent years with the customer no longer being viewed as a king who must be served and obeyed, but more as a long-term partner who shares a common interest with the business (however, that still does not stop some of them continuing to be a pain in the butt).

In Chapter 11 we discussed the issues of customer perceptions and the importance of creating long-term customer relationships at the business start-up stage. In this section we will examine further the issues of customer relations, and more specifically, the understanding of customer perceptions as a critical factor in the development of future business strategy, with developing policies to meet those needs, and with creating an effective system of communications with customers. It matters little how brilliant an owner-manager is in devising long-term strategies for the business if those strategies are incompatible with the needs and perceptions of the customers, as the customers will simply buy elsewhere if they feel that the business is not meeting their needs.

The importance of customer retention

In any business, there will inevitably be a turnover of customers, with a proportion dropping out each year and having to be replaced by new ones. In the case of retail customers for example, this natural wastage will normally occur as a result of changing customer needs or tastes, their purchasing power or residual income, their changing ages (e.g. children growing up, or workers retiring), or geographical movement. A less-natural wastage can also occur as a result of increased activity or aggressive pricing by competitors, or the company itself failing to give the customers the levels of quality and service they require.

For most small businesses, the sales force performs four main functions: servicing existing customers, persuading existing customers to purchase more, replacing customers lost through natural wastage, and obtaining new customers to expand the business. It is obvious therefore, that if the firm can reduce the amount of time and effort expended by its sales force on replacing lost customers, then the time saved can be applied to both persuading existing customers to buy more, or to finding new customers to expand the business. The most obvious way to achieve this saving is by ensuring that the customers receive the standards of quality and levels of service which meet their needs and perceptions, thereby giving them no reason to take their business elsewhere. It is true that a percentage of customers will always buy on price alone irrespective of the service they receive. However, the vast majority of buyers are aware that as well as being price conscious, it is equally important to consider other factors such as the quality of products or services, reliability and convenience of supply, product support and warranty facilities. These factors will inevitably have a cost to the supplier, but as the simple example in Case study 18.1 illustrates, the potential returns can far outweigh the costs in the longer term.

Case study 18.1

Xavier Onassis runs a small business that imports and supplies Mediterranean foods to Greek and Italian restaurants. In recent years, he has had an average of 100 regular customers that generate between them sales revenue of £1,000,000 p.a. His overheads are £400,000 p.a., and his variable costs are 45% of sales revenue. He loses an average of 20% of his customers each year and employs two salesmen at a cost of £50,000 p.a. to replace these and to service existing customers. At the end of year 1, he decides that the business is going nowhere as his salesmen use all their spare time replacing lost custom. On investigation, he finds that reasons for losing such a high proportion of his customers are due to problems of reliability and poor service by his staff. He is advised to invest in staff training and to improve his operating and support systems for his customers. This will cost the equivalent of £300 per customer p.a., but will reduce his customer losses to 10% p.a. allowing his sales staff to develop an extra 10% of new business each year. The following table show the impact of his decision:

	Year 1	Year 2	Year 3	Year 4
Number of customers	100	100	110	120
Sales	1,000,000	1,000,000	1,100,000	1,200,000
Overheads	400,000	400,000	400,000	400,000
Variable costs	450,000	450,000	495,000	540,000
Sales costs	50,000	50,000	50,000	50,000
Customer	0	30,000	33,000	36,000
Profit per customer	1,000	700	1,220	1,450
Net profit	100,000	70,000	122,000	174,000

The above case study is a very simple example of how an investment in customer care, although it causes an initial drop in profits, can offer longer-term benefits in the form of increased sales revenue, increased contribution per customer, and increased overall profits for the business. This is an example of the business maxim that "quality costs nothing" in the long term, and customer care is after all, an integral part of the quality policy for any business.

Customer care

Customer service is often described as the way in which we respond to our customers and their problems, which implies an essential reactive process. In contrast, customer care takes a more proactive stance, more akin to a total quality management policy. The concept of customer care builds a policy of awareness and responsiveness to the customer within the provision of the product or service as a whole, and with the explicit intention of avoiding possible problems at a later stage. Customer care is about minimising the occurrences that are likely to give rise to complaint, and responding quickly and positively when complaints do occur.

Customer care is concerned not just with the ways in which the needs of customers are identified and assessed, in terms of the products, goods and services that they require. It is concerned with the customers' expectations of the ways in which those products are provided, delivered, and subsequently supported by the people involved in the organisation. Customer care is about formulating and implementing policies and standards of behaviour and practice, which will ensure that the customers' needs are identified. It is also about developing procedures which ensure that customers are treated politely fairly and positively if and when things go wrong, to ensure that customers are retained rather than lost. Invariably, the customer service policy will overlap with, and reflect the sales and marketing plans, and the quality policy of the business, as it does in effect provide the mechanism by which the quality standards, etc., are implemented within the sales and distribution environment. What must be remembered is that it is impossible to draw up an effective customer care policy without first identifying the factors that the customers themselves care about, i.e. what they expect from the contact they have with your business, and the transactions they make with it.

Customer perceptions and expectations

The best way to appreciate the perceptions and expectations of people who have dealings with your business is to put yourself in their position. Imagine that you are calling on a business, unannounced, with the intention of finding out about their products or services, how they can be of use to you, what benefits they will offer, what they will cost, and how easily you can acquire them. Finally, imagine that you have your chequebook in your pocket, ready to place an immediate order if you can find the right deal. Okay, you arrive at the site, park outside (assuming you can get into the car park), and enter the premises. What do you expect to find?

- When you enter the premises you expect pleasant and suitable surroundings which are clean, welcoming, well-lit, safe and hygienic, and living up to the general image of the business and its products or services.
- At reception, you expect sufficient staff to be available, so that you are not kept waiting. You expect them to show a friendly, interested and welcoming attitude, to be pleasant, and most certainly non-threatening or aggressive. They should also be smart in appearance, competent and knowledgeable. You expect that your dealings with the organisation's staff should be a pleasant experience, and free of problems, antagonism or excuses.

■ From the products, goods or services, you would expect that these should be available when wanted, fit for the purpose for which they were acquired and at a reasonable price which constitutes value for money. Information about the products should be provided as to where the product can be found, and its use and operation, and most important of all, that information should be user-friendly. The product should also be supported by a friendly, helpful and efficient after-sales service in the event of any problems arising; and the response to any problems should be both prompt and positive.

■ When the products are delivered you expect them to be securely packaged, undamaged, the order should be complete and correct in every detail, and the associated paperwork should show the correct prices and discounts, the terms of trade, and should specify that payment is due on the date you have agreed with the vendor. Full information about warranties, or the actions to be taken in the event of problems should be provided along with contact names and telephone numbers.

■ In the event that a problem does arise, you expect to be able to contact someone promptly without being subjected to twenty minutes of the agonising drone of Pan Pipes music interspersed by periodic shunting between the switchboard and various telephone extensions. You expect your problem to be dealt with promptly and politely, and that someone will offer you a quick and practical solution, with minimum inconvenience to you.

■ Overall, you expect the whole process to be pleasant and painless, and you want to complete the transaction with the feeling that you have been treated as an important and valued customer. If you get that feeling you will not quibble too much about minor cost details, in fact you will be likely to consider any extra cost to be more than justified by the high level of service you have received. Most important of all, you will want to come back for more!

Now just pause, and think for a moment. Consider carefully: how does the above description compare with what your customers would find if they were to visit your premises unannounced? What changes do you need to make to bring your own business up to those standards, and how will you implement them? This is the starting point for formulating a customer care policy, but to make it work will require a very detailed scrutiny of all aspects of the business that interface with customers, or which might in some way have implications for the quality of service your customers receive. The Total Quality Management (TQM) concept referred to in Chapter 11 is concerned with ensuring the highest possible quality of every single aspect of the operation of a business, including its staff, its management, its resources, its processes and its customers. Customer care is in effect, the public face of TQM, and like TQM it should incorporate the concept of "quality by design", building aspects of quality into the product or service provision right from the start in order to pre-empt and avoid potential problems at a later stage.

Customer communications

At the end of Chapter 8 we briefly mentioned the importance of establishing good working relationships with suppliers, and how these relationships should work both ways, each benefiting the other. Here the role has been reversed, and we have become the supplier rather than the customer, but the same type of relationships should apply. In the same way that our suppliers are looking to establish long-term stable supply relationships with ourselves, that is precisely what we want to achieve with our own customers, and the key to achieving this is regular contact and open exchange of information.

It is not sufficient to make a weekly telephone call to see if the customer wants to order anything, as that simply constitutes the bare minimum of effort to sustain whatever level of relationship that already does (or does not) exist. Building relationships with customers is about having regular face to face contact, talking to each other to establish points of common interest or mutual benefit, conducting open and honest negotiations, and developing an atmosphere of trust between the two organisations. Going back to the earlier part of this chapter, it is above all about listening to your customers (as opposed to just selling to them) and getting inside their heads to identify their expectations of your business and what it has to offer them. This does require a great deal of time and effort, but that is precisely why you employ sales staff. Any sales clerk can telephone a customer to take the details of an order hopefully without offending or upsetting the customer, but the main skill that separates a top salesperson, from an average one, is their ability to establish and maintain relationships strong long term with customers, which can often involve a good deal of time, effort and perseverance. So, next time you tell the sales assistant to telephone Bloggs & Co for their order this week because you are too busy to call on them, just remember, that one of your rivals might not be too busy to bother!

It is amazing to hear how firms faced with financial pressures always seem to start the cutbacks in two crucial areas. The first is in training, which gives their staff the skills to provide the goods or services for the customers and to interface with them. The second is in sales, which generates the orders and long-term revenue that keeps the business going. The sales staff should form the primary link between customer and supplier, and one of their primary roles in talking to customers is to identify problem areas. Problems invite solutions, solving their problems generates sales income, and providing satisfactory solutions creates trust, boosts confidence and enhances your relationships with the customers. This is because the process of solving customer's problems gives the supplier an opportunity to exceed their customer's expectations. A customer who is impressed when their expectations are exceeded is one who will tell others of their experience, and the great benefit of this is that the customer starts to do your selling for you, and there is nothing like enthusiastic personal recommendation to promote your business!

Summary

The quality and customer care strategy must be based on a number of key factors:

- A clear understanding of the needs, perceptions, and expectations of the firm's customers and an awareness of how these can change.
- The establishment of clear standards of quality for customer transactions and support services, and the staff training to ensure that these can be implemented and maintained.
- Careful design of the goods or services on offer to incorporate quality features or systems that will maximise their value to the customer, and minimise the risk of problems or failure.
- Well-defined lines of communication between the customers and their contact points in the business, and between the various parts of the business which form the supply chain to deliver the goods and services to the customer.
- Monitoring of the above factors to ensure that they are consistent, and that they contribute towards customer retention, to minimise customer losses, and to facilitate the full use of sales resources to be applied to growing current business and developing new business.
- The customer care strategy itself must complement and work towards the overall long-term strategy of the business as a whole.

References

Drummond, G. and Ensor, J. (1999) *Strategic Marketing Planning & Control.* Butterworth Heinemann, Oxford.

Hooley, G. H., Saunders, J. A. and Piercy, N. F. (1998). *Marketing Strategy & Competitive Positioning*, 2nd edition. Prentice Hall, London.

Kotler, P., *et al.* (2004). *Principles of Marketing.* FT Prentice Hall, London.

Paliwoda, S. J. and Thomas, M. J. (1998) *International Marketing*, 3rd edition. Butterworth Heinemann, Oxford.

Further reading

Butler, D. (2000). *Business Planning*, Chapter 11. Butterworth Heinemann, Oxford.

Canning, V. (1999). *Being Successful in Customer Care.* Blackhall, Dublin.

Kotler, P. (2005). *Marketing Management.* FT Prentice Hall, London.

Oakland, J. (1994). *Total Quality Management: The Route to Improving Performance.* Butterworth Heinemann, Oxford.

Rice, C. (1997). *Understanding Customers.* CIM/Butterworth Heinemann, Oxford.

Smith, I. (1997). *Meeting Customer Needs.* IM/Butterworth Heinemann, Oxford.

Stone, M. and Young, L. (1992). *Competitive Customer Care.* Croner, Kingston upon Thames.

Webb, P. and Webb, S. (1999). *The Small Business Handbook.* Prentice Hall/FT, London.

Innovation and intellectual property

Innovation and intellectual property (IP) must go hand in hand in a modern knowledge economy in which any new idea, invention or innovation needs to be protected both for its own value as an intangible asset, and to avoid copying or commercial exploitation by others. Small firms are regarded by government as a primary source of innovation but they often lack the resources or knowledge to properly manage and protect their innovative assets. Innovative ideas are often the reasons why new businesses are created but they frequently find there is a need to share their ideas with others in order to realise their potential on a commercial basis, particularly if they do not have the necessary capital to develop those ideas and bring them to market. This chapter is about the processes of innovation and creativity, and how the value of the new ideas and inventions can be best protected.

Innovation

Henry Ford is attributed with once saying: "If I had spoken to the customers they'd have asked for a faster horse". Ford was the innovator who made the horseless carriage available to the masses at an affordable price in the early 20th century – such a pity about his less innovative option: "You can have any colour so long as it's black"!

A few more thoughts:

■ Both the Roman orator Senacre and American comedienne Ruby Wax have been attributed with the quotation that "luck is what happens when opportunity and preparation collide". In a similar context, Innovation could be described as the result of what happens when opportunity and imagination collide.

- "Madness is when you expect different results by doing the same things ... Innovation is about being different and better" – Bishop and Jones 2002.
- "There is only one admirable form of the imagination: the imagination that is so intense that it creates a new reality, that it makes things happen" – Sean O'Faolain, Irish short story author (1900–1991).
- Every child is an artist; the problem is how to remain an artist when he grows up – Pablo Picasso.

In the list of ten entrepreneurial characteristics discussed in Chapter 1 (Thompson & Bolton, 2005) one of the characteristics described on the list was the fact that entrepreneurs are people who make a difference, and the innovation process is one of the primary ways in which that can happen – the person who is ready to act when opportunity and imagination collide. Innovation is often thought of primarily in the context of new technology, such as advances in medical and scientific research, the creation of new materials as a side product of space technology, the Dyson cleaner, advances in wireless global communications, and growth in computing power and memory from kilobytes to tetrabytes in just a few years. Innovation is just as relevant to service industries for which examples abound – the E-Bay global boot-fair, low cost no-frills flights from EasyJet, Direct Line telephone insurance now replaced by on-line quotes, on-line shopping with home deliveries of groceries from the major supermarkets, etc. However, any form of innovation relies on the basic human ability to think creatively and to use the imagination, and whilst large organisations have the investment and research and development capacity for technological innovation, it is the small firms sector by virtue of its flexibility and entrepreneurial drive that is heralded by governments as the primary driver of future innovation.

We can see that innovation is important to the government and to the national economy, but why is it so important to the business itself? First, because innovative firms tend to grow faster, thereby creating greater profits for the owners and investors. Second, whereas continuous improvement with the business can improve profitability and performance, it is insufficient in itself to keep the firm ahead of the competition. It is innovation that creates competitive advantage and new market opportunities, not just in terms or new products or services but in alternative ways of delivering or offering existing services that offer specific benefits to the customers, or new ways of managing customer relationships. When looking for new and innovative opportunities, it is not just a case of "what can we offer the customers that will give them something better than they have now?" The innovation should examine all aspects of the business operations including customer relationship management, customer retention, and of course listening to what the customers say they want.

Innovation as a process is all about new ideas, products and services by challenging existing thinking, accepted norms and methods of practice to generate alternative, and profitable solutions to problems. It is about anticipating future customer needs, often before the customers are aware of those needs themselves, as per Henry Ford quoted above; and applying new technology to business processes and markets to generate profitable opportunities. Innovation frequently involves the process of connectivity, harnessing network contacts, finding physical and financial resources, bringing together people's knowledge and ideas, and applying those to problems and opportunities to stimulate change and stretch what we do beyond current accepted boundaries. Along with the connectivity goes creativity and creative thinking; sometimes described as looking at the same things as everyone else but thinking and seeing something different. It takes creativity and imagination to look beyond what currently exists and to envisage a new and better alternative; and once that objective has been realised, to come back down to earth to devise a way to achieve the vision at a cost the customer can afford. What innovation is definitely not about is doing the same things differently, such as dressing up the same old product in new colours, or re-inventing old ideas. Innovation goes beyond accepted norms and simply bouncing ideas around the boardroom, or asking customers what they want does not constitute an innovative culture in a business.

Bessant, Pavitt and Tidd (2001) regard innovation as a core business process, "a generic activity associated with survival and growth" that takes place in all aspects of the organisation. Most of the time it involves incremental change "doing what we do better" but it also involves acting on opportunities when they arise, or responding to threats, such as market or legislative changes. The main objective is to create competitive advantage for the organisation, however, there is a tendency in some organisations just to focus on the parts of the organisation that are regarded as important, e.g. the research and development function, because that is regarded as being the place that innovation should come from. This "one-dimensional" management shows a lack of understanding of innovation and a failure to see the innovation process as being relevant to all parts of the organisation, and as both incremental and breakthrough changes alongside each other – continuous improvement that sustains the market share, coupled with the leaps in technological innovation that create new market opportunities and competitive advantage.

Creating an enterprise culture

Jones (2004) describes ten myths about innovation, one of which is that "only small firms can innovate". Whilst they might have more flexible staff structures and the ability to be more responsive to customer needs than some more cumbersome large organisations, it is totally wrong to suggest that small firms have first claim to being innovative. The capacity and capability to be innovative is not an issue of firm size or structure, it is all about having the right type of organisational culture to facilitate innovation, and where creativity and inventiveness are valued and can thrive. Another of his myths is that "innovation is only relevant to a few industries", e.g. consumer products, retailing, pharmaceuticals, and fashion. Apart from the fact that these are each fairly huge and diverse industries, that myth implies that innovation is solely relevant to changing markets for certain types of product, when in fact innovation should be used to create advantages not just in products or services, but in broader aspects of the supply chain relationships. It is also relevant to the operational and communications processes within the business itself. Innovations don't just have to involve large profit-generating changes to products or services, they can also consist of relatively small or minor changes to the way things are done, that will save time or money, or just simply improve efficiency.

In Chapter 20, we will briefly examine some of the barriers to organisational change, and as innovation is fundamentally a change process it tends to be subject to similar barriers within organisations, particularly in terms of peoples' fears and reservations about what may be involved and how any innovation will affect them, and their jobs. However, if we can create the right culture inside the business wherein innovation and creativity are highly valued, encouraged and rewarded and are seen and accepted as the norm in terms of behaviour and performance; then those barriers are removed and cease to be a problem. Furthermore, a business with an enterprising culture that constantly encourages innovation and creativity can become an exciting and stimulating place to work. The Innovation Network (www.thinksmart.com 2004) has produced "ten practical steps to keep your innovation system alive and well":

1. "Remove fear from your organisation. Innovation means doing something new, something that may fail. If people fear failing,

they will not innovate." Fear of failure is probably the biggest barrier to proposing or trying out new ideas or innovations in any organisation, and removing the negative stigma normally attached to failure is a fundamental step towards creating an enterprising culture within a firm.

2. "Make innovation part of the performance review system for everyone. Ask them what they will create or improve in the coming year and then track their progress." When innovation is embedded in the employees personal objectives by negotiation and in agreement with them at the annual appraisal, they are more inclined to buy in to the idea and it starts to become the norm in terms of the expectations of the firm. It is another stage in removing the fear or threat factor associated with something new or different.

3. "Document an innovation process and make sure everyone understands it as well as his or her role in it." It is quite easy for new ideas or innovations to be implemented but subsequently to fall into disuse as people go back to the old ways of doing things. Documentation and appropriate instruction or training is one way to ensure that everyone knows what is expected and is able to deliver it.

4. "Build in enough looseness into the system for people to explore new possibilities and collaborate with others inside and outside the organisation." If staff are to be innovative they need to have the flexibility and the delegated authority to be able to research and try out new ideas and options. At times that may impinge on company processes and procedures (see below).

5. "Make sure that everyone understands the corporate strategy and that all innovation efforts are aligned with it. However, also create a process for handling the outlier ideas that don't fit the strategy but are too good to throw away." There will always be some ideas that do not complement current organisational strategy, or that are simply too far ahead or their time to be used at present. The important thing is to ensure that these ideas are not lost or wasted, and that they are properly recorded so that they can be resurrected in the future if needed.

6. "Teach people to scan the environment for new trends, technologies, and changes in customer mindsets." This is all about opportunity-spotting, and whilst it is not something that can be readily taught in the conventional sense, it is an attitude that can be constantly encouraged, especially if there is an incentive or reward structure for spotting such opportunities.

7. "Teach people the critical importance of diversity of thinking styles, experience, perspectives, and expertise. Expect diversity in all activities related to innovation." Part of the process of creating an innovative culture will involve providing staff with the skills and expertise for creative thought and thinking outside of the box, and time should be made available for such training. Not just on a one-off basis, but with periodic refreshment and reinforcement of the techniques.

8. "Good criteria can focus ideation; however, overly restrictive criteria can stifle ideation and perpetuate assumptions and mindsets from the past. Spend the time necessary upfront to develop market and success-related parameters that will take you into the future." A rather grandiose way of telling us, I think, to set criteria and targets for innovation that are focused on markets and customers for future growth and profit generation. Interestingly the reference to mindsets of the past could be applied to the issue of Standard Operating Procedures (SOPs), below.

9. "Innovation teams are different from 'regular' project teams. They need different tools and different mindsets. Provide enough training and coaching so that when people are working on an innovation team, they can be successful." Perhaps it is not so much the teams themselves that are different, but the enterprising culture in which they operate and the creative skills and techniques that they are encouraged to learn and use.

10. "Buy or develop an idea management system that captures ideas in a way that encourages people to build on and evaluate new possibilities." So many new ideas are lost because they are not captured, documented and subsequently evaluated. No matter how off-the-wall they may initially sound, the strangest ideas can still have elements of merit or value if linked with others or developed in the right way. Idea management is the process of capturing and logging all and every idea that comes up from any person or any part of the organisation, so that they can be considered and evaluated. It may take 500 new ideas to generate or synthesise one new innovation or invention which is fine for larger organisations with specialist research and development functions, although it will probably be too expensive and impractical for a very small firm; but in the latter case what is wrong with keeping a suggestions book where staff can put forward their ideas?

In Chapter 21 there is a discussion of the pros and cons of the family support argument, that the objectives of both the business and the family need to be aligned. One opponent of that view, Yankee Fachler (2003) describes how it is totally unrealistic to expect family support when our educational system has educated out of us all enterprising spirit and has conditioned us to aim for employability in secure jobs. The quote by Pablo Picasso at the start of this section "Every child is an artist, the problem is how to remain an artist when he grows up" strikes a similar vein in that for the past 150 years the UK educational system has generally encouraged conformity as opposed to individuality and creativity. It has been interesting over the past 3 years, to see enterprise included as a compulsory curriculum activity in schools at all ages to re-create the interest and value of entrepreneurial activities, and that as a part of the enterprise programmes in schools, pupils are being encouraged to be innovative and creative in developing business ideas. For mature people in employment it is often a slow and hard process to develop or to regain creative skills, so the school classrooms are certainly the right place for it to start.

It is also an interesting enigma that modern management places such importance on the value of quality systems and good practice in customer care, and the need to gain Investors in People and ISO 9002 accreditations as a badge to advertise to the world that quality is highly valued; but at the same time the quality procedures that are carefully documented to formulate the standards against which the business will be evaluated, can themselves form a bureaucratic straightjacket that can limit innovation and change. This particular example of this is Standard Operating Procedures (SOPs) that are precisely formulated to ensure that activities are always performed in a uniform manner and to a consistent standard. There are some manufacturing firms that regard the SOP as being inviolate and unchangeable, and any potential innovation that might require the SOP to be re-written is dismissed out of hand. One particular medical devices company that comes to mind was highly innovative in other respects, and encouraged and rewarded staff well when they came up with innovations that saved the company's money, or improved productivity, but the revision of SOPs was not something the managers welcomed.

One final thought on innovation

It is often said that the biggest leaps forward in innovation and technological development, take place in times of turmoil, when necessity literally becomes the mother of invention. The classic case is that of the

Second World War 1939–1945 which saw the advent of the atomic bomb and the jet engine, as two major examples of technological developments. But, Orson Welles summed it up best in his role as Harry Lime in the 1949 film The Third Man: "In Italy for 30 years under the Borgias they had warfare, terror, murder, and bloodshed – but they produced Michelangelo, Leonardo da Vinci, and the Renaissance. In Switzerland they had brotherly love, 500 years of democracy and peace, and what did they produce? – The Cuckoo Clock!"

Managing IP

The process of protecting ownership of books and written material, music, designs and inventions, medical products, etc. has been around for a long time, UK Patent laws date back to the 15th century, and copyright laws to 1622. The need for international protection of IP became prominent in 1873 when many foreign exhibitors refused to attend the International Exhibition of Inventions in Vienna because of concerns that their ideas would be copied for commercial exploitation in other countries. This led to the Paris Convention of 1883 (see World Intellectual Property Organisation, WIPO below). With the advent of global internet use and the surge in growth of production and exports (particularly in high-tech products) from Japan and Korea, and more recently from China, India, Taiwan, and other Pacific rim countries; the need for protection of IP on a broad international basis has become much more acute. Coupled with that has been the increased inclusion of intangible assets or IP as an item on company balance sheets, particularly for service industries that do not manufacture tangible goods, and for virtual companies that may not even occupy specific premises. This section of Chapter 19 is concerned with the main methods of protecting IP and how they are used both in the UK and worldwide. At one time individual countries had their own processes or legislation relating to the protection of IP (although some had none) and these were not always consistent with each other. This meant that the inventor of any new product was often faced with the daunting, time-consuming, and expensive prospect of filing for protection of the product or design in many different countries and often in different languages, which for very small or newly established firms was often prohibitive. It is true that there are specialist agents who will undertake that task but obviously their services come at a cost. When international protection was formalised after the Paris Convention, there were still problems of preventing illegal copying of designs in other countries, where even if the

IP protection existed it was hard to enforce at a distance. This was certainly still the case in the earlier days of computer technology where copies of silicon chips designed in the USA were being produced in bulk and sold at relatively low cost from parts of the Far East. It also occurred to some extent in third world countries where cheap copies were made of drugs without licences to produce them, although that situation also involved an ethical argument about the drugs being unavailable to the populations of poor countries who simply could not afford the high cost of buying them from licensed manufacturers.

Protection of IP on an international basis

In response to the various problems and issues relating to the protection of IP across the world, there have been a number of treaties jointly signed by the majority of countries to harmonise the international registration and recognition of patents and copyrights, etc., and to reduce the cost and time involved in achieving international coverage. This is particularly significant when considered in the context of the Dyson vacuum cleaner that involved something like 2000 separate patents in its development. The main international organisations are:

- *World Intellectual Property Organisation (WIPO)*: This is based in Switzerland, and was established in 1960 as the modern successor to the two International Bureaux that were formed as a result of the Paris and Berne conventions. The Paris Convention for the Protection of Industrial Property in 1883 was the first major international treaty designed to help the people of one country obtain protection for inventions, trademarks and industrial designs in other countries; and was signed initially by 14 member states. In 1886 the Berne Convention for the protection of literary and artistic work covered the copyrighting of artistic works, printed material and music, and payment for their reproduction or use. WIPO now has 181 member states across the world, and administers 23 international treaties relating to IP including some of those established by other organisations. The most significant of these is the Patent Cooperation Treaty (PCT), which allows a single international patent application to be made which has legal effect in the countries which are bound by the treaty and which are designated by the applicant. When the application is filed the applicant is provided with information about the potential patentability of the invention via an international search report before deciding which of the designated countries should be covered by the application. The PCT system streamlines the patenting process, and facilitates broad international coverage without incurring excessive costs. WIPO also has a small- or medium-sized enterprise (SME) programme aimed at enhancing their competitiveness of SMEs by increasing awareness of the value of the effective management of IP.

■ *World Trade Organisation (WTO)*: The Agreement on Trade-Related Aspects of Intellectual Property Rights (TRIPS) negotiated and agreed in 1984 to apply to all WTO members, as a way to stabilise the management and protection of IP and to allow for disputes to be settled more systematically. It established minimum levels of protection that each member government has to give to the IP of fellow WTO members, and subsequently introduced a settlement system for disputes over intellectual property rights (IPR). The agreement covers five broad issues:

  (i) How basic principles of the trading system and other international IP agreements should be applied.

  (ii) How to give adequate protection to IPR.

  (iii) How countries should enforce those rights adequately in their own territories.

  (iv) How to settle disputes on IP between members of the WTO.

  (v) Special transitional arrangements during the period when the new system was being introduced.

TRIPS covers a broad range of IP including Copyright, Trademarks, Patents, Geographical indications, Industrial designs, Layout-designs of integrated circuits, and undisclosed information, such as trade secrets. The protection of IP is based on the pre-existing WIPO agreement.

■ *European Patent Office (EPO)*: The EPO handles applications that enable patents to be registered across 31 EC member countries through a single registration process similar to that of the WIPO PCT process.

■ *The Office for Harmonisation of Internal Markets (OHIM)*: Whereas EPO is concerned with patents, OHIM is involved with the registration of trade marks, and designs that cover the European Union area. It is based in Alicante in Spain, and also provides information to European Courts when there are disputes about registered trade marks or designs.

■ *The Universal Copyright Convention (UCC)*: This is administered by UNESCO, and any copyright registered in the UK automatically falls under the copyright protection of UCC in any country, i.e. a member of the United Nations organisation.

Patents

A Patent is a government issued licence that gives an inventor protection for a limited period (e.g. 20 or 25 years for medicinal products) to stop others from copying, making, using, or selling an invention without the user's explicit permission. To become patented, the invention must be new in that it is not already in the public domain; it must involve some form of inventive step or process, and it must have some form of commercial or industrial application. When applying for a Patent to the UK Patents Office (usually via a Patent Agent who would have the necessary expertise to carry out the rigorous search process to verify that the invention is new and innovative and is not previously registered) the applicant would have to provide detailed design drawings and descriptions of the invention, including the scope of the protection being sought under the application. Once the application has been made there is a temporary period (Patent Pending) during which it cannot legally be copied, providing the applicant with protection until the Patent is published. In the UK the patents system is regulated under the Patents Act (1977) as amended by the Copyright Design and Patents Act (1988) and the Patents Rules (1995).

Applications for European Patents (via the EPO) and Worldwide Patents via a WIPO Office, in each case there is a fixed period of protection to cover the invention between the time of application and the time of the Patent approval (or otherwise). This is longer than in the case of UK applications to allow for the extended time needed to carry out international searches to ensure that the invention is actually new and original.

As stated earlier, any inventions, designs or intellectual material produced by employees during working hours belongs to the employer organisation. Patent registration is a means of formally and legally establishing sole rights to an invention, and any competitors who wish to produce the same products will have to do so under licence from the patent holder. However, patents are usually only granted for a fixed period of time, and once this expires, the invention can be produced by anyone.

Copyrights

Copyright law usually relates to printed material, designs, drawings and graphics, electronic data, films and music. It does not protect the idea, so much as preventing the copying of material by giving the owners of the copyright the legal right to sue anyone who breaches the copyright. In Britain, that protection lasts for 70 years. The copyright will usually belong to the author or creator of the material, although where this is an employee of a business, the copyright would normally belong to that business, it having commissioned the work. Copyright protection allows the originator (or their estate) to benefit financially from their creation; hence any use or reproduction requires permission and usually payment. When material is made available to the public, e.g. as library books or musical performances, CDs, DVDs, etc., payment is usually collected by the Public Lending Rights organisation (for books and music or film loan or rental) and the Performing Rights Society for musical performance or use. These organisations calculate average use for each item and arrange royalty payments which are funded by charges to the users.

Copyright does not have to be registered as it is automatic when any material is published or made public, but owners can take precautions to ensure proof of copyright, e.g. by mailing a sealed and dated copy to themselves or their solicitors or agents, and retaining that copy unopened. Copyrights are subject to the Copyrights Designs and Patents Act 1988.

Trade marks

A Trade Mark is a sign that will distinguish the products, goods or services of one provider from those of another, including logos, words, colour combinations, slogans, etc. by which they are associated with that specific provided. Classic examples are the Coca-cola design, the Virgin logo, or the MacDonald's golden arches. In the UK their use is governed by the Trade3 Marks Act 1994, but they must also conform to the EC regulation 40/94 1993 on the Community Trade Mark. Trade marks can also be registered internationally via WIPO.

Trade secrets

Trade secrets are not actually registered like trade marks or patents, but they still need to be protected under confidentiality laws. This could include new designs or inventions under development but not yet ready for patenting. Employees who are working on these or potential investors in new projects may be asked to sign non-disclosure agreements, which if breached, could result in litigation and claims for.

Registered designs

By registering a design for a product or a brand or image, a business can protect itself from having the design copied and used by another company, with the potential redress of legal action for infringement of that protection. Applications to register designs are made via the UK Patents office, and come under the Registered Design Rules 1995 and Registered Design Regulations 2001. The design rights last for 25 years and can be reassigned. There is currently no international registration system for designs. There are also some unregistered design rights which usually relate to a "non-commonplace configuration design of the shape or configuration of articles" (www.intellectual-property.gov.uk), e.g. the distinctive tread patterns on car tyres. Unregistered design rights can last up to 10 years after the articles carrying the design are first marketed, to prevent illicit copying of the designs.

Domain names

With the rapid growth of the internet and the increasing demand for domain names it was just a matter of time before people started to buy up potentially desirable names to offer for sale to the highest bidder. The next step was the purchase of names that businesses or other organisations would want in connection with their business name or activity; which were then offered to those companies at high prices by unscrupulous individuals, almost industrial blackmail, and this led to complaints and litigation. The Internet Corporation for Assigned Names and Numbers (ICANN), is the organisation responsible for the generic top-level domains, such as .com, .net, and .org, and for minimising potential disputes. ICANN linked up with WIPO to produce the Uniform Domain Name Dispute Resolution Policy (UDRP) as a system for managing domain name disputes, and this is administered by WIPO using independent experts to review each case and to make a decision on its merits. This offers a quite fast and relatively low-cost form of resolution, avoiding expensive litigation.

Infringements and remedies

IPR are essentially private in that any infringement is normally a matter of civil rather than criminal law, and therefore the enforcement of those rights usually requires legal action, or at least the threat of that. If infringement takes place on a large commercial scale, such as pirate copying of films or music, then a criminal offence may have taken place; as some aspects of copyright and trade mark infringement for deliberate monetary gain are covered by criminal law, but this is a topic normally requiring specialist legal advice. The most obvious way of publicising the existence of IPR is by marking items to indicate that they are protected, e.g. by the TM Registered Trade Mark sign, or the internationally recognised © copyright sign, or with the Patent number or a Patent Pending label. It is also possible to ask HM Revenue & Customs to seize and confiscate counterfeit goods that have been imported into the UK.

IP audits and valuation as a business asset

King (2003) has identified five questions to be asked in order to understand the IP value of a company:

- What IP is used in the business?
- What is its value (and therefore its potential level of risk)?
- Who actually owns it (could I sue them or could they sue me)?
- How could it be better exploited?
- At what level do I need to insure the IP risk?

The first stage of the audit process is to actually identify just what IP exists in the business and this can often amount to more than is first imagined, including not just registered IP but unregistered designs, logos, unique services, working practices, etc. that give the firm a competitive advantage over its rivals. For some the value in cash terms might be negligible in that it cannot be licensed sold or transferred, but it will still have value to the firm and its investors. For other aspects there will be a real financial value that can be measured and quantified, e.g. by estimating the potential value of licensing or of royalty income over a period of time, or by the sale value of the intangible asset. King emphasises the importance of recognising to whom the value actually accrues – usually just two, a potential buyer and the seller, and their respective valuations may differ substantially. The valuation process is not just a case of estimating a figure for the sales value or income generating capacity of each IP asset. In the same way that any potential venture capitalist will require a firm to go through the process of "due diligence" to ensure that its business, operational, and financial systems are all that they should be, the valuation of intangibles need to be approached with the same due diligence to ensure a realistic and honest valuation so as not to mislead shareholder, potential lenders or investors, and insurance companies.

The valuation may be carried out as suggested on the current sale value or the potential income of the asset over its lifetime. Alternately it could be based on the cost of creating the asset or the cost of replacing it with something equivalent. These are quite simple methods of valuation, but there are others more acceptable to financial institutions, such as the capitalisation of historic profits that links the revenue generating record of the asset with a system of scoring its strength and stability in the market. In the case of trade marks or brand names their value might be measured in terms of the price that can be achieved for the goods with and without the use of the brand, e.g. the difference in revenue and profit potential between Heinz baked beans and Tesco value baked beans. Another way is to compare the net value of the asset with the revenue it generates. In any event, where shareholders funds are concerned, this is an activity best carries out by an accountant who can advise on the most appropriate methods for the business and the type of asset involved.

The purpose of asset valuation can be twofold, first, because the assets are an intangible but still potentially valuable item for inclusion on the balance sheet of the company, particularly if it is looking to raise finance from investors or venture capitalists. Second, it is most useful to be able to identify a value of the IP when it is being registered, both for insurance purposes, and in case of any future possible litigation for infringement of the protection. IP can also have a high value for licensing to other companies, particularly where, e.g. the owner company does not have the necessary resources to break into an export market, but where there is an opportunity to generate income by licensing the product to an overseas manufacturer or distributor. This is often the case with small firms whose IP may be worth more to their bigger rivals than to themselves.

The maintenance of IP registrations can be an expensive process, and towards the end of a product's lifetime, there may come a point where the value of the IP may drop below the cost of maintaining its registration. At this stage it may be worth considering whether or not it is worthwhile to maintain the registration. Similarly if the value of the IP of a product is gradually declining there may be a time when it is worth selling to another business, perhaps an overseas company for which it will still have a value for several years. IP can be a very saleable asset and there are many firms that will pay for that asset particularly when it is young and still offers some competitive advantage to then owner. IP valuation is also useful when there is a possibility of two companies co-operating or possibly merging, to determine respective ownership shares of the new organisation. Apart from its attractiveness to venture capitalists, registered, and protected IP is also becoming an asset against which loan capital can be secured, as has happened in the music industry in recent years where rights to popular music have been effectively mortgaged to raise cash, and this is a trend that we are likely to see more of in the future.

References

Bessant, J. Pavitt, K. and Tidd, J. (2001). *Managing Innovation*, 2nd edition. Wiley, Chichester.

Bishop, P. and Jones, L. (2003). *Promoting Innovation Toolkit.* Winning Moves Ltd, Stone, Staffs.

Innovation Network (2004). http://www.thinksmart.com

Jones, T. (2004). *Innovating at the Edge.* Elsevier, Oxford.

King, K. (2003). *The Valuation and Exploitation of Tangible Assets.* EMIS.

www.bl.uk British Library – intellectual property information.

www.intellectual-property.gov.uk – DTI information website about IP in the UK.

www.wipo.int/about-ip/en/studies/publications/ip_smes.htm – Intellectual Property and Small- and Medium-Sized Enterprises (World Intellectual Property Organisation).

Further reading

Andriessen, D. (2004). *Making Sense of Intellectual Capital.* Elsevier, Oxford.

Cook, P. (1998). *Best Practice Creativity.* Gower, Aldershot.

Coulter, M. (2003). *Entrepreneurship in Action*, 2nd edition. Prentice Hall, London.

Davis, S. and Meyer, C. (1998). *Blur – the Speed of Change in the Connected Economy.* Capstone, Oxford.

Drucker, P. (1995). *Innovation and Entrepreneurship – Practice and Principles.* Elsevier, Oxford.

Howells, J. (2005). *The Management of Innovation and Technology.* Sage, London.

Jones, O. and Tilley, F. (2003). *Competitive Advantage in SMEs.* Wiley, London.

Marr, B. (2005). *Perspectives on Intellectual Capital.* Elsevier, Oxford.

www.innovation.gov.uk – DTI innovation website.

CHAPTER 20

Developing and implementing the growth strategy

So far, we have decided on the direction in which the business will be going, researched the market and planned the sales and marketing activities, decided on the physical and staff resources that will be required and when and how they will be obtained, and finally, we have forecast the cash flow and capital funding requirements and what combination of finance will best match the needs of the business. Now what remains is to put the different parts of the jigsaw together to complete the strategic plan, and of course to actually make it work. The difficulty here being that the implementation stage is probably the most critical of all, and the one that has the biggest propensity for problems to occur, particularly if the sequence and phasing of the implementation are not carefully planned and organised. Hopefully, the right decisions for the future of the business have already been made, but now comes the time to decide how to make those earlier decisions work together.

Getting the timing right

Obviously, before you can start implementing the changes to your business, you need to have the necessary finances in place, but once the money is available and ready for use, where do you start? Do you ensure that all of your capital investment activities are in place to ensure that you have full production capacity before commencing the marketing? This would incur the risk of having the machinery standing idle or only working at half-capacity whilst sales are built up, and draining your working capital in the process. Alternatively, do you start your marketing early while the extra capacity is being installed, and then run the risk of making your customers wait for delivery? This would not be a particularly good advertisement for your business and might well result in the loss of your new-found custom? An engineering or manufacturing firm would have no choice but to install the plant before starting the sales push, as the commissioning of new production systems inevitably involves teething problems that must be sorted if the firm's quality standards and reputation are not to suffer. A wholesale or retail business may need to focus on the provision of adequate space or distribution capacity before the sales push, but may be able to build up its stock levels in line with growing demand. A service business based around people-skills might adopt an incremental approach to implementation, by phasing its recruitment or training and development of new staff to be achieved slightly ahead of its anticipated new custom. This allows the new people to grow into the job with minimal risk to the firm's quality and reputation, and ensures that the financial outlay is quickly recovered, minimising working capital requirements and potential cash-flow problems.

Of course, the perfect scenario would be to achieve a seamless transition from the current level of activity, to operating at the new increased capacity. But any transition from a small to a larger organisation, or any major diversification of activities, requires the careful management of two inherently incompatible media: people and change, and the fact remains that people simply do not like change in their lives, as at the very least it causes inconvenience and usually creates work and at worst it can be perceived as a threat to them.

Change management

This topic could fill a book in its own right, but some owner-managers would probably find themselves too busy to read it anyway, and others would probably claim to know it already, so we will just summarise some of the key factors involved in the subject. The implementation of strategic objectives is usually a difficult process because it almost certainly requires significant changes to occur in the business, and any form of change is a potential source of problems or conflict. Fortunately in smaller organisations, the extent of the changes that are needed is likely to be less, or of less impact, than would be the case in a big company. Furthermore, the change process is often easier within smaller businesses because of the more open and direct lines of communication that normally exist between the staff and management. Similarly, in small firms, the critical but often routine functions or systems that are important to the running of the business tend to be under the close or direct control of the owner-manager. This can be important to the implementation of the new strategies as any problems that arise within these systems during the change process, tend to be noticed more quickly. On the other hand, if the owner-manager does get distracted by operational issues and fails to monitor progress, in the small firm there may be no other person around to spot the problems that are occurring or that are likely to arise.

Before the owner-manager can think about implementing any proposals for expansion or diversification, he or she needs to consider the impact of those proposals on the other people involved in the business, and to gain a perception of their perspectives. For most mortals, change provokes feelings of uncertainty, uncertainty creates fear and apprehension, fear incites negative attitudes and dissension, and before you know it, the whole workforce has become totally demotivated and uncooperative; and why did this happen? All because you probably didn't take enough time and effort right from the start, to tell them what was going on, and how it would or would not affect them! The attitude of owner-managers towards the sharing of information with staff varies widely from those who are totally open about their plans, to those who share just what they feel is needed at any point in time, and the other extreme where they believe that the management of their own business is their prerogative alone, and not to be shared with the staff. It is the latter example of mushroom management that tends to create the most fear when change occurs, and clearly the point when the business is preparing to grow is a time when the owner needs the full support and co-operation of staff, so cannot afford to keep them in the dark.

The effective management of change is a skill most people learn by default or in retrospect, and it is a skill that owner-managers tend to be especially insensitive about and particularly poor at handling. This is usually because the sole focus of their attention is on what they want the business to achieve, and not on how to get the other stakeholders around them to help them in the process. This constitutes yet another aspect of the culture shift that must be made by the owner-manager before embarking on strategic development of the business; by moving away from "what I want the business to do" towards "what we can achieve for the business".

So, the main points that need to be considered when making changes:

- Keep your staff informed of what is happening right from the start. You do not have to tell them every single graphic detail, but by outlining the main changes that will occur you can avoid the sort of speculation and rumour that creates fear and demotivation. Think back to how you have felt in the past when changes were going on around you, and you might then just appreciate their perspective.

- Sell the benefits and advantages of the proposals to your staff. If they are convinced or at least, positive about the purpose of the changes, you will be more likely to gain their full support and co-operation. Play down the aspects of disruption as being just issues of short-term inconvenience, and promote the prospects of secure employment and development opportunities that the long-term profitability of the business would confer. The object of this is to get your staff to take ownership of the changes, because if they do so, then the whole change process will be easier and smoother to achieve.

- Listen carefully to their concerns and objections to get an insight into their perceptions of the change, and respond positively to these. Give them regular opportunities to air their views and specific channels to do so, perhaps a short weekly feedback meeting with representatives or supervisors. This again contributes towards the ownership of the changes, and to breaking down any barriers that might stand between them and what you want to achieve.

- Consult them about details of the implementation as not only does this help with the ownership of change, it will almost certainly throw up some useful or practical ideas that you have overlooked, that could make the implementation easier. You may be the owner-manager but you don't have a monopoly on good ideas.

- At the end of the process, thank them for their co-operation, and if it has been a success, perhaps make a special occasion out of doing so. You might need their co-operation again in the future.

Getting the systems right

In the previous section, there was a brief reference to the essential functions or systems that are critical to the operation of the business. If the strategic objectives of the business are to be successfully implemented, then first, it is critical to identify the systems that will need to be in place in order to achieve them. The key systems will typically be those that actively contribute towards the primary goals or profitability of the business. For example, the production functions that manufacture goods for sale, the people systems in service industries that produce services to customers, and the sales and marketing activities which sell those goods or services to the customers. This is all about having the right resources in place to achieve the objectives. Are the current systems adequate to cope with expansion or diversification? Is there sufficient manufacturing capacity, and do we have the skilled staff to run the machines? Do we have the trained and experienced staff to provide an increased level of services? Have we got the sales and marketing structure in place to create the demand that will take up the newly created capacity? Without these key systems in place, the strategic development of the business will not work, which is precisely why they must be right before we can get started. Although not directly related to producing or delivering the goods or services to the customers, financial systems are also important here. If the business is to grow, then the financial systems will need to be able to cope with that growth in terms of processing the invoices and payments for increased orders, providing accurate reports for credit control, etc. At start-up stage a lot of firms commence trading with a basic financial system (sales, purchase nominal ledger, etc.) and bolt on extras such as stock control or order processing as and when the need arises – the system evolves with the business. When substantial growth is being considered it is worth re-examining the financial systems to ensure that they will be able to cope, and to provide the information that the enlarged business will require.

The second stage is to ensure that the support systems are in place. These are the functions that enable the key systems to operate smoothly, such as the purchasing, stores, administration, and distribution functions, not forgetting the management systems to organise and co-ordinate these. Again, if the current support systems are unable to cope with the planned growth, then supplementary or new resources will need to be installed or developed alongside, or preferably in advance of, the extra demand and output created by the key systems. For example, a doubling of output or sales may create a proportionate increase in the general administration system, to ensure that invoices go out on time, and that customers pay their bills promptly. This may simply involve employing an extra administrative assistant, but equally and as mentioned in the previous paragraph, it might mean upgrading the computerised accounting system, and training staff to operate it. Taking on an extra might be achieved in a few days, but the latter might take several months to become fully operational.

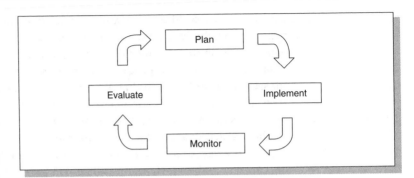

Figure 20.1
The planning and
review cycle.

The third stage is to ensure that adequate monitoring and control systems are in place, both to monitor the expansion of old or the implementation of new systems, and to monitor the efficacy of the whole strategic process and its component parts. Lasher (1999, p. 135) remarks that strategic control is the same as any other form of control; it just has more variables than most. This means that in order to be in control of those variables, the monitoring process needs to be made much tighter. This can be achieved by increasing the level and extent at which each monitoring process operates, perhaps by increasing the frequency of monitoring, or by scrutinising each aspect in more detail. Alternatively, it could be achieved by increasing the actual number and range of monitoring processes that are in use. This would mean, e.g. that the planning and review cycle illustrated in Figure 20.1 might be applied to each of the individual functions and systems that contribute towards the strategic implementation, as well as to the process as a whole. The vital part of the loop is the feedback process that must occur after each evaluation, in order to facilitate the planning of the next stage or activity. Without the feedback to close the loop, any essential changes or modifications that are necessary to make the plans work, are at risk of being overlooked, and minor problems may be exacerbated, or may grow into expensive major problems.

Critical events and stages of implementation

In Chapter 12 we examined the process of planning the implementation of the start-up business plan, identifying key stages and critical actions, and examining potential risks and the contingencies to deal with them. The process for implementing the strategic business plans is basically similar albeit that the implementation may be more complex and may be phased over a longer period of time, particularly where plans involve development of new products, entry into new markets, or perhaps growth by the acquisition of another business to be integrated with the current operation.

In order to implement both the key systems and support systems it will be necessary to produce an action plan (or perhaps a Gannt chart like that shown in Chapter 12) which identifies the critical dates by which each one of these systems must be in place. This is effectively the project planning process that will determine the start dates and completion targets for the introduction of expansion of each system. In a small service business, this may just comprise a series of dates by which new staff must be recruited and trained for their new roles, and the schedule of advertising and promotion activities. In an engineering or manufacturing firm it may entail the employment of a project planning consultant armed with flow charts and critical path analyses. This person would ensure that each part of the new systems is installed in the right sequence and within its own deadline, as any disruption to the timetable might be critical to the installation of subsequent parts of the system. The action plan should be regarded as a means to an end, as opposed to something that once set, cannot be changed. Although it sets the guidelines and targets for the process, it must be flexible enough to account for, and respond to any factors that are beyond the control of the process. The project planning procedures must be, like the workings of each of the systems, subject to the same planning and review cycle if they are to function efficiently.

It is also important when preparing plans for implementation and subsequently reviewing progress, to compare the dates and details with the other main planning tools of the business, i.e. the budgetary plans and cash flow forecasts. In fact, some aspects of the budgetary plans, such as the staged acquisition or release of funds might be the factors that precipitate the next stages of implementation. Any interruption or delays in the implementation could have a major impact on the sales revenue and working capital situation if revenue is not going to be received when expected, particularly when expenditure is still on going. Delays are highly likely to increase overall costs and this could widen any potential cash flow deficit. As mentioned before, it is one of the Universal Laws of Nature (and business) that when managing a new project, whatever might conceivably go wrong will go wrong, and usually at the worst possible time, or when spare cash is at a minimum. Therefore it pays to go through the same risk analysis process described in Chapter 12 to identify likely risks and their potential impact, and to generate contingency plans in case they should happen. Ideally this process should also involve other members of staff or independent and objective advisers (perhaps a business adviser or accountant) to provide a second opinion. Entrepreneurs in small firms can easily become too self-reliant that they overlook the value of an independent viewpoint. Strategic planning as a process requires an examination of the business as a whole, not just from a single perspective (that of the owner-manager) and the objectivity of an outsider can offer a useful balance of views and can sometimes spot issues or problems that the insider may miss.

Keep the implementation in line with the strategic objectives

The main difference between the process of implementing a start-up plan and implementing a growth strategy lies in the role and responsibilities of the entrepreneur or owner-manager. At the start-up phase that person was totally involved in the implementation, both as project manager and as an operational manager, but having made the culture shift from operational to strategic manager, now one of the roles is project managing other staff and resources so that they implement the operational aspects leaving the entrepreneur to ensure that the strategy being employed will achieve the long-term organisational objectives.

The most critical factor to remember is that throughout the whole process of implementing the business development strategy it is imperative that you keep referring back to the strategic objectives for the business, to ensure that whatever you or your staff are doing by way of implementation will be compatible with, and will complement, those objectives. It is very easy to get side-tracked during the implementation stage, perhaps by spotting and pursuing an opportunity that seems like a good idea and that might improve short-term profit, but which will ultimately detract from your longer-term objectives. The best way of ensuring compliance with your main objectives is to build in progress reviews as a matter of regular practice. Regular evaluation of progress and achievement is an important part of the planning and review cycle, and as part of the evaluation you should automatically check that the information and outcomes derived from the monitoring activities are compatible with your overall business development strategy and/or its component parts.

Finally, once the implementation of your strategy is complete, i.e. when you must start to apply the monitoring and review process to the strategy as a whole, to ensure that it continues to work for you, to identify at an early stage any actions that are needed to keep it on track, or any changes that are required to make it work better for you. Strategic planning, whether it is for a large or small business, is an on-going process, and the strategic plan should be a living document to reflect that situation, not just a heap of papers stranded in the bottom of the filing tray. Above all, don't fall back into the old habits of the pre-culture shift days, where the strategic issues are subsumed by the everyday operational aspects of running the business.

References

Lasher, W. (1999). *Strategic Thinking for Smaller Businesses and Divisions* (Chapter 8). Blackwell, Oxford.

Further reading

Barrow, C., Brown, R., Burke, D. and Molian, D. (2005). *Enterprise Development*. Thomson, Harlow.

Burke, R. (2004). *Project Management: Planning and Control Techniques*, 4th edition. Wiley, Chichester.

Butler, D. (2004). Breaking down barriers into training uptake in small firms. *ISBA Conference*, Newcastle.

Drummond, G. and Ensor, J. (1999). *Strategic Marketing Planning and Control* (Chapter 12). Butterworth-Heinemann, Oxford.

Stokes, D. (2002). *Small Business Management*, 4th edition. Thomson, Harlow.

CHAPTER 21

Exit strategies and succession planning

It may seem strange to start talking about exit strategies when a business if still relatively young but in some circumstances, particularly where the business has been established by a serial entrepreneur, a defined exit strategy may even have been incorporated into the original start-up business plan or developed shortly after. Similarly, any involvement of venture capital (V-C) investment in a business would normally define an agreed time and method of exit for the venture capitalists when the initial contracts are drafted. However, for the majority of small business owner-managers, having a defined exit strategy would not be something they would even contemplate in the early years, and may only occur when circumstances such as retirement or health problems force them to start thinking seriously about it. Whereas in the case of a limited company which exists in its own right as a "body corporate" it may be possible to sell the firm relatively easily as a going concern; it can be much harder to value and sell a family business or lifestyle business where the influence of the family or individual family members may be much harder to disentangle, especially, where the goodwill value of the business is closely associated with customer loyalty to just one or two members of the family.

This chapter will start by examining some of the issues relating to family firms, including the two contrasting views about the need for and value of full family support in a new venture. It will also look at the issue of succession planning which again is particularly pertinent to small and family-owned firms, and finally it will discuss some of the issues relating to the planning of exit strategies both in the context of V-C situations, and from the viewpoint of selling the business, whether it be for reasons of health or retirement, or simply to realise the capital value of the firm and to turn it into cash.

The family support argument

It is reckoned that 76% of UK and 85% of EU located businesses are family owned, and a very large proportion of micro-businesses (employing less than 10 staff) involve the owner-manager's direct family in some way, although precise figures for that are not available. This involvement may take one or more of several forms such as paid or unpaid employment, share ownership, partner status whether active or silent, as directors of the company, or/and sometimes as self-employed service providers offering clerical or book-keeping services to the firm to maximise available personal tax allowances in the family. Even when family members are not directly involved with the business, the pressures on owner-managers of starting, operating, and developing the business can impose exhaustive commitment in terms of time and energy, and in consequence can place great strain on family relationships. This is because the needs, priorities, objectives, and expectations of other family members may be significantly different from those of the rest of the family. In this context, it matters not whether the owner-manager is the male or female member of the domestic partnership, as when the business needs take priority the family needs tend to be relegated to a secondary level.

When a new venture is created, not only do priorities change but the stability of the family can be disrupted by changes in routine or long and regular working hours, unavailability, changes in responsibility for sharing domestic workloads, etc. When business finances are tight this may impact on the family finances by reducing available money, and by the stress of knowing that the family may be exposed to financial risk if the venture fails. The owner-manager may sometimes try to conceal problems from the domestic partner so as not to worry them but that often just exacerbates any stress through issues of mutual trust and confidence. Where worries are shared at home this can also result in stress being transferred to the domestic partner. Long and irregular hours put pressure on available time for family activities such as holidays or weekend outings and contact time with children, and the domestic partner is relied on to make the extra effort to re-establish the balance and to manage the home and kids single-handed. Even the use of the home as an office can cause problems when the delineation between work time and home time becomes blurred, and the lack of time to spend with the family becomes more noticeable when the owner-manager is there but is not accessible – "Don't bother mum/dad because she/he is busy working".

Carlock (2001) argues that by ignoring or failing to address the various problems the whole situation just gets much worse, and in the long term it weakens the business and may risk the break-up of the family unit. On the one hand over-emphasis on the business erodes communications between family members, it affects the identity of the family as a cohesive group and damages the loyalty that existed between family members, it erodes time available for the family, and it adversely affects family emotions. On the other hand, over-emphasis on the family erodes the business communications and relationships, it can adversely affect the decision-making processes and performance of the owner-manager (and subsequently the business itself) and it may even limit the long-term strategic options of the business.

Carlock argues that in order for the small business to have the optimum chance of succeeding, the family and the business must be fully supportive of each other, and their respective goals and objectives must be fully aligned, in order to achieve mutual trust and commitment, business effectiveness and family harmony. He proposes the Parallel Planning Process in which the family values, needs, activities, and expectations are planned alongside those of the business at a strategic level, and on a long-term basis by:

- matching family values to management philosophy;
- matching family commitment to business strategy;
- matching family vision to shared business vision;
- matching family enterprise continuity (the involvement of family members in the business) to business succession planning and future exit strategies.

Without maligning Mr Carlock at all, it must be commented that although the principles he espouses are admirable in theory, in the current demographic situation where the nuclear family as we know it is in the demise, and with the pressures of modern competitive business practice those principles may be less than practical and far from realistic. The concept of the Parallel Planning Process was developed in the Mid-west Bible belt of the USA, in an area where strong Christian beliefs and principles still prevail. Arguably, the Parallel Planning Process would probably be of significance in the context of enterprising Asian communities where although the religious beliefs are different, there is a similar ethos of family cohesion, social responsibility, moral standards, and enterprising culture. However, in more cosmopolitan and materialistic multicultural societies, where family discipline, standards, and in particular the expectations of younger generations are very different, it is hard to envisage the application of the Parallel Planning Process being accepted, or being achieved in the majority of family businesses.

The opposing view is typified by Fachler (2003) who adopts a more cynical and pragmatic approach to the issue. It is totally nonsensical to expect a family to run like a business. It is also nonsensical to expect the family objectives to be aligned with those of the business for more than the shortest period of time, because:

- The decision-making processes within the family are totally different (i.e. more emotional and less rational) to those at work in a business.
- Future plans and objectives are likely to change as the circumstances and influences on individual family members change. A family is essentially a group of closely related individuals that have their own lives, and does not operate like a team of employees that are paid to think and work towards the goals of the businesses. If the family had been previously run as a business it would probably have not started a business in the first place.
- Younger offspring are totally incapable of making long-term decision or commitments to succession planning. In the short and medium term their own objectives tend to change radically as they mature, so should not be expected to stay aligned to the business objectives.

Fachler (2003) goes on to claim that "most families are incapable of delivering the degree of emotional support that entrepreneurs crave". He cites the traditional western European education system as having the primary purpose of education people (and their expectations) towards being employable. We are told to work hard at school to gain qualifications that will get us a "good" job, i.e. well-paid and secure, and the total antitheses of being entrepreneurial. It is therefore totally unreasonable to encourage entrepreneurs to believe that no one should start a business without having full family commitment, or that they should automatically be able to expect or rely on emotional support from their families, or that they are naturally equipped to cope with grief and negativity from their families alongside the pressures of starting or running a business.

As the entrepreneurship or self-employment is not the norm in that does not offer the stability and secure employment that we and our families have been educated to expect, Fachler suggests that it is hardly surprising when they act in a negative manner when told of the entrepreneurs ambitions or proposals because it constitute a threat as a departure from the norm. He suggests that in the real world there is a very high probability that any such suggestion is likely to provoke one of the four types of response:

1. Questioning your mental health – "You must be mad!"
2. The put-down approach. "Don't be so damn stupid/irresponsible/foolish!"
3. Outrage – "You've got a nerve/over my dead body!"
4. A threat or ultimatum – "You'll be sorry/try it and I'll divorce you!"

In summary, Fachler's view is that our domestic partners and our families are conditioned to regard self-employment and entrepreneurial ventures as what is essentially a second-class and highly risky form of employment, and inherently threatening to the security and stability of the family, as it lacks prospects and (in the short term at least) is likely to be poorly rewarded. Given that perception how can we possibly expect the family to offer unreserved support and commitment to a new venture? At the very least, his approach and style represents and interesting departure from conventional academic discourse, not the least because of its apparent cynicism, but it is a view also shared by Fleming (2000) who argues that there are seven deadly sins or consequences primarily arising from family relationships that can run a family business into the ground:

- The childhood beliefs (and attitudes) of family members follow them into the business (as per Fachler's view of us being educated to be employable).
- The failure to recognise that the skills required to run a business are substantially different from those required to run a family.
- Some parent are simply unable or unwilling to accept or treat their offspring as equal adults in a business situation.
- The demand for total family loyalty and unswerving support, alongside which can go the failure to treat family members an intelligent and independent human beings with their own ideas. This not only threatens the stability of the family cohesions within the business but it can frustrate the development of new ideas and innovation.
- The attitude or assumption that "father knows best" and cannot be challenged or questioned – again another factor that can stifle business innovation and development.
- Ignoring problems adds to their destructive potential – particularly in the context of family differences and problems as opposed to business issues.

▦   The fact that offspring will often enter the business before having resolve childhood issues or baggage, can affect the way they work. It is interesting that in the heydays of the family-owned regional breweries in the UK (many of the names of which are now lost), the first son who would be expected to inherit the business succession was usually apprenticed to another family brewery in another part of the country to learn the business "from the bottom up" but more importantly to come back into the firm as a mature and experienced adult manager having lost the childhood baggage.

In practical terms, Coulter (2003) suggests that the best-practice option would seem to be to focus on the business as opposed to the family needs, but without loosing sight of the family as having distinct needs of its own, and also as a stakeholder in the long-term success of the business. It is an interesting balancing act that some entrepreneurs can handle better than others. Aside from Coulter, there is also the secondary question, academic or not, that once you engage the family as stakeholders in your business, does engagement that imply that you are accepting your mother-in-law as a stakeholder in your business as well?

Succession planning

It is estimated that only 30% of family businesses survive in that form through to the second generation, and that only 10% survive to the third generation (Coulter, 2003). A very small percentage of family firms grow to become large businesses, i.e. public limited companies where succession planning is not an issue. Even where the originator holds a majority of the shares, it is the control and ownership of those shares and not the total business ownership that is transferred to others, e.g. via inheritance or by the sale of those shares. The majority of small- and medium- sized enterprises (SMEs) are either limited companies in which the originator/entrepreneur or the direct family has a significant if not majority shareholding; or they are family owned sole-trader or partnership businesses which are estimated to account for 76% of all UK Union businesses. For example:

▦   Ownership or succession problems can occur in a number of situations, e.g. where the sole owner or one of the principal partners dies unexpectedly, especially where there is no clear management team or line of management responsibility in place.

- The owner or partner becomes long-term sick or disabled and is no longer able to continue running the business. As in the previous point above, this is again critical if there is a lack of a clear line of management responsibility.
- The owner or one or more partners is approaching retirement age.
- The owner or one of the partners decides that they want to sell up, perhaps because of boredom, wanting a new challenge, or simply to realise the asset value of their business share.
- The domestic situation of the owner or one of the partners changes, perhaps due to impending divorce or to the illness of another family member, forcing them to sell their share of the firm.
- The owner decides it is time to pass the business on to the next generation of the family.

Issues and problems of ownership succession

It is quite often the case that when one or more of these situations occurs, that the family of partners suddenly find themselves in a situation that has never really been considered or discussed before, and suddenly there is a whole host of contentious and inter-related issues that have to be addressed and managed; and many of these issues will contribute further stress and/or distress to the circumstances that have caused the situation in the first place. Some typical problems can include:

- Sudden chaos due to lack of prior planning, particularly where the people involved have never considered (or have deliberately avoided consideration of) the fact that there will eventually come a time when the ownership or management of the business may have to change. The combined pressures of the circumstances, e.g. if the family owner is seriously ill, and the on-going management of the firm plus the management of the change can create huge stress and tension in some family situations, although equally it can draw other families closer together.
- Disagreement as to who should lead or take control of the firm. This is a situation that particularly occurs after the death of the head of the family firm, when the members of the next generation (often prompted by their own domestic partners) find themselves in a situation of conflict over who should

take control of the firm, and over their respective roles and involvement.

- Following on from the previous point, there is often conflict amongst family members as to the future of the business, wherein one may want to continue the family firm whilst others, insist on selling it either because they have no interest in it or because they want to turn it into cash to use for other purposes. This type of situation, where family members have conflicting personal objectives, is potentially the most acrimonious as far as the family are concerned, even if as Carlock (2001) espouses, the family objectives had been previously aligned with those of the business immediately before the situation arose.

- Even where the continuation of the business is in itself not an issue, the situation can arise where family members disagree as to the future direction of the business; e.g. whether it should continue to trade as before, or whether it should start to expand and grow. A lifestyle business that previously supported the originator and his family may not be sufficiently profitable to support the widow and the families of the next generation who have inherited the management of the firm.

- The family members faced with the running of the firm may be totally unsuitable or inadequate in terms of the skills and experience needed to manage the business efficiently and effectively. In the short term this may just be a case of not being familiar with the way the business operates that can be overcome quite quickly. However, if there are severe gaps in the skills or abilities of the family that could damage the long-term efficiency of the firm, then unless that can be resolved, e.g. by bringing in a manager from outside of the family, the firm is at threat. Even the suggestion of bringing in an outsider can create further complications if any family members refuse to accept that necessity, or refuse to allow a non-family member to manage the firm without excessive interference.

- The threat of inheritance tax can be a major issue in the event of the sudden death of an owner-manager where there had been no previous planning or provision to minimise the tax liabilities for the next generation. With the current threshold of inheritance tax at £275,000 and the average house value in the UK being about £220,000 (and much more in the South-east) once other personal assets are accounted for against the balance of the threshold, the balance sheet value of the business does not have to be enormous before it suddenly comes liable to inheritance tax at the rate of 40%, and unless the business has large cash reserves, the inheritors may have to sell the firm to pay the tax bill, or rise a loan or mortgage to keep it.

▓ It is not uncommon for the next generation of a family to be totally disinterested in the continuation of the business. Fifty or even thirty years ago it was the norm for at least one member of the next generation to be groomed to take over the family firm when the head of the family retired or died, but now as most younger people develop their own careers this is not so common. It is no longer realistic for the proprietor to automatically assume that the next generation will want to give up their own careers to take over the business, especially if they have successful and financially rewarding careers of their own. In this situation it can be hard for the head of family to accept that the effort that has been expended in creating and developing the business will not be carried on, and to face the option of employing a manager or putting the firm up for sale.

▓ Where the business is to be continued by one or more family members, the involvement of them in the running of the firm may be demotivating for employees particularly if they lack the skills or experience to do the job well. The employment of further family members would almost certainly be viewed as nepotism and would compound the problem if it deprived employees of any chance of advancement or promotion.

▓ Finally, intertwined with all of the previous issues will be problems of human emotions that inevitably occur in direct and extended families – jealousy, animosity, greed, and potential conflicts of personal ambitions, not just amongst the successors to the business but often aggravated by their own domestic partners or by the extended family; where longstanding family arguments or grievances may resurface after laying dormant for years – but that is just human nature, and there is nothing like a family business to set the family arguing with each other!

Long-term succession planning

In summary of this section, good practice in succession planning follows a number of basic principles:

▓ It should be commenced years ahead of when it is needed, and ideally at the outset of the business. In the case of serial entrepreneurs that would be a normal thing to do as they usually have a target time or stage in the growth of the firm when they will want to sell it on. Other entrepreneurs may be planning a much longer involvement with the firm, but for their own personal financial planning it makes sense to give some thought to if and how the firm will be continued, especially in the event of sickness, death, or retirement.

- The options should also be examined in the context of the overall skills, abilities and personal objectives of the family as a whole that is whether or not they have the necessary skills to take on the business and whether or not they have the interest or inclination to do so.

- If the inclination is present, but the skills are lacking, then actions can be defined to get the necessary skills in place for when they are needed.

- A risk analysis must be an integral part of any succession planning process to identify potential risks and to formulate the necessary contingency plans to deal with them should they arise.

- It is in the best interests of the business and all of its stakeholders that succession plans should be published to remove any possible confusion and to give time to address any objections. The confidence of banks, key customers and suppliers in the future of the firm will be sustained if they are aware in advance of proposed changes and their implications.

- The long-term planning for succession is even more essential now that inheritance tax thresholds have been eroded to the point where the inheritance of any average family property could use up most of the tax-free allowance, leaving the inheritance of a family business liable to be taxed at 40%. In this situation, careful planning to minimise tax liabilities for the inheritors, and the financial impact of that on the cash reserves of the business, should be started as early as possible.

Exit strategies

The Venture Capital context

When most entrepreneurs talk about exit strategies they are usually referring to their own exit from the business, either to sell it to a third party for profit, or as part of planning for retirement to pass it on to a relative, or to install a manager to run it for them. In the context of V-C funding it is the venture capitalists that are planning their own exit from it. For an entrepreneur wanting to rise capital to expand V-C is an attractive proposition as it offers interest-free equity usually accompanied by supportive business expertise from the V-C firm. In return for the risks that they take, V-C companies expect to make their profit primarily from capital growth as opposed to dividends from profits. The investigative process of "due diligence" by the V-C investor is quite rigorous but once completed an agreement is formulated wherein after a specified period of time, usually 3 to 5 years but sometimes as much as 10, the V-C company "exits" the business by an pre-agreed process so that the capital growth can be realised. The method of exit can vary, but typically it would involve one of three options:

1. The floatation of the company shares on the Alternative Investment Market or similar, known as an Initial Public Offer (IPO). This gives the entrepreneur the option of realising his or her share of the growth at the same time if desired.
2. The sale of the business to another firm in the same market, known as a Trade Sale, which usually requires the exit of both the V-C company and the entrepreneur, unless the entrepreneur makes a private arrangement with the purchasing business to stay on.
3. Receivership if the company should fail.

There is also the fourth option in which the entrepreneur buys out the interests of the V-C company for a pre-agreed price, but this would probably require a very substantial loan from other sources that might both be hard to find and even harder to justify to a potential lender, especially if the capital growth has not been as substantial as expected.

Exit strategies: the options

For an entrepreneur wanting to exit the business there are a number of options available:

- *Succession by other family members*: This is often the favoured choice of retiring entrepreneurs, especially if they have worked hard to create what they regard as a family "dynasty" that they want to pass on to the next generation, irrespective of whether or not the next generation actually wants it. Succession by family members allows for the continuation of the business, allows them to retain some financial interest and continued financial returns, and possibly to keep some part-time involvement with the firm that they may have nurtured for many years. However, as discussed earlier in this chapter, it does require two prerequisites:

– First that there are members of the family who actually want to take over the running and management of the business, and this is not always the case, as the entrepreneur's off-spring may already have well-established careers of their own, or simply may not be interested.

– Second, it requires that the successors have appropriate business and management skills and experience to be able to do the job properly without putting the business at risk. The important question that retiring owner-managers fail to ask about their potential family successors is: If these persons were not family members and had applied for a job as managers of my business, would I seriously consider any of them for employment? If not, then why take the risk just because they are related to you?

■ *Interim management*: Where the need for succession results from unexpected death or illness it may be appropriate to appoint an interim manager as caretaker of the business until such times as the family members can either agree on how the succession can best take place, or until the planned successor is able to take up the new responsibilities, particularly if that person is not currently working in the firm and may have to give notice to a current employer.

■ *Appointment of an experienced manager from outside of the business*: Where there are no obvious or willing family successors and the entrepreneur wants to retain ownership of the firm, then this option has to be considered. It allows for the selection and appointment of a manager on the basis of competence and experience whilst leaving the entrepreneur with the power to remove them if necessary. It takes away the day-to-day management responsibilities whilst allowing retention of oversight of the business, and it allows for continued income from the business. The important factor is to ensure that the right person is selected, and in this respect, the entrepreneur might benefit from the opinion of someone outside of the business such as the firm's accountant, at the interview stage to ensure a balanced view of prospective candidates for the job. It may be that there is already a competent manager within the business, so it should not be assumed that it must go to an outsider.

■ *Sale to a third party as a going concern*: At times when there is a buoyant market for buying businesses, or when interest rates are favourable, the sale of the business can be an attractive proposition as an exit strategy. There are two obvious options for the vendor:

 – To offer it for sale to the trade, i.e. other firms, usually competitors in the same market, for whom the purchase could offer an opportunity to expand their market share potential and possibly to achieve cost savings through economies of scale. This would be ideal in a competitive market situation where there are plenty of firms that might be interested in growth by acquisition, but much harder to achieve in a specialist market in which there are just one or two other small suppliers that may or may not be able to afford the asking price.

 – To offer it for sale on the open market. For people who want to establish a business of their own it is often easier to buy and develop a going concern than to start from scratch, albeit that the initial investment cost will probably be higher, but the risk will be lower.

 – In either case the one issue that must be handled sensitively is that of the timing of informing the staff as you may need their full co-operation to take the best value from the sale. Don't leave it until the adverts have appeared in the press or until the first prospective buyers turn up on the doorstep, as that will probably create initial fear or the situation, and subsequent annoyance with you for not being open and honest with them. You may also be missing a trick that the staff themselves might want to combine to make an offer for the firm:

   – *Merger with another business*: In this situation discussions may take place with a rival company for the two businesses to be merged, as opposed to an outright sale to the rival. This could occur where the best-fit suitor company may not be able to afford, or may not want to undertake a high level of borrowing to fund the purchase of the firm, and it also allows the exiting owner-manager to retain a financial interest, and possibly a director's role, in the enlarged business. A merger does not necessarily have to be with a rival, as it could take the form of horizontal or vertical integration, e.g. with a significant supplier or customer of the business. In the case of both mergers and outright sales of the firm the vendor must be prepared to go through a process of due diligence in which financial and operational information about the business is disclosed to the potential purchaser, which can sometimes cause problems of confidentiality with rival companies, especially where information about sales and customers is concerned.

– *Sale to the staff (or other management) of the firm:* This falls into the category of Management Buy-Outs (MBOs) which is the type of situation in which venture capitalists can be keen to invest, particularly if there is capital growth potential in the firm. It is often worth discussing the exit strategy with the managers (if you have any) and staff of the firm quite early, and indicating that they would also be considered as potential purchasers, especially if the firm is in a highly specialised market where prospective buyers could be limited. As an option this can be quite attractive, assuming they can rise the asking price, as the handover of the firm should be much easier when dealing with buyers who are familiar with its workings.

– *Break-up of the business and dispersal of the assets:* This is not a typical situation but can occur where a firm has several revenue generating activities, and where potential trade buyers are only interested in specific parts of the business that relate to their own business activities. For example, in the case of a small but very profitable mobile bar and event catering business, when the business was put up for sale there was no clear buyer for the business as a whole, but several potential buyers for parts of it. In the end, the catering part (assets and goodwill for future bookings, etc.) was sold at an agreed price to one buyer, whilst on the mobile bar side of the business, half of the tangible assets and the goodwill were sold to the second buyer, and the remaining assets were sold to a third buyer. Whilst this may sound like an unnecessarily complex process, the aggregate sale value was worth more than any potential buyer was willing to pay for the business as a whole.

- *Liquidation or disposal of tangible assets:* This is not the same as a forced liquidation where the owners having to sell to avoid legal action because the business has debts or is making substantial losses, it is more a case of voluntary liquidation perhaps because of retirement or some external factors that will adversely affect the future viability of the business. It can sometimes arise when there are simply no buyers interested in taking over the firm, or where there are no potential successors to the owner-manager. It can also occur when for example, the need to exit is prompted by the loss of the business premises, such as the compulsory purchase or redevelopment of the site, or the end on a long-term lease. If the physical location of the business is an important aspect of its goodwill, then loss of the premises might offer no option but to sell of the remaining assets to the highest bidder. If the premises are owned, then they can be sold but might be subject to capital gains tax. Any remaining period of a lease could also be sold or sub-leased. This situation is frequently seen in retail businesses occur due to loss of trade from major supermarkets or similar competition, or where for example it is the customers who have moved away as an area has become run down. Unfortunately, it is often the case of getting out quickly before the business has no value to realise at all.

Whatever exit strategy option is chosen, there is likely to be a need for a transition or handover period when the outgoing owner-manager passes control and responsibility to the newcomer. This can be quite short if the new owner or manager is familiar with the firm and its suppliers and customers, but is likely to take longer if an outsider comes in, particularly if they lack experience. Most incoming owners or managers usually like to take control as quickly and cleanly as possible to make their own impact on the business, but it is not uncommon for an outgoing owner to be contracted to work alongside the newcomer for the first month, or to be available on a consultancy basis for up to 6 months; with the precise arrangement being formalised in the contract of sale.

■ Valuation of the business

The one thing about the valuation process that you can be sure of is that the real value of your business to a potential purchaser, is nothing like the book value shown in your balance sheet. The actual price that a potential buyer is willing to pay will depend on a number of factors including the value of tangible and intangible assets, the profitability both in terms of actual money, and the percentage profit margin, the size of market share controlled by the firm and the number of competitors in the market that want to increase their share, etc., and not least, want the purchaser can afford, and how little they think they can get away with offering.

The issue of valuation was touched upon in Chapter 19 in the context of valuation of intangible assets, and some of the methods briefly mentioned there are the same. The best method for your business will depend very much on the business itself, which is why professional advice is always useful. The three main methods used are:

1. *The asset approach*: where the tangible assets of the business are considered individually, and the values of each are aggregated and then reduced by the tangible liabilities of the business. The values themselves may vary according to the chosen method of valuation, i.e. at original cost, at replacement value, or at fair market price. The method that offers the seller the maximum value may not be the same as the one preferred by a potential buyer. Where property is involved, clearly a valuation at the original purchase price would be unrealistic when property values are constantly rising, so fair market value would be reasonable, but for stick items, original or replacement cost would be realistic. Although the Asset approach is essentially based on the valuation of tangible assets, that situation is changing with the need to incorporate valuable intangible assets such as intellectual property. It is also less appropriate to Internet firms or virtual businesses where tangible assets may be relatively small in comparison with market share, sales turnover, or profitability.

2. *The market comparison approach*: This method compares the performance of the business with that of other businesses in the same market, which might be practical for quoted public companies in large markets but is much less appropriate to form SMEs in smaller or specialised niche markets. This method compares a number of performance factors and the value

attributed is calculated on a multiplier factor of current earnings adjusted for performance against the market average. If the market norm was five times current earnings, but the firm's profit margins were significantly higher it might achieve six or seven times those earnings, but if the margins were lower it might only realise three times those earnings. Clearly this type of valuation will need to be carried out by someone with relevant expertise and experience, and probably more than just a business sales agent.

3. *The income capitalisation approach*: This method incorporates the net present value of the future earnings of the firm over a projected future period, e.g. a "payback" period of perhaps 5 or 10 years. Buyers will typically try to produce a projection of future earnings for their own purposes, incorporating potential cost savings from any economies of scale, although they will be unlikely to want to share that with the vendor. The respective forecasts of vendors and potential buyers are bound to differ with the former being typically optimistic, and the latter being highly cautious.

Use of professional expertise

The complexity of the sale or transfer of management of a business should not be underestimated. It requires a knowledgeable and experienced expert to carry out the valuation, to pitch the asking price at the right level, and to advertise and negotiate the sale on your behalf. It may be better that you choose an accountant to carry out the valuation, and a separate business sales agent to actually advertise and sell the firm. For the legal side of the transactions you will need a solicitor, not just for the conveyancing aspects, but to ensure that your liabilities as a former owner, partner or director are clearly defined, and that you are indemnified against any future debts of the business. This is especially important if the business has any loans or leasing agreements signed by yourself, and that will be continuing after the sale is completed. For personal tax reasons it is worth using a specialist financial adviser or accountant to ensure that you minimise (legally) your potential liabilities for capital gains tax or personal income tax by following appropriate procedures. Although the use of experts can be costly and you may be able to handle some aspects perfectly well yourself, their knowledge and expertise can save a great deal of time and energy, as well as protecting you against future liabilities, and ensuring that the sale, transfer, or closure of the business is tax efficient.

References

Carlock, R. (2001). *Strategic Planning for the Family Business*. Palgrave, Basingstoke.

Coulter, M. (2003). *Entrepreneurship in Action*. FT Prentice Hall, London.

Fachler, Y. (2003). *My Family Doesn't Understand Me – Coping Strategies for Entrepreneurs*. Oak Tree Press. Cork, Ireland.

Fleming, D. (2000). *Keep the Family Baggage out of the Family Business*. Simon & Schuster, Cambridge.

Further reading

Campbell, K. (2003). *Smarter Ventures – a Survivor's Guide to Venture Capital Through the New Cycle*. FT Prentice Hall, London.

Crouch, H. (1998). *Selling Your Business*. Allyear. Saratoga, USA.

Lipman, F. (2001). *The Complete Guide to Valuing and Selling Your Business*. Prima Publishing. Roseville, USA.

Sperry, P. and Mitchell, B. (1999). *The Complete Guide to Selling Your Business*. IoD/Kogan Page, London.

Business review questionnaire

The purpose of the questionnaire is to review the performance of your business across seven key operational areas, and to evaluate each area by grading the firm's performance of a scale of 1 (poor performance) to 5 (very efficient). The success of the process and its value to the business will depend on the evaluation being honest and objective.

The questionnaire should take about 30 minutes to complete. Each section has a list of descriptors (key words relevant to that section) and a number of questions. You should not try to answer every question – use them along with the descriptors, to prompt your thoughts, to help you identify your level of efficiency in each area. There is a Comments box to summarise your thoughts, and another small box for you to enter the grade for the firm's performance in that area. Not all sections will apply to every business, so feel free to omit any sections that are not relevant. You can summarise your score in the box below and identify any areas where training for yourself, managers or staff may be relevant.

Key performance area	Score (1–5)	Training need (Y/N) Who for and comments?
1. Management efficiency		
2. Sales, marketing, and customer relations		
3. Business operations		
4. Finance		
5. Managing staff performance		
6. Innovation, technology, and intellectual property rights		
7. Planning for the future		

Area 1: Management efficiency

Descriptors

Delegation/prioritising/proactive planning/reactive decisions/last-minute rush/personal energy and motivation/management styles.

Points to consider

- Typically, how do you spend your time each day?
- How many hours do you work each day? How well do you manage your time?
- As an owner-manager, how positive and motivated do you feel about your business?
- Do you feel you can trust your staff?
- What examples can you give from the past year where you have delegated responsibility to others, and were they successful?
- If you chose or had to leave the business for 3 months (e.g. sickness or holiday of a lifetime) what would your business look like when you came back?
- Do problems of staff performance only come to light when they are at crisis point?
- When did you last take a holiday?

Comments:

Please grade your business performance on a scale of 1 (poor) to 5 (very efficient) or n/a.

Area 2: Sales, marketing, and customer relations

Descriptors

Winning contracts/successful negotiations/generating new business/ market awareness/effective advertising/generating revenue/sales skills/ customer relationships/customer loyalty/repeat orders/customer turnover/customers' perceptions of the business.

Points to consider

- Why do people buy your products or services?
- Who are your competitors and why do people buy from them?
- How much has your business revenue grown since last year?
- How have your markets changed in the past year?
- When did you last review and update your marketing plan?
- Would your customers regard you as their first-choice supplier?
- Would you say that you have sound long-term relationships with your customers?
- Would they happily recommend you to someone else?
- How much of your sales effort is spent in replacing lost customers?

Comments:

Please grade your business performance on a scale of 1 (poor) to 5 (very efficient) or n/a.

Area 3: Business operations

Descriptors

Efficiency/smooth-running/breakdowns/delays/mistakes/bottlenecks/ frequent changes to schedules/late deliveries/stock levels/health and safety/workplace accidents/numbers of complaints/levels of waste/ returned goods/quality systems and accreditation.

Points to consider

- How well do your operational planning and business processes work?
- Are you faced with frequent or last-minute changes to plans or scheduled work?
- Are you usually able to meet customers' deadlines?
- How often do things seem to go wrong?
- Are there any recurrent problems affecting your operations?
- How much of your money is tied up in stock?
- Have you ensured a safe working environment for your staff?
- Do your members of staff think that quality matters?
- Do you encourage continuous improvement?

Comments:

Please grade your business performance on a scale of 1 (poor) to 5 (very efficient) or n/a.

Area 4: Finance

Descriptors

Book-keeping/annual accounts/profit-margins/break-even/credit control/cash flow/budgetary planning/working capital/need for investment.

Points to consider

- How well do you think you manage your finances?
- Are there any obvious weaknesses in your financial systems?
- Do you know what your break-even sales level is?
- Can you pay the bills when you need to?
- How would your bank manager/accountant describe your current financial situation?
- Do your customers normally pay you on time?

Comments:

Please grade your business performance on a scale of 1 (poor) to 5 (very efficient) or n/a.

Area 5: Managing staff performance

Descriptors

Effective teamwork/staff loyalty/flexibility and co-operation/positive cultures/stability/high turnover/high sickness/industrial disputes/ discipline and grievance issues/high recruitment costs/tribunals/training and development plans.

Points to consider

- Would you say that you have a stable and loyal workforce?
- How many of your staff left last year?
- How many days were lost last year through sickness or absence, and has this level changed recently?
- Do your staff enjoy their day at work or are they clock-watching?
- Do you think your staff would regard you as a good boss?
- What skills do your staff need and how do you help the staff to obtain them?
- Do you think you comply with current employment legislation?
- Are you at risk of industrial or legal action by staff at present?

Comments:

Please grade your business performance on a scale of 1 (poor) to 5 (very efficient) or n/a.

Area 6: Innovation, technology, and intellectual property

Descriptors

ICT systems/customer databases/customer records/financial systems/ e-commerce/e-marketing/knowledge management/data protection/ intellectual property rights.

Points to consider

- Are you making best use of technology to contribute to the efficiency of your business?
- Have you examined opportunities to use e-commerce or e-marketing in the business?
- Is intellectual property important to your business?
- If you were setting up your business again tomorrow, would it be the same as it is now? What would you do differently?
- What investment have you made in new technology in the past 2 years?

Comments:

Please grade your business performance on a scale of 1 (poor) to 5 (very efficient) or n/a.

Area 7: Planning for the future

Descriptors

Business objectives/strategic plans/long-term growth and development/ development opportunities/succession plans.

Points to consider

- How will changes in the outside world, and in your markets, impact on your business?
- Do you know where you want the business to be in 3/5/10 years from now?
- Do you have a clear idea of how you will get to that point?
- Have you considered what finance or investment you will need for the future?
- What important decisions did you take last year that really made an impact on your business performance?
- If you wanted to sell your business tomorrow, could you put a value on it?

Comments:

Please grade your business performance on a scale of 1 (poor) to 5 (very efficient) or n/a.

Index